Governing Perfection

Governing Perfection
Donald S. Prudlo

St. Augustine's Press
South Bend, Indiana

Manufactured in the United States of America.

1 2 3 4 5 6 29 28 27 26 25 24

Library of Congress Control Number: 2024936710

Paperback ISBN: 978-1-58731-330-1
Ebook ISBN: 978-158731-331-8

∞ The paper used in this publication meets the minimum
requirements of the American National Standard for Information Sciences –
Permanence of Paper for Printed Materials, ANSI Z39.48-1984.

St. Augustine's Press
www.staugustine.net

This book is dedicated to all of the fellowship of St. Martha, whose serene management, fidelity, hospitality, competence, and attention to right order have made possible the life of the mind, the achievements of learned leisure, and the fullness of contemplation.

Table of Contents

Introduction

In the beginning, God administrated. The entirety of creation is a miracle of organization, with God himself arranging "all things by measure and number and weight" (Wis 11:20). This marvelous order makes possible the very comprehensibility of the universe. God—who is *Logos*, or reason itself—has created an intelligible cosmos, which can be understood through the rational participation of humans in it. Rightly indeed did St. Thomas echo the sage words of Aristotle, "the office of the wise is to order."[1] This ordering refers to being able to understand final ends or purposes, and to be capable of gauging the relative significances of each, particularly as they relate to the ultimate end of all things: God Himself. Yet before there can be an ordering, there must be a structure in place to facilitate such ordering. There can be no achievement without administration. In every case of a thing achieving its end, there is first the constitutive structures that make such attainment possible in the first place. The chief cause of the order inherent in the universe and in human nature is the government of God. One of the most perfect ways for a rational creature to imitate God is through the exercise of good governance and right ordering. When humans govern, they are performing a god-like activity. When they do it well they are imaging God Himself.

Such an ordering principle has been present from the very beginning, even before the Fall. Adam was called to superintend the

---

1   This statement is critical to all of St. Thomas' thought. He recalls it at the beginning of both of his *Summae*. It comes originally from Aristotle, *Metaphysics*, 1.2 (982a18). It appears in his works no fewer than eleven times.

garden and to name the animals according to their orders. The goodness of governance is then established in a twofold way, by being present in the prelapsarian state and most of all by reflecting the very being of God. Yet governance became problematic as rational creatures exercised their wills to enact disorder. They governed badly, first themselves and then the world with which they had been entrusted. In this sense proper government—both internal and external—become at the same time more important and immeasurably more difficult to achieve. From a Judeo-Christian perspective then, even given the reality of sin, governance and administration are both good and necessary for a flourishing human life.

Government can be divided into self-government and external government. While most would agree that self-government is a necessary and proper thing to have, in the ancient world it was considered the necessary precondition to good external government. Only the man who could rule himself could effectively rule others. This principle, articulated in the first book of Aristotle's *Politics* and assumed as normative until the time of Machiavelli, has been abandoned in the modern world. No longer does there seem to be any connection with a person's moral probity and his eligibility for rule. This is of course an effect of the disorder of sin combined with the intoxicating nature of power. This present book seeks to be an examination of how men and women in the Christian tradition attempted to balance goodness with power in their administration of the Church. Yet, for the followers of Christ does not such a combination seem doomed from the outset? A surface reading of the humility called for in the New Testament seems to preclude the exercise of power by Christians. Christians are called to meekness and deference, to serve rather than be served. It is the princes of the Gentiles who "lord it over" others (Mt 20:25). It would seem that the exercise of power is thereby forbidden to Christians. Yet Christ, the ordering principle of the whole universe, came to teach with authority and issue new commandments. He bequeathed significant power to his apostles to teach and to govern the Church of God. He even recognized the legitimacy of secular governments and their claims to obedience when it did not contradict the Gospel. Christians then find themselves in the seemingly anomalous situation of reconciling humility and leadership, service and authority. Such a harmony looks paradoxical, but like many other paradoxes in Christianity, it might be properly understood in the light of the workings of grace. The saints presented in this book are examples of the concord possible between the two concepts. Yet even beyond this one meets further issues.

One can level criticism from two different directions at any attempt usefully to connect Christianity with the exercise of administrative or governmental power. In the most mundane sense, administration is equated in the modern world with bureaucracy. The art of administration becomes reduced to the *techne* of bureaucracy, as so many other human arts have been diminished into pure mechanism. The massive proliferation of the administrative state is paralleled by astonishing bloat in both public and private institutions. Such developments deaden and flatten human life. Individuals are confronted by an army of nameless minor civil servants, observing arcane and unknown codes that seek to preserve their own petty spheres of power rather than to offer any real service to their constituents. Such a self-perpetuating bureaucratic vision is often parodied, but too often it hits uncomfortably close to the truth. Bureaucracy is a declension of the administrative art, for it takes something good and necessary and reduces it to self-serving ends. It is like a mock virtue that destroys the genuine virtue along with it, as so-called "toxic masculinity" has cast aspersions on fortitude or as puritanism has given a bad name to temperance. Much of modern society tries to adopt a "baby with the bathwater" mentality, whether it be a libertarian desire to destroy existing institutional structures wholesale or a Marxist attempt to abolish such bureaucracies as needless, self-perpetuating parasites. What is needed instead is a revaluation of the goodness and necessity of administration that will lay bare the real problems with a bureaucratic mindset.

The second issue is of more substance. Friedrich Nietzsche rejected the classical and Christian ethical position that all humans acted for happiness. He denies this and rather exalts power as the fundamental end of all human action. This contradicts Aristotle's position that power can only ever have the nature of a means because it does not specify the nature of the object toward which it tends.[2] Thomas concurs with this. He denies that the final end of humans can be power alone, since power, outside of God, is always imperfect in bringing about its effects. Further, he states that power is able to be morally specified as either good or evil, depending on the intention. Indeed, "some happiness might consist in the good use of power, which comes from virtue, rather than in power itself." Anticipating the objections of those who saw perfection in ruling others, Thomas clarifies himself further: "Just as it is a very good thing for a man to make good use of power in ruling many, so is it a very bad thing if he makes a bad use of it."[3] Yet Nietzsche, though going too far, was indeed on to something. Power is seductive and many people seek to maintain or increase it. This is just a simple fact about fallen human nature. Christ came to heal this tendency through his *Kenosis*, or his self emptying of glory, by taking a human nature and dying on the cross. Christianity at the same time knows that power is necessary and that it can be directed toward the good, while at the same time offering a sovereign remedy for the subtle temptations that power brings, through the example of God Himself and through His grace. It is just such a program that I intend to explore in this book, by investigating the saints of the Christian tradition, and by studying their responses to the problems of authority and administration from the perspective of grace building upon nature.

Chapter one studies the origins of Christianity and discusses how the infant Church providentially adopted the administrative mechanisms of the Roman state to achieve her mission. The concept of *Romanitas* combined the administrative skill of the ancient Romans with concepts of virtue necessary for a right ordering of

---

2   A position established ably by Plato and Aristotle, and elucidated by Cicero in *Tusculan Disputations*, book 5.

3   Thomas Aquinas, *Summa Theologiae*, I-II, q. 2, a. 4, ad. 2.

the community. The early Church took these practices, as it also took many from the Hebrews and Greeks, and enriched them. Incarnational Christianity demanded a certain use of material goods for the sake of Christian worship and ministry. Here I examine the activities of four early popes, Damasus I, Leo I, Gelasius I, and Gregory I, and look at their pontifical administrations for examples of holy governance in action. Damasus used his skill to recover the prestige of the Holy See after the reign of a weak pope. He did this by focusing Christian devotion on the martyrs and tying these explicitly to the supervision of the pope. Leo the Great rose through the ranks of the Roman Church through a carefully balanced *cursus honorum* that allowed him to refine his natural talents for administration. In some of the darkest days of Roman history, his consummate skill saved both the city and the Church. Gelasius continued this tradition of strong leadership. It was under his rule that the clear distinction between the Church and the Roman imperial power was made. Finally, Gregory the Great leveraged the administrative achievements of all his predecessors, establishing a papal government whose perimeters would endure into the present day.

Gregory, who himself was a monk, presents a useful bridge to the next chapter, which looks at the monastic orders in the history of the Church and their particular contributions administrative genius. This chapter explores how the Christian concept of perfection can coexist with administration. It traces the movement from isolated spiritual virtuosos, like Anthony of the Desert, to those who began to organize monks into corporate bodies under the rule of spiritual superiors. The first great monastic founder was Pachomius, whose military training and Christian virtue was the first to turn the desert into a city. Basil modified the Pachomian solution in such a way as to emphasize wise moderation and open the spiritual benefits of the monastery to the broader world. In a very real way he "humanized" monasticism, building up a solid foundation from correct religious anthropology. The chapter then follows the importation of monasteries into the West, discussing the governance brought by John Cassian to Gaul and the peculiar conditions found in the Celtic world. Augustine, himself a diocesan bishop, proposed a novel form of "urban monastery" that would later be recognized as the canonical life. I lay a significant focus on Benedict and his Rule as an axial moment in the regularization of the monastic life. His administrative genius is characterized by harmony, moderation, and proper order. Benedict and his Rule need to be situated in their historical context in order to appreciate the numerous contributions of later Church leaders to extend it to Western monasteries. Such a propagation of the Rule was the result of many efforts over the course of centuries. The chapter continues with the constitutional and administrative revolutions created as a result of the Cluniac and Cistercian reforms. It ends with an example of administrative innovation in the order created by Angela Merici, an establishment that shows the perpetual creativity that can be generated by the response to grace while embedded in human nature and the long tradition of the Church.

Chapter three discusses a concentrated period of Church history in the twelfth century that has been referenced by the name of the "Gregorian Reform." The papacy had fallen upon hard times in the 900s and early 1000s and needed to be recalled from its nadir. For this a wholesale administrative revolution was necessary so as to undergird the grand theoretical claims of the reformers. Initially reform was in the hands of lay rulers, but gradually the Church emancipated herself from such domination. The first strong pope in 200 years was Leo IX. It was under his rule that a thoroughgoing reform of the Roman See took place. Leo reinvigorated the ancient practice of synodality, placing the papacy as the visible center of the reforming movement. He was the first pope to undertake extensive travel with the purpose of reinforcing papal prerogatives. In order to reform the Curia, he gathered leading intellectual lights from all of Europe, placing them in critical positions to effect reform at the heart of the Church. These men were given the ecclesiastical title of "Cardinal" as personal vicars of the pope, enabling them to execute administrative reforms in his name. This office became critical to the life of the Church, both in guaranteeing the freedom of papal election while at the same time offering universal representation. Gregory VII, who gave his name to the whole of the reform movement, was a man caught between theory and practice. He strove mightily to implement the high-minded ideals advanced by his coterie, and was the initiator of many key administrative innovations. During his reign he saw the dispatch of powerful legates to carry his papal authority to the corners of Europe, as well as an increasing emphasis on the city of Rome as the center of the Christian world. Finally, there is an analysis of the papacy of Urban II, who did so much to bring the hard work of Leo IX and Gregory VII to fruition.

Following this examination of monastic and papal administration, chapter four is given over to a detailed study of one of the singular achievements in Church history—namely, the foundation and constitutions of the Friars Preachers. First, I discuss the difficulty of inserting a new form of apostolic itinerant preaching into the institutional life of the Church in the twelfth century. Founders such as Norbert, Dominic, and Francis creatively interacted with the canonical and administrative traditions of the Church to avoid heresy and insert themselves within institutional Christianity, all for the good of souls. All the pieces needed for such an institutional transformation began to fall into place around 1200, with the election of Innocent III. For all his administrative brilliance, Innocent knew that unless reform of governance was accompanied by a revolution in holiness, it would result in a dead letter. It was Dominic of Caleruega who drew all these disparate threads together and fashioned the constitutions of the Friars Preachers as a comprehensive, prudential, and enduring testament to administrative genius. Once again, however, the founder had the support of brilliant subordinates. In particular, I focus on the fifth Master of the Order, Humbert of Romans. It was this prescient leader who led the Dominicans through one of their worst crises, one that threatened the very existence of the mendicant movement itself. It was Humbert's prudential and foresightful governance, using the tools bequeathed to him by Dominic, that righted the ship and oriented the Preachers as a fundamental order in the Church even up to the present day.

However well administration and sanctity pair together, they are not always necessarily found united. Chapter five examines several saints who were failed administrators, a fact that does not detract from their holiness, but rather helps to throw in relief how governance is quite a difficult art. Simply because a person is holy does not guarantee good administration. Sanctity may deepen the virtues and talents necessary to governance, but it cannot build where there is no natural and practical aptitude. Here we can see lamentable episodes in Church history of people like the cunning Theophilus of Alexandria misusing the authority of the Church for ambitious ends. In the case of St. Cyril of Alexandria, we can see how even a saint can misuse authority, and that consummate skill in administration, if not prudentially deployed, can easily be frustrated. Yet Cyril matured during his lifetime, and a contrast grew that distinguished his actions from those of his predecessor. Such problems can be compounded when considered at the level of the papacy. Poor papal governance can lead to drastic problems within the Church on earth, and even saintly popes can be terrible administrators. The lamentable events of 1054 in Constantinople provide a case study in terrible governance, on part of both the Greeks and Latins. The events of the life of Peter Celestine show that possession of piety and holiness is no guarantee of success, and that to simply entrust complex governance to a person because of his recognized sanctity is fraught with peril. Coming to realize the depth of his own inability, Celestine resigned the papacy within six months of his election. His reign had been a total disaster. Notwithstanding his holiness, he was utterly unequal to the task demanded of him. Finally, Francis of Assisi throws into sharp relief the Christian paradox of leadership. He vividly demonstrates the difficulty of reconciling humility and the exercise of power. All through his life, in his attempts to govern his new order, Francis was never able to square this circle, an inability which caused serious chaos among his followers for a century.

The final chapter is an examination of the most critical office of governance in the Christian Church—namely, that of the bishop. Ambrose presents an ideal model for understanding the early Christian episcopacy. Though his immediate elevation to the office was stunning, he nevertheless brought with him long experience in the imperial service. In him native talent commingled with grace, producing an astonishingly effective and sanctifying administrative structure. Using Ambrose as a blueprint, I analyze the reign of the retiring scholar Edmund of Abingdon, in thirteenth-century England. His shy temperament cloaked the characteristics of a born administrator and leader. Humble and honest, Edmund knew his shortcomings, and attracted trusted and competent subordinates to rule the Church in England. His success was manifested in the reign of his protege, Richard de Wych, who was also later canonized. I conclude by returning to Ambrose's diocese over 1,000 years later, in the person of Charles Borromeo. By analyzing both his work in successfully concluding the Council of Trent and his active efforts as the reforming Archbishop of Milan, it becomes apparent how examples from the New Testament and the lives of early holy bishops might be incarnated in every age.

In the end this book hopes to draw out the key virtues necessary for elucidating a clearer connection between administration and holiness. It does so through an analysis of the lives and actions of the holy members of the Church charged with such responsibilities. I seek to restore the idea that sanctified holiness is not only possible for those charged with governance of the Church of Christ, but rather is a fulfillment and type of *Christus Rector omnium*—Christ, the ruler of all. Power is a means; it can be used for good or for ill. Serious temptations arise when fallen humans try to exercise it, yet one should not thereby despair of its proper use—that is, when it is subordinated to truth and the common good. It should always be remembered that, in spite of her grumbling, St. Martha made the divine colloquy between Mary and Christ possible. Without her *oikonomia*, her attention to right order and to hospitality, such a meeting could not have been contemplated. Her resignation to her tasks and her humble, practical, and unstinting service to Christ permits Mary to enjoy the "better part." It is good to remember that Martha is a saint right alongside Mary. Administration is very often a burden to those entrusted with it but, considered in the light of Christ's revelation, this creation of order in the midst of chaos is what makes great achievement possible: Just as Martha gave us Mary, so did Ambrose bequeath us Augustine, and Dominic paved the way for the success of Thomas Aquinas. The key for all these holy administrators was not to make governance and end in itself, but a necessary precondition and means for the achievement of the reign of Christ Himself.

Chapter 1
Christianitas and *Romanitas*

In the years following the Resurrection, Christ's disciples carried his gospel throughout the Roman empire and beyond. In every city a handful of converts eventually included numerous households, which then developed into local churches. By the year 100 we find monarchical bishops in each town with a Christian population, assisted by deacons and a rapidly expanding presbyterate. Christianity was to find a ready home in the burgeoning cities of the Mediterranean, among a populace hungry for spiritual nourishment in the midst of civil religion devoid of substance. The new faith brought with it a strict code of conduct, a distinct way of worshipping God, and—in particular—novel ideas for organizing the community. These three aspects were meant to work in unison for the salvation of all: morality, cult, and organization were intended to orient the Church toward its eternal destination. Such development required the careful shepherding of many different graces, talents, and tendencies, all amid plagues and persecutions. In particular, Christians directed their attention to the three mightiest cities of the empire—namely, Alexandria in Egypt, Antioch in Syria, and the center of the world itself, Rome.[1]

---

1   An excellent overview of this period of Church history can be found in Henry Chadwick, *The Church in Ancient Society: From Galilee to Gregory the Great* (New York: Oxford University Press, 2009); Peter Brown *The Rise of Western Christendom: Triumph and Diversity, AD 200–1000*, 10th anniversary edition (Chichester: John Wiley & Sons, 2013); Id., *Authority and the Sacred: Aspects of the Christianisation of the Roman World* (Cambridge: Cambridge University Press, 1995); Robert Markus, *The End of Ancient Christianity* (Cambridge: Cambridge University Press, 1990); and

God willed to become incarnate in the heart of a deeply rooted Hebrew culture that was then experiencing a fruitful interaction with the world of Greek thought, all within the political and legal order of the Roman empire. These three cultural wellsprings were what the infant Christian Church would channel into the mighty river of Western civilization. From the Hebrews she received the scriptures, along with concepts of ethical righteousness, cultic worship, and a linear vision of history. From the Greeks came an intellectual foundation upon which to understand and connect the revelation of God to the realities of the earth. For the earliest Christians, their first language of scripture and preaching was, for the most part, Greek. Hellenistic culture was the good soil in which Christianity was to root. Yet for our present purposes I want to address the contributions and genius of the Latin peoples, offering reasons as to why the third city—Rome—was so critical in mapping divine providence and the unfolding of Christ's mission.

Rome had neither the revelation granted to the Hebrews nor the heights of intellectual achievement attained by the Greeks. If one were to look at the city in the centuries before Christ, there was little to recommend it as a place of world-historical importance. The little town on the Tiber River constantly found itself situated among more powerful neighbors, be it the Etruscans to the north, the Hellenistic kingdoms of the south, or the menacing trading civilization of Carthage across the sea. Yet Rome ultimately found itself at the center of the drama of the West. This is apparent geographically, for the peninsula of Italy extends itself into the center of the Mediterranean, acting as both a bridge and a barrier between Europe and Africa. At the same time, it lies at the midpoint between the East and West. With Spain and the Holy Land at opposite ends of the sea, Rome found itself conveniently situated for the mission that Virgil would later famously bestow upon it:

Walter Ullmann, *The Growth of Papal Government in the Middle Ages*, 4th ed. (London: Routledge, 2009). Also, still useful and eminently readable is Henri Daniel-Rops, *Histoire de l'Église du Christ*.

Roman, remember by your strength to rule
Earth's peoples—for your arts are to be these:
To pacify, to impose the rule of law,
To spare the conquered, battle down the proud.
(*Aeneid* VI.1151–1154)

Yet how far all that seemed from the mud and thatch huts clustered on the Palatine hill eight centuries before. Rome had to carve out a precarious existence, constantly fighting against those who coveted its prime location. While struggling to survive, it also had to resolve its internal politics, finally rejecting the tyranny of petty monarchs and establishing a constitutional rule of law that remains an exemplary political model to the present day. The men of Rome were farmer-soldiers, whose patient perseverance and unwillingness to allow setbacks to dishearten them produced the astonishing achievements of a Roman civilization that eventually stretched from the Atlantic to the Persian gulf, and from the gates of Scotland to the Sahara desert. They were a practical people: builders, lawyers, organizers, military planners, and that most down-to-earth of all professions, farmers. Their society had been in existence for over half-a-millennium before they began to produce native literature and philosophy. They lived in the shadow of the magnificent Greeks and, finding that Hellenistic philosophical speculations lined up well with their familial and social morality, they became the students of Athens. Indeed, they appropriated Greek thought much better than did their Hellenic forbears. At least in the early days, the Romans attempted to live according to the outline of the virtues developed by the Greeks. One could even say that the Romans practiced what the Greeks preached.

As a constitutional republic, Rome valued above all else the work of administration and recognized the supreme dignity of the law. Aristocratic men were trained from birth in the effective running of the city and its holdings, moving from position to position so that when they took their places in the senate, they would have experience in the many diverse ways of governing the Roman people. *Romanitas* for them was a badge of honor, indicating the

Roman approach to doing things, and it was deeply embedded in the social character of the community. Such a concept (first coined by the Christian writer Tertullian around 200 AD) involved a number of different ideas. From their military ideals came the virtues of courage and steadfastness, particularly in defense of the city and the family. Their agricultural nature added to the concept a sense of hard work and prudence. Furthermore, Romans were expected to carry themselves with honor, which betokened the virtue of *gravitas*, a combination of a sense of personal dignity and public temperance. All of this was leavened by a certain "greatness of soul," called magnanimity by the Greeks, which encouraged generosity and good leadership. Finally, the concept of piety was characteristic of the Roman relationship to family, to the broader society, and to religious duties. This reinforced the idea of gratitude for what one did not himself create or even merit, and it engendered serious respect for the customs and practices of one's ancestors. A good Roman was expected to demonstrate piety to the state, whether in public or in military service. Piety toward one's family—and particularly one's parents—was also critical to the Roman system. Finally, one was to observe with rigor the many duties to the gods of the state. All three levels of piety were necessary for the smooth operation of society.

This dedication to *Romanitas* meant that the speakers of the Latin language were eventually able to overcome their more powerful neighbors. While from a historical perspective Rome seemed often on the verge of total defeat, its courage and tenacity served to get it through many dark days. Roman law was renowned for its justice and equity. For one thing, it was public law, common to the community and not personal, beholden to tyrannical whims. Further, it was flexible, being able to adapt to changing conditions, particularly in reference to the tensions between social classes. Given their practical mindset, the most significant development of the legal system was the rise of a professional class of lawyers and commentators who refined and glossed the tradition, ensuring the ongoing validity of the Roman system in the face of the grave challenges that confronted society through the centuries. These jurists were called *prudentes*, from whence we arrive at the term 'jurisprudence,' or the lively integration of the intellectual virtue of prudence with the developing civil law of a society. Their work would remain one of the cardinal contributions of Roman civilization to the world (indeed, codified by Justinian in the sixth century AD, it will become the basis for nearly every legal system in the modern age). Further flexibility was introduced by the rise of customs that abandoned rigid formalism in favor of empowering magistrates with the ability to modify the harsh letter of the law—that is, to balance strict justice with equity. This was done by broadening the idea of law to include those precepts common to all nations, a concept that robustly informed the development of our understanding of the natural law. Romans also understood the necessity of pursuing the common good as opposed to merely private goods. As Roman history progressed, former enemies became allies and eventually citizens, especially as they realized that Rome governed them better than they could have governed themselves. In this way, almost by accident, the Roman republic gained an empire.

While one can certainly see behind many of these developments the sophisticated virtue ethics of thinkers such as Socrates, Plato, and Aristotle, the Romans embodied these philosophical ideas in a practical way that served to provide a stable foundation for the whole of their society. Summed up in the concept of *Romanitas*, this was the very soul of their civilization. When it broke down, as it did spectacularly in the last republican century (133–44 BC), the results were devastating. Indeed, even under the empire, poets and playwrights cast longing glances toward the *Romanitas* of the past, which had by then been replaced by the moral enormities of the emperors, the wolfish dependencies of the lower classes, and the virtual disappearance of serious efforts to reform the Roman character. Indeed, the self-controlled practices of such marginalized groups as the young Christian movement were in a certain sense a living rebuke to the Romans, who had abandoned the commitment to virtue alive in previous generations. For a long time, ethical systems such as Christianity were to exercise as much of a repulsion as an attraction for imperial-age Romans.

Like a moth to a flame, the early Church gravitated toward Rome. The center of a worldwide empire and home to over a million souls, it was logical that missionary efforts would concentrate on such a prize. Indeed, it was the destination of Peter the Apostle, who perhaps arrived in Rome as early as 42 AD, but certainly took up residence here after the Council of Jerusalem in the year 50 when he established himself across the Tiber in the foreign quarters around the Vatican hill and Trastevere. It was not only Peter but also Paul, the Apostle to the Gentiles, who had said, "I must also see Rome" (Acts 19:21). As a result, the two most prominent members of the young Church converged on the imperial city, and there met their respective martyrdoms. This "double Apostolicity" established Rome as one of the epicenters of the Christian world, a fact repeatedly recognized by the early Fathers and Councils of the Church. The providential nature of these events is evident in that the Church, at once both Jewish and Greek, was now also—permanently and ineffaceably—Roman in character. Christianity wove the best of these cultures together. Like three legs of a stool, without Athens, Jerusalem, or Rome, the Catholic Church and Western civilization itself would have fallen. Rome provided a fertile field for sowing the word of God. Converts streamed into the Roman Church from all social classes, including from senatorial families and even the imperial household. While subjected to periodic persecution, for the most part Christianity was left largely unhindered for the first 200 years of its existence, and during this time converts abounded as did the creation of the foundations for the mighty works of faith that would be reared in the future. As Rome became Christian, Christianity became more Roman. This process of inculturation was part of the "Incarnational" character of the Church itself. It took the existing good of a culture and leavened it with the yeast of the Gospel. Just as Christianity bore marks of its Hebrew heritage and its Hellenistic upbringing, so too did the infant Church take into itself the genius of the Roman people.

The real Christian revolution in the ancient world was the recognition of the material body as critical to human dignity. Countless are the ancient religions that pursued spirituality to the detriment of the corporeal. From dualisms like Gnosticism that professed bodily life to be evil, to Eastern religions that viewed all of material existence as suffering, there were a surfeit of spiritual answers to the problems of the human condition. Christianity too affirmed the reality and superiority of the spiritual, but also confessed the goodness of the material world as a necessary corollary. The body was the nexus for the soul's salvation. Only graced works performed by embodied human persons were meritorious before God. The governance of bodies was therefore a key matter for moral consideration. Further, the Church taught that the ordinary ways in which grace was granted were material—namely, water, bread, wine, oil, human bodies. From the beginning Christianity's spiritual mission was mediated in and through an incarnational, material, and bodily reality. This had a marked effect on Christian social attitudes. The Church was to preside over humans in the "wayfaring" state—that is, bodies and souls together striving for salvation. It was to be a physical, visible community of faith whose most precious rituals were material and bodily. Unlike the ancient cultic religions, Christianity embraced material charity as a privileged mode of spiritual striving. It was to be the custodian of the offerings of the faithful who laid up treasure in heaven by endowing the Church upon earth.[2] All of these realities are intrinsic to the nature of the Christian Church, as much an earthly and material thing as it is a heavenly and spiritual one. To teach and to rule the Christian people meant not only the perfection and training of souls, but of human persons who are unified composites of body and soul made in the image and likeness of the one, true God who became flesh to save and redeem humanity, in both body and soul. Spiritual direction was certainly understood to be a noble and necessary good (as it is in nearly all world religions), but the administration of the material and bodily life of Christians was likewise understood—rightly—to be not only good, but necessary, meritorious,

2   Peter Brown, *Through the Eye of a Needle: Wealth, the Fall of Rome, and the Making of Christianity in the West, 350–550 AD* (Princeton: Princeton University Press, 2014).

and holy. As the Romans understood perfectly, it is of.no use to know military theory inside and out if your soldiers are starving on the eve of battle.

The most effective way of organizing and governing embodied persons yet developed was the legal and administrative mechanisms of the Roman government. It was natural that Roman Christians began to employ the techniques and tactics of the Roman society around them. Like their medieval heirs, the early Christians knew that all truth was one, and that wherever it might be found it was the legitimate inheritance of the disciples of the God of Truth.[3] Just as the Church would utilize important insights from Greek philosophy in order to understand more deeply the mysteries of the Holy Trinity and the Incarnation of God, so too would she incorporate Roman legal and administrative genius in order to organize her practical life for the glory of God. Centered around the person of the bishop was arranged a college of deacons and of priests, each with distinct duties. Of particular concern was the provision for the poor. As can be seen in the Book of Acts, the early Christians generously endowed the Apostolic Church so as to give her the capacity to care for the poor and sick of the community (Acts 2:44–45). The Apostles, overburdened by this (necessary) management of temporalities, appointed the first seven deacons whose job it would be to oversee the administration of these material goods. This diaconal model was copied all over the empire, and particularly in Rome,

---

3   In this respect, Tertullian, with his question, "What has Athens to do with Jerusalem?" is an outlier when placed against St. Justin, St. Clement, Origen, and the other ante-Nicene Fathers. Indeed, Tertullian himself uses the classical tradition with alacrity. One could say the whole of the early Church had answered Tertullian with a single word—"everything." Christianity's embrace of the deuterocanonical books like Sirach and Wisdom also testifies to this. The attempts of Adolph Harnack and many others to denigrate the Greeks and affirm a primitive Jewish Christianity untainted by the pagan world have been shown to be fruitless. Christianity was as Greek and Roman as it was Jewish from the very beginning. See Robert Wilken, *The Spirit of Early Christian Thought* (New Haven: Yale, 2003), xvi–xvii.

where the college of deacons remained exceptionally influential. Long before the official legalization of Christianity, people marveled at the efficiency of charitable distribution and the sheer number of people that the Roman Church was able to support, all the while managing to fund other ecclesiastical operations such as cult and burials. The Roman Church from very early in its history had oversight over a number of different classes of people, including clerics, virgins, widows, and orphans, all the way to the fraternity of catacomb diggers (which appears at one time even to have been a minor order). All of these were dependent upon the administrative skill of the Roman Church to run smoothly—that is, to succeed in the task of unifying many diverse people, activities, and goods in view of bringing the entire Church into closer union with Christ her Head. As did bishops all over the Christian world, the Roman See came to follow a familiar pattern: "[T]he bishop as chief pastor of the local Church ... came to represent the fulness of the ministry. He was prophet, teacher, chief celebrant at the liturgical assembly, and chairman of the board of overseers of the Christian 'synagogue.' But he could never perform his functions unaided. It was still the entire church, acting in him as its head and with the deacons and presbyters as the more important organs, that embodied the full ministry of the Church."[4] From the beginning the Church was a *corporation* in the Roman and medieval sense, a group of embodied individuals under the headship of the bishop, whose common end was to bring Christ's saving work into the midst of the world. In order to do this, a vast apparatus of spiritual and social services began to evolve as natural and proper adjuncts of the Christian mission.

It is apparent that all these provisions were in place not only before legalization in 313AD, but even before the dawn of the

4   George Williams, "The Ministry of the Ante-Nicene Church (c. 125–325)" in *The Ministry in Historical Perspectives*, eds. H. Richard Niebuhr and Daniel Day Williams (New York: Harper & Bros, 1956); Cfr. Wendy Mayer and Pauline Allan, "Through a Bishop's Eyes: Toward a Definition of Pastoral Care in Late Antiquity," in *Augustinianum* 40 (2000): 361n57.

great persecutions in the 240s. One of the most beloved of Roman saints was a deacon named Lawrence. No fewer than nine churches in Rome were dedicated to him during the first millennium. When confronted in 258 by the Emperor Valerian and accused of hoarding wealth, Lawrence showed him the massive numbers of poor and sick in Rome supported by the largesse of the Christian community and administered with consummate skill by the Roman Church. Additionally, Constantine's edicts in the 310s demonstrate that much property had been stolen from the Church during the seventy-year period prior to his victory at Milvian Bridge. This meant that the Church of Rome possessed substantial landholdings long before Constantine.[5] The altered legal situation for the Roman Church after the Edict of Milan in 313 was not the beginning of a new age of property and decadence, as was sometimes alleged by older historians, but rather the intensification of a process that had been accelerating since almost the foundation of the Roman Church itself.[6] It would be the practical genius of the Roman Christians, or Christian Romans, that would enable them to order, to manage, and to administer these

---

5   This is made clear in the text of the Edict of Milan in Lactantius, *De mortibus persecutorum*, 48.2–12, and Eusebius, *Ecclesiastical History*, 10.5.9–12. It is reaffirmed in Constantine's letter to the African proconsul Anulinus, 10.5.17, which even includes references to seized "gardens and buildings." See also, Augustine, *Breviculum collationis cum Donatistis libri tres*, 3.18.34, where the Emperor Maxentius ordered that property seized in the persecutions be returned to Pope Militiades in 311.

6   Indeed a "Constantinian Corruption" has been a leitmotif in most works critical of the Catholic Church since the 12th century, finding echoes even in Dante. Such contentions ignore not only the possession of wealth before 313, but also its uncontroversial accrual and use for over 1,000 years. More fundamentally, this critique misses the essential point that a robustly incarnational Church believes humans persons are unities of soul and body made in the image and likeness of God, whose earthly, embodied life requires a moderate and intelligent use of the world's goods for the communication of salvation.

"temporalities" that were so necessary for the relief of the poor, the worship of God, and the maintenance of the ministry. In order to more closely examine the intrinsic connection between administrative excellence and the Church's prolongation of the saving work of Christ the Incarnate Lord, I will offer portraits of four key popes of the late antique Church—namely, St. Damasus (r. 366–384), St. Leo I (r. 440–461), St. Gelasius I (r. 492–496), and St. Gregory I (r. 590–604). Through these four saints in particular, one can see fused together the administrative genius and the holiness prescribed by the Gospel. These indeed were the models of those "wise and prudent servants" whom the Lord set over his household (Lk 12, Mt 24, Mk 13).

Focusing on these four brings both advantages and disadvantages. Each offers a snapshot into the development of papal order as it progressed during the critical centuries after legalization. These four popes were recognized for their remarkable abilities and contributions to the growth of the Holy See. In addition, we are blessed with much more surviving material from these pontificates than from many of their contemporaries. That said, there were many others who might be added to this list of impressive leaders, men such as St. Siricius (r. 384–399), St. Innocent I (r. 401–417), St. Celestine I (r. 422–432), or St. Symmachus (r. 498–514). Indeed, the brilliance of papal leadership from Damasus to Gregory is one of the high points of Catholicism. However, the purpose of the present chapter is not to offer a comprehensive history of early papal administration, but rather to highlight the Roman genius exercised by the most brilliant popes, thereby showing the ways by which they lived lives of sanctity and holiness precisely while ruling the Church in the midst of the world. Such popes were also aided by an increasingly numerous coterie of influential and competent followers who mostly remain nameless: the unknown notaries, archdeacons, and *defensores* of the early Roman Church. This story is their story as well, for the popes knew that they needed a cadre of capable and obedient followers who shared the mission of the burgeoning Church and the commitment to both spiritual and corporal works of mercy.

Damasus: Buidling Memory

By the time Damasus was elected to the Chair of Peter in October of 366, he had already lived a long life of devotion to the Roman Church.[7] Born around 304, he possibly had memories of both the age of persecution and the triumphant entry of Constantine into the city, coupled with the emperor's seemingly miraculous legalization of the Christian faith. Damasus likely entered the service of the Church early on and was assigned to the church of Saint Lawrence, which would later assume his name (now known as San Lorenzo in Damaso), in the heart of the ancient city. While there he lived through the triumph of the orthodox party over Arianism at Nicaea in 325, only to see it suffer a series of setbacks. First, the emperor Constantine abandoned the city after terrible intrafamilial violence (of which he was the author). Decamping to Byzantium, he began work on a "new Rome"—modestly named "Constantinople"—all the while slipping under the increasing sway of Arian holdovers. These Arians increased their influence over Constantine and his sons to such an extent that the whole Church was convulsed by a resurgence of the heresy in the 350s. Damasus was possibly a deacon of the Church when the unfortunate Pope Liberius was taken into exile by the Arian emperor, Constantius II.[8] While in exile Liberius signed several highly ambiguous formularies regarding Arian theology, and unjustly condemned the orthodox hero St. Athanasius. For this reason, he is the first pope in history not to be considered a saint. His exile and vacillation led the emperor to impose an antipope on Rome, Felix II. The compromised Liberius was allowed to return in 358 and, although held in general esteem by the people of Rome, his honor

7   For the most recent treatment of Damasus, see U. Reutter, *Damasus, Bischof von Rom (366–384): Leben und Werke*, Studien und Texte zu Antike und Christentum, vol. 55 (Tübingen, 2009).

8   John R. Curran, *Pagan City and Christian Capital: Rome in the Fourth Century* (Clarendon Press, 2000), 138. The source for this says he "turned back" from accompanying Liberius into this exile, however this may be a slander since the story is found in a very prejudiced source—namely, the anti-Damasan *Libellus Precum*.

and reputation were shattered in the wider Christian community. Upon his return he had to struggle to reoccupy the churches of the city and to remove Felix. Then, in 360, Christianity suffered a further shock—namely, the proclamation of Julian the Apostate as emperor, an aggressive pagan who renounced his Christian baptism and who began to renew the persecutions. Fortunately for the Nicene party, his attention was mostly fixed upon the ascendant Arian faction, whom he attacked and dispersed mercilessly. Had he not died in battle against the Persians in 363, he likely would have trained his sights on the orthodox Nicenes as well. Liberius took the opportunity to receive Arians back into the faith and to reconcile with Athanasius, providing at least a good ending to his hapless career.

Upon the pope's death, the deacon Damasus was elected as the new Bishop of Rome. A man of clear ability and far-reaching vision, he was the perfect man to pick up the pieces after the Liberian interlude and the (all too temporary) victory against Arianism. He needed to restore the prestige and authority of the Roman See after Liberius' compromised papacy and the damage wrought by the Apostate. This was easier said than done since factional politics were rife in Rome and old wounds from the Felician schism had not yet healed. Almost simultaneous with Damasus' election by the Roman clergy, a second election was held in Trastevere that advanced the deacon Ursinus as the new pope. For three years, a desultory struggle ensued that sometimes erupted into open violence. In several instances Damasus was able successfully to appeal to the imperial prefects to ban the Ursinians from the city and to exile their bishop, but the antipope's stubborn followers kept returning and occupying churches. We must be careful in following the details of the conflict because they are only related in partisan accounts sympathetic to the Ursinian schism. What is remarkable, however, is that we can see even in these biased sources how Damasus was able to skillfully negotiate his way to imperial support, with the emperor Valentinian finally upholding his papacy and ordering the remaining Ursinians to be driven out.[9] For the rest of his

9   Ibid., 139–142.

career Damasus faced a barrage of propaganda from the losing side. In 378 they accused him of adultery, a charge that he defeated first before the imperial court, and then at a synod of forty-four bishops in Rome.[10] Indeed it is a testament to Damasus' stature that his admirable qualities come through even in his enemies' scurrilous writing. On one occasion they whispered that he was an *auriscalpius matronarum* or an "ear-tickler of noblewomen."[11] Such sentiments betray Damasus' astonishing success in building up the material legacy of the Roman Church by encouraging pious bequests. While lamentable violence indeed did break out between the parties, Damasus was convinced of three things. In the first place there was a need for unity in the Roman See. He had already lived through a weak papacy and a previous antipope, and he would not tolerate such conditions again. Further, he knew how important imperial support was, and carefully negotiated and leveraged his position, even when the Roman leaders were indifferent Christians. Finally, the struggle with Ursinus had shown him the critical and incarnational significance of the *loca*, or the holy places of Rome, to which he would be devoted for the rest of his career.

Damasus used the administrative power at his disposal in productive and creative ways. Though the exact interpretation of the phrase is vague, it seems safe to say that Damasus was the first to set up a formal archive for the papacy, perhaps even during the time of Liberius. This was established in his new foundation of Saint Lawrence in the Campus Martius at the center of the city. While this may have been a depository for sacred books, if the reading *archivis* is correct, I suspect that it was a centralized repository for the increasing number of papal letters and rescripts.[12] It would

10   Marianne Sághy, "The Bishop of Rome and the Martyrs," in *The Bishop of Rome in Late Antiquity*, ed. Geoffrey D. Dunn (Farnham: Ashgate Publishing, 2015), 45.

11   Curran, 286n177.

12   For the debate on the inscription in question, see ibid., 144n167. See also the forthcoming chapter, Dominic Moreau, "*Ex codicibus et ex antiquis polypticis scrinii Sanctae Sedis Apostolicae*: Canonical Collections and Archives of the Church of Rome in Antiquity" in

fit with Damasus' penchant for increasing levels of administrative organization and centralization. The Roman bishops had been employing notaries for at least a century by this time and had been exchanging letters with bishops throughout the Christian world.[13] Indeed it is likely that St. Fabian (236–250) was the first to appoint notaries for the seven diaconal regions that divided the city. It is notable that these divisions did not correspond to the civil boundaries established by Emperor Augustus, meaning that by at least the early third century the Roman Church had established administrative zones that matched the pastoral needs of the burgeoning community. Under Fabian these notaries were appointed to serve each of the seven deacons, particularly to the end of creating reliable records of the sufferings of the Roman martyrs, an interest that would intensify significantly under Damasus.[14] Indeed under his rule the Roman church asserted its supervision over the celebration of public cult within the city and beyond. Damasus interdicted unauthorized priests from saying Mass, even privately. This ensured proper order within a see that had been racked by heresy, schism, and untoward political pressure.[15]

As an effective leader, Damasus also knew how to discern talent and delegate responsibility. He knew his weaknesses and surrounded himself with clerics who might offset them. He was well aware that he was no theologian, having focused his career on

Brill Companion to the Roman Curia, ed. Donald Prudlo (Leiden: Brill, 2023). See also, Reginald L. Poole, *Lectures on the History of the Papal Chancery Down to the Time of Innocent III* (Cambridge: The University Press, 1915), 14.

13   Detlev Jasper and Horst Fuhrmann, *Papal Letters in the Early Middle Ages,* History of Medieval Canon Law (Washington, DC: Catholic University of America Press, 2001).

14   Thomas F. X. Noble, *The Republic of St. Peter: The Birth of the Papal State, 680–825* (Philadelphia: University of Pennsylvania Press, 1991), 217; Poole, *Lectures on the History of the Papal Chancery*, 7, 12.

15   Kristina Sessa, *The Formation of Papal Authority in Late Antique Italy: Roman Bishops and the Domestic Sphere* (New York: Cambridge University Press, 2014), 210.

administration and diplomacy. Near the end of his life he brought into his employ a brilliant ascetic and theologian, Jerome, as his secretary.[16] Such theological brilliance was an effective enhancement to Damasus' own talents. In spite of this seemingly good fit, Jerome's impatience with the niceties of Church administration and the necessity for diplomatic subtlety paired uneasily with his often-caustic temperament. Damasus was faced with resistance to the foreigner Jerome from within his own clerical establishment, an animosity that the brilliant Illyrian native heartily returned. Knowing that his protege was unsuited for the administrative tasks in which he himself excelled, he prudently resolved to direct Jerome to service more suited to his genius (and to his personality). It was Damasus, Jerome tells us himself, who was critical in directing his attention to the revision of the *Vetus Itala*, the early Latin translation of the Bible, which was to come glorious fruition over the course of Jerome's career as the Latin Vulgate.[17] This was the most significant biblical translations ever undertaken, and it became one of the most influential texts in history, indeed one

16   For Jerome, see Stefan Rebenich, *Jerome* (London: Routledge, 2002).

17   Jerome to Damasus, AD 383, "You urge me to revise the old Latin version and, as it were, to sit in judgment on the copies of the Scriptures which are now scattered throughout the whole world.... The labour is one of love, but at the same time both perilous and presumptuous; for in judging others I must be content to be judged by all; and how can I dare to change the language of the world in its hoary old age, and carry it back to the early days of its infancy? Is there a man, learned or unlearned, who will not, when he takes the volume into his hands, and perceives that what he reads does not suit his settled tastes, break out immediately into violent language, and call me a forger and a profane person for having the audacity to add anything to the ancient books, or to make any changes or corrections therein? Now there are two consoling reflections which enable me to bear the odium—in the first place, the command is given by you who are the supreme bishop; and secondly, even on the showing of those who revile us, readings at variance with the early copies cannot be right." For the history of the *Vetus Itala* and the *Vulgate*, see *The Cambridge History of the Bible*, vol. 1 (Cambridge, Cambridge University Press, 1975).

which was to become the normative version for the whole Latin Church, not to mention the first book printed by Gutenberg. Damasus' leadership is exceptionally evident in this case. Recognizing the ecclesial situation in Rome, he knew that dismissing Jerome from his service was necessary to bring peace to the clergy. Jerome was more suited to a life of private scholarship than public service, and Damasus had the foresight to recognize his aptitude for a project that would be of immeasurable benefit to the whole Church. Two birds with one stone, indeed. For a leader to turn crisis into opportunity like this takes significant courage and prescience. Damasus demonstrated both.

For the majority of his pontificate, his central concerns were peace, stability, and solidifying both Nicene orthodoxy and good papal governance. This is most evident in his extraordinary efforts to organize the churches and shrines of the city of Rome. Indeed, it is not too much a stretch to say that the Christian Rome that pilgrims have encountered from that day up through the present was a result of the Damasan project. Knowing the centrality of the Incarnation, Damasus made it a point to focus his rule on the physical and material churches of his city, pairing them with the martyrs who had shed their blood so as to secure the faith that Christians now received as "sons and heirs, heirs of God and fellow heirs with Christ" (Rom 8:17). The Arians disdained the cults of the martyrs, whereas the various schismatics sought to annex the sacred places to their own use. The pope knew that the cults of the saints were critical links that tied the Church historically back to Christ and vertically to heaven. He needed to secure those outposts as a commander secures strategic points on a battlefield. To that end he began a program to ensure good governance and pastoral administration of the historical parishes of the city. Yet more than that he reached out into the suburban areas, particularly the cemeteries and catacombs, to ensure that the places where the saints suffered, died, and were buried were suitably memorialized. A Church without memory cannot be an incarnational Church, and the sinews of the visible body of Christ ran between altars and shrines in the dense network of lived Christian holiness.

As the emperors increasingly abandoned the ancient city, Damasus took charge. There was a genuine risk of Rome becoming a backwater, while Constantinople and, later, Ravenna and Milan, took center stage. Damasus' astonishing efforts prevented the worst outcomes, and achieved an astonishing transition that set in motion the creation of a new Rome, oriented not around the civic spaces of republic and empire, but around the shrines and places of worship of the new leaven of Christianity. As Curran says, "His lasting contribution to the Christian topography is evidence of a tenacious and embracing vision which was to set him apart from emperors as one of the most important Roman Christians of the fourth century."[18] I would go even further than this qualifying remark, and rate Damasus as one of the most pivotal figures, pagan or Christian, of the late antique era within the city of Rome. He achieved this recognition by focusing on three central pillars of what could certainly be called a well-planned and executed program for a wholesale reorientation of the city. In the first place he made sure to maintain the existing Roman basilicas and property, both those remaining from the pre-Constantinian period as well as the new properties bequeathed by the piety of the Roman emperors after legalization. Related to this was his extension of supervision and concern over the suburban cemeteries, paying particular attention to the catacombs wherein lay the bodies of the early Roman martyrs. Finally, wherever he found such shrines and tombs, he took special pains to memorialize them, and mark them so that anyone would be able to identify the saints as well as their relation to the Roman bishop. It almost goes without saying that such a program would have been impossible had not Damasus been especially adept at the kind of fundraising necessary to sustain such a massive undertaking.[19]

18 Curran, 142.
19 Since the first Roman bishops from the aristocracy date from only the end of the 400s, we can also be sure that 4th century buildings were not built out of the Roman bishops' private or familial wealth. Glen L. Thompson, "The *Pax Constantiniana* and the Roman

The *Liber Pontificalis*, a work first compiled during the fifth or sixth centuries, is a source that contains much that is legendary, but whose careful use can tell us much about the development of Roman ecclesial topography.[20] It contains the sober record, "He (Damasus) searched out and found many bodies of the saints and made them known in poetic verse."[21] Coupled with archaeological findings, scholars can now see Damasus' hand in the construction of Sant' Anastasia on the Palatine (the first church to make its appearance in the heart of the ancient Roman civic space), San Lorenzo in Damaso, Ss. Giovanni e Paolo, Ss. Nereo ed Achilleo, Santa Cecilia, and Santa Pudenziana.[22] He further ensured that the ancient *tituli* or the parish churches of the city were adequately manned by trained, professional clerics. Damasus also moved into the countryside, aligning suburban shrines with Roman parishes, and assigning titular clerics to these outlying places, both to secure the shrines of the martyrs with solid pastoral oversight, and to deny their use by various heretical or schismatic groups.[23]

Perhaps most famously he collaborated with his close friend, the Roman stonecutter and calligrapher Filocalus.[24] This brilliant artist created the elegant Filocalian script, which was used to immortalize the pontiff's epigrammatic verses in dozens of places throughout the city and its countryside. Many of these verses continue to exist in the

---

Episcopate," in *The Bishop of Rome in Late Antiquity*, ed. Geoffrey D. Dunn (Farnham: Ashgate Publishing, 2015), 30.

20   Ibid., 24.

21   "Hic multa corpora sanctorum requisivit et invenit quorum etiam versibus declaravit." *Liber Pontificalis*, i. 212. Cfr. Curran, 193. The first scholarly edition of the *Liber* was by Msgr. Louis Duchesne, *Le Liber pontificalis* (Paris: E. Thorin, 1886–1892). See, Thomas. F. X. Noble, "A New Look at the *Liber Pontificalis*," *Archivum Historiae Pontificae* 23 (1985): 347–358.

22   Thompson, 28–29.

23   Ibid., 35n59, citing Harry O. Maier, "The Topography of Heresy and Dissent in Late-Fourth-Century Rome," in *Historia: Zeitschrift Für Alte Geschichte* 44.2 (1995): 232–249.

24   Filocalus himself says he was "Damasi pappae (sic) cultor atque amator."

very places where Damasus installed them, immortalizing the memories of the saints while tying them to the Roman bishop's oversight of the cults of the martyrs.[25] As one descends into the crypt of San Clemente or comes into the church Sant' Agnese fuori le Mura, the pilgrim is still greeted by the stately inscriptions. Damasus wove himself into many of these epigrams. This was at once canny and Catholic. It tied the memory of the martyrs to the orthodox church, all the while reinforcing papal prerogatives. One can see this in the epigram dedicated to his martyred predecessor, Sixtus II (r. 257–258), where he evokes not only the community of the faithful, both living and dead, but reinforces the proper qualities of the pastor who lays down his life for his flock.[26] Damasus paid particular attention to the cults of Peter and Paul, axial for the claims of the Roman Church. He probably continued the elaboration of the Constantinian basilica over the bones of St. Peter, while at the same time laying the groundwork for the massive five-aisled basilica of St. Paul, which was to stand until the devastating fire of 1823.[27] When pilgrims came to visit the shrines of the Apostles, they would see visual evidence connecting their devotion to the current Roman bishop. It was Damasus' particular genius that connected Peter and Paul not only as grounds to papal claims, but to a broader vision of the providential history of the city itself. In his Epigram at the shrine of the joint apostles in San Sebastiano fuori le Mura he makes some startling claims.[28] In it Damasus repeats the old assertion that Peter

25   Carlo Carletti, *Damaso e i martiri di Roma* (Vatican City: Pontificia commissione di archeologia sacra, 1985).
26   Sághy, 52–53.
27   Curran, 146–147.
28   The history of the cults of Peter and Paul at this spot is somewhat unclear and the subject of controversy. It is likely that a shrine to the double martyrdom of the apostles came to be erected here in the 250s, as can be seen by numerous *graffiti*, probably the origin of the 29 June double feast day. This shrine fell out of favor after legalization since the Apostles could now be publicly venerated at their respective tombs. There is no evidence that supports the old story that their bones were temporarily moved there during the persecutions. Damasus revived the local cult with his epigram celebrating the Concord of the Apostles. See Margherita Guarducci,

and Paul together suffered martyrdom bringing Christianity to Rome, but then he makes a stunning move. "Rome has merited to claim them as citizens. Damasus wished to proclaim these things, O new stars, to your praise." For Damasus, Rome has a new founding at the death of the Apostles, who did not end Rome's mission, but rather elevated its old earthly mission to a heavenly one. They displace the earlier twins Romulus and Remus, as well as Castor and Pollux.[29] The Apostles are bestowed with that most honored title in the pre-Christian world: Roman citizens. Rome is vindicated not only in a Christian sense, but in a world-historical one. This was no mere *translatio imperii*, but rather a wholesale takeover.

To say Damasus was successful is an understatement. Christianity had been hard at work weaving together the strands of Jerusalem, Athens, and Rome, and this pope arrived on the scene and affixed an exclamation point to this undertaking. His patient work of diplomacy, administration, reconciliation, building, and memorializing was to be staggeringly rewarded. His careful cultivation of the Church in its local context had empire-wide consequences that echo down through history. Beside his enduring monuments to the martyrs that still make up the fabric of Christian Rome, he added the luster of the Latin Vulgate. Yet more than this, in the last years of his life he found a faithful emperor and lived to see the triumph of Nicene orthodoxy enshrined in the imperial law. When Theodosius the Great (r. 379–395) and his co-emperors issued the *Edict of Thessalonica* in 380, they not only established the Catholic Church as the sole legal religion of the empire, but they also outlawed all other religions. However, being a legal document, a definition was necessary. The document thereby defined the legal, Catholic religion as follows:

> It is our desire that all the various nations which are subject to our clemency and moderation, should continue to

The Tomb of St. Peter (New York: Hawthorn Books, 1960), chapter 6. This continues to be debated by archaeologists and historians.
29   Sághy, 54.

the profession of that religion which was delivered to the Romans by the divine Apostle Peter, as it has been preserved by faithful tradition and which is now professed by the Pontiff Damasus and by Peter, Bishop of Alexandria, a man of apostolic holiness. According to the apostolic teaching and the doctrine of the Gospel, let us believe in the one deity of the Father, Son and Holy Spirit, in equal majesty and in a holy Trinity. We authorize the followers of this law to assume the title Catholic Christians.[30]

It is not hard to see what a stunning testimony this was to the patience, prudence, and perseverance of Pope Damasus. Few popes have had so much foresight. His active administration and providence allowed the Church to thrive after the convulsions of the mid-fourth century through his careful attention to diplomacy, his adept crisis management, and his ability to look beyond merely contemporary concerns. The prudential governance of his own see proved a model for others, and his preservation of the memory of the faith, in both its spiritual and material forms provided a pattern for many later bishops to follow.

Leo and the Defense of the Common Good

In the half-century that elapsed between the death of Damasus and the accession of Leo the Great, the Church continued its evolution, one that paralleled the administrative developments of the Roman See. The interlude included many capable and prudential pontiffs, including Siricius, Innocent I, Zosimus, and Celestine I, whose strong leadership created a stable and professional ecclesiastical establishment. During that interval two Ecumenical Councils met, Constantinople I in 381 and Ephesus in 431, the latter memorably condemning Patriarch Nestorius of the imperial city and

---

30   Edict of Thessalonica (380), inscribed in the Theodosian Code, XVI.1.2. Translated in Henry Bettenson, *Documents of the Christian Church* (London: Oxford University Press, 1943), 31.

recognizing Mary's title as Mother of God. The period also saw the
golden age of Patristic writing, as the brilliant Cappadocian Fathers
gave way to such men as St. John Chrysostom and St. Augustine.
It was especially the latter who set his stamp on the thought of the
Latin Church, and whose life we will have occasion to revisit.
While the Church was going from strength to strength, the political
situation was far from ideal. The defeat of the Roman legions at
the battle of Adrianople in 378 sounded the death knell of the
supremacy of the elite Roman legions. For the next 1000 years the
battlefield would be dominated by the cavalry of the new barbarian
peoples then migrating into Europe. In spite of the reign of the
Catholic emperor Theodosius, subsequent Roman leaders were
weak and divided, often themselves adhering to various branches
of heretical Christianity. The Rhine border had been breached in
the winter of 406–407, and new peoples began to immigrate into
the old empire, prodded by the advancing Hunnish hordes from
the far east. The Romans had for many years been outsourcing
their protection to such barbarian mercenaries, a policy that
betokened a dying civilization. The wars of the fifth century were
largely ones fought between various peoples, rather than simply
being confrontations between Romans and barbarians.

In 410 the unthinkable happened. Frustrated by the broken
promises of various emperors, the Gothic peoples under Alaric descended upon the city. For three days the Goths sacked Rome,
though they were prevailed upon to spare most of the churches, for
they had been converted to an Arian form of Christianity that was
to plague Italy for the next century.[31] The shock was complete. No
foreign army had set foot in the city for 800 years. Everything that
seemed to be permanent was thrown into chaos. Jerome, Damasus'
secretary, heard of the fall from his cave in Bethlehem. "My voice
sticks in my throat and, as I dictate, sobs choke my utterance. The

---

31   The pope at this time, St. Innocent I, had gone on a mission to make
     peace between Alaric and the weak emperor Honorius at Ravenna.
     Honorius' vacillation meant the peace efforts failed, and the city was
     sacked in Innocent's absence.

City which had taken the whole world was itself taken."[32] That same year the legions had abandoned Britain in order to guard the remaining empire in continental Europe. Barbarian warlords contended for scraps from the increasingly debilitated emperors of the West, as they confronted one another for control of the remaining provinces. The city of Rome found itself increasingly abandoned by the secular authorities, and yet the popes remained and rebuilt upon the foundations of the pagan city. It would be due to their careful leadership that both the church and the city would continue to survive such times of crisis.

The Roman bishops were chosen exclusively from among the Roman clergy for the first five centuries of Christianity. Indeed, the Church had developed a system whereby young clerics would be taken into minor orders and given various responsibilities that would train them for rulership. Once again, we see a legacy derived from the tradition of Roman administrative genius. During the republic, from a very early time, a complicated bureaucracy was set up that ensured good governance in the city. This regarded not only military and diplomatic matters, but also such humble tasks as the maintenance of the sewers and the delivery of grain. It was thought that in order to be a good governor one had to have experience in every area of Roman administration. To that end they developed a series of offices, each with increasing levels of responsibility and each requiring various skillsets. These offices were manned by the aristocratic patricians of Rome. While the patricians held the balance of political authority and had the privilege of governing, in the early republic this was balanced by a sense of serious responsibility. Upon the Roman upper class devolved the responsibility for the stable functioning of the community. They were expected to spend the whole of their lives in unremunerated public service, for their wealth and position betokened a concomitant need to care for the community. A Roman patrician was expected not only to serve in the army and learn how to command therein, but he was also expected to finance his own armor and horses. At the conclusion of military

32   St. Jerome, letter 127.12.

service, he entered the *cursus honorum* or the course of offices to be undertaken before one could rise to political leadership. They would learn about building and maintaining the Roman infrastructure as well as studying the management and deployment of other citizens. They would be schooled in diligent recordkeeping and careful attention to the law, but also pursue experience in public speech. After a patrician had completed all of this service, he was eligible for the highest offices in the state. As long as the Roman patricians balanced their power with this refined sense of their duty to unpaid public service the republic thrived.

It is no mistake that the Church began to develop a parallel system that looked very much like an ecclesiastical *cursus honorum*. Indeed, when St. Ambrose of Milan compiled his book on the various ministries of the Church, he named it *De Officiis*, the exact title used by Cicero for his famous work.[33] While the name *cursus honorum* was never used, we can see its practical implementation in the various offices in the Roman Church, and how they were used to provide on-the-job training to clergy at various stages of their careers.[34] By the second century one notes the full panoply of minor orders in the Church, many of which had to do with practical functions of running an ecclesiastical establishment. At puberty young men were tonsured and made porters and lectors, offices dealing with the mundane tasks necessary to running a *titulus* (titular church), with a particular emphasis on the literacy required both for the celebration of the liturgy and for routine Church administration. While there seems to be no evidence of clerical schools at this period, it is likely that these teenaged clerics were given a solid grounding in at least the fundamentals of the liberal arts. At this point they were expected to marry and regularize their domestic

33   St. Ambrose, *Ambrose: De Officiis*, ed. Ivor J. Davidson, 2 vols. (Oxford: Oxford University Press, 2001).

34   Geoffrey D. Dunn, "The Clerical *Cursus Honorum* in the Late Antique Roman Church," in *Scrinium* 9.1 (2013): 120–133. This disappointingly brief article does not really address the relation to the Roman *cursus* at all, and does not tie the *cursus* either to Ambrose or ordination.

lives, after which they would be raised to the offices of exorcist, acolyte, and subdeacon.[35] This point about domesticity has been stressed in recent scholarship, which suggests that the model for the development of Roman administration was based on the classical Greek concept of *oikonomia*, or domestic economy.[36] In this Aristotelian conception, a man could not be expected to be a prudent administrator who could not adequately manage his own household. Having been tested in all of the offices requiring ecclesial, domestic, and pastoral oversight, only then was a man qualified to be made a bishop. It seems that by the fifth century the model of the Roman householder had been adopted by the Roman Church (to wit the phrase "the household of the faith").[37] By the late fourth century there was a need to reassert this *cursus*, which had become the default of the Roman Church, for two salient reasons. In the first place, some were being raised far too quickly to the Episcopate; witness Ambrose himself, who went from unbaptized pagan to Bishop of Milan over the course of a week. Not all such suddenly intruded candidates were as successful as Ambrose, and there needed to be a relief valve to test them.[38] Furthermore, this century saw many aristocratic and wealthy converts entering the Church, including many with extensive civil administrative experience.[39]

35   Ibid., 122. This was by the time of Pope Siricius, and likely even earlier. See also, Julia Hillner, "Clerics, Property and Patronage: The Case of the Roman Titular Churches," in *Antiquité tardive* 14 (2006): 59–68.

36   Kristina Sessa, *The Formation of Papal Authority in Late Antique Italy: Roman Bishops and the Domestic Sphere* (New York: Cambridge, 2014). See also, Georg Schöllgen, "Hausgemeinden, Oikos-Ekklesiologie und monarchischer Episkopat. Überlegungen zu einer neuen Forschungsrichtung," in *Jahrbuch für Antike und Christentum* 31 (1988): 74–90.

37   Sessa, 274. See also, Hartmut G. Ziche, "Administrer la propriéte de l'église: L'évêque comme clerc et comme entrepreneur,"in *Antiquité tardive* 14 (2006): 69–78.

38   Dunn, "The Clerical *Cursus Honorum*," 133.

39   T. D. Barnes, "Statistics and the Conversion of the Roman Aristocracy," in *The Journal of Roman Studies* 85 (1995): 135–147.

These were natural candidates for leadership positions in Christianity, but the councils and popes of the century were careful to make sure that these too were found worthy, through a *cursus* appropriate to them, to ensure their spiritual maturity.[40]

One such figure who advanced through the normal *cursus* and proved himself exceptionally adept at the *oikonomia* of the household of God was Leo. By the 420s the young Leo was already archdeacon of the city, in charge of coordinating with the seven diaconal superintendents of Rome's ecclesial fabric.[41] He successfully completed many missions for the papacy, both within and outside the city of Rome. In the city, he organized the charitable outlays of the papacy, all the while administering the finances of the Church. He likely was personal aide to one or more popes. He proved especially competent as a papal delegate, able to balance competing interests and resolve conflicts to the credit of the Church. One of his signal victories was restoring friendship between Aetius, the *Magister Militum* in the West, and Albinus, the praetorian prefect, having done this at the request of the emperor.[42] Indeed, early in his career he already had correspondents all over the Mediterranean. John Cassian himself dedicated his work on the Incarnation to the young deacon around the time of the Council of Ephesus in 431. As Daniel-Rops explains:

> St. Leo has all the characteristics of a born leader. Clear-sighted, exact, and methodical, he possessed the kind of brain which instinctively analyses the most complex problems and finds the practical solution to them. He was a firm, unflinching character; the hostile situation never had the slightest effect on him; when everything

40   Ibid., 126, 131. Indeed Dunn proposes no fewer than three distinct *cursus*, one appropriate to those baptized in infancy versus later converts, and one dependent upon social class.

41   For Leo see the comprehensive work by Susan Wessel, *Leo the Great and the Spiritual Rebuilding of a Universal Rome* (Leiden: Brill, 2012), 36. See also, Bronwen Neil, *Leo the Great*, Early Church Fathers (London: Taylor & Francis Ltd., 2009).

42   Ibid., 37.

was on the verge of catastrophe he remained steadfast, and his wonderful serenity brought peace of mind to those troubled folk around him.[43]

Clearly, Leo was marked out for his skills early on, and the clerical *cursus* enabled him to hone his talents.

Leo's vision for governance can be called a dynamic interconnection between *Christianitas* and *Romanitas*. In terms of *Romanitas*, Leo took the best of the Roman tradition and transformed it. He exemplified the virtues spoken above in terms of gravity, constancy, firmness, and discipline, with a legal emphasis on an equity that balanced clemency and severity.[44] Such a mind valued law and practicality, with a view to getting things done in the best and most efficient manner possible. To this was added the leaven of *Christianitas*. As Wessel says, "he confidently brought his model of a compassionate, feeling Christ to bear upon the anxieties that his congregations suffered in light of the barbarian invasions. Politics and theology coalesced profoundly."[45] In this vision his *Romanitas* was seasoned with mercy and compassion, ideas which were not foreign to Roman law with its emphasis on equity and *clementia*, but which acquired a stunningly new valence in the light of Christ. Leo knew that Church law was the vehicle through which mercy could be extended, while at the same time it was critical for forming and disciplining the Christian people. Indeed, Church law and its emphasis on precedent was more flexible than the civil law of the Romans and ensured that the wisdom of the past could be employed and modified to fit new situations.[46]

In the year 440 Leo was on another diplomatic tour of Gaul. So highly respected was he in the city that, upon Pope Sixtus III's

43 Henri Daniel-Rops, *The Church in the Dark Ages*, trans. Audrey Butler (London: Dent, 1960), 102.
44 Philip A. McShane, *La "romanitas" et le Pape Léon-le-Grand: L'apport Culturel des Institutions Impériales à la Formation des Structures Ecclésiastiques* (Tournai: Desclée, 1979), cfr. Wessel, 3.
45 Wessel, 2.
46 Ibid., 156.

death, Leo was elected as the new Roman Bishop *in absentia*. For twenty-one years he would reign, bringing with him his wealth of experience gained in the clerical *cursus honorum*, a living monument to the unification of *Christianitas* and *Romanitas*. As administrator and diplomat, he was well aware of how different interests needed to be coordinated, both inside and outside of the community. Though he was confronted with numerous challenges during his eventful rule, he was able flexibly to adapt and overcome, always taking into account imperial concerns, the conditions brought about by the advance of the Huns, the needs of the Christian people, and the specific challenges of integrating a Christian aristocracy into the fabric of the Roman Church.[47]

Three specific challenges can be cited that establish Leo's strategy and his sanctity. In the first place, there was the terrible problem of the barbarian incursions. The Huns, unlike previous peoples migrating into Europe, were exceptionally violent and swift. They were not even Arian Christians, like the Goths, and so could not be prevailed upon by any appeals to Christianity. To this related Leo's second challenge, the collapse of imperial authority in the West, and the inability of the Roman legions to defend huge swaths of territory in the Latin world. All of this left Leo not only as one of the last remaining substantive magistrates, but also made him increasingly responsible not only for the spiritual, but the temporal health of the people of Rome. Finally, there was the seemingly endless supply of new heresies coming from the East, this time in the form of an overreaction against Nestorianism called (by its critics) Monophysitism. Leo had to meet each of these challenges, sometimes all three at once, to preserve the precarious successes that had been accruing since the legalization and the defeat of Arianism.

Leo's conception of governance was at the same time very exalted at the top while being extremely flexible at the bottom. He, like all Roman bishops, prized unity, and placed the supremacy of

47   Michèle Renée Salzman, *The Making of a Christian Aristocracy. Social and Religious Change in the Western Roman Empire* (Cambridge: Cambridge University Press, 2002).

Roman civil and canon law at the center of his program. Yet he was careful always to solicit advice and to govern through proper channels so as to make the implementation of the law as seamless as possible. Therefore, Leo granted wide latitude to his vicars, both civil and ecclesial. They, like himself, had risen through the system and had proven themselves trustworthy. In a period when correspondence was not only slow, but threatened by barbarian incursions, the pope urgeded his local officials to use their best judgement. He "had a fluid concept of power and leadership that granted autonomy to provincial officials that not only permitted but required them to solve independently all but the most thorny problems."[48] This encouraged local devolution of Roman authority, while retaining the supremacy of the Roman See. Leo was convinced that entrusting the enforcement of canon and civil law to persons worthy of such a charge would create a virtuous cycle, widening the *cursus honorum*, increasing the opportunity for solid administrative formation and fostering good governance, all the while respecting the privileges of the Petrine See.

In order to ensure as good as communication as was possible at the time, Leo employed the burgeoning administrative apparatus of the Holy See. While it is difficult to trace the discrete origins of some of the officers of the papacy, we know that they date from an extremely early period. We have already seen notaries appointed in the early third century. Under Leo (probably earlier) we witness the office of the *Primicerius Notariorum*, who would become one of the most significant officers of the Roman Church.[49] He oversaw the college of notaries who, with increasing professional rigor, produced reams of documents, letters, deeds, declarations, and manumissions. At least from Leo's time, they were in charge of what became known as the Register, or the official calendar of documents produced by each papacy.[50] We know that *defensores* were

---

48   Wessel, 39–40.
49   This Primicerius would rule, along with the Roman archpriest and archdeacon, during a *sede vacante*. Poole, *Lectures*, 15.
50   Wessel, 26.

in existence by the time of Leo, and likely had been present since the reign of Damasus. These *defensores* were lawyers trained in civil and canon law whose job was to defend the legal rights of the various churches of the city. They too had an imperial model, the *defensores civitatis*, who provided free legal counsel and representation for poor residents of the city, in order to defend them against the depredations of the rich.[51] Leo was extremely wary of political faction, which he considered to be poisonous in the Church, undermining the unity and loyalty of the people of God.[52] He insisted that the *cursus* be followed, meaning no one was to be promoted out of turn, even if popular. In addition, by this time the pope had permanent ambassadors, as opposed to simply temporary delegates (which Leo himself had been). He appointed his assistant Julian as *Apocrisarius* to Constantinople.[53] In his letter of appointment, Leo gives us some idea of his diplomatic principles. He advised Julian against interference in the court or in matters of the church in Constantinople, yet at the same time he was to be assiduous in communicating news about both, and to refer all significant decisions to Rome.[54]

Leo had to deal with a number of different ecclesiastical challenges during his tenure, notably those stemming from heresy. There were still Priscillianists and Pelagians about, not to mention the ongoing challenge of the Arian barbarians. Yet the single greatest challenge was the delicate matter of Monophysitism then bubbling up in Constantinople and Egypt.[55] While the West was busy

---

51   For ecclesial *defensores*, see Balthasar Fischer, "Die Entwicklung des Instituts der Defensoren in der römischen Kirche," *Ephemerides Liturgicae* 48 (1939): 443–454.

52   Wessel, 131.

53   Apocrisarius was the equivalent to a papal ambassador (or papal nuncio today), it had a special name because of its status as the intermediary between a bishop and the imperial court.

54   Wessel, 333.

55   While the content of Monophysitism is not the focus of this chapter, one should specify its tenets. It was an excessive reaction against the heresy of Nestorius, condemned at Ephesus in 431. Ephesus

confronting Atilla the Hun, events in the East quickly spun out of control. When the partisans of the Monophysites (who preferred the term "Miaphysites") attempted to hold a council at Ephesus in 449, they not only employed violence against the orthodox party— including the papal legates—but essentially caused the death of the holy Archbishop of Constantinople, St. Flavian. Leo was livid. Now was not the time for flexibility or vacillation. Having been informed firsthand of the so-called council, he denounced it in no uncertain terms as a "Robber Synod." Leo personally undertook to write a "Dogmatic Epistle" stating in clear and plain terms the orthodox doctrine that Christ was one person with two natures—one human and one Divine. He communicated his decisions to the emperor, who ensured the safe conduct of Leo's legates and the elaboration of a new Ecumenical Council in 451 at Chalcedon. Leo instructed the Council that it was to accept his Dogmatic Epistle as the definitive vision of the orthodox faith, which it did. However, he instructed his legates to exercise clemency and mercy for all those who wished to abandon Monophysitism and return to orthodoxy. He wrote, "I have wanted that such moderation be observed amid contentious views and sinful jealousies that, while indeed no excisions or additions to the completeness of the faith should be permitted, yet the remedy of pardon should be granted to those who return to unity and peace."[56] As long as the faith was preserved, Leo was prepared to receive all with open arms and with forgetfulness of past offenses, even those who had stained the

---

condemned the proposition that there were two distinct persons in Christ, and affirmed the unity of Christ's personhood, a divine person. For this reason Mary can truly be called the "Mother of God" since she was mother of the second Person of the Blessed Trinity. Taking their reaction too far, the Monophysites began to deny the full humanity of Christ, maintaining that not only was there one person, there was only one nature—a divine one—in Christ. Denying Christ's full humanity threatened the Incarnation and the redemption, so the Church needed to address this new, opposite heresy.

56   Leo, Ep. 95.2. Cfr. Wessel, 298.

reputation of the Church in the Robber Council. He was even sensitive to the possibility of mistaken impressions, ordering his legates to reaffirm the condemnation of Nestorius, so that Monophysite partisans would not think the whole of the thrust of the Council was directed against them alone. This policy of forceful doctrine and practical moderation won back nearly the whole of the East, with the exception of some intransigent Egyptian bishops. His vision of ecclesial justice was the practical marriage of *Christianitas* and *Romanitas*, an insistence upon the law as servant to salvation. As Wessel states:

> A guiding principle rather than a rigid formula, the justice that Leo conceived of emphasized the capacity of ecclesiastical procedure to facilitate a just and flexible outcome according to the facts of individual cases. Because people were morally ambiguous, the laws that they interpreted and the discipline they administered were to be governed by juridical guidelines that incorporated the intent behind the law. That law was to be followed in every instance scrupulously, but never blindly.... The compassionate application of the law demonstrated that Petrine justice operated in the actions of the Apostolic See.[57]

The final crisis that Leo had to face in the midst of all of this ecclesial politics was to attempt to prevent the Hunnish barbarians from destroying his city. Within living memory of the sack of Alaric, all of Italy was shaken at the prospect of another harrowing invasion of the peninsula. Such fears rapidly began to materialize when Atilla—the "Scourge of God"—invaded Gaul. There he was met by Aetius, the *Magister Militum*, who had assembled a varied group of Visigoths and Roman soldiers, and who bravely faced Atilla down at the Battle of the Catalaunian Fields in 451. While this saved Gaul, Atilla continued his marauding, now with his

57 Wessel, 293.

sights firmly set on Italy. So terrified were people of his coming that the residents of the coastal Veneto fled to the marshes of the lagoon to avoid his wrath, thus planting the seeds for what would become the city of Venice. Atilla implacably marched into the Italian Peninsula. The Roman emperors were bereft of military support and thus the road to Rome lay open, presaging a sack that would make what occurred in Alaric pale in comparison. As a last resort the emperor sent Leo, with only a small group of men, to try to forestall what looked to be inevitable. It is shocking that Valentinian III, who had retreated to Rome from Ravenna, sent the elderly Roman Bishop to do his own job (indeed, later this shadow of a Roman Emperor would kill Aetius, the hero of the Catalaunian Fields, with his own hand). Many modern historians have downplayed the significance and implications of such an event. Here was the aged Leo, bearing no weapons, with a small retinue, coming to face the man who had raped and pillaged his way across Europe, killing bishops upon their own altars. Leo was nearly the last representative of the old Roman order, with no military force to back him up, standing against the conqueror from the East. We have no record of what they said, but we do know that immediately after the meeting Atilla took his army and attempted to exit Italy with all possible speed. Later legends credited visions of Peter and Paul with swords backing up the words of Leo. By any definition, the Roman bishop had saved his people.

Leo's suffering was not over. The Vandals amassed a force that besieged the city in 455. Speeding Rome's later decline, they knocked down the aqueducts that kept the city supplied with fresh water. Leo saw the writing on the wall, and once again went to negotiate with the invader. The Vandals were at least heretical Christians. Leo convinced them to spare the inhabitants and not to burn the city, as long as they were permitted to sack it. It seems that Genseric and his Vandals largely kept to the agreement, the best that Leo could hope for under the dire circumstances. Though a few buildings were burned, and some citizens carried off to Africa as slaves, Rome, bloodied and emptied of inhabitants, managed to survive and Leo's reputation as a savior of the city was further cemented. That Leo was still able to govern his local church, much less correspond with the worldwide body of Christians, is astonishing. In his dealing with the barbarians, he was putting Augustine's *City of God* into practice all the while quelling rumblings of imminent apocalypticism among his flock. Patience and foresight were what was required here, a vision that lasted beyond the devastation of the mere present, and which saw a future beyond one individual lifetime. Leo and Augustine together saw the integration of the new peoples into a new Christendom, not simply an add-on to a tired pagan empire, but a new civilization built from the ground-up. Leavened by the wisdom of the three great cities—Rome, Athens, and Jerusalem—Leo and Augustine envisioned what would become Christendom.

Gelasius: Refining the Law

The moribund Western empire breathed its last in 476 when even the pretense of having an emperor was dropped. Henceforth Italy would be ruled by Ostrogoth Arian heretics, with whom the local Catholics maintained a wary peace, which occasionally broke out into persecution (such as when Boethius was unjustly tried and martyred). The impotent Eastern Emperors (hereafter referred to as Byzantine) were powerless to stop them, and often simply accepted the *de facto* rule of the newcomers. The Christian East had problems of its own. Beside dealing with barbarian incursions, the emperors also had an ongoing problem with Monophysitism. In order to end this quarrel and promote unity, the Emperor Zeno issued the *Henotikon* in 482. It was in effect an attempt to overthrow the Council of Chalcedon that tried to reduce the orthodox faith to a "mere Christianity" that simply affirmed the Nicene Creed without further additions. The Roman Church saw through this attempt to undo an Ecumenical Council and promptly condemned the *Henotikon* and excommunicated the Patriarch of Constantinople, Acacius, in 484. This lamentably led to a schism that endured until 519.

An axial figure in all this was Pope Felix III (r. 483–492). We know that Felix was the first recorded pope from an aristocratic, senatorial family.[58] Such individuals brought with them their *Romanitas* along with a comprehensive approach to governance and administration, modeled on the Roman householder. It was under Felix and his successors that the machinery of Roman ecclesial administration reached a perfection that would be unequaled by the courts of Europe for hundreds of years. It was Felix who excommunicated Acacius and intervened forcefully when Emperor Zeno tried to depose the orthodox patriarchs of Antioch and Alexandria. Rome was demonstrating its exceptional independence. No longer under the sway of imperial Constantinople, she was able freely to exercise a position of remarkable leadership. From the time of Felix's reign forward, we begin to benefit from a rising numbers of surviving papal documents. While letters and rescripts had been pouring from the papal *scrinium* for over 100 years, it is only during his reign that scholars begin to have a critical mass with which to work. For example, we know that in Felix's correspondence with the emperor we have the first papal document directed to someone outside the clergy.[59] It seems clear that Felix was aided by a team of notaries and secretaries, who assisted him in drawing up his epistles. It was one of these who would later succeed him as pope.

St. Gelasius I (r. 492–496) was given but a brief pontificate, but it was of axial importance for the development of the machinery of papal government and for the theory of the papal office.[60] While the Acacian schism persisted through his reign, Gelasius continued

---

58   Sessa, 276.

59   Bronwen Neil and Pauline Allen, *The Letters of Gelasius I (492–496): Pastor and Micro-Manager of the Church of Rome* (Turnhout: Brepols, 2014), 11.

60   For Gelasius, see ibid.; Walter Ullmann, *Gelasius I. (492–496): das Papsttum an der Wende der Spätantike zum Mittelalter* (Stuttgart Hiersemann 1981); and, J. Taylor, "The Early Papacy at Work: Gelasius I (492–6)," in *Journal of Religious History* 8 (1975): 317–32.

the hard line taken by his mentor, Felix. Though this meant that the schism would last nearly a generation, it ended with Roman success, as the Acacians were defeated, and the orthodox Justin and Justinian took up the Byzantine throne. Indeed, in response to this crisis, the pope summarized all his predecessors' achievements and became "the most radical and cogent theorist of papal monarchy to that time."[61] While keeping an eye on universal problems of governance and jurisdiction, Gelasius' main problems were of a more local nature. In the first place, he had to negotiate the management of the Church in the absence of strong imperial control, and in the midst of a barbarian Arian kingdom. As a result, more and more of the Roman people began to turn to their bishop for leadership. Crises were manifold during this period, including economic instability, rampant crime and violence, and a chronic shortage of qualified clergy. This meant Gelasius had to handle an increasing administrative load, which he skillfully navigated through salutary innovations. It was during his reign that a watershed was reached in the development of canon law and in the financial apparatus of the Roman Church. It is astonishing what Gelasius was able to achieve in such a short pontificate, leveraging the achievements of all the popes since the legalization of Christianity, and setting a course that would endure well into the middle ages. It is probably no mistake that he was the first pope in history hailed with the title "Vicar of Christ."[62]

While the pope was unsuccessful at healing the Acacian schism, the issue did give him a platform to reinforce and refine the claims of the Roman See. Ever concerned for right order and for the preservation of the faith, a famous decretal is attributed to him that reasserts not only the books that were considered canonical but also approving works of the Church Fathers, and indicating heretical or apocryphal documents by name.[63] Beside being a precious window into the

---

61 Taylor, "The Early Papacy," 317.
62 Gelasius, ep. 30.15; cfr. Neil and Allen, *Letters of Gelasius*, 50.
63 Gelasius, ep. 42; cfr. ibid., 157–169. The attribution of this decretal to Gelasius is uncertain, as it likely reached its final form in the

development of the biblical canon and the status of various writings around the year 500, the letter is careful to deftly weave in claims for the primacy of the Roman See. Collecting the sentiments of the popes of the previous hundred years, the letter asserts Roman primacy by reference to the Petrine commission, noting that most other bishoprics arose only in post-Apostolic times by imperial or synodical decree. In a Damasan move, it then undergirds the Roman claim by bringing in the martyrdom of St. Paul whose presence, with Peter, guarantees that Rome has "precedence over all the other cities of the world." The decretal then nods to the claims of Antioch and Alexandria, hallowed by their Petrine origins, but lesser than Rome according to Peter's definitive decision. Conspicuous by its absence is Constantinople, which had claimed not only precedence over the ancient Eastern sees, but even equality with Rome itself. The letter cleverly defuses the imperial city's claims not only by ignoring them, but by oblique reference to its posterior foundation and non-Petrine origin, unlike the allied sees of Alexandria and Antioch, within the context of the Acacian schism (centered in Constantinople). This document underlines the positive claims of the papacy while minimizing the legitimacy of its schismatic opponents. It reinforced the papacy's allies, all the while maintaining a studious silence in breaching topics that would unsettle the imperial authorities. It was a diplomatic *tour de force*. And what is more, it provided a basis for Roman primacy even *after* the schism was ended. All in all, it was a monumental work of prudential audacity.

Gelasius also knew how to seize a historical moment. For years the papacy had labored in the shadow of the Western Roman emperors. Now that imperial order had collapsed there, it was a perfect moment to make a declaration regarding the proper orientation of the Church to the state. In the West there had always been a certain amount of freedom and spiritual authority exercised by the

second quarter of the 500s. That said, it is a clear reaffirmation of Gelasian principles, and seems to reflect the situation on the ground during the Acacian Schism. It was not widely circulated or cited until the 9th century.

Church, for example when St. Ambrose excommunicated Theodo-sius the Great. Augustine's thoughts on the subject in the *City of God* dovetail with these exalted notions of ecclesial liberty. The East, however, had begun to labor under its besetting vice of cae-saropapism. Often outbreaks of heresy and schism resulted from overzealous emperors intruding upon properly ecclesiastical spheres. Gelasius knew that the time was ripe for a decretal that would establish the proper boundaries of each realm, and hopefully clarify the correct relations between the two. The emperor at the time was the capable Anastasius. While he had Monophysite sym-pathies, he could not openly manifest them for fear of the orthodox population of the city. Gelasius sensed this and addressed his fa-mous Epistle 12 to him.[64] Written in the elevated and formal style developed by the professional notaries of the papal *scrinium*, the letter begins with flowery praise of the Roman emperor whom, while being honored, is still styled by the pope as "son." He then presumes to instruct the emperor with his enduring "two powers" doctrine. The earth is ruled by the power of the Church in spiritual things and by the kingly power in material things. The spiritual power, because of its eternal mission, is superior to the earthly, yet it does not claim authority over purely material matters. This crisp crystallization of Augustinian doctrine became the constitutional pattern for the West for nearly 1000 years, and provided an anti-dote both to caesaropapism and the possibility of a papal theoc-racy. It was also in essence a final declaration of independence by the Western Church from temporal interference, to which, despite many attempts to hedge its power, it has adhered since that time. As he wrote in a subsequent letter, "Mark this well, when the see of Blessed Peter pronounces judgement, no one is permitted to judge that judgement."[65]

Despite Gelasius' involvement at the very highest levels of power in Church and state, it must be said that the bulk of his ef-forts and correspondence dealt with immediate and local needs.

---

64 Gelasius, ep. 12; cfr. ibid., 73–80.
65 Gelasius, ep. 13, cfr. Daniel-Rops, 108.

With more and more of the administration of central Italy and the city of Rome falling *de facto* on the papacy, the Roman See was forced to take a more active role in governance. In the first place, Gelasius, as head of the clergy, had to face many challenges emanating from a society in which disorder was increasing rapidly. In certain cases, he was compelled to intervene in the politics of local churches in order to interdict or redress senseless acts of violence. As was seen in the pontificate of Damasus, violent scenes could shake the church internally as well as externally. Human imperfection and sinfulness flourished even within the sacred precincts. It was Gelasius' responsibility to rectify such incidents whenever they occurred. One particular instance concerned the diocese of Squillace in Calabria.[66] There, over the course of a few years, two bishops were driven to death by the machinations of an ecclesial faction. Shocked by reports that the Archdeacon Asellus had permitted his epileptic bishop to be trampled in a riot, the pope ordered that he be suspended, but only pending the result of an investigation. It was only when a second bishop was murdered that he ordered the neighboring bishops to intervene as visitors and deprived the native clergy of their rights as parochial pastors, and commanded that the lay instigators be handed over to the civil authorities. Only pending the results of their personal investigations did Gelasius finally issue sentences of suspension and excommunication for the culprits. These epistles demonstrate something key about Gelasius' style of governance. He ruled principally through law and administration, rather than by papal fiat.[67] Indeed his chief methodology for governance was through proper procedure in the papal courts, which he streamlined and wherein he exercised special care.

Gelasius' term saw significant development in canon law and ecclesial procedure. Although the right of appeal to Rome was ancient and venerable by this time, the pope innovated further,

---

66 See the four epistles (36–39), in Neil and Allen, *Letters of Gelasius*, 187–190.
67 Taylor, "The Early Papacy," 317.

making his court a personal one, not bound to rigid procedure. If the nature of the case demanded it, Gelasius could omit any number of established procedures and try it himself, integrating what was known as procedure *cognitio extra ordinem*. Instead of seeing the papacy as a mere court of final arbitration, it changed during his tenure into one which could initiate cases on its own, a procedure that would find its place in the Civil Law of Justinian, and in forthcoming processes of canonical inquisition.[68] In addition, by the 400s, Church and civil courts were working in parallel. The massively overburdened civil courts had come to be seen by the people as favoring the upper classes. For this reason, the poor flocked to the *audientia episcopi* or the Church courts where they might find sympathetic ears for redress of their complaints. Gelasius and his officials used this court to enhance and stabilize the position of the Church in a period of civil disorder, and as a result, served as a steadying hand for the broader society in uncertain times.[69] The introduction of various systems of Germanic law beside the traditional Roman codes gave Gelasius a prime opportunity. His *defensores* and officials were able to use the differing codes to open up a space for canon law to grow. Germanic law was essentially personal, as opposed to the territorial law envisioned by the Romans (requiring the plaintiff to sue only in the defendant's court). Gelasius adopted this Germanic idea into canon law, effectively removing territoriality. When added to the universal nature of Christianity, what Gelasius and his advisors blazed the path for was a *universal and personal* law for the whole Church, with the papal see as the operative court for final appeals, as well as retaining the right to initiate causes anywhere it desired. In addition, the presence of numerous overlapping codes made it possible for a new canon law that applied only *personally* to clerics, independent of secular jurisdiction, thus furthering the liberty of the Church.[70] This brilliant legal maneuvering set an enduring stamp on the legal

68   Ibid., 323.
69   Neil and Allen, *Letters of Gelasius*, 24.
70   Taylor, "The Early Papacy," 325.

thought of the Roman Church, and undergirded many future developments in both the civil and canon law of the Western world.

While Gelasius—being a Roman—was a man of law, he also knew that it must be balanced with clemency and equity. For instance, he was willing to accede to the public reconciliation of the compromised ambassador to Constantinople, Misenus, who had complicated the Acacian schism. His predecessor had put conditions upon his absolution that had become impossible to fulfill. Realizing this, and convinced by Misenus' genuine repentance, Gelasius restored him back to his full episcopal rank, an act of mercy that called forth the title "Vicar of Christ" from the bishops assembled at the synod to receive him back. Yet Gelasius knew that this act of mercy was at the same time a visible exercise of papal sovereignty, absolving the subject from a penance imposed by a previous pope.[71] He also showed himself willing to bend in times of crisis. Well aware of his responsibility to ensure pastoral and sacramental oversight for his flocks, he was challenged by the increasing dearth of priests due to the political and social realities of the time. While he wisely gave temporary relaxation of the stringent rules of the ecclesial *cursus honorum* so as to ensure the access of Christians to the saving sacraments, he still insisted that, given the lack of qualified clerics, at least six months must elapse before ordination as a kind of verification of moral uprightness. Even in times of emergency, he could not allow untested men to see to the spiritual needs of the Church's children. Despite granting this pastoral exception, he insisted upon instant return to the pristine and ancient rules of priestly probation once the crisis was past.[72]

He was also credited with reforming the "temporalities," or the estates of the Roman Church, which were scattered throughout the central Mediterranean, but increasingly focused on central Italy and Sicily. To that end he initiated the *Polypticum*, which was a kind of census and rationalization of papal holdings, to

---

71   Neil and Allen, *Letters of Gelasius*, 41.
72   Taylor, "The Early Papacy," 318.

streamline the holdings of the patrimony of St. Peter. Within this impressive administrative mechanism were included clerical and official salaries, as well as payments to the cemeteries, charitable institutes, and monasteries, not to mention a thorough record of papal taxation. So comprehensive was this effort that it was still being used in the ninth century as the basis for the governance of papal lands.[73] As preparatory to the great *Polypticum*, Gelasius finally established the traditional division of donations that would endure for centuries. In order to avoid corruption, he developed the system known as the *quadraticum*. First developed under Pope Simplicius nearly twenty years previously, it was Gelasius who standardized it for the future. Under this system all donations to the Church were to be divided into four quarters. The first quarter was reserved for the bishops (the *cathedraticum* tax that continues to be assessed to the present day). He specified that this was not simply to gild the bishops' wealth, but was to be a ready fund to meet immediate needs such as food relief and the ransom of prisoners. The second quarter was for the salaries and needs of the clergy, while the third quarter was reserved for the maintenance of the fabric of existing churches and the construction of new ones. The final quarter was always reserved to the poor. The extreme efficiency of this system ensured a constant supply of material goods both to meet the current and ongoing needs of the indigent and to provide sufficient wealth for the governance and advancement of the Church.[74]

Though only pope for four years, Gelasius was able to leverage the achievements of his predecessors and set the papacy on a very firm footing. His decisions echoed for centuries. He was good in a crisis, and yet was always able to keep one eye on the future. He never let an opportune moment go to waste and, while he governed by means of the law and the courts, he was not afraid to exercise mercy when the occasion demanded it. Still, he has come under

---

73 R. A. Markus,. *Gregory the Great and His World* (Cambridge: Cambridge University Press, 1999), 121.
74 Neil and Allen, *Letters of Gelasius*, 18, 22.

criticism in current scholarship. Some have criticized him for grandiosity or pomposity in terms of the language his official letters. While it is true that he uses a style of elevated language that would come to predominate in curial documents, he did so for a reason. These letters were written with an eye to preservation and to the future. Their formality helped to establish their authority, and also gives evidence of possibly the most advanced college of notaries at the time outside of the imperial palace. He is also accused of perpetuating the Acacian schism by insistence on the prerogatives of his see. While the schism did endure long after his death, it is unlikely a change in Gelasius' tone would have effected a reconciliation any sooner. Given the circumstances he deftly used the situation both to reassert the rights of his see and to crystallize a vision of Church and state relations that would come to dominate in the West. Finally, his most recent students, in their excellent study of his letters, have labelled him a "micro-manager." I am not sure they establish the reality of that epithet in their works. Gelasius had his hand in many different areas, yet he also recognized the significance of the rule of law, the conditions on the ground, and the independence of civil power. While he was certainly detail oriented, I do not see this as necessarily tending toward an effort to control things on a microscopic scale. Gelasius was a man of large vision, whose foresight extended to local realities. We must also admit that his ability to govern in such a discrete manner was only aided by the incredible professionalism that had developed in the Roman Church administration over the previous 100 years. When we say that Gelasius governed, what we mean is that by the year 500, the popes had assembled an impressive apparatus for so doing. Notaries, *defensores,* archdeacons, and a cadre of rectors and other administrative professionals stood ready to execute the decisions and traditions of the Roman See in all areas of Church life, now qualitatively *on par* with the civil government. If anything, Gelasius was no "micro-manager," rather a "macro-manager," one who combined holiness and the oversight of a true bishop, and whose mission was aided by a "cloud of witnesses" dedicated to both the man and the office.

Gregory: Ruling the Christian People

It was fortunate that Gelasius had so clearly delineated the proper relations between Church and state, for the sixth century would see many attempts by governments to suborn the papacy. Though the Ostrogoths were largely content to let the Roman bishops alone, all this changed in the 530s when a resurgent Byzantine empire invaded Italy and captured Rome. For the next 200 years papal elections would require imperial confirmation.[75] While the Acacian Schism was favorably settled in 519, Caesaropapism was still in full flower in the East. During the reign of Justinian the Great (r. 527–565) the Monophysite heresy sprang forth again. Justinian was distracted by his massive plans to reconquer the old empire, build Hagia Sophia, and renew the Roman Law. He therefore left domestic and ecclesial matters in the hands of his wife, Theodora, who was a Monophysite sympathizer, and worked to insinuate her coreligionists into positions of power throughout the empire. She was even able to secure the selection of Pope Vigilius (r. 537–555). Vigilius was an ambitious and venal man, who agreed to help Theodora approve of Monophysitism if she supported his campaign for the papacy. When he was successful, one of the most astonishing about-faces in history occurred. Not only did he refuse to approve Monophysitism, but he recondemned it as heresy, thus drawing the ire of Theodora who died before she could get her revenge. While Justinian was personally orthodox, his Byzantine caesaropapism resulted in much civil interference. In fact, it was almost a necessary precondition to election to the papacy that one had served as *Apocrisarius* to the imperial court. It was one such ambassador who became a reluctant pope in 590.

75 For this period see: Andrew J. Ekonomou, *Byzantine Rome and the Greek Popes: Eastern Influences on Rome and the Papacy from Gregory the Great to Zacharias, A.D. 590–752* (Lanham, MD: Rowman & Littlefield, 2009). See also, George E. Demacopoulos, *The Invention of Peter: Apostolic Discourse and Papal Authority in Late Antiquity* (Philadelphia, PA: University of Pennsylvania Press, 2013).

Gregory I (later awarded the cognomen "the Great"), was born around 540 to an old Roman family with aristocratic and senatorial connections.[76] The Rome that he grew up in was then the Rome of the Byzantine revival. His father had been the prefect of the city, and his mother and two aunts would later merit the title "saint." Indeed, a remote ancestor was likely Pope Felix III. Gregory's connections made him a member of one of the most powerful and notable families in both the ecclesiastical and civil worlds. Yet in spite of this, Rome continued to fall into ruins. Life in the city alternated between a series of barbarian sieges and periodic plagues that devastated the remaining population (including a particularly severe outbreak in 542, in which approximately one-third of the people perished). A sack by Totila the Goth in 546 probably saw the family removing to their Sicilian estates, at that time safely under Byzantine control. He was likely given as good an education as was still available at the time. He became well acquainted with grammar, rhetoric, and logic, as well as imperial law. Indeed, such were his abilities (and the state of public order at the time) that he too was made civil prefect of the city in the early 570s. Yet Gregory constantly felt the pull of a deeper call. Monasticism was then blossoming throughout the Western world, beckoning to spiritually serious people of a life lived in the antechamber of heaven, away from conquest, plague, and the bustle of temporal life. When his father died, he transformed his family villa on the Caelian hill in Rome into a monastery, the site of which can still be seen at the church of San Gregorio Magno. There he hoped to bury himself in the living death of the monastic life, deep in prayer and contemplation. Yet it was not to be. A man of such manifest talents and

---

76 The bibliography on St. Gregory is vast. Some more recent, synthetic works are: Matthew Dal Santo and Bronwen Neil, *A Companion to Gregory the Great* (Leiden: Brill, 2013); John Moorhead, *Gregory the Great* (London: Routledge, 2005); R. A. Markus, *Gregory the Great and His World* (Cambridge: Cambridge University Press, 1999); and, Jeffrey Richards, *Consul of God: The Life and Times of Gregory the Great* (London: Routledge, 1980; repr. 2015).

of such a noble line could not be permitted to be lost from the Church in an hour of need.

In 579 Pope Pelagius stirred the young man from his monastic seclusion, ordained him a deacon, and sent him on the delicate mission as *apocrisarius* to Constantinople. Gregory was by no means easily reconciled to this change. Repeatedly in his career he laments being taken away from his life of retired contemplation, and thrust again among the multifarious problems of the world, particularly the thorny issues of administration. How deeply he felt this can be seen in numerous passages, but none more touching that this:

> Since assuming the burden of the pastoral office my soul can no longer recollect itself with ease, because it finds itself dispersed among a multitude of cares. I am forced now to busy myself with the affairs of the various churches, now with the needs of monasteries, now to investigate the conduct of this or that individual; there are times when I must concern myself with worldly matters, repair the ruin brought on by the barbarian invasions, try to prevent wolves from destroying the flock committed to my care.... [A]t times I must bear with some whom I know to be plunderers, and even go out of my way to meet them, so that charity may be maintained.[77]

In Constantinople he proved himself adept, using the easy manners of the aristocracy to accomplish his tasks. The monastic Gregory still knew how to network. As *apocrisarius* he made friends with noble exiles and eminent families, royals, and court physicians. He knew the two emperors, Tiberius and Maurice, personally and was godfather to latter's eldest son. All in all he made many friends, ones whom he could call on later for help when issues with Constantinople surfaced. He likely became spiritual advisor to numerous members of the highest echelons of society. Yet he preferred the company of monks and surrounded himself with

---

77   Cfr. Richards, *Consul of God*, 87.

Greek monastics when not at his official duties.[78] Little did it occur to Gregory that he was planting the seeds in his own mind of a spiritual revolution in terms of living the Christian life. While in Constantinople he defeated the sometime Patriarch Eutychius, who denied the palpability of the resurrected body, a distasteful episode that apparently soured Gregory on writing advanced theological works. Ekonomou thinks that his tenure as *apocrisarius* was a failure, given he was not able to obtain much immediate material aid for Italy.[79] However when one looks at the long term, the experience that Gregory acquired, not to mention the extensive contacts he was able to make and maintain, would suggest that it was more of a success than has been admitted.

It was probably obvious to everyone in the Roman world, Gregory excepted, where this was all going to lead. When his patron, Pope Pelagius II, died in 590 the Roman clergy and people of Rome elected him by acclamation as their new bishop. Gregory was horrified. Indeed, he tried to leverage his old connections to try to get Constantinople to *refuse* their approval of the election, a request that his old friends—likely delighted by his election—denied. The new pope was immediately confronted with crisis after crisis. He quickly became apprised of how much the city had grown to depend on the papacy: "Under the color of the episcopate I have been brought back to the world and here I labor under such great earthly cares as I do not recall having been subjected to even in my life as a layman."[80] Most pressing was the periodic return of the plague, which had carried off his predecessor, and to which a huge number of his flock were succumbing. Legend records Gregory's liturgical procession to beg for divine aid, during which he saw the Archangel Michael sheathing his sword over Hadrian's tomb, which ever after has borne the name Castel Sant'Angelo. Together with the new pope's liturgical piety one finds a mind of administrative genius, whose efficient reformation of the temporalities of the Church

78   Markus, *Gregory the Great*, 10–11.
79   Ekonomou, 12.
80   Gregory, ep. I.5; cfr. Markus, 13n58.

probably did as much to end the plague and ensure a constant stream of supplies for his people. Bronwen Neil is very perceptive when she says, "Gregory's administrative responses were always informed by pastoral considerations.... [H]is first concern was the preservation of the social order in order to facilitate the salvation of souls."[81]

In the absence of a strong central government, many of the day-to-day administrative details of governing Rome and its environs had simply fallen upon the Roman Church.[82] Byzantine interest was too sporadic and had been punctuated by various barbarian uprisings. Yet the people of the city needed to be housed and fed. It is no surprise that many scholars have noted that the Roman papacy of the sixth century seems to lack sustained attention to external matters. In the absence of a central government and thrown back upon its own resources, it was as much as the Roman bishops could do to make sure the city survived at all. We have already seen how Pope Gelasius had put the administration of what was called the "patrimony" on a sound administrative and financial footing, particularly the rich papal lands in Sicily whose annual grain shipments were critical for the survival of the city. Later chroniclers note that Gregory himself was a careful follower of Gelasius in this regard.[83] When some-

---

81 Bronwen Neil, "The Papacy in the Age of Gregory the Great," in *A Companion to Gregory the Great*, eds., Matthew Dal Santo and Bronwen Neil (Leiden: Brill, 2013), 2.

82 "The papal administration had, by the time of Gregory I, assumed, or had been assigned, responsibility for provisioning Rome." T. F. X. Noble, "Morbidity and Vitality in the Early Papacy," in *Catholic Historical Review* 81.4 (1995): 531.

83 Richards, 265. For the temporal holdings of the papacy under Gregory, see: Hartmann Grisar, "Ein Rundgang durch die Patrimonien des heiligen Stuhles um das Jahr 600," in *Zeitschrift für katholische Theologie*, 1.3 (1877), 321–360; Edward Spearing and Evelyn Mary Spearing, *The Patrimony of the Roman Church in the Time of Gregory the Great* (Cambridge: University Press, 1918); and, Vincenzo Recchia, *Gregorio Magno e la società agricola* (Rome: Studium, 1978).

thing is functioning well, there is no need to replace, but only modify according to circumstance. "The machinery for governing the Roman Church's lands was large, complex, well-controlled and on the whole both efficient and humane. It secured the revenues needed for meeting the expenses of a considerable ecclesiastical establishment as well as for furnishing the resources needed for a far-reaching program of charitable assistance of the needy, and for monks and nuns."[84] Key for Gregory's scheme was getting his people into place as quickly as possible so as to ensure the smooth running of the estates. In the first place he made sure to quickly appoint bishops to vacant sees in Sicily soon after his election. In order to aid them he made liberal use of the "rectorate," a sort of vicar of temporalities to coordinate the Church's lands across different dioceses to ensure efficiency and eliminate corruption. Gregory was careful to invest his new bishops and rectors with significant vicarial powers so that they could deal with issues as they arose. He also made sure to rotate the rectors as much as possible, to give them experience in different areas, and to prevent them from entrenching their power and becoming subject to corruption. He also eliminated the plague of pluralism, a move which vastly increased rectorial efficiency.[85] Given the distance and lack of communications, his rectors thereby possesed significant powers, and in response to this he required careful accounting and reports of their efforts. He knew that they would have to make hard decisions, including levying taxes on the poor agricultural laborers who tilled the Church's lands. His advice to them was simple, "Let justice season your humility, and your humility make your justice agreeable."[86] He knew that the rectors were key to the whole economic system of the papacy and of Rome. From them came the money and material resources necessary to perpetuate the *quadraticum* that supplied not only the Church's needs, but those of the poor who, in Rome at the time,

---

84   Markus, 123.
85   Richards, 93, 130.
86   Cfr. Markus, 118.

increased daily. Scholars are unanimous in the regard in which they hold Gregory's administration of the papal lands:

> The Register testifies eloquently to the meticulous care with which he administered the estates of the Roman church, suggesting yet again that background in civil administration and estate management which has already been postulated. His execution of these duties provides one of the best demonstrations of the synthesis of *Romanitas* and *Christianitas* that was the hallmark of everything he did. *Romanitas* can be seen in the efficient and painstaking fulfilment of his role as landlord in the best traditions of Rome. The Register shows time and again his scrupulous fairness, attention to detail, and mastery of every myriad aspect of estate management. *Christianitas* can be seen in the application of Christian charity to temper the stern demands of absolute justice, and in the objective of his patrimonial administration. He regarded it as something to be run not for the profit of the church but for the alleviation of hardship and want among the poor.[87]

Gregory considered that he held the estates of the patrimony in the name of the poor, and that this was their primary inheritance. His efficient management was therefore not optional—rather, it was a duty owed to them by the very nature of the papal office. He went beyond the *Polypticum* and created a census of all the poor in Rome, by name, age, and particular need. He also instituted a system of receipts to ensure that each received his due and so that there was enough for everyone. His management was so effective that there was a copious supply of money and material for each subsidy in the *quadraticum*. Clerics and Bishops were treated very well, and received annual gifts of gold and vestments from the pope. While Gregory would go to nearly any length to relieve the poor, he

87   Richards, 126.

stopped short at selling the sacred vessels of the Church, again as held in trust for the worship of almighty God. All the religious houses (which included increasing numbers of monasteries) were more than adequately supplied, in addition to satisfying the needs of the poor. Gregory carefully shepherded the surplus so that there would be money left over in times of dearth. He was especially kind to refugee religious, and in one famous incident provided a subsidy for no fewer than 3,000 refugee nuns out of his own substance. One commentator opined that during his rule "the Church was like a great open granary."[88]

With this foresightful creation of a surplus, Gregory could also help charity "go in reverse." When the crops failed or the yield was poor he could offer rent reductions or even commutations through his rectors to the agricultural inhabitants of the papal estates, while still having enough for the relief of the city. He proportioned taxation to production and standardized weights and measures to reduce corruption. He refused to charge peasants exorbitant rates to contract Christian marriage and made sure that those who committed minor crimes would not be subject to confiscation, and that their families' inheritance rights would be confirmed. All these measures "amount in effect to a Bill of Rights for Church tenants.... Gregory ordered that his instruction be read out to them publicly, and that they be given copies of his rulings so that their rights might be preserved."[89] Gregory came to be known, with total justice, as *prudentissimus paterfamilias christi*, the most prudent father of Christ's family. Such a brilliant title would have been impossible without his consummate management of the skillful members of the Roman church whose proficient management skills served to succor the poor, comfort the sick and homeless, and provide for the due worship of God and the dignity of the clergy.[90]

88 Daniel-Rops, 227.
89 Richards, 137.
90 For an excellent breakdown of many of these instances, see ibid., 95ff.

Sometimes Gregory is called "the Last Roman." Indeed, he is a bridge between the late antique world and the medieval, yet for him *Romanitas* and *Christianitas* still went hand in hand. He saw his legal work as making the law—something valuable in itself—bow before humanity, through which the Rome of the Caesars would be preserved through St. Peter.[91] We can see several instances where his adherence to the law might be modified by mercy and equity. On certain occasions he alienated lands donated to the Church to avoid having families fall into indigence, even though this was expressly against canon law.[92] He often modified and softened Church rules in order gradually to effect reforms. For example, Gregory was insistent that ordination to the subdiaconate be accompanied by the vow of celibacy. Previous popes had insisted that any married subdeacon be stripped of his office, but Gregory saw the utility of a more gradual approach. He allowed currently married subdeacons to continue their ministry, but made celibacy obligatory for new ordinations after 591.[93] Yet still the law as a whole was most necessary, for it provided both the framework for social and pastoral activity, and was the shield of the weaker elements in society. Incarnational Christianity demanded law, but its administration by men of zeal, prudence, and mercy. Such administration was at its most profound level, a service that mimicked the Kenosis of Christ Himself; Christ is the leader who empties Himself for the flock. While all Christians served Christ, the bishop was in a special manner a servant of the community of servants, and the distinct virtue of such servants was humility. This humility drove Gregory toward charity to all, even the powerful, using the language of humility, read in his favorite title "Servant of the Servants of God."[94] This helped Gregory defuse tensions

91   Ibid., 85.
92   Richards, 109.
93   Ibid., 110–111.
94   For these themes see Greogry, ep. 130, 157, 217, along with an examination in: Markus, 30. See also George E. Demoacpoulos, "Gregory the Great and the Sixth-Century Dispute over the Ecumenical Title," *Theological Studies* 70 (2009): 300-321.

both inside and outside of his Church. He was able to maintain good relations with the emperors and the Patriarchs of the East, and his humility seasoned his continuing presentation of his papal claims. Still, under certain conditions, he could apply the full force of the law when necessary. He did not hesitate to suspend recalcitrant and disobedient clergy, and deposed no fewer than six bishops for malfeasance during his tenure.[95]

Within Rome itself he faced an entrenched ecclesial bureaucracy: the diaconal college of Rome, charged with the governance of the Church's regions in the city. Gregory wanted to model the Church in a more monastic direction, away from the secular clergy. In the first place he reformed the papal household. This was technically independent of the administrative apparatus of the city, and pertained more closely to his own person. To refashion this body would be a proving ground for a wider reorganization. He banned laypeople from his domestic arrangements and surrounded himself with clerics, and particularly with monks.

This finished, he was able to focus attention on the larger issues of the local Church. The deacons had become too powerful, particularly their head, the archdeacon. Gregory was able to use the occasion of a scandal to remove his predecessor's archdeacon. With this done, he turned his attention to the college of deacons as a whole. The college had apparently become a relative sinecure, with most deacons being appointed because of their singing voices. Gregory reassigned some of their liturgical functions to subdeacons, and insisted that they perform their traditional job of managing the distribution of alms. He also elevated the papal *defensores* to the status of a college by themselves, with their own *primicerius*. In this way he enhanced the power of the *defensores* and notaries, yet at the expense of the over-powerful deacons.[96] Although he ran into some opposition, at least during his pontificate he was successful. He wanted his officials to conform more fully to his own ascetical temperament. The secular clergy of Rome

95   Richards, 115.
96   Ibid., 93.

reacted against such tendencies after Gregory's death, and the monasticization of the Roman papacy would have to wait for centuries. In any case his curial reforms lasted, and a more stable balance of power was reflected among the officials of the Roman Church.

By the time of Gregory, we can see how far the Roman Curia had developed.[97] Though it certainly might be dated back to the first centuries of Roman Christianity, it had attained an astonishing maturity. Under Gregory, a clerical *cursus honorum* returned. The sixth century had seen tendencies to nepotism, inheritance, and deference to social standing in appointments to Church positions. Gregory began to reverse that. The papal curia of the time can be conveniently divided into four fundamental departments. The first was the chancery, or *scrinium*: the body of papal officials who dealt with the massive correspondence and growing archives of the popes. This chancery was headed by a *primicerius notariorum* who was assisted by a *secundiciarius*. Their supervision extended over two increasingly distinct areas. The first was a college of notaries (probably the oldest type of official in papal service). These were skilled in the management and production of documents, a science which had achieved an astonishing level of sophistication by Gregory's time. They produced decretals and epistles, processed donations, interfaced with the lawyers, and ensured the continuity of message through papal terms. From among the notaries, a pope usually chose a *chartularius,* or a personal private secretary. The second branch of the chancery was dedicated to the preservation and cataloguing of the mountain of correspondence, and these were

---

97 "Papal Curia" is an anachronism. It does not acquire that title until at least 1089, during the reign of Urban II. Lajos Pásztor, "L'histoire de la curie romaine, problème d'histoire de l'Eglise," in *Revue d'histoire ecclésiastique* 64 (1969): 353–366. However, it is a convenient placeholder for describing the apparatus of papal government, particularly given the mature form it had reached by this time. By using this term, I do not mean to suggest that the "curia" of the year 600 was equivalent to, or as developed as, that of 1100.

to become the church's archives and library, themselves splitting into two different branches after Gregory's death.

The second body was the college of *defensores*, created by Gregory himself, to deal with the legal issues of the Church. These too were headed by *primicerius*. While these primarily made sure legal forms were followed in the transfer and retention of real estate, they also defended the Church's interests against the state and against private litigants. It is likely that the first formal canon lawyers were taken from among these.

In the third place was the financial ministry, headed by an *arcarius*. This official was in charge of the *Polypticum*, as well as being responsible for assessment, taxation, collection, and management of the goods of the Church. It is likely the rectors would come under this office. Though not mentioned at this time, a *sacellarius* was likely already in place, who served as the payroll master for the distribution of the goods of the church. One could speculate that the papal almoner also took his origins there, but he might have also come from the papal household.

This "household" was the final branch of pontifical administration. It was headed by the *vicedominus*, or the head of the pope's residence, likely in charge of the *cubicularii*, or the chamberlains (butlers). The *vestiarius* was entrusted with the pope's personal wealth and activities, whereas the *nomenclator* and his associates served as masters and coordinators of papal liturgical ceremonial.[98] None of this includes the vast apparatus that was being constructed to govern secular Rome, including an army of judges, proctors, legates, and soldiers.

Gregory obviously had much on his plate. Yet he did more than mere reorganization and streamlining. Gregory had a vision for administrators. While he lamented being taken from his monastery and thrust back into the world of affairs, he also knew that such

---

98   For thorough examinations of papal governance in this period, see Noble, *The Republic of St. Peter*, 212–230; Poole, *Lectures on the Papal Chancery*; and, Bronwen Neil, "The Papacy in the Age of Gregory the Great," in, *A Companion to Gregory the Great*, eds. Matthew Dal Santo and Bronwen Neil (Leiden: Brill, 2013).

condescension was necessary for the pastors of the Church. Indeed, it is to Gregory that we must credit the first (and one of the best) evocations of the "mixed life" in Christian history. He knew that the ministers of the Church needed more than simple administrative know-how. Nor was it enough for a pastor or governor to be simple, pious, and holy. Some sort of fusion was necessary for the proper running of the Church of God. Just as human nature was both body and soul, the proper governance of the Church demanded attention to the whole human person. Incarnational Christianity demanded governors who were "shrewd as serpents" yet "innocent as doves" (Mt 10:16). For him the life of the monk trained the virtues and educated the mind, giving a person practice in reading and understanding the scriptures, with the further end of teaching when one was called to do so. Drawing on Augustine and John Cassian, Gregory pleaded that our common human condition drew together the contemplative life of Mary and the active life of Martha. To return to the active life was a ministry of compassion for him.[99]

Gregory did not immerse himself in speculative theology, but rather laid a groundwork in his letters and sermons for the practical life of leadership in the Church of God. Most significantly he wrote the *Pastoral Rule* (*Regula Pastoralis*), which collected his meditations and experiences on pastorship, a capacious term which included all positions of leadership, responsibility, and administration, particularly concerning the rule of God's people. While not deep theology, it was exceptionally penetrating. As Wallace-Hadrill writes, "No westerner before him had looked as he looked at the work of a bishop, the art of arts, the art of the government of souls; or had traced a bishop's motives in accepting office, even to the roots of self-deception."[100] He was a deep spiritual writer, but not a profound original thinker. In this he was exceptionally suitable as a pastor, someone who could deeply identify with the spiritual sicknesses of his people. He was well aware of the delicacy of a pastor's position, having had extensive experience as a diplomat, abbot, and

99   Markus, 18–27.
100   Andrew Wallace-Hadrill; cfr. Richards, 261

diaconal secretary. Pastors had the difficult duty of learning "what to speak, to whom to speak, when to speak, how to speak, how much to speak."[101] This was often hard for the priesthood, inured to leadership and, increasingly, deriving from the upper echelons of society. Gregory thought a monasticization of the priesthood would ease this issue. He wrote, "Nothing is as hard for one in the order of the priesthood as to temper the mind's rigor by compassion, changing attitude according to the persons concerned."[102] A certain flexibility had to mark the mind of the pastor, something amply demonstrated in his missionary efforts to the Angles.

While the origins of the English mission are difficult to discern historically, we know that Gregory was its prime mover.[103] Gregory intended from the very beginning for the mission to be led by monks, choosing Augustine from his own monastery on the Caelian hill. Knowing the distance the missionaries would have to travel, he insisted that Augustine cultivate contacts with the Frankish churches, who might provide him more immediate material assistance.[104] This was a delicate and unique undertaking. It was the first mission sent from and sponsored by the Roman See (though some missionaries had obtained approval from Rome before this date). One of Augustine's companions was the Abbot Mellitus, who would succeed Augustine as the second Archbishop of Canterbury. In his letters to Mellitus, Gregory sends forth his pastoral vision, as well as his prudence. One of the chief problems of the English mission was that the country had fallen back into paganism after the departure of the legions in 410. While the mission effected many conversions, consternation ensued about the proper attitude toward pagan temples. On such a critical issue, the missionaries turned to Rome. At first Gregory considered it inappropriate that such buildings, redolent of pagan worship, be allowed to stand. He

101 *Regula Pastoralis*, cfr. Markus, 29.
102 Gregory, *Homilies on Ezechiel*, 1.11.28; cfr. ibid.
103 For a thorough analysis of the mission, see: Henry Mayr-Harting, *The Coming of Christianity to Anglo-Saxon England*, 3rd ed. (State College, PA: Pennsylvania State University Press, 1991).
104 Markus, 178.

dispatched a letter to Mellitus to this effect. It is clear that the question bothered the pope, however. After mulling it over, he had a complete change of heart, wrote a new letter, and dispatched a post rider with orders to supersede his previous instructions. The people's worship in the old temples, albeit misguided, was sign of a naturally good religious impulse. In order to avoid uneasiness among the new converts he proposed a new strategy. Bless the temple with holy water, purify it and remove the idols, then set up an altar to say Mass. Thereby the peoples' natural religious sentiments would not be offended, and that which they worshiped in images and shadows would now be done in "Spirit and in Truth." Gregory was not a man of practical principles so fixed that his mind could not be changed. This small decision probably significantly speeded the reconversion of England. As he wrote in another letter, "It is the height of stupidity to think oneself the first in such a way as to spurn to learn the good things one may come across."[105] For him, pastoral rule meant flexibility with regard to changing conditions on the ground.

In the end Gregory presents a fitting bookend to the papacies studied here. During the 300 years between the legalization and his reign, the popes devised systems of governance that preserved the best of the Roman system, seasoning it with the salt of Christ's message. Gregory set a pattern by preserving what was essential, streamlining anything for the sake of greater service, and being innovative and flexible when the situation demanded it. In many ways, in both word and example, Gregory presents the image of the "ideal pastor." It is fitting to end this chapter with his own words.

> Our Creator and Disposer so arranges all things that anyone who might become exalted by the gift he has been given is humbled by the virtue he lacks. He so orders things that while He raises one up by the grace He bestows on him, He makes him inferior to another by granting some other gift to another. So each should

---

105 Gregory, ep. ix. 26; cfr. Markus, 74.

recognize that someone lower than himself may yet be his better in respect of some other gift. Though he may know that he has the precedence over others, let him place himself beneath others in respect of other respects. All things are so ordered that while all possess different gifts, yet through the mutual requirements of charity, these gifts become shared by all.... Hence Paul said, "Serve one another in love" (Gal. 3:13). Love will free us of the yoke of sin when it subjects us to one another through mutual service in love.[106]

---

106 Gregory, *Moralia in Iob*, xxviii.10.22; cfr. ibid., 30.

Chapter 2
Ruling the "Better Part"

Christ, in His restoration of human nature, has provided His followers a pattern for perfection. He left the vertiginous injunction, "Be perfect, as your heavenly Father is perfect" (Mt 5:48). From the foundation of the Church men and women had been drawn by that call to excellence. It mirrored the appeal of the ancients to *arete*, and yet surpassed it in every way. In Christ was the living incarnation of *arete* itself. Socrates had asked what it meant to be a good human, and Christ had given the world the answer. Men and women by the hundreds and thousands heard and followed that call, going beyond the basic demands of moral existence to seek out the life of perfection here on earth. As the Church reflected on the call to perfection, she began to discern that in order to live such a life the example of Christ must provide the pattern. It was no mere spiritual journey or ineffable experience. Christ had lived an embodied life that perfectly integrated soul and body, and those who followed His counsel to perfection had to try to do the same. Christians knew that the choice was not one between a good life and a bad life, but between a good life and a better one. Earthly possessions, created by God and developed by human genius, were goods in a genuine sense. Yet with our disordered affections such goods could distract us from God if not managed well. It is better to imitate the Son of Man "who had nowhere to lay his head" (Lk 9:58; Mt 8:20). Christ was poor on earth, and so those who would follow Him in the life of perfection too would give up their material possessions to follow him. Early Christian believers also knew that to live the chaste life of the angels, to anticipate heaven "where they neither marry nor are given in marriage" (Mt 22:30) was also the path to a single-hearted pursuit of God. Finally, Christ presented an image of perfect submission to the Father, for "He was obedient even unto death" (Phil 2:8). In order to pursue the life of perfection one had to set aside the good of self-will so as to follow Christ in uprightness and purity, learning to align one's will with His. These three paths to holiness became known as the "evangelical counsels," for they were not demanded as a condition of salvation, but rather for those called to pursue the surer path to perfection on earth.

At first these choices were highly individual, as only some chose lives of exceptional poverty or chastity. Though all of the ingredients were present in the primitive Church for living the life of perfection, it took centuries for it to cohere into a developed movement.[1] The life of *askesis* or self-denial was a path well known

---

1   The literature for monasticism is vast, indeed so much that a one-volume introduction has proven impossible to generate. We must approach the issues from different directions. For its origins, see the classic study in Karl Heussi, *Der Ursprung des Mönchtums* (Tübingen: Mohr, 1936). More recently, foundational studies on social and cultural histories are found in Peter Brown, *The Cult of the Saints: Its Rise and Function in Latin Christianity* (Chicago: University of Chicago Press, 1981); Id, "The Rise and Function of the Holy Man in Late Antiquity," in *Journal of Roman Studies* 61 (1971): 80–10; Id., *Society and the Holy in Late Antiquity* (Berkeley, CA: University of California Press, 1982), and Id., *Through the Eye of a Needle: Wealth, the Fall of Rome, and the Making of Christianity in the West, 350–550 AD* (Princeton, NJ: Princeton University Press, 2014). See also, Marilyn Dunn, *The Emergence of Monasticism From the Desert Fathers to the Early Middle Ages* (Malden, MA: Blackwell, 2007). The magisterial work by Adalbert de Vogüé, OSB, is foundational: *Histoire littéraire du mouvement monastique dans l'antiquité*, 12 vols. (Paris: Éditions du Cerf, 1991–2008). Also useful are works by David Knowles, *The Religious Orders in England*, 3 vols. (Cambridge: Cambridge University Press,) 1961–62, and the brief and impressionistic, *Christian Monasticism* (New York: McGraw-Hill, 1977). Another approach, broad in scope, but with interpretive issues of its own, is Jean Décarreaux, *Monks and Civilization, from the Barbarian Invasions to the Reign of Charlemagne*, trans. Charlotte Haldane (London: Allen & Unwin, 1964).

to ancient philosophical schools and provided a pattern for early Christians to assume and elevate to a supernatural level. As long as the specter of persecution hovered over the young Church, however, there was little opportunity for sustained meditation on the proper way to organize such a way of life. For the first three centuries martyrdom was the *ne plus ultra* of holiness, not only guaranteeing admission into heaven, but fulfilling Christ's blueprint of perfect charity: "Greater love than this has no one, than to lay down one's life for one's friend" (Jn 15:13).

Yet the persecutions were only sporadic and usually local, and here and there an individual could be found who felt called to a higher path. The most famous of these was Anthony of Egypt (250–356).[2] Born of a wealthy Christian family going back generations, he had grown increasingly uneasy, particularly as the Roman state began more systematic persecutions. One day in Church he was struck by the tragic gospel of the rich young man in Luke (Lk 18:18–30). The man asks Christ what he must do to attain eternal life. Christ lists the commandments, which the man had kept entirely intact. He presses upon the Master for that which he still lacks. "Go, sell all you have, and give it to the poor, and you will have treasure in heaven." The rich young man sadly turns away, "for he had many possessions." The gospel's message was like a bolt to the heart of Anthony, himself also a "rich young man." Anthony resolved not to delay. He sold his family patrimony and—after making provision for his sister—retired to live as a hermit in the desert. He would become the father of many (monastic) nations.

2   Anthony was not the first of the hermits, but the publication of his biography by St. Athanasius popularized the movement, and it can be partially credited with spreading monasticism in the West, following its translation into Latin in 374. The critical edition (which also defends Athanasian authorship) is G. J. M. Bartelink, *Vie d'Antoine*, Sources chrétiennes 400 (Paris: Cerf, 2011). This work had an exceptionally broad appeal, as can also be seen by the role it played in Augustine's conversion. See also, David Brakke, *Athanasius and the Politics of Asceticism* (Oxford: Clarendon Press, 1995).

Yet Anthony was a spiritual virtuoso, a solitary mystical genius with no intentions beyond his own salvation and perfection. Even so, such was his charisma that people began to make their way into the desert to seek him out for counsel and advice. Others began to attempt to imitate him, and a path was beat from city to desert. The eremitical life of the hermit had been established, yet such a life was difficult in the extreme and subject to its own seductions. Few indeed are they who could live apart from the common concourse of humanity. We are 'social animals' according to Aristotle, who speaks of the man who can live by himself as being "either a beast or a god."[3] This solitary life was all but impossible except for the heartiest of souls, and then only when accompanied by extraordinary graces. Even today, while the life of a hermit is recognized by the Church, it is exceptionally rare, and subject to careful ecclesial oversight. Solitude gives space for temptation and self-will, while depriving the hermit of mutual concourse and support, or even the communal celebration of the Christian sacraments (and most early hermits were not priests). While a grace-filled figure such as Anthony could and did thrive, for the majority even of those seeking the life of perfection, such efforts seemed superhuman.

The Cenobitic Revolution

In the early Church the Apostles and their successors had found it necessary to organize and occasionally restrain excessive manifestations of charismatic activity (1 Cor 12). In the past some have lamented what they consider to be the "institutional flattening" of such spontaneous expressions of faith. Perhaps, they speculate, the ordering of such phenomena and their subjection to supervision is actually the suppression of the Holy Spirit. Yet from the very beginning a pattern emerged. New and surprising eruptions of the leaven of the gospel either found a home within the institutional church or separated altogether from it. Inevitably, the latter option led to marginalization and, in most cases, extinction. These spiritual movements required a

3   Aristotle, *Politics*, Book 1, 1253a 27–29.

symbiotic relationship with the Church visible. Just as the Church exercises dominion over embodied persons, so too do their various spiritualities, doctrines, and modes of worship come under her purview. Far from being a restraint upon evangelical zeal, the Apostles were certain that institutional oversight of these expressions of faith was necessary. They could only flourish when they were properly ordered, both internally vis-à-vis correct belief and proper ritual, and externally in regard to the broader Church and to its government. One can tend to forget that the institutional Church itself is guided by the Holy Spirit with the power of governance precisely to oversee these expressions of faith. Indeed, the charisma of leadership belonging to the Apostles implicitly contains within it all other spiritual gifts.[4] The spiritual gifts confer aspects of interior sanctification, all of which is subsumed under the responsibility for the salvation of souls entrusted to the Church. As a solicitous mother watches over the first steps of her child, she is careful to remove obstacles and establish boundaries. There is no dichotomy in Christianity between law and gospel, as Martin Luther taught. Rather, both work together for the good, both free and enrich human persons, and both are necessary for the proper functioning of the Body of Christ on earth.

Similar to the new religious movements of today was the burst of evangelical energy let loose by the ascetics of the third century, whose standard bearer was Anthony. By the hundreds, men and women streamed out to the desert for advice and counsel. Many, struck by the spiritual seriousness of the ascetics, decided to remain. At first scattered at the edges of civilization, in ruins and cemeteries, virtual cities of religious began to form. While some, like Anthony, could marshal the astonishing grace and holiness needed to face the loneliness and temptation of the eremitical life, many could not. There was increasing disorder. Opportunistic peasants and escaped prisoners mingled with the holy. Some sought refuge merely out of fear of persecution. There was a lack of discretion in the visits of members of the opposite sex. An increase in the desert population placed agricultural strain on what was already an area only

4   *Lumen Gentium*, 12.

marginally fertile. While some found legitimate guidance under renowned and eminent spiritual masters, many could certainly say with Isaiah that "all we like sheep have gone astray; we have turned every one to his own way" (Is 53:6). The ascetic dream was in danger of being occluded from two directions. In the first place was the frightful difficulty of the eremitical life, detached from human society and reliant upon persons who were as remarkable as they were rare. On the other hand, there was the threat from below, of unworthy and dissolute individuals who often poisoned the atmosphere of self-denial and restraint. At the very least, the life itself was threatened by the throngs of faithful Christian souls who simply followed holiness out into the desert for intercession and aid.

Often Church history shines with those who use holiness to channel the energies unleashed by new Christian movements, and to insert them stably and safely within the confines of the Church of Christ. They are akin to the vinedressers who, finding a productive but wild plant, carefully and patiently graft it onto the thriving root stock of the vineyard. By the early 300s, the situation in Egypt was deteriorating by the day.[5] Not only was the Church nearing the crest of the Diocletianic persecution, disorder and lawlessness afflicted the ascetics of the desert as well. Into this world stepped the Coptic ex-soldier Pachom (known by the Greek version of his name, Pachomius). He had experienced the order and precision of the Roman army, dominant for centuries because of its discipline, skill, and leadership. Yet he had also tasted the charity of the Christian community, which gave without expecting recompense. He decided that he would use his talents to marshal a new type of army, a host for the Lord. He saw opportunity in the midst of chaos. Diocletian's economic reforms were short lived. Depression

---

5   See Derwas J. Chitty, *The Desert a City: An Introduction to the Study of Egyptian and Palestinian Monasticism Under the Christian Empire* (Oxford: Blackwell, 1966). For Egypt in this period, see Roger Bagnall, *Egypt in Late Antiquity* (Princeton, NJ: Princeton University Press, 1993); and id., *Egypt in the Byzantine World, 300–700* (Cambridge: Cambridge University Press, 2010).

and inflation stalked the land, depopulating formerly prosperous estates and resulting in massive unemployment. Pachomius had apprenticed himself to an experienced anchorite named Palamon for training in this new life. Around the year 315, given the breathing space provided by the Edict of Milan, Pachomius launched his plan. He called out to dispossessed Christians to treat their misfortune as gain, and to follow him into the desert where he would create a new kind of Roman villa, one dedicated to the service of the Lord. Twice he tried this new endeavor, but his young communities failed. Yet each time he learned, adapted, and improved, such that on the third attempt at Tabennesi he struck gold. He balanced asceticism with communal living, and leavened it with strong leadership. He saw that the labor of simple Christians might be turned to spiritual good, while also granting them safety and security in their old age. He had brilliantly elided practical concerns with the spiritual, all directed toward the end of salvation in what came to be known as the cenobitical state (*koinos bios*, the common life).

These monks (*monachos*, or solitaries, first recorded in a papyrus of 324) lived and worked together under the absolute authority of their *abbas*, Pachomius.[6] One of the most significant innovations was the creation of an enclosure wall.[7] This had several purposes. It provided protection to the community from desert raiders—who would continue to be a problem for hundreds of years—thus granting safety to those within for the accomplishment of their work and prayer. It also created a visible boundary between the sacred and profane, one of the most basic of religious impulses. It was tangible, separating people bodily from those outside, leading to the final effect, which was an increased *esprit-de-corps* for

---

6   Henry Chadwick, *The Church in Ancient Society: From Galilee to Gregory the Great* (New York: Oxford University Press, 2009), 401. *Abbas* later became anglicized as "Abbot". An excellent introduction to Pachomian monasticism and its significance can be found in Heinrich Bacht, "L'importance de l'idéal monastique chez saint Pachôme pour l'histoire du monachisme chrétien," in *Revue d'ascetique et de mystique* 126 (1950): 308–326.

7   Bacht, "L'importance," 316.

the monks found within. It was a reminder of separation and exclusion from the outside world, and served to orient the monks both physically and spiritually. Given his military formation, Pachomius organized his monks into camps of 30 to 40 individuals each. They were divided according to their various crafts, with about 10 men subject to a foreman who reported to the master of each house, all of whom in turn were under Pachomius' absolute direction.[8] All in all it was a military style chain of command that emphasized mutual trust and subordinate responsibility. Pachomius, as abbot, had authority to move monks wherever they were needed, so a key aspect of the whole enterprise was obedience to the spiritual superior.

> The mutual contact with others, constantly watched over by their superiors, would develop the souls and personalities of the monks by enabling them to practice a larger number of virtues. Pachomius was the man of genius who by organizing such communities of cenobites, instituted a way of life that was to be more favourable than that of the anchorites.[9]

It is possible that by Pachomius' death, as many as 5000 monks lived under his direct rule. With such astonishing manpower and unity of direction, much fallow land was made arable, leading to a virtuous cycle whereby more monks could be accommodated. He even had two nunneries under his supervision, all supported by the production of his very efficient monastery (although he rigidly segregated the sexes). He had turned the desert into a city.

Even in this primitive monastery tensions were bound to arise. Like many religious foundations after his, success could also present dangers. Monasteries were probably the first economic institutions

8   C. H. Lawrence, *Medieval Monasticism: Forms of Religious Life in Western Europe in the Middle Ages*, 3rd ed. (London: Pearson, 2001), 7–8; Bacht, "L'importance," 317.
9   Décarreaux, *Monks and Civilization*, 77.

in world history that actually generated wealth and capital through the application of industry and cunning. Wealth might bring danger, so St. Pachomius (and his successor, St. Theodore) were careful to make sure to make religious observance fundamental. Work was necessary but secondary to the main mission, which was the salvation of the individual monk. Labor was but an interval between the prayers of the community. To this end Pachomius appointed an economic proctor.[10] While it is uncertain whether this position was occupied by a layman or a monk, it liberated the abbot from excessive concern for the economic activities of the monastery, particularly those relating to external exchange and trade. Pachomius' main purpose was spiritual leadership. This left him free for a regular circuit of visits to all his subordinate houses within the monastic complex, meeting and advising the individual monks personally and giving spiritual conferences. At regular intervals the whole community would assemble, particularly for high feast days. At these semiannual meetings, all of the superiors would have to give an account of their particular houses and charges, and submit themselves for correction by the abbot. All of this was governed by something truly novel, for Pachomius authored a Rule to help govern his people.[11] This was the first time in Christian history that a form of life was organized and articulated by a spiritual master for the governance of a monastic community. This is yet another example of Roman genius, for written law was ever a guarantee against tyranny and oppression. Pachomius knew that a written law could embody the spirit he wished to leave his brethren and would hopefully be a guarantee of future faithfulness and a testament to the spiritual monument he bequeathed. Its originality lay not only with the monastic chain of command that he founded, but the very form of the monastic establishment itself, which for over nearly 1700 years has

10 For the place of work and economics in the Pachomian establishments, see: Heussi, *Der Ursprung*, 126–128.
11 This Rule exists primarily in the Latin translation done by St. Jerome. See the collected works of Pachomius in: *Pachomian Koinonia*, ed. Armand Veilleux, 3 vols. (Kalamazoo, MI: Cistercian Publications, 1980).

remained largely the same. The houses were to be spread evenly throughout the compound, all of which were oriented toward a focal point that included a Church, a common dining hall (refectory), and a hospital for sick monks. Provision was also made for a guest house, entrusted to serious and devout monks who could tend to the many faithful who came for respite and for advice. It had the added benefit of channeling visitors to a common area and controlling their movements, so as not to disturb the bulk of the community in their daily endeavors. In terms of discipline, Pachomius brought together the regimented life of the army and allied it to the mortifications of the desert. The monk's combat was to be an internal one. Pachomius used work intervals to make sure the monks avoided the temptations of sloth. Severe punishments could be meted out for acts of disobedience, but the most feared punishment of all—exclaustration—was terrible enough to keep the monks largely in line.

Pachomius had deftly solved several key issues involved in pursing the life of perfection. He had removed the spiritual—and occasionally social—elitism of many of the hermits, and allowed a place where Christians of any station might come and focus on their own salvation. While there was provision for teaching illiterate monks to read, this was primarily directed to the purposes of worship. In no sense was this foundation a precursor of intellectual labor. The monk was to work and pray in an atmosphere of security, laboring for personal salvation in a like-minded community.[12] Pachomius had solved problems related to chastity and individual poverty by living a common, enclosed life. The ready obedience of the monks to the Rule and to Pachomius personally guaranteed the maintenance of discipline and order. A spiritual entrepreneur, Pachomius had seen an opportunity and seized upon it, establishing the common life as the fundamental bedrock of the search for perfection for both men and women. While hermits would have a place in the future, it would be a small one, reserved for very specific vocations undertaken after much discernment. Though he did not intend it,

---

12 Graham Gould, *The Desert Fathers on Monastic Community* (Oxford: Clarendon Press, 1993).

Pachomius' solution was to have a profound influence in translating Christianity from an urban phenomenon into an evangelical tool that would penetrate into the countryside. Rural monasteries became bases from which to combat the remnants of paganism within the empire.[13] Pachomius' genius was to bring the pursuit of salvation from the cave to the common room, opening up the charismatic path blazed by men like Anthony and Paul the Hermit to Christianity as a whole, an endeavor only made possible by his foresight, organization, and constant search for the common good.

The Rule Makers

In spite of its originality, or perhaps even because of it, the Pachomian system was not easily exported. It remained a solution to the local, contextual situation found in Egypt at the dawn of Christian legalization. While Egypt remained the cradle of monasticism, the Pachomian Rule never extended beyond his own communities. Indeed, as time went on his successors became more and more harsh, imposing severe penalties on disobedience, and occasionally rendering their monks into mobs in the service of a too-fundamentalist reading of Christian providential history. They would play pivotal roles in anti-heretical and anti-pagan activities throughout the fourth and fifth centuries, in ways not always to the credit of the monastic institution. Yet at the same time the *ethos* of the desert became enshrined not in rules, but in collections of stories and sayings, copied and spread throughout the Christian world, such as the *Apophthegmata Patrum* or the *Lausiac History* of Palladius from 420.[14] In this way, stories of ascetic heroism

---

13   Chadwick, 401–402.
14   For the *Apophthegmata Patrum*, see *The Anonymous Sayings of the Desert Fathers: A Select Edition and Complete English Translation*, ed. John Wortley (Cambridge: Cambridge University Press, 2014). For the *Lausiac History*, see Palladius, *Palladius of Aspuna: The Lausiac History*, ed. John Wortley. Cistercian Studies 252. (Collegeville, MN: Liturgical Press, 2015). These and other stories, such as the *Life of St. Anthony*, were assembled over time into a

became part and parcel of the future history of spirituality, while being rigidly separated from their historical Egyptian context. This allowed the religious founders of the West access to the spiritual and ascetical knowledge of Egypt without being exposed to the particular tensions that caused the decline of Egyptian monasticism as a whole.

It is common in both history and hagiography to fall into a fallacy known as "telescoping." This means assigning an extraordinary influence or significance to one individual in order to explain a complex situation more easily. To a certain extent this was true of Anthony and Pachomius. There were anchorites before Anthony, but he was the most famous. The project of Pachomius was one of trial and error, and during his life there were other communities in the process of formation, and development continued after his death. Yet such stories are intricate and tend to cast received wisdom in a bad light. In the interests of truth and accuracy some of the legendary stories need dismantling.[15] Far from downplaying historical "founders" however, this exercise demonstrates how men like Basil, Augustine, and Benedict were part of a powerful evangelical tide, and that they, each in his own way, were able to channel it for the good of future generations. At the same time, like the popes of the previous chapter, no saint or founder is an island. They are aided at all times by the tradition of the past, by collaborators in their present, and by devoted followers in the future. The achievements of such things as the "Basilian" monasteries of the East, the "canonical" life outlined by Augustine, and the "regular"

work called the *Vitas Patrum*, which exercised a remarkable influence on later religious foundations for nearly a millennium. See the commentary in Décarreaux, *Monks and Civilization*, 91.

15   Philip Rousseau takes this approach in his work, *The Early Christian Centuries*, (London: Taylor & Francis Group, 2002). However, this attempt is marred by his idea that "institutionalization" means the emptying of the charismatic power of the early foundations. In addition, he is rightly suspicious of the "founder" model, but at times goes too far in downplaying the historical reality of such figures.

communities of Benedict were historical watersheds. They too could be considered as gospel vines, richly provided for by the deeply rooted practices and doctrines of the Church and aided by the collaboration of many confreres, which crystallized the experiences of the dynamic fifth and sixth centuries, the axial age of Christian monasticism.

Basil of Caesarea (330–379) is a figure of supreme stature in the history of Christianity, particularly in the Eastern Church.[16] Himself a model bishop, he was a force to be reckoned with in terms of the achievement of Nicene unity. As the key figure among the Cappadocian Fathers, he also served to complete the Trinitarian doctrine with his defense of the full divinity of the Holy Spirit. Particularly in the Eastern Church, many liturgical traditions have come down bearing his name, but for our present purposes, it is his contributions to monasticism that echo most deeply. While in the Western tradition of monasticism there have arisen a virtual panoply of orders and approaches, to this day in the Eastern churches monasticism is universally recognized as "Basilian" in its inspiration.[17] Indeed Basil was one of the first generation of bishops who had been inspired by the monastic movement.[18] In a certain sense, such men wanted to bring the desert into the city. At the same time, Basil was a man of his age, adept at political maneuvers and raised in an atmosphere of the Greek classics and philosophy. Taking all this into account, his personality reflected the attempt to create an ideal

16 For Basil, see Philip Rousseau, *Basil of Caesarea* (Berkeley, CA: University of California Press, 1994).

17 Though later monks renewed and distilled the Basilian spirit (such as St. Theodore the Studite), Eastern monasticism remained Basilian at heart, though governed through centuries of received custom.

18 Some older, but still useful considerations of Basil and monasticism are Emmanuel Amand de Mendieta, *L'ascèse monastique de Saint Basile: essai historique* (Maredsous: Éditions de Maredsous, 1948); Margaret Gertrude Murphy, *St. Basil and Monasticism,* Catholic University of America Series on Patristic Studies, Vol. XXV (New York: AMS Press, 1930); and, W.K. Lowther Clarke, *St. Basil the Great: A Study in Monasticism* (Cambridge: Cambridge University Press, 1913).

balance between Athens and Jerusalem. So many of the ancient pagan thinkers had themselves embraced asceticism, and had called for virtuous moderation. Basil experienced the life of the monks as living out this ancient calling, though immeasurably raised (and indeed made possible) by the grace of Christ. For him, the word "philosopher" was functionally equivalent to "monk," for such men had fused the ancient ideal with the new spirit of the gospel. They had found in Christ a pattern and a fulfillment.

Born into a prosperous family that had already been Christian for generations, Basil was able to take advantage not only of the best schools in the Eastern empire, but also from the increased preferential treatment of Christians following Constantine's conversion. He attended school in Alexandria, meeting both his future friend, St. Gregory Nazianzen, and a bitter enemy, Julian (later "the Apostate"). By the 350s he was well on his way to a prosperous career in law and rhetoric. In 357, after an encounter with a serious ascetic, Basil had a conversion experience and was baptized, but was still held back from full adherence to the life of perfection. Goaded by his elder sister, St. Macrina—herself an ardent ascetic—Basil finally made the commitment to pursue an ascetical life. To that end, he began an itinerant journey around the monasteries of the Middle East, during which he toured the Pachomian settlements of Egypt, where he admired the organization and discipline that so characterized that region. Yet at the same time he worried that such monasteries were in danger of becoming "going concerns" focused on production, whose immense numbers of monks reduced the kind of personal interaction and spiritual direction needed for progress.[19]

Basil also visited the flourishing monastic communities of Syria and Palestine.[20] It was there in particular that he found many hermits and ascetics then undertaking astonishing and unusual

19 Décarreaux, *Monks and Civilization*, 97.
20 Monasticism had come to the Holy Land almost contemporaneously with its establishment in Egypt. See John Binns, *Ascetics and Ambassadors of Christ: The Monasteries of Palestine, 314–631* (Oxford: Clarendon Press, 1994).

feats of penitence, for instance those who strove never to sleep, or who lived their lives on the tops of ruined pillars, meters above the ground and exposed to the weather. Basil came to two serious conclusions from these experiences. In the first place, excessive asceticism had made some mentally unbalanced, and competition for spiritual extremes tended to instill the vice of pride among such men. They did not observe the mean between feasting and starvation, and as such were bad "philosophers." Basil knew that a pursuit of holiness, in a real sense, means moderation. Competitive fasts were enervating to both body and spirit. On a deeper level, however, Basil—while certainly admiring the holiness of many of the hermits he met—nonetheless considered that their activities were calculated only to benefit themselves. They had little opportunity to exercise the virtues built by the common life. Such men often had "angular" characters that made them nearly impossible to be around. Reading the stories of the desert fathers often gives one the impression of prickly figures, polemical and short-tempered (one could even point to St. Jerome as an example of the eremitical style of manners). Basil knew that life in community required the practice of all the virtues, and indeed established the possibility that the monk who had "rounded" his edges in the unending challenges of the common life might actually attain a higher level of holiness than his more singular brethren. Even further, ascetics ran from the world and so deprived themselves of the opportunity of practicing charity, particularly the corporal works of mercy directed toward the world beyond the monastery gate.[21] Basil was convinced by the packed guest houses of the Pachomian establishments, no less than from the line of devotees that made St. Simeon Stylites find higher and higher pillars, that the needs of the broader Christian (and indeed human) community was dire, and that monks were placed in a prime position to bring the gospel to life. They could aid the world, even when they retired from it.

Such meditations informed Basil's approach to the religious vocation. Yet apart from practical experience, Basil was a sublime

---

21   See the meditations in Décarreaux, *Monks and Civilization*, 96–97.

theologian. He was vividly aware not only of the inherent dignity of human nature, but also its capacities when sanctified by grace. He wanted the Christian life to be "likeness to God as far as possible,"[22] a Platonic sentiment, exalted by the example of Christ and the gifts of the divine Spirit. Like many early fathers before the Pelagian affair, he was very optimistic about human nature, especially when informed by the spiritual gifts of grace. Men and women were to use this inherent goodness to orient their lives toward perfection in order to achieve sanctity. Basil was also familiar with contemporary heretics and one can detect reactions to them in some of his monastic rules. He knew that the violent asceticism of the Manichees was at heart anti-Incarnational. They fasted because they thought the world evil. For Basil this was a perversion of our human nature, created good in the image of God. Indeed, he also permitted monks to eat any sort of food, provided it was simple and inexpensive. This too was directed against the Manichees, religious vegetarians who rejected meat as reproduced by the devilish mechanism of sex. In many cases the monastic life was a declaration not only against lax Christianity, but a standard for orthodoxy. In the East, the monasteries would remain bulwarks of correct doctrine in the centuries to come. All of this presupposed a solid understanding of human nature, for Basil knew that any leadership or organization must start with a proper understanding of human anthropology illuminated by the light of Christ.

Armed then with both theory and practice, Basil made it one of the purposes of his life to reform and regularize the ascetical communities of Cappadocia and Syria. He transitioned from an earlier devotion to the solitary ascetic to a comprehensively communitarian view of the religious life.[23] Basil left no formal Rule. Rather, his considerations on the monastic life were instead the

22 Homily on the Creation of Man, 1. 17. Cfr. Chadwick, 336.
23 See the careful works of Anna M. Sivas for Basil's monastic vocation and her careful editing of the Rules. Particularly, The Asketikon of St Basil the Great (Oxford: Oxford University Press, 2005). For Basil's emerging vision, see chapter 4, "The Emergence of Monasticism in Fourth-Century Anatolia," 51–101.

result of conferences he gave for ascetics, organized after the manner of question-and-answer sessions. These were then copied out by stenographers and compiled into texts. It does seem that Basil himself put the finishing touches on these collections. The primary sources for the monastic life then come as a finished product from Basil's own hand. These are the *Small Asketikon* and the *Great Asketikon*. The *Small Asketikon* was the first attempt at collecting the saint's thoughts on the monastic life and reached a finished format by the year 366. This version was exceptionally influential in the West, due to its Latin translation by Rufinus of Aquileia after 397, being used extensively by both John Cassian and Benedict. The *Great Asketikon* represented a further augmentation and tailoring by Basil in his later years, possibly as early as 376, and formed the basis for much of Eastern monasticism after that date. It this sense, while it is inaccurate to speak of a formal "Rule," Basil is still able to offer a portrait of the common life that encourages creative interaction, while at the same time provides a broad schema for living the life of holiness.

The work begins with a discussion of the universal Christian vocation of holiness, before leading the questioning ascetics deeper into the monastic life. These initial areas are focused upon charity as the fundamental commandment, presaging Basil's emphasis on community life, in which charity is most efficaciously exercised. Throughout the text he weaves his masterful understanding of human nature with scripture, building the picture of an ideal, balanced, charitable seeker of perfection. He points out blind spots in the lives of solitary ascetics, particularly with the lack of interpersonal interaction. Deceived by such absences, the ascetic may falsely think he has achieved the heights of perfection, and may be blinded to vices that could be corrected by oversight and community.[24] Basil gives some of the first instructions for the testing of applicants, so as to assure that they will integrate fruitfully into the community, and are not arriving under false pretenses.[25] Basil's

24   *Small Asketikon*, 3.27–33; cfr. Ibid.
25   Ibid., 6.2–11.

monastery is based on the constant practice of self-control, in moderation and humility, and reinforced by supervision and fraternity. Basil is always on the lookout for the common internal good of his monks as well. The instructions lay down general principles without delving into specific determinations. He refuses to lay down a common standard for food, saying that the old and those with difficult occupations should receive according to their needs, leaving everything to the discretion of wise overseers.[26]

Basil shows his brilliance in making these practical counsels of spiritual value. The rules he lays down are for spiritual growth, and the act of regulation and administration in service to the community is itself a work of grace. Clothing too should be at the same time simple, yet common to the whole brotherhood. It is to be a habit that demonstrates externally the internal purpose of the monks, betokening order, humility, and community life. He wisely counsels regular obedience, but eschews following any order that is evil and dishonorable it itself. In this, and in many other places, Basil evinces a respect for the innate dignity of the subordinate. Commands are to be according to nature and the gospel, for in following those two guides one discovers the way to perfection. Yet at the same time, Basil is extremely harsh on the spiritual virtuoso, such as one who fasts so ostentatiously that he refuses to eat with the community.[27] Fasting should be done in common, and for the good and edification of all.[28] Likewise, Basil expects a centralization of charity, in that no brother is to undertake to give food or clothing to the poor, except those who fulfill that specific office in the monastery.[29] Unlike later rule-writers, Basil has little to say about the abbot or superior. The model he gives is that of a child's nurse, who is at the same time protective and corrective, while weighing all decisions based on the charge's maturity and competence.[30] He does not neglect correction,

26   Ibid., 9.1–8.
27   Lawrence, *Medieval Monasticism*, 9–10
28   *Small Asketikon*, 89.1–93.1.
29   Ibid., 98–99.
30   Ibid., 15.1–3.

proposing in this case the figures of father and physician. At times the correction may sting, but it is done with the end of salvation in view, and for the subject's own good and growth. Though Basil himself was extremely well educated, he does not set up the brotherhood as a place of learning and forbids a monk from undertaking study on his own, yet still he provides a way whereby the superior, should he find such a person useful, may give the monk permission to read.[31]

The flexibility inherent in such a system make it extremely well-suited for deployment in many different times and contexts. It was at the same time so spiritually deep—while remaining humane—that it became the normative rule (used in a loose sense) for the entirety of the Christian East. Further than that, it served as a fundamental inspiration for the burgeoning monastic enterprises of the West. He also pioneered in personally creating and supervising monastic institutions. He counseled several practices that would become common in the future. In the first place, he did not want monasteries in the middle of desert wastes, but near (and eventually even in) the cities of the East. In that way they could practice the search for perfection while at the same time providing support for the poor and spiritual sustenance for the city dwellers. Basil also practiced episcopal supervision once he became bishop of Caesarea.[32] He would visit and correct the various monastics in his territory, indeed the outlines of the *Asketikon* came from just such spiritual conferences. He also established the principle that monasteries should be small enough that each monk was known to the others and so that the superior could counsel each personally. Not only did this enhance the family community, but also allowed new monasteries to be spun off when a certain number of inhabitants was reached. Finally, he insisted on hospitality for guests, already a well-established practice in the houses of Palestine and Egypt. His

---

31 Ibid., 81.1–2.
32 Paul Jonathan Fedwick, *The Church and the Charisma of Leadership in Basil of Caesarea* (Toronto: Pontifical Institute of Mediaeval Studies, 1979).

innovation in this area was to open the gates even to non-Christians, including pagans. This was an especial help in familiarizing the broader world with the novel life of the monks, and allayed very real suspicions about their way of life.[33] Very quickly Basil's foundations became centers for the efficient distribution of charity, and their voluntary inmates, questing after perfection, began to offer the social services that monasteries would become known for over the next 1000 years. Such services included leprosaria, homes and schools for orphans, infirmaries, and workhouses.[34] Basil's foundations, and the holy men who followed him, established a pattern that would be critical for the expansion and articulation of the monastic life in the future.

Inexorably, the pull of monasticism drifted to the West as well. All during the fourth century there existed strong affinities between the East and West that permitted the movement of persons and ideas. Athanasius was probably the first, with his *Life of Anthony*, who broached the topic of monasticism for the Latins, but he was not the last. Westerners too made their way East, and the letters and translations of St. Jerome and Rufinus of Aquileia raised enthusiasm for the life of the monastery in new lands. Gaul was one of the first to feel the influence. St. Martin of Tours formed one of the first communities in Marmoutier in the 370s, and his enthusiastic biographer, Sulpicius Severus, made sure that a Western example of monasticism was made widely known. This work went on to have exceptional influence in the Western Church, popularizing the idea of a "confessor" saint rather than a martyred one. There were Greek emigrants as well. The most notable was St. John Cassian (ca. 360–ca. 435).[35] When still a young monk, Cassian

---

33   For these, see Chadwick, 336–338.
34   David Knowles, *From Pachomius to Ignatius: A Study in the Constitutional History of the Religious Orders; The Sarum Lectures* (Oxford: Clarendon, 1966), 4–5.
35   Cassian, sometimes associated with Semi-Pelagianism, is nonetheless a saint of the Church. His feast has been celebrated for over a millennium in Marseilles, and he is found in the Roman Martyrology (2004) on his feast day of 23 July. He is widely honored and celebrated

departed his house in Palestine and visited the hermits of Egypt, absorbing their wisdom and teaching. He later moved across the Mediterranean to Gaul, the cradle of Western monasticism. There he compiled two works of enduring importance for monastic history. The first was the *Conferences*, which was cast in the form of talks to monks in which he communicated the thought of the desert fathers and discussed the interior life. It would be a constant companion of later founders such as Benedict and Dominic. His second work was the *Institutes*, which discusses the practicalities of community life and provides a road map of virtues for building perfection. It was perhaps issued to bring some sense of order to the rather anarchic world of Gallic monasticism, and found particular purchase at Lerins, which would become a beacon of Eastern-style cenobitical life for the West.[36]

One man deeply affected by the call to perfection was the young searcher Augustine (354–430). He himself relates how stories about the power of Athanasius' *Life of Anthony* could be life changing. After his conversion he resolved to lead a monastic life, first in Italy and then back home in Africa. Yet time and time again he found himself called back into the active life. Even when he was constrained to become bishop of Hippo in 396, he did not abandon his love for the pursuit of perfection. Like many of his fellow bishops, he lived in an age of the "monastic episcopacy," for many of them were formed in or attracted to the cenobitical life. Many sought the moral purification of their regions, based on the ascetic ideals of the monastery. Augustine tried a different and altogether original tack. He wanted to form his diocesan clergy along a

in the Eastern Catholic Churches as well. The semipelagian crisis occurred long after his demise. While the doctrine itself was condemned at the Second Council of Orange in 529, the Church continued to treat him as a holy man. Indeed the "crisis" did nothing to tarnish his reputation as one of the most profound spiritual thinkers in the history of Christendom.

36   "Cassien ... opposa au caractère vague du monachisme occidental gaulois la mûre sagesse des règles orientales." Bacht, "L'importance," 311.

monastic model.[37] He did this certainly to raise the general tenor of his priests, but there were other reasons. In an age when celibacy was becoming more common among the priesthood, loneliness and lack of community could enervate a presbyterate, while physical separation from the bishop could mean the rise of faction and dissent. He began an experiment in which the celibate diocesan clergy of the city would retire each evening to the cathedral, where they would live, eat, and pray with the bishop as a quasi-abbot. In the morning, spiritually recharged, they would scatter to their pastoral duties. Augustine had developed the first prototype of an urban monastery,[38] which in later centuries would come to be called the "canonical life." After the saint's death, one of his followers culled a series of organizing principles from one of Augustine's letters to nuns. This would later become the so-called "Rule of Augustine." It was the first attempt in history to bridge the active life of Martha with the contemplation of Mary. Augustine's Rule was forgotten for centuries, but would prove to be one of the fundamental contributions to the organization of religious life in later times. This was indeed the age of long-germinating seeds, later to blossom with considerable consequence and profit. We shall have occasion to revisit both Augustine and his Rule later in this work.

During the fifth century monastic roots spread wherever Christianity was found. An astonishing outpouring of evangelical energy in Ireland proved to be pivotal for the reestablishment of order in Western Europe under such luminaries as St. Columba and St. Columbanus. Irish monasticism was of a particular kind, far more austere and ascetic than most Western monasteries. They introduced several aspects of organization that would later become common. In the first place they emphasized smaller establishments, governed by abbots who were in sacred orders. While it may be

---

37   Adolar Zumkeller and Edmund Colledge, *Augustine's Ideal of the Religious Life* (New York: Fordham University Press, 1986).

38   Indeed not only that, but as Décarreaux points out, also a center for evangelization, catechesis, and one of the first seminaries. Décarreaux, *Monks and Civilization*, 122.

obvious to us that the leader of a monastic establishment be ordained so that he could lead his monks in prayer, this was by no means common in the early Church.[39] Irish monasteries tied governance to the possession of the sacred character of ordination, for they recognized that within the power of the priesthood was the charism of governance itself. While the Irish monasteries sometimes went too far in granting power to their abbots (indeed sometimes Irish bishops were themselves merely choir-monks) this principle embedded itself as a fundamental basis of monastic order. Perhaps most significant for the future, the Irish monks rigorously organized the moral life into penitential books, which heralded the rise of private confession.[40] Indeed, as strange and distinct as Irish monasticism was, it provided a window into what the gospel might do in an area unaffected by the old Roman imperial system. It showed the adaptability of the monastic model to a pastoral people who had no experience of Roman administration. Still, the excessive asceticism of the harsh Irish missionaries needed leavening. While they are indeed to be credited with reviving Christian life in a chaotic time, further influence was needed to bring their enthusiasm into proper balance.

This balance, as has happened so often in Church history, came from the tradition of moderation inherited from the Greco-Roman philosophical synthesis, and made practical by the Roman genius for organization, all united in a proper appreciation of Christian anthropology. All the above efforts to understand and advance the life of perfection find their pinnacle in the axial figure of St. Benedict of Nursia (480–ca. 540).[41] Here again, however, we are presented with a history that has been telescoped by piety

---

39 Most Egyptian monasteries, for example, relied upon supply priests from the outside for the celebration of the Eucharist. For Irish monasticism, see Lawrence, *Medieval Monasticism*, 39–65.

40 Hugh Connolly, *The Irish Penitentials and Their Significance for the Sacrament of Penance Today* (Blackrock, Dublin: Four Courts Press, 1995).

41 For Benedict, see: Adalbert de Vogüé, OSB, *Saint Benedict: The Man and His Work* (Petersham, MA: St. Bede's Publications, 2006).

and the long passage of years. To some Benedict seems almost a superhuman figure, establishing order out of chaos, and laying down principles of monastic rule that have not yet been exhausted. There is some truth to this, for anyone who had read the terse Rule that goes under his name can see the proportion, balance, and spiritual depth that it exudes. In order to form a proper picture of the place of Benedict, we need to *correctly* see him in his context. In the first place, Benedict was the heir of a rich tradition dating back two centuries and more. He knew the Rule of Pachomius well, but also the customaries of other monasteries, particularly the Gallican Rules of St. Caesarius of Arles. At the conclusion of this Rule, he recommends the writings of both Cassian and Basil. He is clearly dependent upon works that had been, by his time, long in circulation.

Nor was Benedict properly the founder of Italian monasticism, which itself dates back to the later 300s (and in some isolated instances even earlier).[42] Indeed the most intractable problem in terms of the writing of his own Rule is its relation to the "Rule of the Master," itself an Italian product. This Rule is diffuse and disorganized, a sort of hodge-podge of institutional customs and spiritual admonitions. It is likely that this Rule formed the basis for Benedict's efforts.[43] The masterful organization of the Roman Church, detailed in the last chapter, was also very much in the

42   Georg Jenal, *Italia ascetica atque monastica: das Asketen- und Mönchtum in Italien von den Anfängen bis zur Zeit der Langobarden (ca. 150/250–604)* (Stuttgart: Hiersemann, 1995).

43   The literature regarding source criticism of the *Rule* is an industry in itself. For an introduction, see David Knowles, *Great Historical Enterprises, and Problems in Monastic History* (Edinburgh: Nelson, 1963), 137–195; The debate over the right order of authorship still goes on, and Marilyn Dunn gives arguments for why Benedict may still be prior to the "Master." See her, "Mastering Benedict: Monastic Rules and their Authors in the Early Medieval West," in *English Historical Review* 105 (1990): 567–583. Recent scholarship, however, has tended to accept Benedict's dependence. See Adalbert de Vogüé, *A Critical Study of the Rule of Benedict* (Hyde Park, NY: New City Press, 2013).

background of Benedict's own thinking.[44] In very many ways St. Benedict was a compiler, not an original thinker. Yet this realization should not cause us to think less of him, for it is the very source of his genius. As a founder he, like Janus, is able to look both backward and forward. His depth in the sources, and his awareness of contemporary problems allied to a firm understanding of human nature, allows the implementation of his thought in different times and places. Genius is not necessarily original; indeed, much brilliance has to do with the deployment and enactment of existing material for the common good and in accord with the best practices and principles. It demands the ability to cast off what is unnecessary and the strength to see to the heart of a problem. Benedict's mastery of the sources enables him to see farther. It is in his administration that one glimpses the breadth of his genius.

Benedict's Rule, written in quickly vernacularizing low-Latin, is presented in what David Knowles called "lapidary brevity." Assembling the received wisdom of the tradition, Benedict wanted a simple text and way of life, a "most elementary rule for beginners."[45] In seventy-three paragraph-sized chapters he lays out his vision of the monastic state, the search for perfection, and the internal ordering of such a life. Benedict too experienced fits and starts to his own vocation. Like Pachomius, he was persecuted by those who had vowed obedience to him, also failing in two attempts to found a monastery. To that was added the hostility of secular clergy, who viewed with wary eyes the increasing popularity of the monastic state.[46] Yet he learned from all setbacks and made a third attempt on the 1700-foot summit of Montecassino, halfway between Rome and Naples. It was out of the way, well protected, and the site of an ancient temple to Apollo that he destroyed. There he made his new foundation, one that—many centuries later—

44 Knowles, *The Religious Orders*, vol.1, 9.
45 Rule of St. Benedict (hereafter Regula, cited by chapter), 73.
46 Exemplified in the terrible character of the local priest of Subiaco, Florentius. He tried both to send prostitutes to disperse Benedict's community, and to poison him. Décarreaux, *Monks and Civilization*, 219.

would be recognized as one of the stabilizing pillars of western civilization. Yet in his time Italy was in total disarray. The peninsula was wracked by wars. The rule of the Arian Ostrogoths was repeatedly challenged by a resurgent Byzantium, and Rome was the prize. Order on a large scale was simply impossible, but one might, if careful, construct a well-regulated community away from urban centers, with a unity of focus and purpose. This is just what Benedict set out to do.

The chief characteristic of such an establishment was its independence. Benedict expected the monastery to be self-sufficient. It would have all the possessions required to farm and to supply however large a community it might intend to have.[47] In order to assure this Benedict established one of the fundamental reorientations of the monastic program. While the life of the monk was one of contemplation, and the true *Opus Dei* was still the Divine Office, all monks were called upon to work.[48] This often meant manual labor. Benedict had a most profound understanding of human nature. From his experiences, monks who attempted to spend all their time in prayer became by turns sullen or slothful. Alternation of work and prayer would not only allow the monks to support themselves, but to exercise their bodies as well as their minds, each time returning to prayer with refreshed energy. It was a practical, Roman approach to an "incarnational" problem. In Benedict's prescriptions we can see the seeds of the doctrine of the dignity of labor. He also added a third activity to communal prayer and manual labor—namely, private spiritual reading. This would become the *Lectio Divina* of the Benedictine tradition. It implies literate monks, and consequently some sort of educational apparatus to train young novices in the rudiments of grammar. As such, it presages the astonishing intellectual and academic undertakings to come, though this was beyond Benedict and would only come to pass in the future.

The Rule was a monument in institutional history, for it can be called the first purposely written constitution that the world had

47 Regula, 66.
48 Regula, 48.

ever seen. Beside humility and moderation, another of his prime concerns was institutional order. Confronted at the same time by a collapsing civil society and a Roman Church quickly becoming adept at ensuring internal church order, Benedict strove to make his little world a place of peace and discipline. The axis of this would be the office of the abbot. This superior was to have absolute and total control over the monastery and rightly expected ready and instant obedience from his subordinates. What seems at first glance an absolutist monarchism is somewhat tempered. Benedict gives three models for the religious superior.

The first is fatherhood. The administrator as father seeks nothing for those under his rule but their absolute good, yet in order for them to attain goodness and maturity he must sometimes use discipline, always tempered with love and focused on the end to be achieved. Benedict also constantly reminds abbots that as "fathers" they are responsible for their "children" and will be judged strictly on their rule by the just judge. It is a warning to all those placed in positions of responsibility "because he has undertaken to govern souls, he must one day render an account of them."[49] This admonition, repeated constantly, within a Christian context is meant to be a powerful check on voluntaristic arbitrariness in abbatial rule. The second model he gives is a military one, "soldiers under a holy obedience." Just as secular soldiers must obey their general without murmur, so the monks, with much higher purpose, ought to obey their superiors as if these were Christ, for they are meant to be an elite force directed to the end of salvation. Finally, Benedict gives the striking image of the monastery as a "school for the Lord's service." The abbot is to be a schoolmaster (a much more disciplinary position at that time than now), but even the teacher is to act only for the ultimate good of the students. The three models of leadership that he proposes are, then, all interconnected: father, military leader, and schoolmaster. All are characterized by their attention to the ultimate end, and the common good of the whole. By placing "father" first, however, Benedict emphasizes the imitation of God

49   Regula, 2.

the Father, with leadership seen as an expression of charity. In making this connection, Benedict also shows the abbot himself to be under a superior, and therefore ruling only in accord with the law of God, which he may not transgress. It is a fundamentally Christian check on arbitrary rule.

Even given the subjection of the abbot to God, the temptations of power are still subtle and ever-present. There are some earthly limitations under which even Benedict's monarch-abbot must labor. In the first place, each abbot is to be elected by a democratic vote, whereby the majority of the community freely chooses who will rule over them. While after confirmation of election the abbot is supreme, this still marks a key moment of participatory concurrence in the life of the community. After election the abbot is obliged to consult the community whenever there are matters of import at hand.[50] While the abbot is always absolutely free to make the final decision, Benedict recognizes the utility of asking the advice of subordinates, and in particular the senior members of the community. In the case of visiting monks, should they see anything amiss, they are encouraged to report it to the abbot.[51] If the community elects an abbot who is disorderly or unruly, in exceptional cases the local bishop may be called in to depose him and install a steward. This is the only instance where Benedict refers to outside interference in what is supposed to be a perfectly self-contained world.

Knowing the reality of sin and imperfection, Benedict provides one extraordinary relief valve in case of dire emergency.[52] Perhaps most fundamental to the dignity of the monk is the unspoken assumption that the superior cannot demand obedience in anything that contravenes the divine law. The absolute abbot is then utterly bound—but it is the divine law that constrains him. Benedict even gives a method of redress when an impossible order is given. That he considers potential impossibility as less serious than cases of

50   Regula, 3.
51   Regula, 61.
52   Regula, 64.

immorality indicates that Benedict never foresaw the kind of mindless obedience he is sometimes charged with demanding. If a monk considers an order impossible, he is permitted in all humility and reverence to discuss it with his superior and to make rational arguments.[53] Benedict, a true master of human nature, tries his hardest to avoid such impossible situations in two ways. In the first place he makes very few discrete rulings, leaving such matters as food and clothing largely up to the local superiors who have specific local knowledge. Apart from than that, however, he constantly counsels adaptation to the needs of each monk. "Every age and stage of intellect ought to have its own appropriate degree of discipline,"[54] and "Let him [the abbot], according to the character and intelligence of each, mould and adapt himself."[55] Benedict's Rule is spiritually deep because he recognized two realities simultaneously. Human nature was the same in all and unchanged through history, permitting a deep knowledge of the heart. Yet at the same time human persons, embedded in contexts and bodies, are all unique and demand the individual care their dignity deserves. The monasteries of the Christian world were one of the first places where integral human development on an individual scale could take place. It was a locus for the salvation of body and soul together.

In spite of Benedict's reluctance to lay down specific rules, he was insistent on the outline of governance at the monastery. Though the legislation is scattered throughout the Rule, one can glean a general overview of his ideas on proper institutional order. At the heart of his project is his desire to avoid all faction such that the unanimity of the brotherhood in charity might spring forth. He cautions monks not to make themselves patrons over other monks, for fear of dissention.[56] He also enforces an astonishing equality,

53   Regula, 68.
54   Regula, 30.
55   Regula, 2.
56   Regula, 69. Patron-client relationships were the fundamental social structures of the pre-modern world. The interdiction of such intermediate power networks was critical to the proper foundation of the monastery, and of itself strikingly modern.

largely alien to this time period. Monks are totally to put away any worldly rank or status. They are to be ranked solely according to their dates of profession. Benedict is even wary of the place of priests in his communities, a reticence we have seen in older rules. While their priesthood is to be given respect, in all non-liturgical functions they are to adhere to the same order as the rest of the monks.

His concern for factionalism is made plain in legislation about the provost (the prior, or second in command). It appears that in some monasteries the prior was selected at the same time as the abbot, or sometimes appointed from without. At times certain priors felt that this made them a competing power to the abbot, which introduced grave divisions into the monastery.[57] Benedict is insistent that the prior is to serve at the pleasure of the abbot, he is to be "his man." In this way the abbot claims a trusted subordinate, beholden only to him, and preserves the unity of fatherly rule in the institution. He also foresees the selection of deans, in the case of larger houses, who can be set over a smaller group of monks for the sake of discipline and advisement. Here again we find echoes of Pachomius' military organization.

For Benedict the role of Cellarer is central. This position was to be sort of a minister of the temporalities. Since Benedictine houses were economically self-sufficient, and often quite large, this meant that such a position was delicate and required great trust. It allowed the majority of the monks to attend to their spiritual duties, with knowledge that their earthly needs were being addressed. Benedict exhibits his organizational brilliance in enumerating some (but not all) of the lesser offices of the monastery, including kitchen staff, porters, and readers. In all of these he shows his moderation and respect for human nature. The kitchen staff is to eat early, so as not to hinder them during table service. The reader should receive a cup of wine and water, with some bread in it, to keep his spirits (and voice) up during the public lections. Even in food and drink, Benedict was strict but flexible. Sick brethren could eat meat

57   Regula, 65.

if they needed it. Portions were to be allocated based on need and work schedules. Most famously, a monk was to be allowed a *hemina* of wine each day, though even that might be increased at the abbot's discretion.[58]

The three words that summarize Benedict's approach are harmony, moderation, and order. The monastery exists for the good of the community as a whole and its residents must strive to maintain the internal common good. In light of this, a special emphasis is laid upon the reception of new members for the house. Benedict is the first to give explicit regulations for what will become known as the novitiate. In the first place a postulant is not to be given immediate entry, rather he must manifest his request at the monastery door over the course of several days in order to demonstrate his seriousness. He is then permitted to stay in the guest house for several days to become accustomed to the climate of the monastery. After this he is permitted to move to the dormitory of the novices under the supervision of a senior monk (not yet a novice master, but certainly moving in that direction). He is to remain in the monastery for no less than a year. On three occasions the Rule is read aloud to him to remind and confirm him in his dispositions. Only at the end of such a year, having demonstrated perseverance, is he then permitted to make his profession. During this ceremony he not only vows to observe the evangelical counsels, but adds to them a fourth—peculiarly Benedictine—vow of stability. This means that he is to remain for the rest of his life at the monastery of his profession. One cannot overemphasize the significance of this vow for the equilibrium of Benedictine life. It anchored persons and communities, and bound them together across generations.

The founder also gave particular emphasis to the punishments for disobedience. Corporal punishment was not so much dreaded as what were considered the greater punishments of excommunication from the common refectory and common prayers. Worst of

58 Scholars still disagree on how much a *hemina* is, with many suggesting a half-pint, though I think it likely more. For food legislation, see Regula, 39–41.

all, and reserved only for the gravest, repeat offenders was the penalty of exclaustration, or permanent banishment. When one considers what contemporary society was like outside the walls of the monastery, this may have very much seemed like a death sentence, and served as a serious deterrent to wrongdoing. And yet the Rule, which would give its name to the "Regular" life of religious, was intended to be a flexible document, and an "elementary rule for beginners." It was to establish the parameters of the garden Benedict wished to plant. For further spiritual growth, the humble Benedict pointed past his Rule and back to Pachomius, Basil, and Cassian. Once firmly established in the Rule, only then could one mount to the height of perfection. The Rule was the necessary administrative skeleton upon which the life of perfection wrapped its flesh.

Rules, Reform, and Renewal

In looking at the legacy of the Rule we must be realistic. It was written for a discrete community at a specific time and place. Indeed, the foundation it was meant for—Cassino—itself was sacked and its community dispersed a little over a generation after Benedict's death in the 540s. The Lombard eruption from northern Italy led to the attack on the great monastery in 570. The monks scattered, with many finding their way to Rome. While older scholars suggested that the Cassinese community became a leaven to the monasteries of Rome, there is little direct historical testimony. Gregory the Great, Benedict's biographer, only mentions once that Benedict wrote a Rule, and even the evidence of Benedictine practices at Gregory's own monastery on the Caelian is spotty at best.[59] Yet it is Gregory's Benedict that has become

---

59 Lawrence laconically says of Gregory's biography, that it "evidently contains all that was known about him (Benedict) at Rome at the end of the sixth century, possibly rather more than was known." Lawrence, *Medieval Monasticism*, 19. See also Knowles, *Religious Houses*, vol. 1, 18.

familiar. Gregory likely did have first-hand information from people who had known the Cassinese founder, and through him Benedict's name became famous, beginning that long historiographical telescoping of the sources of Western monasticism into the person of Benedict himself.

Yet the dispersal of the monks did not result in a concomitant expansion of the Rule. Local customaries were still followed in Italy, using a mishmash of different sources. In the wider European world, there were hundreds of monastic houses, some following Irish usages, some Eastern, some Gallican, yet all affected by local situations and creating customaries on the fly. We can say with certitude that Benedict had no personal vision beyond his small community of perfection at Cassino. There is no provision in the Rule for foundation or supervision of other monasteries. If the Rule were to have any chance at survival, much less spread, its internal genius would have to be realized gradually and with great difficulty across centuries. As will be seen in the future, without dedicated followers and stalwart reformers, Benedict's Rule would have disappeared entirely were it not for a series of events that were kicked off by Gregory's immortalizing hagiography.

The Rule began to circulate, primarily north of the Alps, by the second half of the 600s. While there is no evidence that the original Roman monastic mission to Britain was Benedictine, still in their struggle against native Celtic influences in the Church, saints such as Wilfrid used the Benedictine Rule as a Roman influence to counterbalance what they considered to be aberrant religious practices.[60] It appears that the abbeys of Ripon and Wrexham were purposely founded as 'Benedictine' houses from the 670s.[61] The movement began to catch on. St. Benedict Biscop (who had taken his name in honor of the founder of the Rule), founded the houses of Wearmouth and Jarrow. While it appears that Biscop created an eclectic

60   Henry Mayr-Harting, *The Coming of Christianity to Anglo-Saxon England*, 3rd ed. (State College, PA: Pennsylvania State University Press, 1991).
61   Lawrence, *Medieval Monasticism*, 57.

Rule, he held the *Regula* in very high esteem. Indeed, one of the most powerful catalysts for the spread of the Rule was Jarrow's most famous son, the Venerable Bede (ca. 672–735). This brilliant monk lauded Benedict and his Rule in his many works, seeing it as the logical terminus for all monasticism purified of Celtic particularities. Yet for all the suspicions about their practices, Celtic missionaries nonetheless played a pivotal role in the reconversion of Western Europe, particularly in the Merovingian lands. St. Columbanus had revivified many monasteries, and brought with him the tradition of independence from episcopal oversight. Yet his penitential practices were extreme, and it seems that soon after his death foundations like Luxeuil began to temper the regime with Benedictine moderation.[62] The unfolding awareness of the Rule evoked a veneration for the man himself, and in an act of pious theft (far from unheard of in the Middle Ages) the monks of Fleury conducted a daring raid on Montecassino to steal the bones of Benedict and bring them back to Gaul. They claimed success, whereas the remaining few hermits on Montecassino asserted that they had only accessed an outer tomb, which then led to claims of his body being in both locations.[63]

It is an unexpected reality that enthusiasm for Benedict and his Rule seems to have started in northern Europe and only tardily migrated back to Italy. In 718 a Brescian monk named Petronax made a pilgrimage to Rome and, encouraged by Pope Gregory II, continued on to the tomb of Benedict.[64] There he found a few hermits

---

62   Ibid., 47.

63   See Patrick Geary, *Furta Sacra: Thefts of Relics in the Central Middle Ages* (Princeton, NJ: Princeton University Press, 1978), esp. 146–149. It seems that Montecassino has the better claim. The Fleury raiders may only have ransacked an outer tomb containing other monks' bones. The local knowledge of the Montecassino hermits may have been decisive in this case.

64   While little is known about the second founder of Montecassino, there was a conference whose proceedings have proven very difficult to access: *Petronace da Brescia nel XIII centenario della rinascita di Montecassino (718–2018). Atti della giornata di studio (Cassino,*

gathered around the shrine. He decided that he would rebuild the foundation, which had lay in ruins for over 150 years, according to the original intent of the founder. St. Petronax was an extremely able organizer and managed to assemble funds from nobles and churchmen throughout the peninsula. Indeed, drawn by the magical name of Benedict, he was soon joined by northern monks, keen on drinking from the fountain at its source. In the first place came St. Willibald from the Anglo-Saxon world. He had spent nearly a decade in pilgrimage, becoming one of very few contemporaries to reach the Holy Land in the early 700s. When he returned to Italy he spent ten years (729–739) as a monk at Cassino, serving in various offices and giving St. Petronax the benefit of his experience in successful Benedictine foundations. Later joining the order was St. Sturm, who lived at Cassino from 747–748. He would later become the founding abbot of the mighty imperial monastery of Fulda in Germany. Both Sturm and Willibald participated in the massive missionary effort of St. Boniface to Christianize Western Germany. Boniface made it his policy to found monasteries according to the Rule, both for its moderation and utility, as well as to solidify the connections with Italy.

The reconstitution of both community and Rule that happened at this extraordinary time was then a two-way street. Northern customs blended with the remaining memories of the practice of the Rule. Two developments occurred that profoundly changed both Benedict's vision and the future of monasticism itself. In the first place much more provision was created for the ordination of monks to the priesthood. Next, the monks were increasingly occupied by liturgical or literary work, meaning that the original requirement for manual labor began to wane.[65] Thus by a somewhat circuitous route the Rule had come back to life. By 770 the first commentary will be written. From Montecassino, moribund for 150 years, came much of the energy for the conversion of Germany,

Palagio badiale, 23 novembre 2018), ed. Mariano Dell'Omo. Miscellanea Cassinese, 87 (Montecassino, 2019).
65 Knowles, *The Monastic Order in England,* vol. 1, 19.

and for the expansion of the Rule in ways even Benedict did not anticipate.

The ascendancy of the Rule was established by its patronage under the Carolingian dynasty. In their lands we see all councils after 742 referring to the Rule whenever legislating for monks. Charlemagne himself was instrumental in mainstreaming Benedictine life in his drive to regularize all civic and religious matters in his kingdom.[66] It must be stressed that Charlemagne was no imposer of uniformity. Just as he wisely permitted local customs to continue, so too he did not want to extinguish the legitimate practices of the monasteries. Rather, he was interested in creating a standard against which to measure and remedy abuses in the system. In 787 he sent representatives to the abbey of Montecassino to obtain an authentic copy of the Rule, which could then be copied by the royal chancery, in the same matter as he had begun to circulate Roman liturgical books.[67] Indeed it was the very "Roman" character of the *Regula* that attracted Charlemagne, who harbored universalizing ambitions.

Yet Charlemagne's predilection was compromised by his own actions and those of his nobles. Already by this time endowment of a monastery with property did not mean permanent alienation, but the repurposing of capital that could be used and distributed by the king. Monasteries became commodities and holding companies for kingly (later imperial) interests. None of this should detract from their genuine religious concerns, for they expected their bequests to be rewarded richly by the prayers and masses of the monks. But such arrangements had a stultifying effect on the

---

66 For Charlemagne, see the exhaustive biography by Janet Nelson, *King and Emperor: A New Life of Charlemagne* (Oakland, CA: University of California Press, 2019).

67 Lawrence, *Medieval Monasticism*, 70. For the Roman influence on Benedictinism, see Joachim Wollasch, "Benedictus abbas romensis: Das römische Element in der frühen benediktinischen Tradition," in *Tradition als historische Kraft: interdisziplinäre Forschungen zur Geschichte des früheren Mittelalters*, eds. N. Kamp and J. Wollasch (Berlin: 1982), 119–37.

religious life of the houses, as lay proprietors took substantial portions of monastic income and rendered the negotiations between proprietor and community enervating and often litigious. In order to rectify such a situation, new processes would have to be developed and new approaches applied in order to realize the life of monastic perfection in its fullness.

One of Charlemagne's most notable traits as a leader was his ability to recognize talent and to delegate authority to trustworthy subordinates. He found worthy men throughout (and beyond) his empire and empowered them with the authority they needed to enact reform. Charlemagne was convinced that the Rule of Benedict was the key to the regularization of monastic life in his kingdoms. Inspired both by Benedict and by the success of the Rule's implementation in Anglo-Saxon lands, he empowered subordinates to bring his reform to reality. He found a trusted monk for this task in yet another Benedict, this time St. Benedict of Aniane (ca. 747–821).[68] While in some senses Benedict of Aniane was a second founder of Benedictine monasticism, we must also credit the intense energy and single-minded collegiality of Charlemagne and his court, particularly the support of the sympathetic education advisor, Alcuin.

This new Benedict had become a monk seeking a life of extreme austerity, but to the extent that he drew rebuke from his own abbot. Sensing that the monasteries of Gaul were too lax, Benedict of Aniane withdrew by himself to live the life of a hermit. His asceticism drew followers, which helped to temper his more puritanical side. Experience smoothed the rough edges, and he came to see the Rule of his namesake as the most efficient means for leading a community of perfection, and in it he discovered his own balance in its moderation. With this realization he founded the monastery

---

68 For what can be known about Benedict of Aniane biographically, see Rutger Kramer, *Rethinking Authority in the Carolingian Empire* (Amsterdam: Amsterdam University Press, 2019), especially chapter 4, "*Caesar et Abba Simul:* Monastic Reforms between Aachen and Aniane."

of Aniane in 782, placing it immediately in donation to Charlemagne. This was a canny move. Not only did it disintermediate the local bishop and nobles, but it involved Benedict intimately in the politics of the Carolingian family, which he was able to leverage significantly in his drive to reform the monasteries of the kingdom. He became intimately associated with King Louis of Aquitaine as one of his closest advisors. When Louis succeeded his father as Holy Roman Emperor in 814, Benedict was by his side. Benedict knew well how to manipulate the levers of power in order to obtain the recognition of the Rule, and did not disdain to employ royals and aristocrats in his pursuit of reform. His presence at court resulted in acquaintances from around the empire. This included bishops and abbots who themselves solicited him eagerly for reformed monks to help in their houses.[69] Indeed one gets the impression that this ascetic and dedicated monk could indeed be named the patron saint of networkers. While it would have surprised the first Benedict, his Rule became established by the power of the state, an authority his Benedictine heir would leverage with consummate skill in the task of purifying the religious houses. He demonstrated the axiom that power was morally neutral unless specified by an end. The employment of state power for the subvention and support of the Church was considered absolutely essential in the early Middle Ages, and when managed carefully, as Benedict of Aniane proved himself capable, it was possible to secure a great many spiritual and material blessings.

Louis and Benedict together worked out a plan to establish a new imperial monastery near the capital of Aachen called Inda.[70] He did this for several reasons. Personally, Louis (known to history as "the Pious") wanted a spiritual retreat close to the palace. He also designed it as his final resting place. The more immediate motivation was to provide a platform from which Benedict of Aniane could more efficiently conduct the reform of the monasteries, and

---

69   Kramer, *Rethinking Authority*, 191.
70   Later in history, after it had acquired the bones of Pope St. Cornelius, it became known by the name "Kornelimünster."

be in frequent attendance on Louis at court.[71] Benedict and Louis seem to have used Inda as a training ground for elite monks who would in turn go back to their monasteries to instruct and reform them.[72] It is likely that Benedict of Aniane also collaborated in the copying of the exemplar of the Rule brought back from Cassino by Charlemagne's agents. In this way he reinforced the personal training of the monks with the authority of the definitive Rule, copied and assessed against the authentic text kept at the Imperial archives. Benedict did not stop there. He convinced Louis to assemble two synods of the abbots of the realm, in 816 and 817. In preparation for these meetings, he labored to create two works of supreme importance. The first was the *Codex Regularum*, which was a compilation of all the available Rules made before Benedict. He followed this with the *Concordia Regularum*. This second work sought to be a sort of harmony of all the Rules, a proto-scholastic project of reconciling authorities so as to demonstrate how they all found their fruition in the Rule of Benedict.[73] With both text and legislation at his back, he and Louis sent out inspectors to investigate the lives of the religious houses. They were not to impose— rather, they set out to encourage and model. Benedict quashed no local customs, but was rather convinced that the inherent superiority of a life lived according to the Rule would be its own persuasion. In this he was largely correct. Yet in one case, Benedict essentially failed. He tried to convince Louis to ensure the freedom of abbatial elections. Monasteries had been suffering significantly under the patronage system that assigned lay proctors to govern

71 Kramer, *Rethinking Authority*, 179–180.

72 There is a dispute about whether this was the original intention, or if it was simply because there were so many monastic visitors who stayed there. Either way, the phenomenon was real. Inda became the hub of a Benedictine revival. Ibid., 181.

73 Ibid., 183. See also, Colleen Maura McGrane, OSB, "The Rule Collector of Aniane," in *American Benedictine Review* 63.3 (2012): 267–283; and Suzanne Dulcy, *La règle de saint Benoît d'Aniane et la réforme monastique à l'époque carolingienne* (Nîmes: A. Larguier, 1935).

religious houses. According to the spirit of the Rule, Benedict wanted these abolished and power returned to the monasteries themselves, freed of lay interference. However, the economic pull of the religious houses and their deep integration in the social fabric meant that later emperors and nobles would continue the lamentable practices that sapped the religious vigor of the houses. Benedict's was a good idea that would have to wait for its day.[74]

This new Benedict was a master of many facets of administration. He had a practical workshop born of experience, first at Aniane and then at Inda. Like his patron Charlemagne, Benedict was no micromanager. He trained good people and sent them out to accomplish their functions. He knew how to operate in the corridors of power and was unafraid to seek allies and protectors for his mission. "The story of his life is not the glorification of an individual reformer, but of a person who learned to work within a given system, and who learned to make people listen in spite of himself."[75] Comfortable both in the practical world of politics and legislation, he did not ignore the theoretical as his writings give clear testimony. He had a firm grasp of the first principles and, animated by the spirit of the first Benedict, intrepidly went forward bringing order and harmony to the monks of the Empire. For all of that, however, Benedict of Aniane was not a constitutional innovator. He was content to make his monasteries and the Rule the models for others to follow, rather than assert any organizational impositions within the houses themselves. Constitutional evolution would come, and in stunningly new ways.

The Rise of (an) Order

By the year of Benedict's death in 821 many of the luminaries of the Carolingian court had already passed to their reward. Each emperor subsequent to Charles the Great was weaker than the last, and imperial power waned. Sensing weakness, external enemies began

74   Kramer, *Rethinking Authority*, 206.
75   Ibid., 213.

to renew their attacks on the borders of Christendom: Muslims to the south, Magyars to the east, and Vikings to the north. These enemies, especially the Norsemen, tended to focus raids on the monasteries, which were known as centralized repositories of wealth, for many had become focuses of pilgrimage in their own rights. Without clear central leadership, the initiatives of Louis and Benedict became essentially dead letters. Local nobles were often as predatory as the invaders. The Church too suffered an immense loss as a result of increasingly weak leadership. Even the papacy was not immune. The Church of Rome became a battleground for the petty nobility of central Italy, and a series of inept, incompetent, and outright immoral figures thrust themselves into the See of Peter. East and West drifted farther apart, and society began to unravel. This new age of iron was not propitious for regular observance, and even houses which had tasted the reform were afflicted by the need for mere survival. Whole communities were disrupted and forced into dispirited wandering for new homes. In 883 the Muslims pillaged throughout central Italy and murdered the entire community at Montecassino, which was again abandoned for no fewer than sixty years.[76] Even something as seemingly permanent as the Benedictine presence in the Church was not assured in any time or place. It had to be lived and restored, time and time again, by men and women who were dedicated to the orderliness it brought and its potential for holiness.

It is almost a truism of Church history that each age gets the saints that it needs. Around the turn of the year 900, a young canon of a noble family named Odo, well-educated and comfortable, chanced one day to pick up the Rule of Benedict. He came away abashed at his community's failure to live up to what was called "an elementary rule for beginners." His canonry, site of the tomb of St. Martin of Tours, was one of the wealthiest in Christendom. Chastened, he abandoned his well-endowed position, and wandered the country, looking for a house that observed the Rule. He could not find one until he was told of a holy Abbot named Berno

---

76   Lawrence, *Medieval Monasticism*, 79.

who ruled the small monastery of Baume in the remote Jura mountains. There the Rule was observed in its integrity, and the reforms of Benedict of Aniane were kept alive. There he finally found a fully Benedictine life. The Rule had, once again, endured. In 909 a local nobleman, William III of Aquitaine, expressed a desire to found a monastery for the good of his soul, and was convinced that only a house of the strictest observance would do. Referred to Berno, they settled upon a rolling valley in a place called Cluny.[77] There Berno, Odo, and a few other monks moved to undertake the establishment of the new foundation. Two things made this endeavor different. In the first place, the monastery was placed directly under the patronage of St. Peter. While this stratagem had been used in the past, it would be Cluny that would leverage it to exceptional success.[78] It meant that Cluny was to be directly dependent upon the Holy See. While it is certain that neither William nor Berno foresaw the marvelous symbiotic relation that would develop centuries hence, they did know that such a donation would free the monastery from the interference of the local bishops (who were often as relaxed as the religious houses of the time).[79]

But William, urged by Berno, went further. He perpetually disclaimed the right to interfere in the governance of the monastery in any way. Berno had achieved the dream of Benedict of Aniane, and had liberated the Rule not only from the decadent local ecclesiastical authorities, but also from depredations by the state. He

77 Studies on Cluny, while not as extensive as that on the later Cistercians (except in the area of art and architectural history), can be found in Marcel Pacaut, *L'Ordre de Cluny: 909–1789* (Paris: Fayard, 1986); H. E. J. Cowdrey, *The Cluniacs and the Gregorian Reform* (Oxford: Clarendon, 1970); Barbara Rosenwein, *Rhinoceros Bound: Cluny in the Tenth Century* (Philadelphia, PA: University of Pennsylvania Press, 1982); and, ID., *To Be the Neighbor of Saint Peter: The Social Meaning of Cluny's Property, 909–1049* (Ithaca, NY: Cornell University Press, 1989).

78 Ibid., 80.

79 Nor did they likely expect much oversight or advantage from the papacy, then mired in a century of corruption. Knowles calls it "an attachment to a wraith or a vacuum." *From Pachomius to Ignatius*, 10.

had acquired a most fundamental right. At his death only the members of the community would elect his successor, and it would remain that way in perpetuity. Cluny was fully and finally an independent Benedictine house, able to govern itself and manage its own affairs with no external impediments. Finally, a garden had been planted in which the Rule could freely blossom.

Odo peacefully succeeded Berno upon the latter's death in 926, and set his stamp firmly on the Cluniac community. Indeed, much of what later comes to be seen as "Cluniac" customs, that spread so far and so rapidly, was a result of his focus on the house's mission. It was he who prescribed the practice of silence in the cloisters to a far greater extent than before, and strictly enforced the so-called "Grand Silence" after Compline. He also laid heavy emphasis on the vocal prayer of the monks. By Odo's time the notion of manual labor as found in the Rule had become obsolescent.[80] While some monasteries had transmuted the obligation to intellectual work or the copying of manuscripts, other houses had simply slipped into lassitude. For Odo, the proper object of the monk in seeking to define the *Opus Dei* was the liturgy. He eliminated as many obligations external to this as he could. In addition to the standard divine office, Odo added psalms and prayers while increasing the solemnity of the ceremonial. These developments also occurred at the time when the doctrine of purgatory was in fruitful development alongside the increasing presence of monks who had received priestly ordination. Cluny was one of the first to establish an extensive program of private masses to complement the solemn community celebration of the Eucharist. A plethora of witnesses, both lay and religious, testified to the magnificent and harmonic symphony of divine praise that Cluny modelled. It was called the *ordo districtus*, or the "busy community," by St. Peter Damian, for

---

80 The monasteries could do this because of the multitudes of *coloni* or workers who would come to affiliate themselves with a monastery, live and work on its land, in exchange for prayers. These became the "neighbors of St. Peter" who provided the manual labor necessary for the dedication of the monks wholly to liturgy.

there was almost no time at all spent apart from the worship of God, the highest activity that a human could perform, executed with military order and discipline. It was this vision that inspired people all over Europe, from monasteries wishing to reform the regular observance to laity looking for pious foundations to endow and pray for them. Cluny was to become one of the main anchors for the revivification of European Christian society.

This devotion to divine observance was coupled with astonishing stability. Free to elect the best man for the position, Cluny installed a number of exceptionally fine and long-lived administrators. St. Maieul (r. 942–994), St. Odilo (r. 994–1049), and St. Hugh I (r. 1049–1109) give evidence for this. During a period of 167 years, Cluny had only *three* abbots, each one of them a brilliant ruler and saint. This astonishing holiness in stability is one of the key underlying reasons for Cluny's success. One tends to forget—in a democratic and bureaucratic age that seeks to replace leadership at regular short intervals—what kind of balance and living institutional memory could arise from such a system. Cluny was truly to be a "city set on a hill." Admirers and imitators were not long in coming, even during the time of St. Odo. By the end of his life he had already been introducing Cluniac practices into other French monasteries. Even then he would meet opposition, such as when the monks of Fleury, alerted to his arrival, met him armed with clubs and pikes. After three days he won them over with his humility, and was able to gradually reform the house. Yet in one instance he encountered a serious difficulty. While on occasion a whole community would approach him for reform, still there were hundreds of monks "stranded" in less-than-perfect houses who were prevented from tasting the benefits of the reform. Since Benedictine monks took a vow of stability to their original houses, it would have been the height of disobedience for a monk to abandon his monastery. Odo considered the problem, and knew it could not be solved by reference to the Rule only. He therefore—for the first time—took advantage of his community's dependence on Rome and went to see the pope. Premodern Catholics knew that, even though a pope might be unedifying and corrupt, yet he still possessed the keys of

St. Peter. The occupant of the Holy See at the time certainly fit that bill. John XI (r. 931–935) was a man dominated by his corrupt mother, Marozia, and his brother, Alberic II. Excluded from any share in the civil governance of Rome, John tried to involve himself in ecclesiastical affairs alone, with limited success. Odo approached him seeking to work out a way to receive monks who wanted to live the regular life of Cluny.[81] He obtained a declaration from John that the life of Cluny was a *vita perfectior* or a more perfect life than that lived by the monks in many contemporary monasteries. It had long been a principle of Church law that a person could always elect to take a harder path than the one a person was bound to by vows (this was however a one way street; one could not choose a less perfect path, but only pass to a more difficult one).[82] By declaring Odo's community to be a "more perfect" way, it allowed the monks in other monasteries to freely abandon their relaxed houses and affiliate themselves with the Cluniac movement. This had a stunning effect. Not only were the bad monasteries depopulated of good members who were inclined to follow the Rule, Cluny was energized by the arrival of hundreds of men absolutely dedicated to living the reformed Benedictine life. Odo's clever use of a papal declaration, undergirded by an ancient principle of Church law, was ingenious. One by one the bad monasteries either ceased to exist, or finally were permitted to affiliate with the reform movement. Though I cannot attribute any genuine foresight of this development to John XI, this decision presaged many future ones in which papal power was extended dramatically, by affiliating the Holy See with the powers of spiritual reform and by disintermediating corrupt or indifferent abbots and bishops.

81 Since this was considered a matter that only involved monks, and in distant France, Alberic II did not interfere.
82 See Summa Theologiae, II-II, q. 186. A. 7; Gratian, Decretum, Pars. II, c. 19, q. 2, can. 2, citing a decretal of Urban II. For the authenticity of this letter of Urban, see Kenneth Pennington, "Gratian, Causa 19, and the Birth of Canonical Jurisprudence," in *La cultura giuridico-canonica medioevale: Premesse per un dialogo ecumenico* (Rome: 2003): 215–236.

Indeed, Cluny seemed almost surprised by its own success. It had followed the path of many other reformers in trying to be a beacon to others, a sort of monastic exemplar to which people could repair when trying to reform their own houses. Still, they were afflicted by the lack of any sort of external constitutional ordering in the Rule itself. In Benedict's original conception, each house was to be sovereign and independent of all others. Benedict of Aniane had tried a more centralizing approach, but as it depended upon a tottering civil authority it was not of extended duration. Given that many monasteries were literally throwing themselves at Cluny, some sort of administrative revolution became increasingly necessary. By the death of Maieul in 994, five houses depended upon Cluny, yet by the time of Hugh at the turn of the twelfth century perhaps as many as 2,000 existed in some sort of relation to the motherhouse. The Cluniac empire happened accidentally and was certainly not foreseen from the beginning. Therefore, the mother monastery had to respond to a situation in real time and on the ground. While later religious reforms would have the leisure to work out complicated constitutional arrangements, Cluny had no such luxury. It would be St. Odilo, and especially St. Hugh I, who would essentially create what came to be known as a "religious order" in the Church, a development of astonishing significance in the history of Christianity.

Odilo was called the "archangel of Monks" by Fulbert of Chartres.[83] He spent much of his life travelling. Indeed it was an ironic reality that for most of these monastic reformers—who so treasured the life of stability and silence—that they were constantly on the move and in demand as counselors to bishops, kings, and popes. During his reign the reform spread from France into Germany and Spain. This happened both by free acceptance of the Cluniac customs by local houses, or the entrusting of monasteries by their lay and episcopal proctors in an act of donation.[84] He also

83 Lawrence, *Medieval Monasticism*, 88.
84 In fact there were an number of different ways in which a house could be affiliated with Cluny beside the two mentioned, including

continued to exert pressure on the Apostolic See, and was successful in obtaining a series of bulls that successively reduced and finally eliminated all rights of the bishops to supervise Cluny, making it absolutely subject only to Rome. He began a system that was brought to perfection by St. Hugh I. Cluny was faced with the problem of ensuring the fidelity of all these new houses to the reform. Abbots could of course occasionally visit during their itinerant journeys, but this was not enough to ensure stability of commitment.

Therefore, the principle became established that the Abbot of Cluny was to be sort of a supreme superior of all the monasteries. Every member of each monastery, including the abbots of such houses, were to exercise obedience to the motherhouse at Cluny. To those of us familiar with the hierarchical ordering of religious societies this may not seem surprising, but it was an absolutely novel and quite shocking development. Even the Rule itself foresaw the monarchical abbot, with no one above him (save the shadowy and distant presence of the local bishop). Never before had abbots been subjected to the rule of other abbots. When monks made profession in any of the houses subject to Cluny, their vows of obedience were not to their local superiors, but to the Abbot of Cluny. Whenever a superior was needed he was appointed by the motherhouse, and indeed occasionally came from Cluny itself. These sorts of houses became the first "priories," headed by an official known as the "prior." While some monasteries retained the authority to elect abbots, these in turn had to be ratified at Cluny. Order was maintained by a constant travelling network of monks and abbots, both to and from Cluny. Indeed, each monk was required at least to visit Cluny at some point.

David Knowles, among others, has pushed back on the idea of calling this a "religious order" because this suggests a constitutionally regulated group of equal houses, and established, written

those being merely influenced by Cluniac customs and ceremonial. See Knowles, *From Pachomius to Ignatius*, 13–14.

systems of governance.[85] There is certainly some truth to this. As said above, the system developed organically in response to issues as they arose. It was logical that a number of different levels of commitment to centralized governance would come about. Knowles is right in suggesting that this system emerged within a genuine context that involved the Benedictine idea of family Rule (extended over a much larger space), with current political ideas of the relation between lord and vassal. It is certain that Cluny saw the priories through the lens of vassalage, as indeed obligations like an annual subvention and personal obedience to a remote lord were part and parcel of the existing socio-economic system. This system valued the Rule of persons rather than legal abstractions. Later in the Middle Ages, with the rise of the Roman law and the increasing internationalization of the European landscape, the time would be right for the formalization of such structures of governance, but Cluny was the right answer at the right time. A monk was personally related to his spiritual father at Cluny, and subject as a vassal to the church at Cluny. It is not overreaching to suggest that some of the ecclesiology of the Gregorian reform and the medieval papacy was inspired by this Cluniac model of a "universal ordinary." All of this providence and foresight made Cluny the spiritual engine of eleventh-century Christendom, producing scores of bishops and several popes. As the eyes of the Church were upon it, Cluny benefitted immensely from the charitable largesse of the Christian people. It produced one of the most magnificent buildings in world history, the Church of Cluny III, with a 531-foot nave and a ceiling upwards of 100 feet high. (St. Peter's would be slightly redesigned in the sixteenth century, just to make sure it was longer than Cluny III.) Yet such unmitigated success led to a loss of its original stringency. Cluny remained respected and powerful, but by the 1130s it had become comfortable, though not corrupt. Almost like clockwork, new voices began to rise once again seeking the call of perfection found in the evergreen boughs of the Benedictine Rule.

85   Ibid., 12.

The Gregorian reform of the eleventh century had many of its roots in Cluny, yet also harnessed extensive new spiritual energies coursing through Christian Europe at that time. The stabilization of both Church and state had brought with it a burning desire for purification and reform at all levels, targeting especially the practices of clerical concubinage and simony. In the broader world a new predilection for poverty and austerity were beginning to make itself felt, ushering in new reforms and related movements.[86] Yet within the walls of the monastery lurked subtler temptations. The wild success of the Cluniac foundations produced pushback in several areas. They were exceptionally wealthy, particularly the motherhouse. While this did not necessarily threaten the individual poverty of the monks themselves, it did allow them to live as a community in comfort and security, amidst immense architectural and liturgical splendor. Indeed the latter reality also provoked a response from those who wanted a purified and simplified liturgy—both the Mass and the divine office—pruned of the many additions that Cluny had added to it. Both taken together had meant that Cluniac monks had essentially abandoned the life of communal labor recommended by the Rule itself in favor of nearly ceaseless liturgical supplications. Furthermore, the abbot of Cluny had become an imperial presence, subjecting hundreds of other communities to his oversight. This did not seem to comport with the original vision of the abbot as the father of one house. Hence, once again, a movement started that sought simplification according, as they saw it, *ad apicem litterae.* This meant that they would seek out the observance of the text of the Rule in as literal and absolute a manner as possible, to the last jot.[87] A key figure in this was St.

---

86   Herbert Grundmann, *Religious Movements in the Middle Ages,* trans. Steven Rowan (Notre Dame: University of Notre Dame Press, 1995; 1935).

87   Incidentally, this was increasingly a concern even outside of the monasteries—the rising scholastic movement gave exceptional importance to texts, as opposed to oral tradition or custom. The study of the text itself was key. One can see this also in focus on the Bible, "the sovereign textbook of the schools," and the intense

Robert of Molesmes who, around 1075, abandoned his position as abbot of a Cluniac monastery to join a group of hermits in the Burgundian wilds. Robert brought austerity and the Rule, and of course, endowments followed. Eventually a group of rigorists persuaded Robert to again flee from the abbey he himself had established. Robert seems to have been genuinely devoted to holiness but relatively unstable. They moved into an even more remote area, called Cîteaux. There they founded what they called the "New Monastery" with the purpose of a literal living-out of Benedictine life according to the bare text of the Rule. They were characterized by a white habit (as opposed to the black of the Cluniac monks) and by the dedication of each of their churches to the Blessed Virgin. Eventually the pope himself had to order Robert back to Molesmes (for an abbot to abandon two houses was really beyond the pale), leaving the small community to face many material and spiritual hardships. Two of Robert's followers successively became abbots of the house, the most influential being the Englishman St. Stephen Harding (r. 1109–1133).

It was, in reality, Stephen who was the administrative genius behind the Cistercians. He is obscured behind the colossal figure of St. Bernard of Clairvaux (1090–1153).[88] Indeed there is much that the massive personality of Bernard tends to conceal. It is not too much to say, however, that the arrival of Bernard and his companions in 1112 at the gates of Cîteaux really did stabilize a group that was on the razor's edge of survival. These new numbers enabled the Cistercians to spin off daughter-houses, the most famous of which was Bernard's own Clairvaux, where he reigned (mostly remotely) as abbot for nearly forty years. Yet it was Stephen who set the tone, one of those brilliant administrators whose contributions unjustly seem to pale against the original founder Robert and

attention to both canon and civil Law around the same time. For the Scholastic moment, see R.W. Southern, *Scholastic Humanism and the Unification of Europe*, vol. 1 (Oxford: Blackwell, 1997).

88   For an overview of Bernard's astonishing career, see G. R. Evans, *Bernard of Clairvaux* (New York: Oxford University Press, 2000).

the brilliant son Bernard. It seems the desire for absolute poverty and austerity was part of Stephen's special program. He ruthlessly stripped Cistercian churches of adornment in order to more fully focus on the divine office and the Mass, and adopted an extremely streamlined liturgy purified of Gallican accretions (still celebrated in places as the Cistercian rite).[89] He rigidly forbade the acceptance of any property or endowment that would involve his monks in external affairs. When a monastery was founded, the brethren explicitly specified it was to be in "wasteland." This meant unproductive territory that had little to no value. By the patient labor of years, the Cistercian order turned thousands of hectares of sterile land into vastly valuable real estate, changing the face of Europe in so doing. Stephen eschewed the acceptance of any rents, tolls, feudal obligations, parishes, or tithes. This was entirely consonant with the tenor of the 1100s, which sought conformity to Christ through the material poverty lived out by his apostles.

Nonetheless, Stephen and the brethren did make some changes not expressly foreseen by the Rule. St. Benedict had approved the ancient practice of child oblation, whereby parents offered children to the monastery as a gift. The Middle Ages were coming to see the significance of freedom in the undertaking of vows, and the Cistercians—like most groups after them—acquiesced in this social movement that tended to discourage involuntary oblation. Stephen wanted people in his monastery who had freely and fully embraced this particular way of life, not to mention his desire to relieve the community of the burden of teaching and training such youths. In so doing the Cistercians were able to underscore the development and significance of the novitiate.[90] Perhaps of even more consequence was the expansion and institutionalization of the *conversus*. Many institutions before the Cistercians had lay brothers, but it was they who created an institution that was streamlined, efficient, and popular. Peasant and largely illiterate men freely affiliated themselves to

89   Archdale A. King, *Liturgies of the Religious Orders* (London: Longmans, Green, 1955).
90   Knowles, *From Pachomius to Ignatius*, 28.

Cistercian convents, and were permitted to attend (but not sing) in choir. They participated in the spiritual life of the community, freed the monks for their primary task of praising God, and attended to the manifold material necessities of the house. The idea of monks alone supporting themselves entirely from their own labor—even given the streamlined Cistercian rite—proved almost immediately to be untenable. The Cistercians provided separate dormitories, refectories, and workhouses for the *conversi*. In this way they were able to harness the rising lay desire for lives of penance and holiness, and integrate them fruitfully within Cistercian life, not to mention providing new opportunities in a world where the population was expanding rapidly. In many houses the lay brothers outnumbered the professed monks 2–1 or even 3–1. Without the lay brothers, the "wastelands" would never have been turned into the massively productive territories they eventually became.[91]

In order to support and maintain such a novel expression of the religious life, Stephen was compelled to introduce constitutional innovations. The expression of the arrangements created to govern the Cistercian order are embedded in the *Carta Caritatis*, or the "Charter of Charity." This was first compiled before 1118 and subsequently modified significantly over the course of time, but the main inspiration certainly comes from St. Stephen.[92] Indeed in the form it comes down to us, it has been called "not a constitution given to the order by the first fathers, but a skillful summary of decisions that had been made successively."[93] One can discern several

---

91 Lawrence, *Medieval Monasticism*, 176–177.
92 This document has gone through some of the most thorough source and text criticism of any document from the Middle Ages. For an introduction to the controversy, see Constance H. Berman, *The Cistercian Evolution: The Invention of a Religious Order in Twelfth-Century Europe* (Philadelphia: University of Pennsylvania Press, 2000). While I would disagree with her position that the Cistercians are more evolutionary than revolutionary, this book is an excellent introduction to the issues. I would, however, agree that the Cistercian "order" is a product of later historical development.
93 Knowles, *From Pachomius to Ignatius*, 26.

stages in the evolution of Cistercian organization. In the first place there was a sort of (good) crisis that came out of the arrival of Bernard and his kinsmen to the monastery. Cîteaux could no longer support them, and so was in the position of needing to found daughter-houses. Yet it wanted to eschew entirely the Cluniac model of an imperial abbot. Each abbey needed to have a sovereign abbot, as the Rule maintained. In addition, Cîteaux had no interest in taxing new establishments to gild the original foundation (as Cluny did, albeit modestly). Harding forbade any such contributions, yet at the same time made himself spiritually responsible for the new foundation, stipulating that all the practices of the new house must conform exactly to those at Cîteaux. As the number of new foundations grew, Stephen knew he needed a better system, while yet preserving independence of the houses from episcopal interference. To that end he instituted one of his most original innovations—namely, the chapter general. Each year the abbots would all convene at the motherhouse for a general chapter of faults, corrected by the Abbot of Cîteaux. As time went on this became more of a meeting, rather than a general session for correction, where the abbots discussed the main challenges facing the group. Eventually the assembly became so large that its business was delegated to a smaller body of *diffinitors,* who then presented legislation for formal approval by the assembled abbots. Harding also knew that if he was to avoid the fate of the 'imperial' abbot of Cluny, he had to delegate responsibilities. By this time the order had been growing so quickly that the daughter-houses themselves were making new foundations. He made the abbots of these houses directly responsible for the oversight of any new foundations established under their auspices, thereby creating a pyramidal system of delegated authority, a corporation of compaternity and filiation, which provided oversight and independence, at the same time securing the rights of each individual community, creating numerous religious families all descended from the great motherhouse at Cîteaux. This had the effect of creating self-sustaining communities while assuring commonality of observance. It was an exceptionally foresightful system that looked forward to the establishment of administrative provinces in later reforms. Such efforts paved the way for radically new ways of reimagining the religious life far into the future.

"Ruling" in New Contexts

Some of the most successful saints have been those who have cooperated with graces in such a way that they are able to harness the needs of their times for the good of the future. Often these have to negotiate the occasionally constricting demands of their contemporary societies, and adapt in agile and flexible ways to meet the demands of the moment. St. Angela Merici was one such axial figure. Working in the context of late medieval Catholicism, she was the author of a movement that would transform the early modern world and the place of women religious in it. While the evolution of her "company" as it was called was pulled in many new directions after her death, it was her patient leadership at its beginning that enabled the group to accumulate the necessary resilience to meet new demands.[94] At once practical and yet focused on divine providence, she did not allow fixed ideas to inhibit her administrative creativity. She responded to situations on the ground and, through many vicissitudes, formulated enduring and creative solutions.

Born near Lake Garda to an agricultural family of the middle class, Angela had a pious upbringing.[95] This was interrupted,

[94] Indeed one of the barriers to studying Angela was the substantive evolution of her order *after* her death, leading many scholars, particularly the Ursulines, to "read back" later Ursuline practices into Angela's life, attempting to discover their later apostolates in her work. Another issue is that the major scholarly work on her comes from the mid-1960s and so are concerned with making sure the Ursuline charism elides with new conceptions of the religious life coming from Vatican II. Both lenses tend to distort the historical Angela.

[95] The biographical material on Angela is surprisingly sparse. See Philip Caraman, *Saint Angela: The Life of Angela Merici, Foundress of the Ursulines (1474–1540)* (New York: Kennedy, 1963); and the more recent, but also more limited, study in Querciolo Mazzonis,

however, when she lost her father at age 14, followed by her mother three years later. She was compelled to develop virtues of self-reliance and independence.[96] Her uncle and aunt took her in at this point in her life. They were of the solid stock of Italian townspeople who were at once both pious and practical. They bequeathed to Angela an appreciation for solid virtue honestly lived, along with an attitude of suspicion toward the whims of religious fashion and mystical fanaticism. She developed a studied disdain for the many self-proclaimed female visionaries so common in pre-Reformation Italy, believing their souls to be in danger because of the rigidity derived from their presumed certitude.[97] Hers was an incarnational spirituality, focused on the holy places of the life of Christ and the tombs of martyrs and saints. These were "fixed stars" that could orient her in union with the historical Church and, later, fortify her society against the new religious dissidence from the north.[98] She would carry all these attitudes with her for the rest of her life, and they would be formative for her future foundations. As an adolescent,

Spirituality, Gender, and the Self in Renaissance Italy: Angela Merici and the Company of St. Ursula (1474–1540) (Washington, DC: Catholic University of America Press, 2007). Foundational is the rigorously scientific, but somewhat dated, study: Teresa Ledochowska, O.S.U., *Angela Merici and the Company of St. Ursula*, trans. Mary Teresa Neylan, O.S.U., 2 vols. (Rome: Ancora, 1967). See also Giuditta Garioni Bertolotti, *S. Angela Merici, vergine bresciana, 1474–1540*, 3rd ed. (Brescia: Queriniana Brescia, 1950). For an older, more comprehensive bibliography, see *Beiträge zur Darstellung und zur Geschichte des Ursulinenordens*, VII (1934) and X (1937).

96 Mazzonis, 12–14, Ledochowska, 10.
97 Mazzonis, 24–25; Ledochowska, 20.
98 Angela particularly was devoted to the practice of pilgrimage. She made the extremely difficult journey to the Holy Land, where she experienced the terrible penance of a temporary privation of eyesight, a trial that taught her patience and detachment. While she recovered after the journey, she never lost a taste for travel, later going to Varallo, Rome, and visiting the tombs of other Italian saints. See Caraman, 58.

she was affiliated with the Franciscan third order, an association that certainly influenced her later vocation, without defining it. She was particularly attracted by its spirit of detachment and its commitment to apostolic works.

Given her initiative and her relative freedom, she began to undertake an organization of the pious activities in her area. She knew that in order for things to be accomplished she needed to have the help of citizens of social stature. As such she began to move among the highest echelons of the city of Brescia, making contacts, asking for alms, and creating friendships. It seems Angela moved with an easy grace among the rich and powerful, and she was never at a loss whether speaking to duke or pope. This social facility served her well. Her unfeigned holiness drew the pious aristocracy toward her. The situation of the clergy in Italy in the year 1500 was generally corrupt, and Brescia was a microcosm of the larger situation. Its bishop, Paolo Zane, reigned from 1471–1531 and was almost never in residence. The cathedral canons were wholly corrupt in the absence of episcopal supervision, and most of the priests did not perform their duties with diligence.[99] The female monasteries were ruled by "grand dames" and were often mere boarding houses for the children of the aristocracy.[100] At the same time the vast majority of society was still solidly dedicated to the Catholic faith—particularly the liturgy, social charity, and community solidarity it provided. Among the upper-class laity literacy was rapidly increasing and they eagerly consumed religious literature and provided generous subventions for Church construction and other pious endeavors. She also possessed that venerable key to the hearts of Italian city-dwellers— namely, the ability to mediate peace, a quality that made her known far and wide. Angela knew that the spiritual energy of northern Italy was in the hands of this eager laity, and as such she smartly affiliated herself with them in a symbiotic relation of benefit to both. The laity received a saintly friend whom they could trust with their secrets and treasures, and Angela obtained counselors and advocates at the

99   Ledochowska, 35.
100 Caraman, 164.

highest levels of society.[101] Angela thus entrusted nearly the whole of her work to the laity, and only later to priests who had garnered her confidence. This was merely one aspect of the reality of the situation. Angela never spoke a word against the institutional Church, and always showed herself a faithful daughter of Rome, but in her practicality she often had to keep the clergy at a prudent distance.

Her initial idea was to create a female analogue to the brothers of "Divino Amore" who were charged with running the houses of pious works. With her practical sense, Angela saw how such a foundation might solve many problems then plaguing northern Italy. In the first place there was the issue of young women who lacked the means to either enter into marriage or provide the dowry necessary to enter a late Medieval convent. Left to their own devices they had few other alternatives than a desperation that often drove them to lives of vice. At the same time there was a growing demand for education, particularly among the urban middle class. While opportunities existed for young men in the academic, clerical, and professional fields, women were left terribly underserved. Furthermore, there was a desperate need to organize labor and alms for the execution of the many works of charity necessary at the time. Many foundations of hospitals, orphanages, and leprosaria had been individually and independently established. Cooperation was limited since they had to work within their own constricting structures. What was needed was an adaptable workforce that could be deployed where needed given various times and conditions. In particular, there was much need for women to work with the female patients at the hospitals, since the brothers, in the name of modesty and religion, could not do as much for these. At the time, the need was particularly acute in the places known as *incurabili* where the sickest patients suffered at the point of death without anyone tending them (especially in light of the new plague of Syphilis that was spreading through Europe, a disease whose nature made few willing to minister).[102] In one fell

101 Ibid., 33.
102 Ledochowska, 63.

swoop, Angela's assembling of a "company" of women could solve all of these problems in a comprehensive way.

Already known for her holiness, she began to attract women who would be interested in such an active life. Her vision developed slowly, and indeed some commentators allege that she was tardy in answering the divine call. However, what really emerges from a study of her life is the careful prudence she exercised in the creation of what was a wholly new reality in the history of the Church.[103] News of Angela's good work spread quickly, and when she met Clement VII during the 1525 jubilee, he suggested that she be made superintendent of all the *luoghi pii* (charitable institutions) in the city of Rome. Angela was convinced that the time was not ripe and that her vocation was in Brescia. In an act of pious shrewdness, she left the holy city that night to return home, fearful that the dawn might carry a papal command with it.[104] She later evaded similar appeals from the city of Cremona, and remained fixed on the deliberate development of her tiny band in her home city. Patiently her little group grew—focused as they were on the active apostolate—and so did their circle of friends and supporters. In 1530 she acquired a house near the Church of St. Afra, run by the canons of John Lateran, giving her a Roman connection somewhat disassociated from the Brescian clerical establishment. There she dwelt with twelve initial followers. Within two years they had made another corporate pilgrimage to Varallo, after which they stabilized themselves under the protection of St. Ursula of Cologne.[105]

At length, in 1532, the aged Bishop Zane died, and he was replaced by the accomplished Venetian Cardinal, Andrea Corner. While he too was rarely resident due to his service for the Holy See, he nonetheless pushed for reforms. He had good vicars, yet the power of such upright men was limited given the

103 Caraman, 80.
104 Ledochowska, 73.
105 Varallo was a pilgrimage destination that sought to reproduce the sites of the Holy Land.

episcopal absence. They had little power to reform the clergy on their own. In appealing to Angela's growing society, the vicars were able to make an end run around the diocesan institutions, and effect reform-from-below. Indeed, it would be Cardinal Corner who would later canonically recognize the group on 8 August 1536.[106]

For the establishment of an order Angela needed to have clerical associates. Besides her cordial relationship with the canons of St. Afra, she had cultivated friends among the reformed elements of the Brescian clergy. Among these was Gabriele Cozzano. He was known as an exceptionally discreet priest, an efficient administrator behind the scenes, and absolutely devoted to the woman who was called "Mother." It was he who would aid Angela in reducing her vision to a formal Rule. He would remain as director of the company even after her death, and his aid to the fledgling enterprise was invaluable. His intimate knowledge of Angela's intentions enabled him to shepherd the young group through troubled waters, so that it emerged in the Baroque period as a significant force in the Church. Cozzano was always self-effacing. For people in that age who had trouble believing that such a revolutionary form of life could be the product of a Brescian woman, he was always careful to say, "There is nothing of mine in the Rule."[107] Indeed Angela may be credited with the first Rule for women by a woman in the history of Latin Christianity. It was Cozzano and Cardinal Corner who gave the advice to create a group as only a loosely bound association of female religious, leaving ample room for any possible new directions that might emerge from the looming ecumenical council. Angela acquiesced, and their wise prescription in this matter allowed her little band the space to evolve and conform to the later decrees of the Council of Trent.[108]

One of the innovations that Angela brought was that the company was to be open to all women, regardless of social class. This

106 Ibid., 109.
107 Ibid., 100.
108 Caraman, 182.

was remarkable at a time when female religious houses were dominated by the aristocracy, with women of the lower classes relegated to the position of domestics or lay sisters. No dowry was required to join her company—rather, they relied upon support from their lay friends in the secular world. Governance in the house was based solely on a spiritual meritocracy underlined by democratic elections in which all votes were equal regardless of past social class. A spiritually advanced woman from the lower classes might indeed have religious rule over someone of a higher social station than her own, a truly unique development. While in the short term this tended to depress vocations from the daughters of the noble classes, as time went on the spiritual quality of Angela's society began to draw these as well.[109] This liberated young women from the necessity of having a dowry for either marriage or an enclosed convent. In spite of this departure from traditional practice, the Mother had no desire to upset the social fabric. Indeed, in her initial plan, those young women who joined her were to continue to live in their homes under parental authority. Such an arrangement indeed increased social harmony. With the delicate question of dowry removed from the family's anxiety, the spiritual growth and deployment of the young women could continue apace, while respecting the traditional avenues of authority.

Given the novelty of this form of life, Angela was left with two problems. The first was a question of supervising and governing a company so dispersed throughout the city of Brescia. On the other hand, given this delicate beginning, to whom could she look for guidance and advocacy in temporal matters that were certain to arise? Angela brilliantly crafted a two-tiered society. On one hand, widows who desired to participate in her apostolic works affiliated themselves with the Ursulines and became part of a group called the "Matrons" (also called "Lady-Governors"). These continued

---

109 Mazzonis, 84–85. He also makes the apposite remark that the nobility likewise did not want their daughters there because the lack of claustration did not provide enough of a protection against scandal that their aristocratic sensibilities demanded.

to live in their homes and were directed to dispose of their time, wealth, and talent in support of the second group. These were the "Virgins," or the young women who joined the order at the canonical age (or even before, with parental consent). The novelty of such an arrangement was that the matron-widows were to be placed over the temporal concerns of the virgins. It was they who controlled finances and almsgiving. However, the spiritual formation of the young women was only to be done under Angela or other mature virgins. The Mother thus effected a religious division of labor, that freed the Virgins from the burdens of temporal administration, and likewise safeguarded their education and formation. In addition, Angela was practical enough to understand that, while the matrons could take care of most internal temporal affairs, given the conditions then obtaining, she also needed advocates on the outside. For this reason she selected a number of her close friends as male guardians. They would be in charge of legal advocacy and defense of the sisters' rights in the public square.[110] All of this ensured proper governance, while leaving the virgins free to pursue their apostolic and spiritual duties.[111] Finally, in order to assure proper supervision, Angela divided the city of Brescia into four districts and appointed four mature virgins as *colonelle*.[112] These officials would be in charge of supervising those virgins who still lived in their homes. They would direct the daily activities of the virgins, and make requests of a temporal nature to the matrons, should it become necessary. However, Angela instructed the *colonelle* to use their own initiative as much as possible, so as not to pester the matrons needlessly.[113] In this way the rudiments of an administration were established, all that was

---

110 It is also notable that, even given the support of Cozzano and Bishop Corner, Angela did not entrust the office of guardian to clerics. In her own quiet way, she was making a point about the current state of clerical discipline.

111 Ledochowska, 143.

112 Ibid., 116. The use of this military term likely corresponded to Angela's conception of the army of martyrs under St. Ursula.

113 Ibid., 142.

needed was the formalization of the group after the granting of episcopal approval.

In light of this, on 18 March 1537, the first chapter general of the Ursulines met and unanimously elected Angela as Mother General.[114] Angela, shrewd as always, worked to make sure this first chapter would be on as strict a legal basis as possible, including employing a notary and ensuring detailed recordkeeping. After her election she proposed the selection of a sort of executive council that could deal with quotidian matters that would not require the presence of the whole community. For this the sisters elected four virgins and five matrons who would serve as Angela's advisory committee. Anything that they enacted was to be considered as having been decided by the whole company.[115] She stipulated that whenever there was a vacancy in the position of Mother General, or the need for significant legislative activity, a chapter general would be called. All elections in the order were to be based entirely on democratic and meritocratic principles, without consideration of persons.[116] While the Mother ardently believed that the plan for the society came from God himself, she did not thereby consider herself exempt from consultation, discussion, and experiment.[117] She knew that God's plan was enacted through human intermediaries in particular contexts. For her, grace indeed built upon nature. Angela was also never imprisoned by a fixed idea. Her form of life evolved naturally from the conditions in which she and her sisters found themselves, and she could not have doubted that such changes would continue to happen even after her death. It was for this reason she left such a wide latitude in her instructions. For instance, in the Rule there is nothing about the Mother General (save some regulations for her canonical election), nor is there anything about the *colonelle*. Her Rule was written solely for the organization and direction of the

114 Ibid., x.
115 Ibid., 111.
116 Mazzonis, 30.
117 Ledochowska, 103.

Virgins. She did, however, leave a *Testament* that was directed personally to the Mother Superior, and left a series of informal counsels to the *colonelle*. These loose instructions allowed for future adaptation. It was imperative that such a novel society would have the ability to be as agile as possible to meet eventual unforeseen challenges.

In the end, Angela's Rule was one written in collaboration with her advisors, her spiritual daughters, and her lay friends.[118] It was written in response to historical realities and was adaptable given changes in such conditions. As an example of such creativity, her virgins did not undertake solemn, perpetual vows. They only made a public promise to live a stable life in the order. This set them apart significantly from the older orders, but at the same time lifted a significant burden of conscience from them. It was also the product of a society that saw the performance of good works as more valuable when undertaken freely, rather than under the aspect of a formal vow.[119] She was also insistent that merit should always be the qualification for election in the company, and that a leader should be "mature in mind rather than advanced in years." She would have no automatic promotions, for not only was social inequality prohibited, but also the tyranny of seniority. As regards property, she had no compunctions about receiving it and holding it for the good of her order and its apostolate. While she took much inspiration from the example of St. Francis of Assisi, it did not prevent her from seeing the practical utility and even necessity of property for a group of female religious.

When she was elected Mother General, she only had three years of life left to her. While initially she only wanted to serve as

---

118 At the same time Angela was very careful never directly to seek advice from anyone within the company regarding the formal Rule. She did not want anyone in the society after her death to claim to know her mind, thus prudently eliminating a significant cause of schism. Ibid., 135.

119 While this is not theologically correct (see *Summa Theologiae*, II-II, q. 88, a. 6), it accurately reflects the voluntarist tenor of the age. Caraman, 140.

counselor and treasurer, by the end of her life the position had come to resemble religious superiors in other orders. With great diplomacy she began a slow surrendering of her authority, parceling out her government so that the order would continue to function as it had before her death. As a final sign of her flexibility, she short circuited the Rule and personally appointed the next Mother General. In this she presciently foresaw short-term difficulties and worked to prevent them. Deprived of her transparent holiness and example, she recognized how a society made up mostly of lower-class women might be handicapped after her passing. Accordingly, she appointed an aristocratic countess, Lucrezia Lodrone, who had been widowed at a young age and who possessed an immense fortune and an assured social position. She was wholeheartedly committed to the company and of high spiritual quality. In appointing Lucrezia, Angela made sure that her society would have the shield of social prominence at the top of its governance, without sacrificing spiritual quality. In so doing she quieted many of the vicious tongues of Brescia, that were bridled only so long as she lived.[120]

After Angela's death the Ursulines continued their astonishing expansion all through northern Italy and beyond. Even so, they were forced to confront the realities of the post-Tridentine Church and its insistence on regularization and claustration of female religious. While there are certainly aspects of social control involved in their transition, given the context of the times, such was necessary for their survival and indeed their success. Their incorporation as a standard religious community allowed the continuance of their apostolic work from a centralized location. Their success with women of the lower social classes meant that they were quickly marshalled to further the Tridentine project of lay formation and education, and they became the female correlative to the Jesuit order in the formation of young women. Angela's group came to have a significance in the European world and beyond because of

120 See the comments in Cardinal Tisserant's introduction in Ledochowska, xi.

this pivot to an educational mission. Her native good sense and intelligence had established the possibility of an active female apostolate for the first time in history, and their insertion into the cloister ensured their reputation for orthodoxy both in the eyes of the Church and lay society at large. Even if Angela had foreseen neither the exclusive commitment to education nor the entrance of her sisters into the cloister, still her spirit of detachment and her willingness to adapt according to conditions meant that she likely would not have protested. She inserted into her leadership a spirituality born of both virginal purity and maternal tenderness, the genesis of a two-fold vocation that was to have profound implications in the religious life. It was her greatest achievement to bequeath that spirit to her daughters and to the Church-at-large. In her charge to governors in the Rule, she exhorts them to "behave with such love as they owe to the very dear spouses and beloved children of Jesus Christ, striving to enfold them in a maternal tenderness; not looking on them as mean and ordinary women, but loving and recognizing in them the God for whose love they have undertaken their charge."[121] Angela's gift to the religious life of the Catholic Church is her enduring emphasis of the maternal characteristics of leadership and administration, something that came to be realized in ways she never even conceived, but which remain rooted in her spirit.

The search for perfection takes on many interpretations and forms throughout Christian history, and the religious life took root in many different soils. It was not a linear history of unbroken success, but the hard and punctuated story of setback, reform, corruption, and rebirth. We may well ask, then, what these religious men and women were about. It is best here to quote Cardinal Newman:

> He (St. Benedict) found the world, physical and social,
> in ruins, and his mission was to restore it in the way, not
> of science, but of nature, not as if setting about to do it,
> nor professing to do it, by any set time or by any rare

121 Angela, *Rule*, cfr. Caraman, 166.

specific or by any series of strokes, but so quietly, patiently, gradually, that often, till the work was done, it was not known to be doing. It was a restoration rather than a visitation, correction, or conversion. The new world which he helped to create was a growth rather than a structure. Silent men were observed about the country, or discovered in the forest, digging, clearing, and building; and other silent men, men not seen, were sitting in the cold cloister, trying their eyes, and keeping their attention on the stretch, while they painfully deciphered and copied and re-copied the manuscripts which they had saved. There was no one that 'contended or cried out,' or drew attention to what was going on; but by degrees the woody swamp became a hermitage, a religious house, a farm, an abbey, a village, a seminary, a school of learning, and a city. Roads and bridges connected it with other abbeys and cities, which had similarly grown up; and what the haughty Alaric or fierce Attila had broken to pieces, these patient meditative men had brought together and made to live again.[122]

It is the story of people embedded and embodied in distinct contexts, taking perennial wisdom concerning grace and human nature and applying it on the ground in new circumstances. People, even those living in the "antechamber" of heaven, were beings of body and soul, marred by original sin and in the process of being repristinated through grace. They had to be governed and their lives demanded administration. They needed order so as to effectually reach their ends. In all this we can see the rules, especially that of Benedict, not as some sort of straitjacket that rendered their followers unthinking or less than human, but rather as the organ of endless creativity and challenge, a platform that was not dispensable, but rather the *sine qua non* of an intimate

122 John Henry Newman, *Historical Sketches*, 2 vols. (London: Longman, Greens, and Co., 1890), 2, 410.

following of Christ. The *Regula* established the so-called "regular life" as the pathway to a more profound evangelical realization of the possibilities of a graced humanity—an existence that is organized, perfected, and lived out by saints in every age of Christian history.

Chapter 3
Prophet, Priest, and King:
Administrative Reform from the Top

The monasteries have always proven to be spiritual powerhouses of Christian life. The desire for reform often flowed outward from them and affected the broader society.[1] While the monastic renaissance proceeded apace under Benedict of Aniane and the wise abbots of Cluny, the Christian world simultaneously found itself in dire need of reform of other types. In surveying the tenth century, corruption and lassitude can be found at every level of Church and state. The depredations of Vikings, Magyars, and Muslims still were a constant menace. Vicious internecine warfare weakened many kingdoms, especially given the utter collapse of effective imperial authority. Local lords ruled over their subjects, both lay and clerical, with fists of iron. The laity, while rich in liturgical and devotional piety, lacked any access to anything beyond the most primitive catechesis. Meanwhile, the regular life languished and clergy found themselves woefully unprepared for the coming commercial revolution and attendant urbanization. Many canons had settled into comfortable lives as noble retainers, enjoying not only steady incomes but living openly with women. Bishops were inextricably bound to local lay authorities through ties of wealth and kinship, often deferring to them even in matters of spiritual rule. Despite the energy emanating from the reorientation of religious life, unreformed monasteries still abounded.

---

1   Uta-Renate Blumethal says of the coming reform, that it "is best described as an expansion and deepening of monastic concern for religious renewal." Id., *The Investiture Controversy: Church and Monarchy from the Ninth to the Twelfth Century*, (Philadelphia: University of Pennsylvania Press, 1988), 65.

Ecclesiastics of all sorts were oppressed by an astonishing amount of lay proprietorship that made them effective tenants in their own churches, with all the spiritual and administrative confusion this entailed. Indeed, numerous churchmen coming from the post-Roman gift economy had made offerings to lords clerical and noble to secure their own ordinations and positions. These problems went all the way to the top.

From a Catholic perspective, the worst situation of all was the state of the papacy itself. Following the strong reign of Nicholas I (r. 858–867), the Holy See found itself increasingly the pawn of rival Italian families. A traditional beginning to this period of papal somnolence is marked by the terrible "Synod of the Corpse" in 897, when the body of Pope Formosus was disinterred, clothed in pontifical garments, and subjected to a "trial" for alleged canonical misdeeds.[2] The situation did not improve after that. The period from 904–968 is known as the *saeculum obscurum* or the "shadowy age." This is not only because of a paucity of documentation, but on the grounds of the general reputation for corruption that came to be attributed to the holders of the Apostolic See during that period. While it is clear that much of the lurid details of the period come from biased enemies of the Roman popes and their families, we still cannot escape the evidence of their localism, nepotism, and general lack of fitness for office.[3]

---

2   For this episode, see Michael Edward Moore, "The Destruction of Pope Formosus: Papal History in an Age of Resentment (875–897)," in *Ecclesia et Violentia: Violence against the Church and Violence within the Church in the Middle Ages*, eds. Radosław Kotecki and Jacek Maciejewski (Newcastle upon Tyne: Cambridge Scholars Publishing, 2014), 184–208.

3   Many of the events of the so-called "pornocracy" have been challenged by historians. See, Bernard Hamilton, "The Monastic Revival in Tenth Century Rome," in *Studia Monastica* 4 (1962): 35–68; and, id., "The House of Theophylact and the Promotion of the Religious Life Among Women in Tenth-Century Rome," in *Studia Monastica* 12 (1970): 195–217. Both are reprinted in id., *Monastic Reform, Catharism, and the Crusades, (900–1300)* (London: Variorum Reprints, 1979).

The religious life of the city suffered considerably. By 932 only 19 working monasteries and convents remained in Rome, fewer than half the number of a century before.[4] Any febrile attempts at a revival came largely from the Theophylact family, which dominated the papacy for its own ends. Indeed, even the few attempts of the contemporary popes to legislate for reform seem to have been inspired by the laity. The otherwise hapless John XI (r. 931–935) extended the privilege of exemption to Cluny, but this was likely only due to the personal predilection of the *de facto* ruler of the city, Prince Alberic II, towards St. Odo. John XI was himself the brother of Alberic, who appears to have governed through the inept pope in both civil and church matters. The power of appointing bishops of Rome throughout this period was entirely in the hands of the Theophylacts. In the greatest indignity of all, Alberic contrived to promote his own son as John XII (r. 955–964). This was perhaps the nadir of the two millennia history of the papacy. John was only eighteen years old. He was more interested in hunting than in ecclesial administration, and did not hesitate to lead troops and mutilate enemies. While the obscene story about his death at the hands of an outraged husband is of suspect provenance, we do know that he died of stroke or apoplexy in his mid-twenties. Yet even then the story of the Church moves in strange ways, as we will see. Seeds were germinating in the ever-fertile soil of Christianity that would lead to bountiful harvests.

While the See of Rome was in such dire straits, the rest of Europe was slowly coming to its senses. In addition to the gathering force of Cluniac reform, the global situation also began to steady itself. The medieval warm period—in addition to advances made in farming—led to a virtuous cycle of economic production and population growth that would last for hundreds of years. This would lead to increased urbanization and the commercial revolution that would propel European power and wealth. External borders too were stabilizing. The Muslims had been checked in both the Iberian peninsula and in Italy (in the latter case by an army led

4   Hamilton, "Monastic Revival," 45.

personally by Pope John X himself). The pestilential raids of both Vikings and Magyars were ended by their conversions to the faith and their integration into the cultural unity of Christendom. They became forces for Christianity instead of against her mission.[5] All of this gave Europe breathing room. Alfred the Great of Wessex and Alfonso III of Castile had pushed back the tides in their countries and had established security in their realms.

Perhaps the most significant political achievement was the rise of the Ottonian dynasty in Germany, the first effective imperial presence in a century. In 962—as a testament to the enduring appeal of Rome even during such dire times—Emperor Otto I arrived to be given the imperial crown by the dissolute John XII. This new German emperor and his successors would reform both Church and state within their territories, providing a basis for fundamental progress in the future. In the Île-de-France, Hugh Capet became king in 987, founding one of the longest dynasties in world history, one that lasted until 1830. These developments provided significant stability in the heart of Europe. The lay world was in the process of significant and positive transformation, whereas the papacy remained mired in local politics and occasional depravity. Yet this was still a profoundly Catholic age. The laity, as happens from time to time, took matters into their own hands to promote a thorough-going reform. United with the energies flowing from the Cluniac foundations, it was the lay nobility who began to promote a religious purification.[6] Their piety and deep Christian principles convinced them of the necessity for reform, yet the manner in which they undertook it led to serious questions and generated deep divisions. This is true of any movement in the Church that does not involve the clergy, for such efforts often attempt to subordinate their rightful sphere of independence to the laity. The aristocratic

5   Indeed the Normans (the converted Vikings of northern France) restored or founded nearly as many monasteries as their pagan forefathers had destroyed.

6   For a brief introduction, see John Howe, "The Nobility's Reform of the Medieval Church," in *American Historical Review* 93 (April 1988): 317–339.

vision of reform often lacked order and prudence and—while certainly moved by genuinely spiritual motives—it was inevitably tied up with the nobles' desire to increase wealth and stability, while also projecting their respective power.

Eventually the sorry situation of the papacy attracted the attention of the resurgent Ottonians. When in 996 Otto III travelled to Rome to seek coronation, he took advantage of the death of John XV to appoint his own cousin as Pope Gregory V (r. 996–999). Otto continued this pattern with his installation of the scholarly Sylvester II (r. 999–1003). Otto minced no words about this appointment. He declared that "we have elected, ordained, and created" Sylvester as pope.[7] The Ottonians had aggressively embraced a hierocratic vision of Christendom that placed the emperor at the top. He was to be both *Rex et Sacerdos* (King and Priest). This was a concept that had menaced the Church ever since legalization 700 years prior, and which was most perfectly manifested in the caesaropapism of Byzantium. In the name of reform, the emperors had introduced unwarranted and—in Western terms—unprecedented interference in the internal government of the spiritual authority. This period has rightly been called "the Church in the power of the laity."[8] In a certain sense their assertion of power over the papacy was merely a logical extension of the way the Ottonians and their retainers treated other church offices. Since bishops were significant civil figures as well, the state considered it had a vested interest in their appointments. During the tenth century, most episcopal designations passed through the hands of kings. When such rulers were interested in Church reform, this was occasionally beneficial. Even in these cases, though, the new incumbent had divided loyalties at the very least and tended to favor the civil power to whom they owed their careers.

7   Walter Ullmann, *The Growth of Papal Government in the Middle Ages; A Study in the Ideological Relation of Clerical to Lay Power* (London: Methuen, 1962), 244.

8   As in the volume of the Fliche-Martin series: Emile Amann and Auguste Dumas, *L'Église au pouvoir des laïques: (888–1057)* (Paris: Bloud & Gay, 1948).

This attitude trickled down to lower levels of nobility and clergy as well. The Seigneurial Revolution had led to a large-scale privatization of churches and clerical offices. This created a massive lay intrusion into ecclesiastical revenues, much of which was then redirected away from the support of the Church and of charitable enterprises into the hands of private owners. This system was called "lay proprietorship," whereby the local lord owned the church with its attached benefice and income. He had nearly complete rights to dispose of it as he saw fit: exchanging it, selling it, mortgaging it, or donating it, with the single stipulation that it would only ever be used as a church.[9] He would then effectively hire an officeholder to fulfill the clerical duties and pay him a stipend out of the income, while retaining the rest for himself. In the early medieval ceremony for accepting any office there was always an exchange. The one who received the office was expected—in terms of a gift economy—to make an offering for the benefits conferred upon him.[10] As the monetary economy grew it became more and more apparent that this was a "transaction" that appeared to involve paying for spiritual gifts.[11] This privatization and apparent "lay investiture" of spiritual power set the stage for a correspondingly grave reaction.

Otto III died in 1002, leaving behind a succession crisis in Germany. Control of the papacy lapsed back into the hands of the clans of Rome, with the Crescenzi and Theophylacts punting the papacy back and forth, all the while keeping the Holy City in their iron grip. Still, the lure of Rome and reform came increasingly to occupy men's minds. It was even possible, on occasion, to see sainthood in this "reign of the laymen." Emperor Henry II (r. 1014–1024) cooperated

9   Blumenthal, *The Investiture Controversy*, 5. See Hans Erich Feine, *Kirchliche Rechtsgeschichte: Die katholische Kirche*, 5th ed. (Cologne: Böhlau, 1972), 160–182.

10   For this concept, see Lester Little, "From Gift Economy to Profit Economy," in *Religious Poverty and the Profit Economy in Medieval Europe* (Ithaca, NY: Cornell University Press, 1978).

11   Colin Morris, *The Papal Monarchy: The Western Church from 1050 to 1250* (Oxford: Clarendon Press, 1991), 28.

with the otherwise impotent Pope Benedict VIII (r. 1012–1024) to hold a reforming synod at Pavia in 1022 that condemned selling spiritual goods and forbidding clerical concubinage. In the absence of solid ecclesial leadership, and in light of St. Henry's premature death, the council remained a dead letter.[12] Yet St. Henry also appointed many reform-minded bishops and encouraged a top-down reorientation of the imperial monasteries in Germany.[13] The Ottonians preferred employing clerics in administrative capacities, not only because they were better educated but because such expertise leveraged their own imperial power against that of the nobility. Clerics too enjoyed this royal protection since it saved them from the predations of the aristocrats and the danger of the alienation of Church property. Indeed, these privileges came to be seen as liberty of a sort.[14] Yet this was still Church government by lay fiat. The quality of the reform depended solely on the piety of the royal officeholder.

12   Ibid., 375. For a revisionist assessment of the reigns of the "second Tusculan period," see Klaus J. Herrmann, *Das Tuskulanerpapsttum (1012–1046): Benedikt VIII., Johannes XIX., Benedikt IX* (Stuttgart: A. Hiersemann, 1973). He is perhaps too revisionist, however, as Benedict IX was a truly bad pope. Sometimes ignoring negative assessments—even trustworthy ones—Herrmann gives excessive emphasis to minor evidence of administrative ability, such as the decision to switch from outdated papyrus to more contemporary parchment. He also praises the Tusculan chancery for dropping the old Roman curial hand in favor of a minuscule that everyone (even north of the Alps) *could read*. This is like praising someone for not using a fax machine today. Indeed, this is paralleled in the current papal practice of sending *telegrams* to heads of nations over which the pope's plane flies. As Blumenthal presciently says, "despite some recent revisions, the consensus is still that the last Tusculan popes were hardly zealous reformers." Id., *The Investiture Controversy*, 71.

13   "He (Henry II) was the personification of a monarch who, appointed by God to rule His people, had, in his function as supreme protector to take care of all their interests. And since his empire was Christian, Christian interests came before every other consideration." Ullmann, *Papal Government*, 250.

14   Blumenthal, *The Investiture Controversy*, 35.

The next emperor, the Salian Conrad II (r. 1027–1039), treated the church as a subsidiary corporation from whence he drew literate bureaucrats. He had little interest in reform other than the administrative efficiencies this might bring, and gave little care to founding or improving imperial monasteries. Conrad lacked the religious sense of St. Henry, and so between the two of them they demonstrated the possible strength and essential weakness of the *rex-sacerdos* system.[15] It was not a situation that could endure given the underlying principles of the papacy and of the tradition of Western Christendom. In the vacuum of imperial power in central Italy, the Theophylacts regained control and continued to treat Rome as their own private domain. Their followers would occupy the papacy until 1045.

The next emperor, Henry III (r. 1046–1056), was a mean between Conrad and his namesake. While he truly desired reform in the Church, he still also acted for the sake of peace and the preservation of his own power. For him, royal authority and Church renewal went hand in hand.[16] This renewal still required some intervention by the Holy See. Even in the midst of turbulent papacies, the emperors still required a Roman coronation for their own legitimacy. At the start of his reign Henry was confronted by a bitter schism in which three men contended for the papal title. The old pope, Benedict IX (r. 1032–1045), was the last of the Theophylact family to hold papal office.[17] In 1045, alleging his widespread immorality, he was driven out and

15 Blumenthal is inclined to mildly excuse Conrad, since he was measured against the increasingly strict reforming movement of his time, a standard to which Henry II was not held. Ibid., 49.

16 Ibid., 50–52.

17 This period(s) of Benedict's reign(s) still poses matters of debate. In some papal lists he appears as pope on no fewer than *three* separate occasions. It is clear he was legitimate pope from 1032–1044, when he was forced out of the city. He returned in 1045, then tried to resign to get married. He then rescinded his resignation in 1047 and tried to rule until 1048, when he definitively resigned and later died, apparently repentant, at the Greek abbey of Grottaferrata. This career alone would demonstrate the need for serious reform, even if the most lurid accusations against him were set aside.

replaced by a member of the rival Crescenzi clan. He was able forcibly to regain Rome, but then decided that he would much rather marry than trouble himself to remain pope. The few Romans who desperately sought a reform saw an opportunity to get rid of both the rival candidates. Benedict used his resignation as leverage to get the nascent reform party to pay off the money he had spent in being elected pope and in maintaining his position. The man who spearheaded the raising of the money was a young monk named Hildebrand, who was in the household of the reform-minded John Gratian, Archpriest of the Lateran basilica. They gathered the money and paid Benedict off. He promptly resigned and was replaced by John Gratian as Pope Gregory VI (r. 1045–1046). The reform of the Church, which had been speeding along among the monasteries and bishoprics of the north, had finally it seemed reached the Holy See. Yet all was not well. Henry III was present in Italy for most of these antics, viewing it all with a very jaundiced eye. Henry wanted to be certain that his coronation was by the real Bishop of Rome, and the reform party, in their zeal, had made a miscalculation.

In an atmosphere where "simony" was becoming one of the dirtiest of social words, many looked suspiciously at the 'transaction' between John Gratian, Hildebrand, and Benedict IX. It appeared to be money in exchange for a papal resignation (in order to get married no less!). Was this not a financial agreement that trafficked in the most sublime gifts of the Holy Spirit? It was in the eyes of many people an attempt of John Gratian to buy the papacy itself. Despite Hildebrand's and Gregory VI's obviously good intentions, public opinion sensed hypocrisy. After 100 years of "imperial priesthood," Henry would not tolerate it. He travelled to Rome and called the Synod of Sutri in 1046 to decide the claims of the three rival popes (for by this time Benedict had repented of his 'simoniacal' resignation and wanted to return to power).[18] This council was

---

18   For this episode, see Morris, *The Papal Monarchy*, 83–85; and, Pius Engelbert, "Heinrich III und die Synoden von Sutri und Rom im Dezember 1046," in *Römische Quartalschrift für christliche Altertumskunde und Kirchengeschichte* 94 (1999): 228–266.

fraught with implications. It had the appearance of a lay emperor sitting in judgment over the papacy itself. Handled indelicately, it might have proven the final nail in the coffin of the liberty of the Church in the West. Had the emperor been an Otto III or Conrad II, the issue could have unfolded quite differently. Yet Henry was truly dedicated to reform and—along with all good Christians—sincerely desired to obtain a purification of the Petrine See.

The delicacy surrounded Gregory VI in particular. He was a good man and was seen (then and since) as the legitimate pope. The claims of Benedict IX and the Crescenzi pope (Sylvester III) were dismissed out of hand, and they were declared deposed.[19] It appears that the synod also convinced Gregory VI that his own election had been due to simony.[20] He was not deposed by the synod, but voluntarily and freely resigned, having admitted the simoniacal nature of his elevation.[21] This left the Roman See vacant. Henry III sought hence to remove the papacy from the incompetent hands of the Roman clans permanently. To that end he appointed Suidger of Bamberg as Pope Clement II by imperial fiat (though he did in fact observe the forms of election by the Roman clergy and acclamation by the people). Clement in turn crowned him as Holy Roman emperor. In order to perpetuate the settlement, Henry obtained from the new pope the right to nominate Bishops of Rome in the future. As high-handed as this procedure was, it ensured stability and

19 This is a bit problematic since Benedict IX *had* been a legitimate pope. This deposition was clearly based on 1) his simoniacal election, 2) his dissolute life, and 3) his resignation in 1045.
20 Almost all subsequent legislation up to the present day has invalidated appointments or elections that occur due to simony. Julius II (ironically) even made simoniacal papal elections invalid. Pius X overturned this, confirming a simoniacal papal election. Even as recently as *Universi Dominici gregis* (1996), simony resulted in *latae sententiae* excommunications for involved participants in conclaves, but at the same time confirmed a simoniacal papal election. It is a serious canonical problem.
21 While pressure was clearly applied to Gregory, he never rescinded his resignation. It was made without any conditions.

provided a platform for future reform. It disintermediated the troublesome Theophylact and Crescenzi clans. It ensured a string of several transalpine popes who were not beholden to local politics, who had a commitment to reform, and who possessed intellectual vision that extended beyond the horizon of the Alban hills. While later generations would be uncomfortable with such direct imperial involvement, it appeared providential at the time. At last, the Roman papacy had the breathing room it needed to undertake housecleaning that would propel it back to its position of leadership in Christendom.[22] Because of this, historians have had the opportunity to view a thorough reform of the Roman See, effected in three very different yet complementary ways. By looking at how three occupants pushed forward a unified vision of the common good in a variety of ways, one begins to appreciate the complexities and possibilities involved in administrative reform in the Holy See.

The Prophet

Clement II and his successor Damasus II were both very short-lived. Each was German and—though the Roman families

---

22   This period of Reform is sometimes termed "Gregorian" after Pope St. Gregory VII. While indeed he was a leading mind, his were not the only ideas, nor the only approach, to these complex issues. Therefore, following Colin Morris, I will restrict "Gregorian" to the actual period of his papacy. Morris, *The Papal Monarchy*, 82. The bibliography of this period is immense. Besides the studies of Morris, Ullmann, and Blumenthal referenced above, see also Mary Stroll, *Popes and Antipopes: The Politics of Eleventh Century Church Reform* (Leiden: Brill, 2012); I. S. Robinson, *The Papal Reform of the Eleventh Century: The Lives of Pope Leo IX and Pope Gregory VII* (Manchester: Manchester University Press, 2004); Werner Goez, *Kirchenreform und Investiturstreit: 910–1122* (Stuttgart: Kohlhammer, 2000); Giovanni Miccoli and Andrea Tilatti, *Chiesa Gregoriana: ricerche sulla riforma del secolo XI* (Rome: Herder, 1999); and Johannes Laudage, *Gregorianische Reform und Investiturstreit* (Darmstadt: Wissenschaftliche Buchgesellschaft, 1993).

impotently stewed about it—imperial control ensured that the Holy See would be stable and committed to the vision of the papacy as a reforming and far-reaching institution. The real spark for renewal came when Henry nominated the Alsatian Bishop Bruno. Bruno was a cousin of the imperial family and hailed from a long line of courtly churchmen, with long experience in the realities of politics. He had led troops when he was young and was well versed in traditions of strong leadership. He became associated with spreading the reform of Cluny, and was gradually numbered among the partisans of the reform movement.[23] Henry did not even bother to come to Rome this time, but merely nominated Bruno from a council at the imperial city of Worms. To his credit, the nominee withheld consent unless the forms of election were observed in Rome itself. To that end he travelled to Rome as an unshod pilgrim, where he was rapturously received by the Roman people who both appreciated such dramatic gestures and were relieved that the endless internecine warfare between Roman families was coming to an end. Bruno was canonically elected as Pope Leo IX (r. 1049–1053), with the enthusiastic support of Hildebrand who joined his party after having followed the ex-pope, Gregory VI, into retirement. This Leo, later canonized, would prove the hinge upon which the reformation of the papacy turned. He would dedicate the whole of his short career to the purification of the papacy and its court, restoring it to a leadership position in Christendom that had been largely vacated for nearly 200 years.

Leo turned the full force of his charismatic personality into re-vivifying the papal office. He did this by channeling the deep-seated desire for reform that was coursing throughout Europe, gaining strength and steam for the previous fifty years. Rome had been laggard in responding to this desire, but it was realistically the only fount from which a thoroughgoing reform could be sustained in

23 For the Cluniac influences on reform, see H. E. J. Cowdrey, *The Cluniacs and the Gregorian Reform* (Oxford: Clarendon Press, 1970).

the whole of the Christian world. To that end Leo focused on the two main problems facing the Church in the minds of the reformers. In the first place was the ever-present danger of simony. The rise of the monetary economy had transformed the old exchange of offerings into financial transaction, underlining the appearance that an office-seeker was literally paying for the spiritual gifts of the Holy Spirit. This new transparency alerted people to the dangers inherent in the system and led to a serious reaction. Simony came to be seen as the most ancient of errors, condemned by the Apostles themselves in the Book of Acts and named after Simon the Magician who sought so purchase the healing gifts of Christ's followers:

> Now when Simon saw that the Spirit was given through the laying on of the apostles' hands, he offered them money, saying, "Give me also this power, that any one on whom I lay my hands may receive the Holy Spirit." But Peter said to him, "Your silver perish with you, because you thought you could obtain the gift of God with money!" (Acts 8:18–20)

The sense of urgency was underlined because of later confrontations that were reported between Peter and Simon in Rome, which is found in well-known apocryphal literature and corroborated by the Church Fathers. Armed with such authorities the battle shifted one thousand years into the future. Leo was now Peter, and he confronted not one but many Simons who sought to bribe and bridle the Holy Spirit. The new pope was exceptionally fitted for such a task, being a mesmerizing preacher and backed by conviction and deep theological learning.

The second serious threat to the purity of Christianity was the issue of clerical unchastity, something the reformers also traced to the New Testament. This they understood under the malleable term of "Nicolaism," a heresy condemned in the Book of Revelation; "Yet this you have [to your credit], you hate the works of the Nicolaitans, which I also hate" (Rev 2:6). In the Middle Ages, the common interpretation of the sect was that they were partisans of sexual immorality.[24] Given the issue of clerical celibacy and the widespread practice of concubinage and other forms of unchastity, this issue took on deeper significance in the eleventh century. The practice of celibacy had arisen among the early monks, who traced the practice to Christ and then Paul.[25] Since monasticism provided the spiritual energy for the clergy, it was natural that monastic practices came to be seen as prototypes for virtuous Christians. By the fourth century, the Western Church had been requiring vows of celibacy for the grade of deacon and higher, and this meant at times the separation from existing wives. While the Eastern Church continued to permit marriage before ordination, the law of the Westerners came to prioritize celibacy.[26] Over the course of centuries stricter laws came into force, such as lowering the requirement for celibacy to the subdiaconate and enforcing separation as a condition of ordination for previously married men. A serious setback occurred in the chaotic 800s and 900s. While Church law still strictly required celibacy, it was honored more in the breach. Bishops and priests fathered sons and sought to pass on their benefices. Such nepotism was even seen in the Roman *saeculum obscurum*. When the reformers arrived, observance of the vow of chastity came to be no less than a battle

24   Humbert of Silva-Candida (of whom more hereafter) was Leo's one advisor who knew Greek and who coined the contemporary usage of "Nicolaism." While he attributes it to an early deacon named "Nicholas," one cannot avoid the etymology of the word in Greek: "Victory of the Laity."

25   For a contextual analysis, see Peter Brown, *The Body and Society: Men, Women, and Sexual Renunciation in Early Christianity* (New York: Columbia University Press, 1988); and Helen L. Parish, *Clerical Celibacy in the West, c.1100–1700* (Farnham: Ashgate, 2010).

26   Even so, in the Eastern Church only a celibate was permitted to be ordained bishop, leading to an extensive "monasticization" of the whole Eastern episcopacy. In neither church was marriage *after* ordination ever permitted.

cry.[27] Since most of the reforming clerics were formed in the monastic tradition, their observance of celibacy was a prime way to differentiate themselves from other clerics, whose betrayal of their vows came to be portrayed an open indicator of their contempt for reform and for Christ. Given the general overlap between those who obtained office through simony and those who kept wives or mistresses, it became easy to lump the two problems together and to make them the focal points for all efforts of reform.

Leo's particular administrative approach to the problem was two-fold. In the first place he combined personal presence with the calling of synods.[28] Synodality had been an intrinsic part of Church governance ever since the earliest days of Christianity. It was the normal way of creating law, exercising oversight, and making difficult decisions. It was participative, deliberative, and authoritative. Leo's innovation was to make the papacy the centerpiece of such synods. This in itself was unusual. Outside of Church councils held in or near Rome, the pope had rarely made himself a personal presence. Indeed, the Ecumenical Councils of the first millennium were conducted almost entirely by papal legates.[29] Leo centered his

27   Critical for this period are the essays in Michael Frassetto, *Medieval Purity and Piety: Essays on Medieval Clerical Celibacy and Religious Reform* (New York: Garland Publishing, 1998).

28   For the texts of these reforming synods, see Karl Joseph von Hefele, *Histoire des Conciles, d'après les documents originaux (nouvelle traduction française faite sur la deuxième édition allemande corrigée et augmentée de notes critiques et bibliographique)*, trans. and edited by Dom H. Leclercq (Paris, Librairie Letouzey et Ané, 1907), volumes 8 and 9. See also, Georg Gresser, *Die Synoden und Konzilien in der Zeit des Reformpapsttums in Deutschland und Italien von Leo IX. bis Calixt II. 1049–1123,* (Paderborn : Ferdinand Schöningh, 2006).

29   The lack of papal presence at these Councils might be seen as a support to Eastern Orthodox ecclesiology, however the delegation of papal ambassadors to preside at councils indicated that the pope was apart from, and superior to, any Council. Indeed, many times the Roman legates were priests or deacons who nonetheless held the

synods on the person of the pope, reinforcing not only his authority in the minds of the participants, but providing a platform whereby he could extend his ideas for the reform. Here again, the vision was animated by an appeal to the New Testament. Peter would again appear in the midst of the Apostles, leading, counseling, and some-times reproving them. At his first Synod, held in Rome just after his election, he denounced simony like a prophet of old. He struck such terror into the hearts of his guilty listeners that the Bishop of Sutri died on the spot, vainly attempting to clear his own name. Like Peter's confrontation with Ananias and Sapphira, the Book of Acts seemed to be coming alive in the person of Leo. He measured the temperature of the Church and found that shock therapy was necessary in order to shake people out of their torpor. Leo inherited a garden that was run riot with weeds and wild overgrowth. A wise gardener knew that radical (with the sense of "to the root") tending was needed before fresh growth was possible. He did not flag in his duties.

Leo's style was governance by personal presence, not merely decree. Following the successful launch of his program in his own diocese, he turned north. After holding a synod in Lombardy, he traveled back to Germany and the Emperor. While there he healed a nascent civil war and continued his campaign against abuses.[30] In October 1049 Leo held a massive council in Reims,

---

presidency of the Councils over bishops. Even at Vatican II the pope was not present except ceremonially. John XXIII watched the proceedings on closed-circuit TV.

30   Reform and mediation were always found together in this period. Blumenthal, *The Investiture Controversy*, 13. Peacemaking was considered essential to any true healing of Christian society. Indeed, some of the very roots of the reform were to be found in the "Peace of God" and the "Truce of God" movements to end feuds and strife. See the essays in Thomas Head and Richard Landes, *The Peace of God: Social Violence and Religious Response in France Around the Year 1000* (Ithaca, NY: Cornell University Press, 1992). See also, Hartmut Hoffmann, *Gottesfriede und Treuga Dei* (Stuttgart: A. Hiersemann, 1964).

with members coming from all over Western Europe. There, like a hub radiating to the spokes, he denounced simony and unchastity, causing some bishops to flee. Within weeks he was through Alsace and Bavaria. In his wake bishop upon bishop, emboldened by Leo's charisma, banished the clerical concubines and began processes that would lead to the extinction of simony in their territories. He continued in this way for the next two years. He was a force of nature. He understood, as perhaps no pope has until John Paul II, the necessity and utility of personal papal presence. A physically present leader prevents equivocation, draws out the truth, and is able to activate reforms in an embodied manner. The papacy had not been a living presence in Europe, particularly north of the Alps, since the time of the early Carolingians. Leo bridged the space between Rome and the rest of Europe personally. Yet when he came north after his election, he had a secondary purpose: to bring the leading figures of the reform back with him to Rome.

Leo's time in the holy city had taught him that reliance upon the local Roman church was impossible at that moment. While the common people supported him, the Roman clans lurked in the background, menacing not only his reform but his very rule. They were the ones who occupied the main offices of the Roman Church, the pastors and deacons who held the city's parishes and deaneries. Even the small native Roman reform movement had been quashed by Gregory VI's resignation after his simoniacal elevation. There simply was no reform party left in Rome. If he wanted to have solid advising, he needed to look elsewhere in the universal Church. In the north Leo cemented alliances with local bishops who were committed to the reform. They would serve as his eyes and ears on the spot in their local churches.

Yet he also gathered a group of disciples and brought them to Rome. The radical reformer-monk Humbert of Moyenmoutier was made the Cardinal-Bishop of Silva Candida. Hugh the White, a monk from Lorraine, became Cardinal-Priest of San Clemente, while the Cluniac Stephen would become a trusted papal associate and ambassador. He appointed a canon, Udo (Odo) of Toul, as

Papal Chancellor and Librarian of the Holy Roman Church. From Flanders, Leo called Frederick, a man who would become his closest advisor and follow Udo as chancellor. He also brought Hildebrand, then a subdeacon, to manage the Lateran Palace. As a native Italian, Hildebrand could interface with the city and local power structures. Even though he was associated with the disgraced Gregory VI, Leo sensed great things in him. Hildebrand would later become pope himself, giving his name (Gregory VII) to the whole of the reform.

Leo also maintained close contact with another Italian light, St. Peter Damian. Though Peter held out against being appointed a cardinal until 1058, he nonetheless was one of the guiding stars of Leo's reform. The talent gathered by Leo was extraordinary. He assembled a team of administrators that would be the envy of any pope. "Leo flooded Rome with a coterie of reformers from across the rest of Western Christendom, some from inside the empire's borders, others from outside, representing all the main strands of contemporary Christianity: the cathedrals, the monasteries, and even the more radical wing."[31] At the same time, Leo acted prudentially. He continued to appoint cardinals from the Diocese of Rome as often as he promoted a foreigner. This meant that the clans continued to receive official recognition. Yet this came with one key difference: Leo did not entrust them with any responsibilities. They were mere placeholders meant to mollify the Roman families, while Leo's men got the real work done. One of the most brilliant features of St. Leo's leadership was this ability to recognize and attract supremely talented men, and to delegate to them the responsibility for different areas of the reform.

What made all of this possible was the office of cardinal. Behind this ecclesiastical title lies one of the most innovative administrative reforms in the history of Christianity.[32] In the first place, "Cardinal"

---

31   Peter Heather, *The Restoration of Rome: Barbarian Popes and Imperial Pretenders* (Oxford: Oxford University Press, 2014), 382.

32   A good starting point is Stephan Kuttner, "*Cardinalis*: The History of a Canonical Concept," in *Traditio* 3 (1945): 129–214; See also,

is merely an ecclesiastical title. It is not of divine institution, and functions only as an appellation for a close papal collaborator. As such it is malleable and can and has been used in a number of different contexts. In the early Christian centuries, the term "cardinal" was very loosely applied to various clerics of the Western Church.[33] As time went on it came to be more closely associated with the clergy of Rome alone. From the earliest days, Rome was distinguished from every other see in the world because its liturgical life did not spring from a single cathedral, but could be found dispersed around the city in a number of churches.[34] These churches were called *tituli* and—given the absence of a cathedral until the donation of the Lateran palace in the fourth century—the pope rotated his liturgies around such "stational" churches (titles still to be found in contemporary liturgical books today). By the fifth

Rudolf Hüls, *Kardinäle, Klerus und Kirchen Roms 1049–1130* (Tübingen: 1977); Charles Lefebvre, "Les origines et le rôle du cardinalat au moyen age," in *Apollinaris; commentarius iuridico-canonicus* 41 (1968): 59–70; Peter A. B. Llewellyn, "Le premier développement du collège des cardinaux," in *Recherches de science religieuse* 67 (1979): 31–44; and Helene Tillmann, "Ricerche sull'origine dei membri del collegio cardenalizio nel XII secolo. I. La questione dell'accertamento delle origine dei cardinali," in *Rivista di Storia della Chiesa in Italia* 24 (July-December, 1970): 441–464. In this section I am telescoping somewhat the evolution of the Cardinalate from 1050–1120 for the sake of explanation and clarification. For an older account, see Francesco Cristofori, *Storia dei cardinali di Santa Romana Chiesa, dal secolo V all'anno del signore MDCCCLXXXVIII* (Rome: Tipografia de Propaganda Fide, 1888).

33 There is an etymological and ecclesiological debate on the purchase of such a term at the time, whether the person was a "hinge" attached to a particular church, or had been transferred to a church ("incardinated"), or was simply the rightful possessor of a church. See the discussion in Kuttner, "*Cardinalis*," 129–133. Kuttner inclines to the interpretation that a "cardinal" bishop or priest was one transferred to a new place. Such a reading makes what happens in the 11th century an even more traditional development.

34 Ibid., 146. Morris, *Papal Monarchy*, 165.

century 25 traditional *tituli* had become fixed as the parishes of the Church of Rome.[35] In the 700s the weekly liturgy of the Cathedral of St. John Lateran came to be governed by the bishops of the seven "suburbicarian" sees.[36] During that time the names "Cardinal-Bishop" and "Cardinal-Priest" came into common usage. To these were added the seven deacons who served in the early papal household and the seven archdeacons in charge of the charitable divisions of Rome for fourteen total "Cardinal-Deacons."[37] By the 800s the title of cardinal had transformed from a description into a dignity. For years these titles had been in the hands of locals, promoted from within Roman families for their own ends and purposes. It was Leo's genius to repurpose these appointments so as to provide provision for foreign advisors to offset the power of the Latin families. In this way the pope circumvented the idea that such foreigners were not from the Roman clergy by literally *making them* members of that same clergy (or "incardinating" them).

Yet there was an even broader vision behind this. The whole of the reform movement sought the "liberty of the Church." What they meant by this was essentially the liberation of the priesthood from lay control, either from the corruption of concubinage or the enervating system of lay proprietorship.[38] In order to do this what they needed was the freedom to select their own men, in their own ways, totally independent from outside interference. The principle for this had already been laid down by the independent election of Cluniac abbots. Local and closed elections allowed a community to choose the best man for the job, for only such a group was in the position to make judgements regarding its own internal common good. If the papacy was ever to be free it needed liberation from the corrupt and self-serving Roman clans, while also carefully weaning itself off imperial dependence. There had been

35 This was later increased to 28 to accommodate the later major Basilicas.
36 Ostia, Albano, Palestrina, Porto, Silva Candida, Gabii, and Velletri.
37 The title "cardinal-deacon" was not in use until much later, dating to around 1100.
38 Ullmann, *Papal Government*, 296.

essentially no free papal elections for 200 years, and even before that there had been interference from imperial governments, both Carolingian and Byzantine. The liberty of the Church would never be fully realized given such a state. For this reason the reform party began to design a new system to ensure the integrity of papal selection, not to mention keeping the office in the hands of the reformers.

Yet there was a problem prescinding from this. Since the dawn of the Church, the right to elect the pope had been in the hands of the Roman clergy. The pope, after all, was their bishop, and therefore they were the ones who were most interested and informed about the possible successors. Yet as the papacy developed into a more worldwide institution, and as the traditional Roman clergy fell into the hands of the venal clans, the situation became increasingly intractable. Therefore, the reformers created one of the most brilliant "legal fictions" in history. Since the members of the Roman clergy had appropriated the title cardinal as a dignity, and since the cardinals were the clergy of the pope, then he could distribute such titles freely within his own city. Instead of assigning a Roman priest to a titular church, Leo and his successors began to install prominent foreigners. These technically became pastors of the traditional suburbicarian sees and of the Roman parishes. As such, they became "incardinated" into the Roman clergy and, given their cardinalitial titles, were thereby empowered with the traditional right of casting a vote for the new pope.[39]

Providentially, the reformers were given an opportunity with the death of Henry III in 1056. His successor was only six-years old and therefore set for a long period of regency. They had to act quickly because the Roman clans also sensed the opportunity and

---

39   This "legal fiction" continues to the present day. Each cardinal is still installed as the titular pastor of a Roman Church. One can see their coats of arms on ecclesial facades all over the city. While they do not have any pastoral responsibility, they are still expected to say Mass there when in Rome, and to offer some subvention, particularly for maintenance and restoration.

attempted to reacquire the papacy at the same time, creating a short-lived schism. In 1059, given the imperial situation, Hildebrand came up with a system whereby the Cardinal-Bishops (by that time nearly all "reform" men) selected the new pope, who was then confirmed by the other cardinals and the people of Rome.[40] The man they elected was Nicholas II (r. 1059–1061). Given the incipient schism of the Roman families, Nicholas and Hildebrand quickly called a synod to ratify the new election procedure. The result of this was the bull *In Nomine Domini,* which guaranteed election by the Cardinal-Bishops (later modified to include all cardinals).[41] In its essence this remains today the legislation governing papal elections. The reformers had achieved a coup. In one fell swoop they had not only destroyed the potency of the Roman clans, but they had effectively disintermediated the emperor from meddling in papal selection. Yet this new type of procedure was destined to have an even larger effect after the twelfth-century rediscovery of Roman law. The Roman law principle, "what touches all must be approved by all," began to make its way into the canon law of the West.[42] This means in effect that if a matter touches the whole of the community, then the whole of the community (or its representatives) must be consulted. Today this principle undergirds all Western constitutional law. Since the papacy was of Churchwide importance, then the selection of the pope ought to involve the whole of the Church. For this reason, cardinals came to be

40   By 1060 at the latest all the Suburbicarians were from the "reform" party. Blumenthal, *The Investiture Controversy,* 76.
41   Morris, *Papal Monarchy,* 92.
42   See Yves-Marie Congar, O.P. "Quod omnes tangit ab omnibus tractari et approbari debet," in *Revue historique de droit français et étranger* 81 (1958): 210–259. The principle formed the basis of representative government in the central Middle Ages, and even came to be inserted in canon law by Boniface VIII, *Liber Sextus* 5.12.29. Constantin Fasolt, "Quod omnes tangit ab omnibus tractari debet: The Words and the Meaning," in *Iure Veritas: Studies in Canon Law in Memory of Schafer Williams,* eds. S. Bowman and B. Cody (Cincinnati, OH, University of Cincinnati, College of Law, 1991), 21–55.

appointed from across Europe and then across the globe, assuring universal representation at this most pivotal of moments. Yet all of this was done in line with the tradition for, even today, a cardinal hailing from a far corner of the world still bears the title of pastor to a Roman *titulus*, and as such he has become part of the Roman clergy. While guaranteeing the traditional right of the Roman clergy to elect their bishop, the reform party enabled the College of Cardinals to open up to the world. It is difficult to overestimate how far reaching this administrative innovation truly was. Not only did it guarantee the freedom of papal elections in the future, it also ensured the virtual presence of the whole Church, providing a model for political representation that has become part and parcel of Western culture.

The King

The successors of Leo benefitted magnificently from the groundwork that he had laid, but there were still many implications to work out. Now that the papacy had achieved a measure of freedom, what did that mean for Church governance and administration? Of particular concern was how relations with civil officials were to be conducted. In the background of all these issues one finds the unquestioned leader of the reform party—namely, Hildebrand (created cardinal in 1059). He was the hub through which the intellectual arguments of the reformers were deployed into practical action within the papal court. He skillfully managed the progress of reform, particularly the disputed papal election of 1061 and a rapidly developing crisis in Milan. It was Hildebrand who would guide the reform for the next twenty-five years through the reign of Alexander II (r. 1061–1073), and then into his own term as Gregory VII (r. 1073–1085). During his tenure the ideology of reform became more and more focused, and various administrative ideas coalesced into an increasingly coherent program. While Hildebrand was a shrewd manager and decisive leader, at times ideology ran away with him causing difficulties both for himself and for the reform as a whole.

Much of that was in the future when Hildebrand successfully defended Alexander II against a schism brought about by the disappointed Roman clans. Taking advantage of temporary imperial weakness, Hildebrand made sure to fortify the papacy against the inevitable approach of a period when there would be a strong leader at the head of the empire. The popes had known for hundreds of years that they needed some form of temporal defense. The key was to make sure that protectors did not turn into usurpers. He knew that a revived imperial throne would attempt to recapture its influence over the Holy See. In light of this, Hildebrand pivoted on his position with regard to secular protection. To counterbalance German authority, he engineered a new alliance with the freebooting Norman barons of southern Italy.[43] The (mostly) converted descendants of the Vikings, the Normans had come to southern Italy seeking land and fortune. They caused no end of disorder in the south, while at the same time menacing the papacy. They had gone so far as to capture Pope St. Leo IX and hold him until he recognized their overlordship of the south. Recognizing the Normans as a much more potent and immediate threat, Hildebrand and Alexander II decided that the best way to manage their precarious position was to make peace. Knowing that the Normans would not beat their swords into plowshares, they decided to redirect their energies from attacking the Church and innocent civilians into a more productive direction. They authorized the reconquest of Sicily from the Muslims, which had the effect of further sanctioning the Norman rule in southern Italy, moving them to take the papacy under their protection, and eliminating a longstanding threat to Christendom's southern flank in the Mediterranean. There is in fact some argument to be made that their authorization of the Norman invasion of England was to eliminate simony and reform the Anglo-Saxon church.[44] In any case, the English Norman kings too became political allies of the papacy. All of these moves had the effect of blunting the possibility

43   Blumenthal, *The Investiture Controversy*, 82.
44   Ibid., 149.

of German interference, yet they are likewise examples of the far-seeing political thinking then percolating around the Roman Curia.

Of equal concern was the developing situation in Lombardy. Milan was one of the largest cities in Europe, and one of the first to benefit from the nascent commercial revolution. It was one of the most strategically located places on the continent, roughly halfway between both Rome and Germany. Long ago Charlemagne had conquered it, but traces of German rule quickly disappeared after his death, leading to a sense of independence that would lead to Milan becoming one of the chief anti-imperial cities in the coming centuries. This did not mean that Milan was, by default, politically aligned with the papacy. Indeed, the streak of independence went back long before the Carolingians to the early ages of Christianity, where Milan had not only been a late capital of the Roman empire, but had achieved precedence in the West second only to Rome under the rule of St. Ambrose. The "Ambrosian Church" was distinguished by a fierce self-sufficiency. While it deferred spiritually to Rome, Milan maintained a separate liturgical rite, different from the rest of the West, and its bishops were among the most mighty in the Catholic Church. It was truly a city to be reckoned with.

Given this independence and pedigree, Milan was often on the forefront of social, economic, and religious movements. The same sentiments making themselves felt at the top of the church also began percolating among the laity. We have already witnessed the commitment of certain aristocrats to the reform. In Milan, the impetus came from a different direction. The desire to purify the Church had risen from the working classes themselves—including the newly urbanized laborers and shopkeepers who began to desire more from their spiritual lives than the relatively comfortable secular clergy could offer.[45] While there was certainly a sort of class

45 For the history of this movement, see the essays in *La Pataria. Lotte religiose e sociali nella Milano dell'XI secolo*, ed. P. Golinelli (Milano, Europìa – Jaca Book, 1984); Alfredo Lucioni, "L'età della

tension between these new burghers and their clergy (themselves often associated with the noble families of the city), matters went much deeper. Fired by the reform of the monasteries and the papacy, a new religious sense began to dominate in Milan. Tired of venal and corrupt clergy, and particularly offended by violations of vows of chastity, the laity of Milan began to agitate for reform. By the 1050s a sort of lay strike had been organized.[46] In what one could describe as a "reverse interdict," many of the townspeople of Milan absented themselves from the liturgies sung by those who were married or considered simoniacal. They petitioned other, purified areas to send them priests, and they began to attend only masses offered by these reformed clerics. Donations and offerings to the local churches dried up. Events began to move more quickly since in 1061 Anselm of Lucca, a reformer familiar with the situation, became Pope Alexander II. He retained his affection for the Milanese movement, and he and Hildebrand cannily coopted the *Pataria* (as it was called) as an example of reforming zeal.[47] Alexander even sent a battle-flag to the leader of the group, Erlembard.

The *Pataria*, now enjoying papal approval and the absence of serious imperial interference, went on the offensive and drove out all the simoniacal clergy from the city. Matters were beginning to get out of hand. When the two leaders of the *Pataria* were murdered, the papacy treated them as martyrs, and cults sprang up

Pataria," in *Diocesi di Milano*, eds. Adriano Caprioli, Antonio Rimoldi, and Luciano Vaccaro, vol. 1. (Brescia: 1990), 167–194; H. E. J. Cowdrey, "Archbishop Aribert II of Milan," in *History* 51(1966): 1–15; and Giovanni Miccoli, "Per la storia della Pataria milanese," in *Bulletino del Istituto storico italiano per il Medio Evo* 70 (1958): 43–123.

46   Morris, *Papal Monarchy*, 104. In 1059, Hildebrand threw his whole weight behind the movement, and got Nicholas II to authorize the liturgical strike. Blumenthal, *The Investiture Crisis*, 95.

47   Blumenthal suggests Alexander II did not personally identify with the *Pataria*, but his actions (even if encouraged by Hildebrand) seem to challenge this idea. Id., *The Investiture Controversy*, 96.

around them (Sts. Arialdo and Erlembard).[48] The papacy here was playing a dangerous game. Though it had achieved the purification of the Milanese Church on its own terms, there were to be far reaching consequences. Movements like the *Pataria* had the revolutionary potential not only to reform the church, but to overthrow the whole social order. Further, in many people's minds, such radical reform was beginning to appear dangerously close to heresy. While papal approval had saved the Milanese movement, in later years the term *Patarene* would come to be synonymous with heretic.

Hildebrand and Alexander preferred carpet bombing to precision warfare. While indeed there were large masses of unreformed clergy, their widely cast nets often caught some who were willing to reform, generally, but had not yet done so for various reasons. Moderates were alienated by these campaigns. The reformers regularly threw loosely defined accusations of heresy around. While it is true that there was no precise scholastic definition of heresy at that time, many reformers used it as a catch-all title for those who resisted the reform in any way. Some of the reform party, such as Cardinal Humbert, equated simony with heresy itself.[49] Simony in his mind invalidated the sacraments performed by those guilty of this practice. The implications were staggering. He held that if, for example, a bishop 100 years prior had purchased his office, then all priests ordained by him, and all sacraments performed by them, were *ipso facto* invalid. Whole regions might have been without the sacraments for decades. Humbert was the most radical in this, and many realized that he

---

48 Morris, *Papal Monarchy*, 100. For the hagiographical *vita* of St. Arialdus, see *Monumenta Germaniae Historica. Scriptores,* 30.ii, 1047–1075.

49 Gilchrist is of the opinion that only the most intemperate of reformers (eg. Humbert) equated simony with heresy. See John Gilchrist, "'*Simoniaca haeresis*' and the problem of orders from Leo IX to Gratian," in *Proceedings of the Second International Congress of Medieval Canon Law.* Monumenta Iuris Canonici 1 (1965): 209–235.

was going too far. Simony was a corrupt practice certainly, but corruption was not heresy. St. Peter Damian (as fiery as he could otherwise be) was to be the voice of reason in this case. As papal legate to Milan, he permitted all repentant simoniacs to return to their offices. He argued for the validity of their orders, a gesture of real reconciliation that enabled many who were formerly guilty back into the good graces of the Church.[50] St. Peter Damian, through his mediation, saved the peace of the Church. It is possible that he presented this to Alexander II and Hildebrand as a *fait accompli*. Given their radicalism it was an uncomfortable solution. They deftly saved papal face by confirming the decision, but mandated that in the future simony would invalidate the conferral of orders.[51] A good advisor, working on the ground, had preserved the common good of the Church while at the same time enhancing papal authority and furthering the cause of the reform. Notwithstanding this, the reformers—both moderate and extreme—had tapped into a vast reserve of public sentiment. Their sponsorship of the *Pataria* set the stage for papal leadership in reform movements into the following centuries. It cemented a deepening relationship between the popes and the rising cities of Italy. They had correctly read the "signs of the times" and the *Pataria*—

---

50   Morris, *Papal Monarchy*, 103. The correspondence of Peter Damian has been expertly edited and is a treasure trove for the reform movement and the period as a whole. See Peter Damian, *Letters*, eds. Owen J. Blum, Irven M. Resnick, and Kurt Reinde, in 6 vols. (Washington, DC: Catholic University of America Press, 1989–2005).

51   Without knowing it, St. Peter Damian had coupled good policy with solid theology. If one is tempted to blame Humbert, Alexander II, and Hildebrand, we should remember that Augustine's anti-Donatist writings were not known at this time. They were treating the issue of invalid orders *de novo* as it were. It is a testament to St. Peter Damian's depth of theological knowledge and holiness that he was able to reproduce Augustine's timeless solution to the same problems. See Patricia Ranft, *The Theology of Peter Damian: "Let Your Life Always Serve As a Witness"* (Washington, DC: Catholic University of America Press, 2012).

which might have turned into a revolutionary anti-ecclesial move-ment—was instead mainstreamed into the Church, providing spir-itual energy to Milan, to Rome, and to the Church-at-large.

When Hildebrand himself came to be elected as pope in 1073, he carried with him decades of experience in the struggle for Church reform. He was sublimely convinced of the rectitude of his own movement and, as pope, pursued a mystical identification of himself with the Apostle Peter.[52] While this had been latent in many pronouncements of the papacy for centuries, Gregory elevated Leo-nine and Gelasian sentiments to the level of governing principles. As the voice of Peter on earth he saw himself as a purifying fire. He was a terror to evildoers and an enigma to many moderates. His often-intemperate invectives alienated many would-be sympa-thizers and occasionally irritated even his supporters.[53] He was pas-sionate and single-mindedly committed to the triumph of the Roman Church (which he equated simply with the triumph of Christ in the world). While more of a doer than a thinker, he was able to leverage the insights of the brilliant minds of the reform and reduce their insights to practical action. It was he who distilled much of the ideology that came to be normative for the papacy and for the development of Church-state relations in the Middle Ages. During his lifetime papalist ecclesiology was already being ex-pressed in terms of the "sun and the moon" and the "two swords" theories. In the first case, drawing from Genesis, the world is ruled by two lights, a greater and lesser. The spiritual power, being directed to an immortal end, is immeasurably greater and produces

52 Blumenthal, *The Investiture Controversy*, 117.
53 He could be acerbic even to those good men whom he thought were going too slow. He chastised St. Hugh of Cluny for a lack of love for the Roman Church. Even St. Peter Damian said of him that he was "an intrinsically worthless piece of iron but with the irresistible effect of the magnet, drawing everything into its field." Gregory VII was an elemental personality who saw all reality in contrasting terms of black and white. As Blumenthal remarks, "Hildebrand was definitely not a mediocre personality." Id., *The Investiture Controversy*, 116.

its own light. The earthly power is a lesser power, for it rules the world darkened by sin, and only receives what light it has from the sun.

The second conception is drawn from an obscure line in Luke's gospel, just before Christ was arrested. "And they said, 'Look, Lord, here are two swords.' And he said to them, 'It is enough'" (Lk 22:38). Medieval interpreters took this to represent the two powers that were sufficient to govern the world, the spiritual and temporal swords. Commentators noticed, however, that it was the Apostles who had the two swords. Therefore, all power must be in the hands of the Church, which in turn grants the temporal sword to an earthly ruler. The corollary to this position was that the Church—since the temporal sword belongs to her by nature—can take that sword back from a sinful or heretical king and give it to someone who will uphold the Church and the moral law. Such ideology animated the second stage of reform. The purification of the church not only required the elimination of simony and concubinage, but also demanded the removal of any lay supervision over spiritual realities. This would involve a direct attack on royal prerogatives, the lay proprietorship system, and the entire Ottonian-Salian system of *rex-sacerdos*.[54]

As the 1070s started, the issues came to be more clearly defined. What had seemed normal in the previous century now appeared to be not only simony, but unwarranted lay intrusion into the Church. If the mission of Christianity were to succeed, the Church required freedom from external influence. The previous twenty years of papal reform had been leading up to a climactic encounter between papacy and empire. When he became pope, Gregory decided upon the path of confrontation. He considered that only the direct defeat of the German emperor would bring about the ecclesiastical liberty he so desired. Henry IV had entered upon his majority in the year 1065. Up to that point, he had been forcibly shuffled back and forth between his rather ineffectual mother, Agnes, and churchmen of various levels of quality.

---

54 Blumenthal, *The Investiture Controversy*, 118.

Instead, one of the prime regents during this period was St. Anno of Cologne who, though occasionally high-handed, demonstrated that sanctity could still be found in combining ecclesial and royal service together.[55] The young Henry was faced with a number of challenges at the start of his reign, not the least of these being a massive uprising in Saxony. This occupied much of his time, so Gregory had a freer hand in the first years of his reign to interface with the local churches. While he did this with the intention of re-inforcing the good principles of the reform, even sympathetic northern churchmen bristled at being treated as mere "bailiffs" of the pope.[56] His high-handed maneuvering led German bishops to the brink of schism by 1076, particularly galled by his continuing support of the anti-imperial *Patarene* rebels in Milan.

Henry, for his part, was finally able to pay attention to Italy in 1075 after putting down the Saxon rebellion. At the insistence of his nobles, he forcefully intervened in the Milanese church to put an end to strife and bloodshed, directly appointing a new bishop on his own authority. Gregory reacted instantly (as he was inclined to do). He accused Henry of consorting with excommu-nicated men, which was indeed true. He also saw the danger of an imperial appointment to one of the most important sees in Christendom—in Italy itself no less—and against the popular cause Gregory himself had championed for so long. Using these pretexts, Gregory proceeded to "go nuclear." He counselled the emperor to remember his place and—should he fail to do so—he would be summarily excommunicated and relieved of his royal dignity. Henry responded in kind. He began a propaganda cam-paign of vituperation against Gregory filled with invective, essen-tially denying the validity of the pope's election. Yet in the court of public opinion Henry came off badly. The young emperor's backing of the schismatic German bishops prompted a response

55 . For St. Anno, see the proceedings contained in: *Sankt Anno und seine viel liebe Statt: Beiträge zum 900 jährigen Jubiläum,* ed. Gabriel Busch (Siegburg: Reckinger, 1975).
56 Morris, *The Papal Monarchy,* 114.

from the common people (who saw Gregory as a champion) and the nobles (who sensed weakness in Henry and a chance to resume the struggle against imperial encroachment). Gregory had cleverly unified the two transalpine forces that could successfully challenge the emperor. Just as he had leveraged the power of the *Pataria* in Milan, so was he now doing to the Church in Germany. A council of nobles, bolstered by the newly claimed papal power to dissolve their oaths of obedience, demanded Henry reconcile with Gregory. The emperor's entire reign was at stake. Gregory began to travel to Germany but stopped at the mountain stronghold of his strongest supporter, Countess Matilda of Tuscany. There in the tiny keep he waited for Germany to come apart at the seams.

Henry IV was taken aback by the force of the sentiment against him. Astutely, he immediately acceded to their demands and went across the Alps to seek reconciliation with the pope. Had he not done so, Germany would have descended into anarchy from which it would have been most difficult to recover. After forcing the penitent emperor to wait several days outside in the snow, Gregory received him, heard his confession, and absolved him of his excommunication, which resulted in Henry IV's continued ability to rule. It was one of the most powerful scenes in history: the temporal ruler of the Christian world, backed by armies and retainers, kneeling in the snow before the spiritual successor of St. Peter. Yet that was not to be the end of the story.

Before word of the emperor's absolution had crossed the Alps, some were taking matters into their own hands and, in Gregory's name, went about raising rebellion. Henry would spend the next three years quashing them, irritating the emperor greatly and putting the pope in a very difficult situation. By 1080, Henry had had enough. He was now secure enough in his position that he cast off all obedience to Gregory and appointed an antipope. Gregory's position worsened while his intransigency grew. He condemned all forms of lay investiture that involved the direct granting of the symbols of spiritual authority by the laity. Elections were to be freely conducted according to local custom by the clergy and people, and were all subject to confirmation by the Holy See.[57] It is a testament both to Gregory's foresight and stubbornness that today this seems normative for Catholics. It was far from being so in the 1070s—in fact, it was considered revolutionary.

Gregory's aggressive employment of another administrative novelty began to undermine his support at Rome. He recognized that the 'personal touch' of Leo, while effective, was also exceptionally time consuming, not to mention dangerous. It was his conviction that Rome, as the center of the world, ought to be the place to which the world came. It would not do to have the pope constantly travelling about. It might compromise his dignity and occasionally endanger his safety. To that end he evolved two significant administrative reforms. The first was the reinforcement of the requirement for metropolitans to travel to the Holy City for the personal investiture with their *pallia*.[58] This requirement was meant to cement their relation to the Holy See and their devotion to St. Peter, while at the same time ensuring that even the most important archiepiscopal sees acknowledged that they were dependent ultimately on Rome and not on their local churches or secular officials. Eventually this would evolve into the requirement that all bishops come to Rome every five years to make a visit *ad limina apostolorum* ("to the threshold of the Apostles"). The centralizing and organizing effect this had on the Church was immense. Now all the bishops would personally encounter Peter within his own context, in the midst of the city of emperors and martyrs, at the tombs of the very Apostles themselves. Their devotion to Peter and his successor would be deepened, and the pope and his advisors would get a constant stream of on-the-ground information for the practical governance of the Church. It cost the papacy nothing, and

57　Ibid., 118–119.
58　Ibid., 55. The pallium is the thin strip of white wool, embroidered with crosses and worn around the neck that symbolizes archiepiscopal dignity and metropolitan authority. It is worn by the archbishops within their own dioceses, while the pope wears his worldwide.

created a significant amount of both spiritual and symbolic capital.

The second innovation also had to do with a lack of papal travel outside of the city. Europe was getting larger every day as the frontiers were pushed back. The pope could not be everywhere, nor correct every problem personally. To that end the papacy innovated the concept of *legates*, or papal ambassadors.[59] There were precursors for this position, such as the ancient *apocrisarius*, representative of the pope in Constantinople, not to mention various ad hoc appointments throughout history. It was the Gregorian reformers who refined this office into a brilliant administrative tool. Trusted advisors and bishops would be empowered with papal authority to intervene in local problems throughout the Christian world. This brought papal government into immediate relations with the local churches, strengthening their ties, and enabling the papacy to end intractable conflicts that could not be settled on the local level. It also ushered in one of the most significant governmental innovations that continues to echo today—namely, the professional diplomatic service, still today a point of pride for the papacy, and duplicated by every nation on earth.

Yet as with all innovations, there was initial resistance. Local churches, particularly the traditional metropolitan sees, chafed under this increased centralization of oversight and were irritated at the concomitant reduction in authority it betokened. Neither were secular officials thrilled. They formerly could treat with the papacy from a safe distance. Yet when a churchman arrived invested with the authority of St. Peter and inserted himself into the

---

59 To say that papal legates were key to the Reform is an understatement. Many significant studies have been done on individual ones, eg. Kriston R. Rennie, *Law and Practice in the Age of Reform: The Legatine Work of Hugh of Die (1073–1106)* (Turnhout, Belgium: Brepols, 2010); Stefan Weiss, *Die Urkunden der päpstlichen Legaten von Leo IX. bis Coelestin III. (1049–1198)* (Cologne: Böhlau Verlag, 1995); and, Kathleen G. Cushing, *Papacy and Law in the Gregorian Revolution: The Canonistic Work of Anselm of Lucca* (Oxford: Clarendon Press, 1998).

court, the papacy became a much more present force. Never had popes conferred so much authority in subordinates, who essentially became vicegerents of the papacy within their assigned territories. The nature of legatine system also meant that Gregory had to rely on his own inner circle of trusted advisors. Of course, he had assembled a genuinely first-rate team who were massively effective at advancing the Gregorian mission.[60] This 'inner circle,' however, deprived the traditional Roman clergy of their positions surrounding the papal court. The local clergy found themselves frozen out as it were, while foreigners had the pope's ear and were endowed with unprecedented powers. In 1084 the excluded clergy had had enough—thirteen local cardinals and a number of papal officials abandoned Gregory and went over to the imperially-created antipope, who then obediently crowned Henry as emperor. Gregory was driven to take refuge in the Norman city of Salerno where he died. His last words were, "I have loved justice, and hated iniquity. For that reason I die in exile."

In reviewing the administrative history of this potent and history-changing papacy several observations are apparent. Gregory was a difficult personality, invested with a singular commitment to the idea of his own authority. He acted as a true "papal monarch." He was convinced that he was doing the work of God in purifying the Church to ensure that it had the liberty to continue His mission. In terms of subsequent history, we can witness how successful he was. His reign was the hinge of the fruitful papal centralization of the Middle Ages and led to the creation of an effective central administration for what would become a worldwide Church. His struggle to free the Church from lay involvement secured its liberty through many subsequent challenges.

By using the principles of ecclesiastical freedom developed by Gregory and his circle, the Church was able to navigate future challenges to its activity in the world on behalf of the gospel. Indeed, he was finally accorded the honor of canonization in 1728 as the final seal of approval of the holiness of his life. At the same time,

60   Morris, *The Papal Monarchy*, 111.

none of that was apparent at the time of his death in 1085. The means Gregory chose to achieve his ends—while always having the common good of the Church at heart—never seemed to rise beyond the level of shrewd prudence. At times he had an exceptional comprehension of the situation on the ground, such as in his patronage of the *Pataria* and in his sense of the German situation in 1076. Yet he was often blinded by an inflexible intransigence that eventually led to the squandering (at least in the short term) of what he had sought to achieve. Gregory saw the papacy through the lens of rulership and obedience, which is undoubtedly part of a Catholic vision, but not in its fullness. He could run roughshod over moderates and allies alike and, unlike Leo, tended to alienate the particular church over which he was also the head. He laid down enduring principles, many of which have become part and parcel of Catholicism, yet his administration betrayed a vision that would only come to fruition in the future. He had a strategic mind, but his tactical implementation left much to be desired. He bequeathed a disunified Church and a divided Christendom, while also providing his successors with the tools necessary to effect a renewal and transformation.

The Priest

The high-handed actions of Gregory and his failure to govern consultatively put his followers in a difficult spot upon his death in 1085. While the Cardinal-Bishops were still on the side of the reform, the majority of Cardinal-Priests had switched allegiance to the imperial antipope, Clement III (r. 1080–1100). Clement was a competent leader, and held the allegiance of central, eastern, and northern Europe. He too governed with an eye to purifying the church, yet at the same time he was most certainly the emperor's man. The legitimate Roman line could not even govern the city of Rome, from whence Gregory himself had been forced to flee. The reform party was again divided between moderates and fire-breathers (those after the mold of Gregory and Humbert).

A year of wrangling ensued until the elevation of the moderate Victor III (later beatified). He had been the reforming Abbot of Montecassino, continuing the monastic emphasis that had been at the basis of the whole reform. Unfortunately, he was very short-lived, dying in 1087. The Roman papacy again had to confront a *sede vacante* while the power and influence of the antipope increased. In the little town of Terracina, halfway between Naples and Rome, the remaining cardinal-bishops elected the suburbicarian Bishop of Ostia, Odo of Châtillon, as the new pope.[61] He took the name Urban II.[62] Odo had been a pupil of St. Bruno, the founder of the Carthusians, and himself had held the office of grand prior of Cluny. He had been a personal attendant to Gregory VII and so had drunk deep draughts of the reform in both its monastic and papal forms. Urban II would reign until 1099 and finally be beatified by Pope Leo XIII in 1881. It is to Odo that we must credit much of the enduring success of the reform that went on under Gregory's name. Had it not been for his patient management and calm demeanor in facing the inherited problems of the past (both externally and internally inflicted), it is possible that the imperial antipope Clement III would have emerged victorious, ensuring a continuation of the *rex sacerdos* system. Blessed Urban II forms, then, the image of a priest—that is, one who retains the prophetic voice of Leo IX, the necessary theological underpinnings of papal kingship from Gregory VII, but adds to both a thirst for justice that

61 One should remember that, while the schism of the cardinal-priests was disastrous, in terms of papal election they had not yet been raised to the dignity of full electors, therefore the cardinal-bishops alone legally had the right of papal election at the time. The participation of the lower orders of cardinals became normative only later.

62 Most of the focus on Urban has been in the context of the First Crusade. For a broader view see the magisterial work: Alfons Becker, *Papst Urban II. (1088–1099)*, 3 vols., (Stuttgart: Anton Hiersemann, 1964–2012). See also the specific works of Robert Somerville, who focuses on Urban's synods, as well as, Francis J. Gossman, *Pope Urban II and Canon Law* (Washington, DC: Catholic University of America Press, 1960).

was especially seasoned with mercy. In Urban we see the good effects of the reform finally coming to fruition both in the Holy See and in the broader Church.

Urban's immediate concern was to heal the schism provoked by emperor Henry IV. By this time all of Europe was behind the original sentiments of the reformers, and clerical celibacy and the prohibition of simony were becoming realized throughout Christendom. However, the struggle had evolved and entered into a new phase. The key issue became lay investiture. What several generations before had been seen as an imperial effort to reform the Church, was now examined from a different perspective. When a layman handed to a new bishop the symbols of his spiritual office (the ring and crozier) it seemed that it subordinated the Church to the state, and that the bishops were thereby in some way dependent upon their lay lords for the authority to govern the Church. In the minds of the reform party this was utter servitude and completely compromised the liberty of the Church. Having freed the Roman bishops of secular and imperial interference, they now sought to extend the same freedom to the whole Church. This had brought them into such bitter conflict with the emperor that it created a schism. It was Urban's mission to delicately remove the causes for such dissension. He developed a multi-pronged strategy for this. In the first place he maintained the aggressive use of legates, but with modifications. He and his successors recognized that giving them the status of "viceregent" was going too far. The investiture of legates with quasi-papal power to be exercised for an unlimited time left a bad taste in many mouths. It was like sending a bulldozer to tend a flower bed. Therefore, Urban curbed their powers. He insisted that, while useful, legates should be limited in their power geographically and according to duration. In addition, they were best used to settle a specific, temporary problem that was beyond the administrative competence of the local churches. In this way the legitimate autonomy of particular churches could be protected, while at the same time applying judicial use of superior authority to solve thorny problems. He was also able to secure the support of secular princes by agreeing to cooperate with them in the dispatch of legates.[63] The prudent delegation of power to ambassadors was thereby able to extend papal authority while respecting subordinates, and it proved to be an enduring contribution to Church policy.

In terms of internal reorganization, Urban II can fairly be called the father of the modern curia.[64] It was he (assisted by his successors) who streamlined all the spontaneous developments of the previous fifty years and consolidated them into a workable body that was capable of running a worldwide organization. In many ways, the blueprints laid down by Urban continue to function to the present day. It was he who finally did away with many of the ancient offices that had become sinecures, or which were bereft of administrative function.[65] The Sacred Lateran Palace was the heart of the old papal government, and as such it was attached to the stational liturgies of the Roman churches.[66] The reform popes effected a separation between liturgical and administrative functions, and to the benefit of both. Roman priests could thenceforth concentrate on the complicated papal ceremonial, while other officers were detached to focus solely on management of the Church's business.[67] These curial officials were referred to as the "papal chaplains."

63 Morris, *Papal Monarchy*, 125.
64 The word "curia" is first employed in a papal document under Urban II in 1089. Morris, *The Papal Monarchy*, 169.
65 Blumenthal, *The Investiture Controversy*, 78.
66 Reinhard Elze, "Das sacrum palatium Lateranense im 10. und 11. Jahrhundert," in *Studi gregoriani per la storia di Gregorio VII e della riforma gregoriana* vol. 4 (1952): 27–54.
67 Note that this did not mean that curial clergy did not celebrate the liturgy, but it did usually mean they were relieved of *cura animarum*, and thus enabled to focus their whole energy on administrative matters. Interestingly, the curia quickly developed a streamlined liturgical rite, distinct from the highly complex Lateran ceremonial, that would later be copied and standardized at the Council of Trent for the whole Roman Church. For this, see S. J. P. Van Dijk, *The Origins of the Modern Roman Liturgy: the Liturgy of the Papal Court and the Franciscan Order in the Thirteenth Century*, trans. Joan Hazelden Walker (Westminster, MD: Newman Press, 1960).

Given their liberation from excessive liturgical duty and pastoral care, these became a standing body of young men chosen for their administrative talent who were apprenticed to the curia. Quickly they became the elite bench from which the papacy selected its primary servants. Indeed, by the twelfth century, the whole of the Roman Rota would be populated by such elite "chaplains."[68] In the place of the ancient *vicedominus* and *vestiarius*, Urban created a unified office called the papal chamberlain. He was to be the chief financial officer of the Roman Church.[69] Unifying oversight of all the different revenue streams (including estates, exemption taxes, and national donations to "Peter's pence") served to rationalize the curial activity and enable it to bring its influence to bear more efficiently. Urban also reformed the chancery, and retired the old *Liber Diurnus* that for hundreds of years had provided the templates for papal documents. It was replaced by new standard papal diplomatics that employed a style known as the *cursus*, one that was immediately recognizable and of ancient provenance.[70]

There were two fundamental changes in management style that served Urban exceptionally well. In the first place he saw the disastrous effects of a "kitchen cabinet" during the reign of Gregory VII. Relying on private advisors, some of them from outside of the curia or even the clergy, created an atmosphere of disaffection. Indeed, most of Gregory's own cardinals went into schism because of the former's refusal to deliberate with them. Urban carefully worked to create a culture of consultation. While making it clear that he was the primary decision maker, he opened up topics for

68   Ullmann, *Papal Government*, 331.
69   Morris, *The Papal Monarchy*, 168; Ullmann, *Papal Government*, 330.
70   See the discussion in R. L. Poole, *Lectures on the History of the Papal Chancery Down to the Time of Innocent III* (Cambridge: Cambridge University Press, 1915). In spite of its age, this is still a very valuable study, to be read alongside C. R. Cheney, *The Study of the Medieval Papal Chancery: The Second Edwards Lecture Delivered Within the University of Glasgow on the 7th December, 1964* (Glasgow: Jackson, 1966).

discussion and actively sought advice. It was he who advanced the concept of *societas* by assembling the cardinals of all ranks into a consultative body.[71] In a certain sense they formed a cabinet, with whom the pope engaged in regular deliberations called consistories. Urban therefore leveraged the best of both worlds. He retained the monarchical principles of rule inherited from Gregory, while avoiding the latter's mistakes and benefitting from the sound advice of permanent expert colleagues.

Indeed, the brilliance of Blessed Urban went even deeper. In creating a system of administrative apprenticeship among the papal chaplains, he essentially "trained trust." Through intimate association with the government of the Church, Urban was able to raise up successive generations of dependable advisors. This in turn allowed an increase in Roman representation within the college, thus mollifying local interests at the same time. The Roman clergy came to be a reformed and dependable body upon which the popes and the curia could draw upon for talent. At the same time, Urban was able to maintain contact with sympathetic defenders across Europe, using the bonds of *amicitia*. This concept transcended merely personal friendship and united people throughout Christendom in the bonds of a common cause.[72] Urban's model truly was very much in tune with premodern conceptions of monarchy. Kings in the Middle Ages always consulted; they always sought the advice of representatives. Absolute monarchy was an early modern aberration in the history of the West. Even if one could theoretically abstract papal absolutism (as St. Gregory did), one had to measure its efficacy against prudential considerations. Indeed, Urban's flexibility in this matter ended up strengthening the papacy considerably.

The second significant administrative innovation of Blessed Urban was the evolving ideology of dispensation. Indeed, so profound was Urban's use of it that occasionally he has been called the father of canonical jurisprudence and a primary precursor of

71   Ullmann, *Papal Government*, 319.
72   Morris, *Papal Monarchy*, 122.

the nascent scholastic method. While it is true that these claims are excessive, as his predecessors also employed indult and dispensation, Urban did raise it to the level of a governing principle.[73] He wrote that it was occasionally necessary to temper legal strictures or to interpret them differently according to the "needs of the times" or the "qualities of persons."[74] Based on this principle it became easy to distinguish texts that had the character of immutability (such as the dogmatic decisions of popes and councils) from those that were merely disciplinary.[75] While this is a commonplace in Catholic thought today, it was the first time such a clear distinction had been established. One can clearly see the difficulty that the reformers experienced previously in distinguishing between heresy and the practice of simony. Urban's principles put this all into perspective. Yet his brilliance was more profound than merely distinguishing the problems. In asserting the right to derogate or abrogate a law, the pope as the supreme legislator was at the same time claiming superiority over the whole of ecclesiastical positive law. Indeed, in the very exercise of a merciful dispensation, papal and curial authority were effectively underscored. Urban recognized the kind of returns that might be achieved with a judicious use of mercy. To that end he began to offer reconciliation, particularly to those who had, unknowingly, been ordained by simoniacal bishops.[76] In terms of the schism, Gregory's hardline partisans

---

73   Stephan Kuttner, "Urban II and the Doctrine of Interpretation: A Turning Point?" in *Studia Gratiana* 15 (1972): 53–85. He writes that "later political theory would call (it) the doctrine of administrative discretion proper to the making of executive decisions."

74   Ibid., 60.

75   Ullmann, *Papal Government*, 371. Ullman also recognizes that this lays the groundwork for a jurisprudence allied with theology or "juristic theology." Such a development of the science of "distinction" enables the foundation and growth of a plethora of other new sciences. Ibid., 386.

76   Urban allowed a quite generous latitude to the concept of "unknowing." It was only those who specifically bought their offices who would fall under Urban's ban. Morris, *Papal Government*, 124.

demanded that the excommunicated be shunned at all costs. Urban tempered this demand by focusing ire on the leaders of the schism, yet permitting those who abandoned it to return on extremely generous terms.

He also exercised discretion in the political sphere and demonstrated that he could outmaneuver the intransigent. For instance, he secured the obedience of the Nordic countries by siding with King Eric III of Denmark in his quarrel with the schismatic Archbishop of Hamburg. In order to obtain the king's support he separated Scandinavia from the metropolitan authority of Hamburg, an event that not only secured the king's obedience to Urban, but also became a defining moment for northern European self-determination. In many other ways, he was able to chip away at the power of the obstinate Henry IV. In 1093, Henry's son Conrad initiated a rebellion, and had himself crowned as King of Lombardy. Though probably a political calculation, he later switched his allegiance to Urban. The pope capitalized on this by supporting Conrad's claim against his father, cleverly creating a geographical barrier between himself and Henry, and further compromising the excommunicated emperor's position. In 1095, having made substantial gains against the antipope, he moved against Henry directly, yet in a far more strategic way than had Gregory.

Urban appeared at the Council of Piacenza in 1095 as the supporter of Henry's estranged wife, Eupraxia of Kiev. There she publicly accused Henry of numerous sexual sins and infidelities, a propaganda disaster for Henry. Since the papacy had been a traditional defender of the marriage bond, Urban backed Eupraxia, and permitted her continued separation from Henry.[77] In addition, Urban received an embassy from Byzantium at the same council.

---

77 Urban had also backed Queen Bertrada against Philip I of France, even though this compromised the Roman position in that country. On questions of principle and doctrine, Urban exhibited a character of steel. The papacy was the guardian of Christian marriage throughout its history, particularly significant for the rights of women and wives.

The Byzantine army had been destroyed in 1071 by a new Islamic threat, the Seljuk Turks. These were threatening the survival of the entire Greek Christian empire. Alexius I Comnenos appealed directly to the pope for aid. Such an appeal not only significantly bolstered Urban's claims to headship of Christendom, but offered an opportunity to contain the Normans, stop the Islamic threat, and heal the Eastern schism all in one fell swoop. In response, Urban created one of the most original and audacious plans in Christian history.

In order to effect his policies, Urban took a page out of Leo's IX playbook. He knew that in the situation the papacy now faced, personal presence was needed. To that end he began a tour of the north, starting at Piacenza and extending into central France. This culminated at a grand council in the city of Clermont. There he preached on the necessity of coming to the aid of the persecuted Christians of Byzantium and the Levant. It was there he originated the idea of the Crusade, an armed pilgrimage to come to the relief of the Holy Land. His preaching and his idea galvanized Europe. It was the culmination of the Peace of God and Truce of God movements that had been in process for nearly a century. It also cemented the pope's position as the leader of Christendom. No matter what may be said of the prospect or progress of the Crusades, in a very real sense 'Europe' as a concept can be dated not to Charlemagne, but to Blessed Urban II's decision to mobilize all Christians in a common endeavor to liberate the Holy Land. It effectively signaled the death knell of the imperial schism and propelled the Roman papacy to a position of supremacy unchallenged for centuries. It capped the whole of the reform movement. Indeed, even the Investiture controversy itself would be settled within a generation, largely in the papacy's favor. The secular lords were prohibited from investing bishops with symbols of spiritual rule, though they still might hand over symbols of *secular* rule, should a bishop be entrusted with any temporal affairs. It was an equitable solution to both sides, made possible indeed by the grand ideology of Gregory, but made practicable by the solid prudence of Urban and his successors.

In Leo, Gregory, and Urban we can trace three very different leadership styles and approaches to administration. Without any of them the reform would have ultimately failed, yet each of them had strengths and weaknesses. What is certain, however, is that their collaboration, their foresight, their commitment to the common good of the Church, and their dedication led not only to the thorough reformation of the Christian world (particularly the clergy), but to an elevation of papal authority—even though this was not indeed wholly novel, but embedded in scripture and tradition. They paved the way for the achievements of the central Middle Ages, in cathedral and in university, in administration and in art. Walter Ullmann gives a prescient assessment of some of their achievements:

> It was as universal monarchs that the popes partly applied Roman law principles, partly developed them, and partly created new ones, which have since gained universal recognition in international law. The protection of legates; safe conduct of ambassadors; secrecy in diplomatic negotiations; insistence on the adherence to treaties made between secular rulers; condemnation of treaty violations; papal annulment and rescission of treaties and compacts; fixation of treaty conditions; excommunication and deposition of rulers; orders for the release of prisoners; for their humane treatment and that of hostages; protection of exiles, aliens, and Jews; condemnation of "unjust" wars and piracy; confirmation of peace treaties; orders for the free passage of troops engaged in a "just" campaign; orders to rulers to enter into alliances; ascription of occupied territories to a victorious belligerent party, and so forth.[78]

While models of ecclesiology have continued to develop, and while many bemoan the political attitudes of the medieval papacy and

78   Ullmann, 450.

question the motivations therein, papal achievements were undeniable. Not the least of these was the creation of a system of government that essentially endures to the present day. The model of governance they created had a built-in flexibility that enabled it first to become the most advanced court in Europe and then positioned it in good stead to become the administrators of the first worldwide organization in human history. The holiness of the reform was rooted, innovative, and incarnational in the deepest sense.

Chapter 4
Administration as an Art:
The Case of the Friars Preachers

At the height of the Christological controversies, Pope St. Leo the Great explained that Christ "remained what He was, and became what He was not."[1] This could be analogically applied to all successful administrative reforms in the history of Christianity. Maintaining the call of the gospel and fidelity to doctrine allows a surprising openness to novel ways of doing things. Ironically, it is in the failure to follow the gospel and "sound doctrine" that revolutionary ideas are permitted to germinate, ideas which ultimately harm the faith. The words of Christ in Mark 2 can be applied to this phenomenon: "And no one puts new wine into old wineskins; if he does, the wine will burst the skins, and the wine is lost, and so are the skins; but new wine is for fresh skins" (Mk 2:22). In each new age the harvest of the Church brings forth new vintages. When such movements emerged they required new structures. These could not be haphazardly wedged into older systems; such enforced conformity threatened to strangle their evangelical energy, yet at the same time they could not thrive outside the flowing stream of the Christian tradition. Neither slavishly adhering to the past nor recklessly casting it off, successful new movements have always sought to harness the immemorial heritage of the Church. Fresh vines, grafted into Christ in every age, constantly produced new fruit (Jn 15:1–27). This was only

1   A paraphrase of the sentiment of Letter 28, the so-called *Tome of Leo*. Compare with St. Gregory Nazianzen, "What He was He continued to be; what He was not He took to Himself." *Oration* 29.19.

made possible by the patient labor of the vinedressers, who arranged, grafted, and even pruned when necessary for the good of the whole organism. To provide frameworks for these manifestations of the Holy Spirit, careful and prudent provision was needed. No authentically Christian movement is ever really innovation, but rather renovation. The Incarnation is the "one new thing" sought for by the author of Ecclesiastes, for otherwise "there is nothing new under the sun" (Ecc 1:9). Within the body of Christ's Church, everything must be measured against the genuine newness of the gospel, for it is only in recollection of and realignment with its teachings that new movements—each embedded in its own particular time and context—can bear real fruit in bringing Christ's kingdom into this world.

The central Middle Ages were a time of expansion and excitement. It was also a profoundly Christian period, and produced a spirit of reform that surged throughout Europe. After Charlemagne's false dawn, a series of events took place that stabilized Christendom and put the European continent on the path to growth and expansion. We have already seen how the monastic world provided significant ballast for the reestablishment of order. Cluny and later Cîteaux remade the map of Europe, now dotted with thousands of reformed houses living the Benedictine Rule in its fullness. Political security also began slowly to return, as the Ottonian dynasty strengthened in central Europe, the Capetian kings began their long dynasty in France, and new cities sprang up in Italy dedicated to the revival of trade. The external borders steadied as well. The Viking raiders, undefeated in battle, were nevertheless domesticated by their conversion to Christianity. The Spanish kingdoms began, more and more successfully, to push back the Islamic occupiers, and the barbarian eruption of the Magyars was ended with their defeat at Lechfield in 955 and their reception into the Church in 972. A climactic change called the "Medieval warm period" reduced rain and increased crop yield, and was accompanied by the innovations of the second agricultural revolution. Such a superabundance of food led to a population boom that lasted until the coming of the Black Death in 1347. Commerce—desultory at best during the previous half-millennium—began to revitalize, led by the Italian city-states and the Dutch and Flemish ports of the north. Even the papacy had shaken itself out of its two century-long torpor with the election of St. Leo IX in 1049. Europe was poised for a period of prosperity like few seen in history

Yet with comfort came problems. Europe had been largely an agricultural and subsistence culture after the fall of Roman order. Indeed, the monasteries had become models of communitarian self-sufficiency that so characterized the period. As a result of the rising commercial revolution, coupled with exceptional land management on the part of the monasteries, both Church and state experienced an unprecedented surge of wealth. While the Church possessed property long before the Constantinian settlement, still the voices of the New Testament counselling caution about money and riches echoed in the common conscience.[2] Increasingly people began to feel guilt regarding their own material wealth and extended these doubts to the possession of capital by the Church. Parallel to this was a rising tide of lay literacy and piety, which went hand in hand for a desire that the Church be purified in head and members. This purification was set in motion in the Roman See during the Gregorian reform, during which the Roman Church again asserted its independence and once more began to act in a sovereign manner in Christian society.

The Gregorians usefully united their desire to 'clean house' with the lay yearning for a deeper spiritual life and a purified clergy. On occasion, however, enthusiasm out-muscled good sense. When the increasing desire for lay piety met the totally unprepared urban clergy, there could often be fireworks. During the *Pataria* rebellion in Milan in the 1070s, the laypeople threw out the entire presbyterate of their city for corruption and immorality.[3] This movement

2   See Lester K. Little, *Religious Poverty and the Profit Economy in Medieval Europe* (Ithaca, NY: Cornell University Press, 1978); and Peter Brown, *Through the Eye of a Needle: Wealth, the Fall of Rome, and the Making of Christianity in the West, 350–550 AD* (Princeton, NJ: Princeton University Press, 2012).

3   For this remarkable episode, see the previous chapter, and Olaf

had the broad support of the papacy and the Roman curia. At times though, this ardor outstripped official sanction and led to sporadic outbreaks of violence. Further, people in the eleventh century, now living together in cities, practicing crafts and the mercantile arts, and experimenting in novel political forms such as Christian democracy, tended to look askance at both the monasteries with their rural, landed wealth, and the episcopacy with its income and ties to the nobility. Where, they mused, could one read about monks in the New Testament?

As in every age, Christians sought perfection. As they meditated on what form this might take, they began to look at the example of the early Church, particularly the Book of Acts. The heroes of primitive Christianity did not appear to be propertied, cloistered monks, but rather itinerant and poor preachers of the gospel. A new type of devotional life began to emerge: the pursuit of holiness through *the imitation of the Apostles*.[4] Around the year 1100 a stable and confident Europe, secure in its borders, had begun to seek a deeper spirituality. Men around Europe decided to heed the call of the gospel to observe a life of itinerant poverty. One such man was Robert of Arbrissel (ca. 1045–1116).[5] He was animated by the same motives that urged on the Gregorians in Rome; he too wanted a purification and simplification of Christianity. As such he set forth on the byways of medieval France, preaching penitence and immediately gathering throngs of followers. Here was something

Zumhagen, *Religiöse Konflikte und kommunale Entwicklung: Mailand, Cremona, Piacenza und Florenz zur Zeit der Pataria* (Köln: Böhlau Verlag, 2002); and Paolo Golinelli, *La Pataria: lotte religiose e sociali nella Milano dell'XI secolo* (Novara: Europía, 1984).

4   We are still many centuries away from the *Devotio Moderna* of the 15th century, and its new ideas of the "imitation of Christ." Absolutely critical for these 11th and 12th century beginnings of the Apostolic Poverty movement is Herbert Grundmann, *Religious Movements in the Middle Ages*, trans. Steven Rowan (Notre Dame: University of Notre Dame Press, 1995; 1935).

5   The sources for his life are edited in *Robert of Arbrissel: A Medieval Religious Life*, ed. Bruce L. Venarde (Washington, D.C.: Catholic University of America Press, 2003).

genuinely new and far different from the typical, ill-educated parish priest who rarely sermonized.[6] Robert was dynamic and charismatic, answering the contemporary spiritual needs of people in a way of which many in the institutional Church were incapable. He was exciting and new, a traveler who brought news from distant lands and who wove it into energetic preaching. Yet this popularity proved to be its own problem. Robert gained many female followers and, while there was no proof of wrongdoing, women could not simply wander about the medieval world in attendance upon a young, appealing preacher. Robert upset ecclesial norms even more than social ones. There was no extant canonical role for his type of life. While some were sympathetic, there was no category into which he might be placed, be it monk, canon, or secular priest. Clearly there were also issues of jealousy and power involved, and Robert was not proficient enough at stemming the tide of calumny. Eventually he was forced to affiliate his followers into a traditional monastery, one for men and one for women, at Fontevraud.

While acknowledging the sometimes-contemptible reasons for restricting his ministry, many within the clergy really did have a point. The institutional Church was the guardian of doctrine and practice and had to have some say in the governance of religious societies. It was the Church that had the ordained power to grant jurisdiction for the celebration of the sacraments and for preaching. Indeed, the bishop, according to tradition, was the sole person who possessed an inherent right to preach, one which he could delegate to other ordained ministers such as priests and deacons. Further, to hear these novel speakers extolling their own lives as imitators of the Apostles must have stuck in the craws of the bishops, themselves the literal successors to the Apostles. Their very existence as poor, wandering preachers tended to cast the clergy into a bad light. Further, monasteries had proved their worth for over a millennium. Their

6   This is not to stress the corruption of the secular clergy at the time, simply their unambitious moral and intellectual tone. This may have been enough a century before, but would not feed the spiritual hunger of people in the central Middle Ages.

manner of life had come to be received as normative for anyone serious about the pursuit of holiness. Even the New Testament and the deep tradition of the Church argued against such a roving life. Had not 2 Timothy 3 warned against wanderers who insinuated themselves into Christian homes and seduced women? Benedict himself, seeming prophetical in their eyes, had inveighed against *gyrovagues* in the very first chapter of his Rule, excoriating those pseudo-monks who roamed about looking for free food and shelter without discipline or spiritual training. The monks had extensive experience with those who refused proper order and who as a result could easily be filled with pride and self-will. The tradition on this point made sense. Many things would have to happen before another experiment like Robert's would be able to reach maturity in the Church.

One step in the evolution is attributed to a man much like Robert. Norbert of Xanten came from an exceptionally aristocratic background and had achieved the status of almoner of the Holy Roman Emperor, Henry V.[7] One day, confronted by a lightning storm, he had a serious conversion experience. As a result, he sold all he had, abandoned his comfortable position, and embraced the way of the wandering preacher. Unlike Robert, though, Norbert had a more ecclesial bent. Almost immediately he travelled to meet the pope where, given his stature in the Church and state, he likely obtained some kind of preaching license. This enabled him to move about freely, knowing that he was protected by the highest authority, thus circumventing problems encountered by Robert and others. Yet still there was uneasiness and confusion, as many churchmen still had no idea where such a wandering preacher, however licensed, fit within the canonical framework of the

---

7   For Norbert, see Kaspar Elm, *Norbert von Xanten: Adliger, Ordensstifter* (Kirchenfürst. Köln: Wienand, 1984); and A. W. van den Hurk, *Norbert of Gennep and His Order* (*Norbert Van Gennep En Zijn Orde*) (Apeldoorn: Altiora-Averbode, 1984); an older hagiographical biography is Laurence Thomas Anderson, *Saint Norbert of Xanten, A Second St. Paul* (Dublin: Gill, 1955). See also the commentary in Theodore James Antry and Carol Neel, *Norbert and Early Norbertine Spirituality* (New York: Paulist Press, 2007).

Church. Pope Callixtus II (r. 1119–1124) cleverly defused such tension. Recognizing Norbert's qualities, he invited Norbert to create a community and stabilize himself, which the preacher obediently did. While it meant that the life of wandering was over, several decisive principles had been established. He had pioneered the post of a *licensed* preacher after the pattern of the Apostles. He dedicated himself to orthodoxy by defeating the heretic Tanchelm (fl. 1115), indicating that a wandering preacher was not—by that very fact of itinerancy—wayward in faith. Finally, he demonstrated ready obedience, even when the papacy later asked him to leave his new community and become Archbishop of Magdeburg.

The society that he founded was significant as a bridge between the earlier monks and the later friars. They were to be known from their abbey at Prémontré as the Praemonstratenisans (and in later centuries as the Norbertines). Yet Norbert was not content to simply establish another type of Benedictine monastery. While he was absolutely devoted to the celebration of the liturgy (something that often corresponded with doctrinal orthodoxy), he also wanted flexibility. Given the rapid changes then transpiring across the continent, new forms of religious ministry were needed, particularly requiring men who had enough education to confute heresy and who had enough pastoral acumen to tend to the burgeoning populations of medieval cities.

The Rule of Benedict, even in its later incarnations, with its preference for wild, rural wastes, was not amenable to this vision. Norbert needed something more supple for what he had in mind. He wanted access to an active public ministry in the midst of the search for perfection in community. As such he eschewed the Rule of Benedict, and instead adapted a form of life called *canonical*. This life was the spiritual grandchild of St. Augustine, and the Rule attached to his name developed over the course of centuries, particularly under the influence of the Frankish bishop, St. Chrodegang (d. 766). Indeed, some have cited Chrodegang as the source of much of the Carolingian spiritual renewal.[8] Yet his particular Rule

8   M.A. Claussen, *The Reform of the Frankish Church: Chrodegang*

focused on *secular* canons.[9] A canon in this sense was a cleric attached to a church, usually the cathedral church, having the bishop as immediate superior. The idea was to regularize the lives of these urban clerks into a more monastic observance within the canonry, while permitting them time and spiritual energy to undertake duties outside of it. In later centuries this Rule became modified and further supplanted by versions of the Augustinian "Rule" that were more capacious and less tied to monastic observance. Norbert's decision to accept this more malleable Rule was the key to a renovation of the concept of religious life.

For nearly a thousand years the active life had been the realm of the laity and the secular clergy. Monks embraced the contemplative life and for centuries there was little to disturb that division of labor. Contemplatives were known as the spiritual bulwark of the Church, and were renowned for their orthodoxy, even when they became relaxed and corrupt. The active life on the other hand, when not regulated had a tendency to veer into heterodoxy. This was the danger sensed by the Church in the 1100s. The Norbertines split the difference, establishing their orthodoxy and making a beachhead into the active life by becoming *regular* canons—or canons not subject to a bishop, but rather to an abbot—and following a formal Rule. The purpose was to be an auxiliary to the secular clergy, itself a diffuse body that had been slowly reforming since the time of the Gregorians, but one still institutionally unprepared for the urban shift.

As was the case in many congregations, much of the heavy lifting was not done by the founder. He merely bequeathed a vision but gave little in the way of practical orientation. For the source of the resourceful and sagacious constitutions of the Norbertines we must look to the man whom the founder left in charge when he

---

of Metz and the Regula Canonicorum in the Eighth Century (New York: Cambridge University Press, 2004).

9   For these texts, see Jerome Bertram, *The Chrodegang Rules: The Rules for the Common Life of the Secular Clergy from the Eighth and Ninth Centuries* (Aldershot, Hants, England: Ashgate, 2005).

became an archbishop. It is with Bl. Hughes de Fosses (ca. 1093–1164) that one finds the elaboration of the new order.[10] It was he who molded the loose Rule of Augustine into the Constitutions of Prémontré. The founders of the order acknowledged the rising desire for a life of holiness among the laity. Hughes established a strong contemplative foundation that would bring the life and liturgy of the monastery to bear upon the spiritual needs of the age. Even though their main reason for being was not preaching, the laity responded to the Norbertines' liturgical piety and to their ministry. In this Hughes was able to balance liturgy and evangelization. The conditions of the twelfth century demanded some sort of rapprochement between action and contemplation. The laity and secular clergy were reaching deeper into practices of penitence and purification, while the older orders were struggling to carry their lives of holiness into the street.

The Praemonstratensian constitutions provided an organizational framework for this realization. In the first place, Norbert had wanted to ensure regular life, in that all daughter-houses were to be full communities and each with independent abbatial authority, though all would be subject to visitation by the abbot-general at Prémontré. Yet even given that role of oversight, the abbot-general himself was to be assessed by the abbots of the three eldest daughter-houses. Norbert and Hughes retained the legislative general chapter pioneered by the Cistercians, and also made the abbot-general subject to its decisions. While the abbots of the order had lifetime appointments, they were still elected and required to consult senior members of the house. Hughes was paralleling political developments occurring in broader society, by pioneering a delicate balance of aristocratic and democratic elements. He provided

---

10 There is remarkably little work to be found on this key figure. See Hugues Lamy, *Vie du bienheureux Hugues de Fosses, premier abbé de Prémontré* (Charleroi: Terre Wallonne, 1925). Also, see the valuable work (though broader in scope) in François Petit, *La spiritualité des prémontrés au XIIe et XIIIe siècles* (Paris: J. Vrin, 1947).

strong governance while at the same time respecting the dignity of subordinates and the integrity of the house. With these developments, we move ever closer to the contemporary conception of a fully formed "religious order."

Foxes in the Vineyard

Yet not all movements of the 1100s worked themselves out into such thoughtful and enduring institutions. The Gregorian reform and the rise of the imitation of the Apostles unleashed massive spiritual energies into Christendom. People began to expect a renewed clergy, one that lived up to its vows and that was not corrupt. The laity desired more expansive and adapted forms of spirituality. While some entered monastic orders, others modelled their practices after established forms of religious life. Yet still others, such as the merchant-saint, Omobono of Cremona, wanted to live lives of charity and penance outside of religious life.[11] He was followed by many others, movements that would later coalesce in the foundations of the so-called third orders by the mendicants in the fourteenth century, but which also gave birth to hundreds of pious confraternities throughout Europe. Yet all that is to anticipate the story. No such mechanisms were to be envisioned in the mid-1100s. People, newly sensitive to presumed hypocrisy, began to follow the wandering preachers away from their established parishes. Many such preachers were unlettered and unlicensed. A few bandied about revolutionary principles. Indeed, we can trace three broad ideas that sometimes coalesced into serious problems for the Church. These were the problems that serious ecclesiastical administration was inevitably to confront.

11   For Omobono, see Daniele Piazzi, *Omobono di Cremona: Biografie dal XIII al XVI secolo* (Cremona, 1991); André Vauchez, *Omobono di Cremona (+1197)(+1197): laico e santo : profilo storico* (Cremona: Nuova editrice cremonese, 2001); and, ID., *S. Homebon de Crémone: "Père des Pauvres" et patron des tailleurs*, with collaboration by U. Longo, L. Albiero, and V. Souche, in *Subsidia Hagiographica* 96 (Brussels: 2018).

The first we have already touched upon. A general anti-monastic feeling was beginning to penetrate Christianity for a variety of reasons. Monks sought to "flee" the world and tended to gravitate toward rural wastes. They seemed to be running in literally the opposite direction as the medieval laity, who were now flocking to densely populated urban areas for work and chances at prosperity. As people began to consider new roads to perfection and became increasingly more literate, an examination of the New Testament did not turn up much that looked like a working monastery. Rather, what the pages of the Bible seemed to be promoting was a life of wandering preaching and evangelization. How could the monks, who vowed stability and shut themselves in for the remainder of their lives, be living out a scriptural conception of holiness? Christ and his Apostles were not monks, therefore perhaps a better path was one of charity and atonement for sin lived amongst the people, particularly those in dire situations in the new cities. In addition, the religious houses were seen as massive centers of concentrated wealth, which was easy enough to see in a foundation like Cluny. What was harder to see was the massive amount of productive capacity, particularly agricultural, for which they were responsible, not to mention in what ways these were the medieval engines of charity and social welfare. Yet it was the immoveable wealth that attracted attention. While many monasteries by this time were observant and not corrupt, they were nevertheless comfortable, and an entire tradition of Goliardic poetry and satire began to surround the monks, who came to be chastised as proprietors, gourmands, and all-around useless fellows. In many cases these jests were unjust, but regardless indicated sincere popular sentiment.[12]

12 This pointed to a larger issue of anti-clericalism, which was common in Catholic countries, and was easily transferred to the Friars, the Jesuits, and others in later history. It was not intrinsically tied to religious dissent, but rather a common reaction in places deeply attached to premodern Christianity. See the essays in: Peter A. Dykema and Heiko Augustinus Oberman, *Anticlericalism in Late Medieval and Early Modern Europe* (Leiden: Brill, 1993).

This led to the second tendency—namely, an exaltation of the concept of poverty. Of course, the monks individually practiced (or were supposed to practice) poverty, yet they were at the same time members of exceptionally wealthy corporations, ones that assured them security, a home, and food in perpetuity. Looking at the pages of the New Testament, it was clear that the early Apostles worked for their food and lived off of the daily donations of the faithful. Such meditations had not affected Christianity for a long time. When the economy of Europe was local and subsistence-level, there was little opportunity to marshal wealth, and even among those who did have it, there were few ways to deploy capital in any easy way to generate profit. All this began to change as the merchant-cities initiated trade and as the agricultural and commercial revolutions took off. Now investment and profit were not only possible, they were almost guaranteed. A virtuous economic cycle was generated by the 1100s that I would say has not even today exhausted itself.

A newly wealthy Europe began to read familiar gospel passages in a new light. As Anthony of the Desert had been struck to the quick by the story of the rich young man, so too did the spiritually serious members of the incipient middle class begin to fear for the states of their souls. Avarice was a terrible sin, and wealth might endanger salvation. In response to the 'camel and the needle,' had not the Apostles themselves asked, "Who then can be saved?" (Mt 19:25) Meditations on individual sanctity had a way of transferring themselves to a broader ecclesiastical critique. If Christ and his first followers were poor, and if the infant Church in Jerusalem was poor and persecuted, from whence came these mighty ecclesial endowments and estates? Eminent Churchmen held vast amounts of wealth. It was difficult to reconcile this with the picture of the Church in Acts. In another case of historical telescoping, people began to assign the cause of the complex assembling of the Church's wealth to one singular event—namely, the Donation of Constantine.

Though the document itself was spurious, this was not

definitively established until the fifteenth century.[13] It purported to be a grant from Constantine the Great to Pope Sylvester of the entirety of the Western (Latin-speaking) empire. As such it was used to expand papal pretensions, particularly in Church-state debates. It had a kernel of historical truth, in that Constantine did hand over to the pope the Lateran Basilica and certain other Christian sites in the city of Rome. Nonetheless, to many in the Middle Ages this came to be gradually perceived as the fatal moment of corruption for the Church. Even the orthodox Dante sees in this Donation a great fall from purity.[14] Operating side by side with this presumption of corruption was jealousy, not only from the middle classes but also from the rising political authorities of the time, who sought to circumscribe the power of the Church. When preachers who were living a life of poverty came to town, the local clergy compared badly. This was not only due to their lack of skill in making sermons (for they had many other responsibilities, not to mention a dearth of any formal training) but also because they held property. Their laity began to follow these itinerant preachers of penitence, men who were not beholden to the "original sin" of Constantine.

When one combined the search for poverty with a strong desire for purification, the final piece of the puzzle fell into place. The Gregorians had reformed so thoroughly that they impressed their ideals deeply upon a new generation of laity. These reformers had occasionally used excessively harsh language in their righteous attempts to end simony and clerical concubinage. Some of their phrasing might suggest that someone who had obtained ordination through purchase, or who had violated their vow of celibacy could, by those very facts, utterly lose the power of sacramental

13 For a history of the document and its reception, see: Johannes Fried and Wolfram Brandes, *Donation of Constantine and Constitutum Constantini: The Misinterpretation of a Fiction and Its Original Meaning* (Berlin: Walter de Gruyter, 2007).

14 Dante, *Inferno* 19, 115–117.

performance. While men such as St. Peter Damian and St. Gregory VII were too smart to listen to this chain of reasoning to its end, it remains that some of their sentiments could be read in that way, and indeed they were by many. This led to the rise of a novel form of Donatism, the ancient African heresy that asserted only the "pure" could confect the sacraments. If a priest or bishop had compromised the faith, they had—by that fact—lost their priesthood (or indeed never had it in the first place). Augustine had met and defeated their theology in the early 400s when he declared that it was Christ who worked the sacraments through the ministry of men, even unworthy ones. Yet it is an error that is easy to make, and a tempting one in any age of Church history when one is confronted by leaders who traduce their vows. It was no different in the medieval world. The comfortable, perhaps corrupt, clergy could not possibly be the representatives of Christ. The propertied monks and the lax canons were in no way living the life demanded by the New Testament. Therefore, one ought to reject them and embrace those who truly practiced poverty and who lived the evangelical life of wandering preaching. When all three of these ideas merged together, many who held them began to cross the line into doctrinal heresy.

Emblematic of such a combination of issues was the career of the merchant Peter Waldo of Lyons.[15] Fired by the same motivations that had prompted many laity to seek a deeper life of holiness, Peter turned to the New Testament and began living a life of poverty and wandering preaching. He gathered a body of followers and together they travelled to Rome in 1179 to present themselves at the Third Lateran Council. There, in the presence of the pope, they were mocked for their lack of theological sophistication. A

15   For Waldensianism as a movement, see Grado Merlo, *Valdesi e valdismi medievali: itinerari e proposte di ricerca*, (Turin: Claudiana, 1984); Gabriel Audisio, *The Waldensian Dissent: Persecution and Survival, ca. 1170–1570* (Cambridge: Cambridge University Press, 1999); and Euan Cameron, *Waldenses: Rejections of Holy Church in Medieval Europe* (Oxford: Blackwell, 2000).

Welsh courtier-priest, Walter Map, cross examined them and laid bare their ignorance. As a result they were denied the canonical mission to preach. Embarrassed by this rough treatment at the Council, Peter Waldo began on a path that led to a break with the Church, founding the Waldensian movement. Had they simply preached repentance—which indeed was the duty of any good Christian—they would not have been barred. They found it difficult to separate penance from doctrine, and as such were denied permission. Since Waldo considered that the life he had chosen was incumbent upon him as an evangelical command, he disobeyed the Church. This resulted in his excommunication. In one sense the Church was very much in the right. It could not have men ignorant of theology preaching in public and leading Christians astray. Still, the high-handed and sarcastic manner with which they were treated left much to be desired. These men were merely professing what had become common spiritual motivations of the age. Waldo initially had no desire to break from the Church, but only to preach the gospel. It was the inability to think "outside the box" that prevented Waldensians from becoming integrated into Church life in a healthy way. As it was, they became increasingly heretical, forming ideas about the institutional Church and the life of Christians that would anticipate the Reformation by 300 years.

This was a situation with which the Church was profoundly ill-equipped to deal. The West had been largely free of theological heterodoxy for nearly 800 years. Indeed, with the salient exception of Pelagius around the year 400, most heresies were products of the theologically sophisticated culture of the Greek East. When doctrinal error at last began to appear, the Church had little idea of how to respond. On occasion the laity took matters into their own hands and lynched suspected heretics. The civil authorities, who considered heresy to be akin to treason, also took steps to suppress them. Clearly the Church had to do something, but lacked any firm institutional idea of how to go about it. This would require collaboration and an institutional breakthrough of the first order. Fortunately for the Church, many pieces began falling into place around the year 1200.

The Hounds of Heaven

In 1198 the 37-year-old Lothario Conti was elected as Pope Innocent III (d. 1216).[16] He was one of the most brilliant and foresightful popes in the history of the Church, laying the groundwork for developments which have continued to the present day. He was an administrator of genius and a leader of renown. It fell to him to leverage the astonishing achievements of the papacy over the previous 150 years. Indeed, it is probable that no pope exercised more power over the broader society in the entire history of Christianity. Fortunately, on the balance, Innocent used that authority for good. He shared his predecessors' wish for the continued purification of Christianity. Now that the papacy had been thoroughly reformed and possessed of the most advanced court in Europe, Innocent set about using his influence to reform dioceses, orders, and the general life of the Christian people. He was keenly aware of the new movements for sanctification that were bubbling up in the new cities of Europe. He was also deeply worried that heretics might channel those energies in the wrong direction to the detriment of both Church and eternal souls. Innocent III desired a reformation of the Christian world, an improvement in morals, and the worthy reception of the sacraments—and all ordained to the end of salvation. What was needed was a revolution of holiness to accompany a streamlining of law, a centralization of effort, and a coordination of approach. If such could be accomplished, so the pope thought, no force on earth could stop it. Innocent knew he could handle the last three, but he recognized that he needed help on the critical first aspect. Without such a conversion to sanctity, all legal and administrative

---

16 For Innocent, see the essays in John Clare Moore and Brenda Bolton, *Pope Innocent III and His World* (Aldershot: Ashgate, 1999; repr. 2010); see also, *Innocent III: Vicar of Christ or Lord of the World?* James M. Powell, ed., 2nd expanded edition (Washington, DC: Catholic University of America Press, 1994); and Jane Sayers, *Innocent III: Leader of Europe 1198–1216* (London: Longman, 1994).

machinations would be for naught. Yet without adept governmental structures, spiritual energy itself could be wasted and channeled in the wrong directions. He did what he could, deploying saints as spiritual vanguards against heresy. He worked actively to reconcile heretical groups who were amenable to reaffiliation. He also made moral purification of the clergy a priority of his pontificate, but Innocent could not do it all himself. What he needed was an elite cadre of men dedicated to both the doctrine of the Church and to the observation of the precepts and counsels of the gospel. What he needed was men who shared his vision, whom he could deploy to the corners of Christendom and beyond.

Innocent had sought such men in different places. He reconciled Waldensian heretics who wished to reconvert, attempting to undo the institutional failure of Lateran III. Yet these were, and remained, small groups of men who were permitted to preach under the aegis of the Church. He encountered Francis and his small band of followers in 1208, encouraging them but going little further. Indeed, he may have saved the entire Franciscan movement by requesting that Francis be ordained a deacon, which meant that he thereby possessed a canonical mission to preach. It allied the burgeoning movement with the Church, putting it on the road to being the primarily clerical institute it became by its founder's death in 1226.[17] Innocent also tried to institute preachers, particularly against the aggressive heretics of Languedoc and Provence. Yet, although good men, these legates were hampered by their imperious demands for obedience and their wealth, obvious from their garments, attendants, and baggage trains. Such men did not compare well with the poor heretics who lived among the people of the region. None of these precisely embodied what Innocent was looking for when seeking to meet the challenges of the age. He would have to look elsewhere to find a movement that could embody the whole of his ambitious vision.

---

17   For an excellent account of Francis, see Augustine Thompson, *Francis of Assisi: A New Biography* (Ithaca, NY: Cornell University Press, 2012).

The pope had also been active in reforming the episcopate, promoting good men and dismissing those who were irredeemably corrupt. One of the former was the bishop of the modest Diocese of Osma in north-central Spain. His name was Diego de Acebo. He had been busying himself with reforming his diocese, primarily by inviting in the Cistercian order and reorganizing his own church so as to elevate the spiritual tone of his diocese. Being a learned man, himself a product of the rising scholastic tide, he ensured his clergy were well-educated. Yet it was one of his key insights that education alone could not effect a spiritual change of heart—it must be allied with virtue.[18] To that end, he reformed his own cathedral chapter according to the "Rule" of Augustine making his diocese an exemplar of what was possible in the broader reform of the Church. His efforts engendered admiration and trust from both Church and civil leaders. Diego was selected in 1203 for a delicate diplomatic mission to Denmark to arrange a marriage for the King of Castile's son. Accompanying him on his journey was the subprior of his reformed chapter, a man by the name of Dominic de Caleruega.[19] While on their journey they encountered heresy for the first time (it was nearly nonexistent in Castile). These confrontations reoriented the pair significantly by redirecting their

18 Jordan of Saxony, *Libellus de Principiis Ordinis Praedicatorum*, ed. H. C. Scheeben. *Monumenta Ordinis Praedicatorum Historica* 16 (Rome: Institutum Historicum Ordinis Fratrum Praedicatorum, 1935), 4.

19 Recent research has discredited the late medieval identification of Dominic with the noble Guzman family. It was common practice for noble families to "appropriate" saints during this time, mostly for familial "gilding the lily." On the lack of an historical basis for the identification of Dominic with the Guzman family, see Anthony Lappin, "On the Family and Early Years of Saint Dominic of Caleruega," in *Archivum Fratrum Praedicatorum* 67 (1997): 5–26. For Dominic, see M.-H. Vicaire, *Saint Dominic and His Times*, trans. Kathleen Pond (New York: McGraw-Hill, 1964), supplemented by the comments in the series by Simon Tugwell, "Notes on the Life of St. Dominic," in *Archivum Fratrum Praedicatorum*, 65–68.

reforming energies from inside the institution and more actively steering them toward the salvation of souls. Diego began to conceive of the idea of becoming a missionary to the pagans, yet when he applied to the pope for permission to lay down his responsibilities, he was rebuked. The pope needed men like him exactly where he was, in the dioceses of Christendom.

It is here that one of Diego's faults becomes plain. He had a sort of attention-deficit problem that was abetted by wanderlust. Having reformed his diocese, he was ready for new tasks, and could be easily distracted by new ideas. The pope had told him to return to his diocese but had not exactly specified *how*. Taking advantage of the ambiguity, Diego began a long tour through southern France, lodging at Cîteaux for a time and taking the Cistercian habit. He then began slowly to make his way back through Provence, ever with the untiring Dominic at his side. In mid-1206, he met the disheartened papal preachers who had been sent out by Innocent III in an attempt to thwart the growth of heresy. They told him of their marked lack of success and their desire to resign. This gave Diego an idea (not to mention yet another excuse for not returning home). He asked about the beliefs of the heretics (in this case mostly the quite unorthodox Cathars, rather than the somewhat more mainstream Waldensians). He found that the legates had not made any effort to understand their opponents' arguments, considering that they were merely there to recall people to the observance of baptismal obedience. This was a significant breakthrough. By studying the beliefs of their adversaries, Diego and Dominic became skilled at debate.[20] It forced the heretics to confront them directly and on theological terms, rather than dismiss the preachers as corrupt and worldly puppets. Not only this, the legates' speeches were known to be supremely boring. Charged with evangelical fervor Diego and Dominic introduced powerful, heartfelt sermonizing. This engaged the laity and at the same time

---

20 This betrays evidence of the effects of scholasticism, wherein the opponents' positions are considered first, prior to making a counterargument.

played the heretics' own game—the medium of delivery could in fact be as crucial as the message itself.

There was but one further step. Once when Diego went out preaching, things were going along quite well until his opponents challenged his wealth. As a bishop of the Church he had retainers, companions, and probably a security detail, all of whom had to be provisioned and whose belongings had to be carried. As a bishop, Diego wore a jeweled cross and ring, and probably dressed as befitting a modest nobleman. All of this was grist for the Cathars. They denounced him as a hypocrite, an argument that has persuasive power in any period (even if not logically valid). Exceptionally embarrassed by this setback, he made another of his sweeping decisions. He dismissed his whole retinue, put off his episcopal attire, and went as a wandering preacher, taking along only Dominic.[21] This of course shocked the ecclesiastical establishment of the time, including the pope and the legates. However, to their credit, they took the time to see that it was bringing results. After the legates adopted the same stratagem in 1207, they too began to make headway. Though Innocent was a bit scandalized to hear that one of his bishops had put on the clothing of a wandering mendicant, he later warmed to the idea, a testament to his foresight and flexibility.[22]

Diego's and Dominic's main interest was in reconciliation, and in reinserting penitents into the social fabric. As their success increased, however, so did animosity toward them. At times their converts would be the subjects of violence or ostracism. This was particularly acute in the case of the women of noble households

21   This is the account of the foundation of the order given by Stephen of Bourbon, ed., in A. Lecoy de la Marche, *Anecdotes historiques, légendes et apologues. Tirés du recueil inédit d'Étienne de Bourbon, dominicain du XIIIe siècle*, Société de l'Histoire de France 185 (Paris, 1877), 83; see also, Tugwell, *Early Dominicans*, 89, for a defense of this version of the story. I agree with his conclusions.

22   The name mendicant comes from "mendicare," or "to beg." See the essays in *The Origin, Development, and Refinement of Medieval Religious Mendicancies*, ed. Donald S. Prudlo (Leiden: Brill, 2011).

who, after first accepting the faith of the Cathars, returned to the Church but were then cast off by their families. The two intrepid evangelists quickly came up with a solution. They would create a female monastery at Prouille for converted heretics, over which Dominic would supervise and be the chaplain.[23] This would be supported out of Diego's own diocesan revenues, thus providing not only a safe place for female converts, but actually rendering reconversion a much more palatable option. Having accomplished so much, Diego finally gave into the pressure to return to his see, probably thinking that he would make a quick visit so as to acquire funds for making Prouille a base for preaching missions, perhaps even instituting some kind of religious congregation there. Alas it was not to be, for Diego fell ill and died by the end of 1207.[24] Dominic was left almost completely on his own. He found himself deprived of episcopal revenue (except that which was entailed on Prouille), in charge of the new female convent, and in an explosive atmosphere of confrontation that was quickly to degenerate into open violence and war.

While the loss of such a friend and mentor must have been devastating for Dominic, and his position exposed and lonely, it is possible that the absence of Diego's rather scattershot thinking enabled the young canon to come into his own. He had several advantages despite his situation. In the first place he had received a solid religious and intellectual formation in Spain, taking part in reforming efforts and having been trained in the solid observance of the "Rule" of Augustine in an urban setting. He had Diego's brilliant, but rather rambling, ideas on the possibilities of a new *Predicatio* or "preaching mission." Further, Dominic had seen results and had

23 Simon Tugwell, O.P., "For Whom was Prouille Founded?" in *Archivum Fratrum Praedicatorum* 74 (2004), 5–125.
24 The Preachers tried, from the very beginning, to minimize Diego's importance so as to play up Dominic's role. This is most clearly on display in the General Chapter of Valenciennes in 1259, when it orders versions of the life of the saint to strike through Diego's name in certain places (such as the founding of Prouille) and to insert Dominic's name instead. See *Acta*, 1. 98.

made converts, animated as he was by evangelical zeal. More than all that, however, he had a penetrating mind with the laser-like ability to focus and solve problems. His possessed a single-minded dedication to zeal for the salvation of souls, and he spent the rest of his life laying the groundwork necessary for the successful achievement of such a mission. Nothing would prevent the realization of such ambitions, regardless of heretical obstinance, institutional intransigence, or even the pusillanimity of some of his followers. Freed from the shadow of the commanding figure of Diego, Dominic emerged fully matured.

Yet growth came slowly. Prouille was not granted full enclosure and the rights to its endowments until 1212, and as late as 1214 Dominic likely had fewer than ten male followers. The decade after Diego's death was a tenuous time as Dominic carefully negotiated his way through the Albigensian Crusade. Once that was largely concluded after the victory of Dominic's close friend Simon de Montfort at the Battle of Muret in 1213, the way was open for a regularization of religious life in southern France. Someone needed to pick up the pieces left after the bitter conflict and continue the work of evangelization and reconciliation. Dominic needed a new base for his preaching (Prouille was too remote). He turned to Fulk, Bishop of Toulouse, who was overjoyed to have such orthodox men seek his protection. He showered them with material resources and gave them a house in his city and care of the Church of St. Romain. Dominic was treading a path he knew very well, the life of a canon of fixed residence. It is possible that, had the Dominicans stayed locally in Toulouse, they would have become the Canons Regular of St. Romain. The founder was serious about having a clerical institute, with all the obligations to the divine office that implied. Such a bedrock would provide a stable ground to the brethren as they went about their duties. Fulk cleverly delegated his authority as a preacher to the whole community rather than licensing individuals, a practice that cleared away any administrative obstacles to their preaching. In order to cement this new foundation, Fulk had Dominic accompany him to the Fourth Lateran Council in 1215, under the leadership of the prescient Innocent

III.[25] Significant efforts were being made to avoid the mistakes committed at the previous general Council in regard to movements of apostolic preaching. There Dominic and Fulk presented their case. The far-seeing pope responded favorably to their petitions, with the stipulation that they adopt an extant Rule, rather than authoring a wholly new one. This might have meant that the nascent group could have been forcibly assimilated to the Norbertines or Cistercians, which would have cut off the evangelical freshness of Dominic's plan at birth. Yet there is no sign of reluctance or recalcitrance on Dominic's part. A cornerstone skill for good administrators is to "roll with the punches." Dominic did not mourn this as an arrow in the heart of his creativity, but rather embraced the decision as providential.

When he arrived back in Toulouse in 1216 he convened the first Chapter General, where the brethren would make a decision about the choice of Rule. Instead of taking the papal command as an institutional setback, he turned it into an opportunity when he and his brothers adopted the vague "Rule" of St. Augustine, more a series of counsels rather than regulations; it was a form Dominic himself was familiar with from his time in Osma. In his hands he could flexibly mold such a Rule into a religious constitution that preserved the decision of the hierarchical Church, while at the same time adapting his little band to meet every demand of his new evangelical project. It was an administrative move of brilliance, harnessing the existing tradition to fulfill a new need, and adapting the Christian heritage without compromising it. The adoption of the Rule meant that the brothers were now fully within the institution of the Church. As clerics their right to preach was sanctioned by long practice. They maintained the celebration of the canonical hours, but left room for the realization of their real purpose—namely, the preaching of the gospel for the salvation of souls. Their canonical life meant they could be centered in the cities, the location of both the burgeoning universities and the most pressing pastoral needs.

25   Jordan, *Libellus*, 39.

Yet this adoption of the Rule was but a springboard for Dominic, who began a campaign on two distinct fronts to assure the survival of his and Diego's vision for the future of "the preaching." On one hand, Dominic began an offensive to secure as much official sanction as he could. He repeatedly turned to the Roman Curia and the papacy for a series of decisions that would secure his nascent foundation. He had no reticence in using the official channels sanctioned by canon law in the pursuit of the protection of his new order. On the other hand, Dominic labored internally to amplify the Augustinian Rule into a constitutional law for his own order, one that would take the basics of the canonical life while generating something truly new and enduring. The canonical life then was a middle road, but not one that was any less rigorous. Dominic and his brothers chose to follow the strictest observance of the Rule of St. Augustine then in use—namely, the Customary of the Premonstratensians.[26] In many respects the primitive constitution of the order is taken verbatim from that of Prémontré.[27] Again, Dominic is not loath to incorporate the genius of previous generations in the maturation of his plan, for the Norbertines themselves had solved many of the problems Dominic was about to contend with. They embraced the life of urban Europe, ministering in public rather than being bound to monastic retreat. They had developed a flexible and centralized mechanism of government, and they had brought a renewed devotion to the penitential side of the canonical life. The developed Customary of Prémontré was then an ideal prototype for Dominic's constitutions. Yet even in the midst of this critical foundation, one witnesses the astonishing creative breakthrough that came to characterize the order: Dominic's administrative genius.

---

26 For this see: G. R. Galbraith, *The Constitution of the Dominican Order: 1216–1360* (New York: Longman's, 1925).

27 See A. H. Thomas, "Les constitutions dominicains témoins des *Instituta* de Prémontré au début du XIIIe siècle," in *Analecta Praemonstratensia* 42 (1966): 28–47.

Constitutional Discretion

Dominic had one end in view—the salvation of souls. From that perspective he set forth to create a system that would bend all its energies toward achieving that goal. Having clarified the end, he began to look at his context and consider the most efficacious manner of going about achieving his intention. The chief issues of the time were a broad-based ignorance of solid Catholic doctrine, the presence of heresy that threatened to sunder the Christian community, and the inability of the majority of the clergy to meet these challenges. To effectively counter all three meant a commitment to evangelization, particularly in the form of preaching. This had been Dominic's experience throughout Languedoc and Provence. If he could assemble an elite body of preachers, these would offset all three problems. They would counteract the shortcomings of local clergy, resist the pretensions of the heretics, and instruct the faithful all at the same time. This made preaching Dominic's *proximate* end (related to the *ultimate* end of salvation).[28]

Having determined this, he began to ask how most effectually to recruit, train, and deploy his vision of a corps of elite preachers. An effective preacher needed three things: a license, holiness, and education. These would be the three means to reach his proximate end. He also had to distinguish between these three in theory and in practice. For instance, he had dealt with the issue of licensing preachers at least in theory by making his group a band of clerics. He and his brethren would have to negotiate that in practice as the years went on, obtaining licenses from bishops and popes as they made their way throughout Europe. Further, Dominic was well

28 Aptly summed up by Master General Humbert of Romans, "studium est ordinatum ad praedicationem, praedicationem ad animarum salutem, quae est ultimus finis." "Study is ordered to preaching, which in turn is ordered to the salvation of souls—the ultimate end." Humbert of Romans, "Expositio super constitutiones" in *Opera de Vita Regulari*, ed. J.J. Berthier, 2 vols. (Rome, 1888), vol. 1, 28.

trained in the schools of holiness, drinking deeply of the tradition of spiritual formation in the religious life, particularly from the *Conferences* of John Cassian, which he habitually carried. However, it was a different matter when such theories were applied within the cloister, as this setting opened up a number of practical issues that had occupied previous reformers. Most open-ended was the issue of education. He needed to create a flexible system, which ensured that his preachers would be equipped not only to communicate orthodox teaching but also to answer heretical counterarguments. For this reason they needed advanced academic training, something only made possible by the scholastic revolution and the rise of universities throughout Europe. It was toward this that he bent all his efforts. Nothing would get in the way of the kind of scholastic formation that was necessary for effective preaching, and therefore, the salvation of souls.

With all this in mind Dominic set himself to work, single-minded and self-effacing in his effort to achieve the lofty ends of his project. Up to this point much of what he had done had been derivative of others, yet what it demonstrates is how deep in the tradition he was. He wanted to retain the best of what had come before, so long as it promoted and advanced his vision. He demonstrated this in his creative adaptations of the Norbertine constitutions and the Augustinian Rule. For instance, he strengthened the strictures on fasting from the Rule and modified many Praemonstratensian provisions. He retained their preference for urban ministry, a fact that would embed his friars in the very hearts of medieval cities. He also preserved their ideas of centralized and flexible governance as well as their recommitment to penance within the canonical life. Dominic was insistent that his followers retain traditional monastic practices; they were to celebrate the Divine Office when present in the convent and to follow the traditional order of meals. This was enacted for two fundamental reasons. First, the cloister would be the school of holiness needed to inculcate the virtue necessary for a good preacher. Further, the life of community and the trials encountered within it would serve as an effective check on academic pride, and the possibility of a virtuosic individualism detrimental to both the regular life and to the spiritual good of the order. He even expanded the rules for silence beyond the prescriptions of Prémontré. Silence would feed both the life of virtue and be an invaluable aid to study, to which the whole of the order's effort was aimed.

It was this devotion to study that characterizes many of Dominic's breaks from previous legislation. Even though the brethren were bound to the Divine Office in common, they were to recite it *breviter et succinte* so as to return to study and preaching as expeditiously as possible.[29] Further, he definitively abolished the practice of manual labor, an astonishing alteration of something that had been a bedrock component of all western monasticism for nearly 1000 years. While some of the older orders had been deemphasizing such work or delegating it to lay brothers, it was Dominic who simply did away with it. Indeed, not even the Franciscans went this far, and Francis' original vision was that his brothers would live by the work of their hands. Dominic's clerical followers were completely liberated from this stricture. Furthermore, he eliminated the Benedictine emphasis on *Lectio Divina*, which tended toward private sanctification only. Rather, the labor of the Order of Preachers would be to study.[30] The spiritual breakthrough here is that it fulfilled two functions—such labor in study would help to lead to personal sanctification (a revolution in the idea of 'dignity of work') and would at the same time benefit souls. In order to free the friars for loftier tasks, Dominic retained the institution of lay brothers and allowed the reception of lay penitents. These would undertake all of the manual labor and oversee whatever material concerns might come up, freeing the clerical brethren up for study. Indeed,

---

29 One could loosely translate this as "make it short and sweet."
30 This paralleled interesting developments in the lay world, as the commercial revolution gave new meaning to what would become known as "white collar" labor, lawyers, teachers, accountants, etc. Such new professions that did not seem to 'make' anything led to problems fitting them into traditional notions of work. The Dominican thinkers would be at the forefront of justifying such new forms of labor in the coming centuries.

in his vision each house was itself to be an educational center, emphasized by the fact that it not only had a religious superior (the prior) but was also required to have a theological master who gave regular classes (the "Lector").

This was illustrated particularly in Dominic setting his order up on an axis that depended upon Bologna and Paris, the two key academic centers in the medieval world.[31] He was vividly aware of the tradition, and took many cues from the founders of preceding orders. He retained the innovations of unified governance under a single leader from the Cluniac monks, the supervision of that leader by annual general chapters from the Cistercians, and the commitment to the divine office and the common life as modeled by the Premonstratensians. Dominic wisely retained these deep roots in the monastic and canonical traditions and grafted upon them some truly revolutionary constitutional developments. He recognized that each order had its own particular charism, and so he did not hesitate to reject older models of the religious life that hindered his particular ends of preaching and evangelization.

Dominic's constitutional innovations were exceptionally significant in the history of religious administration. Most astonishing was the latitude of dispensational authority in the constitutions. Nearly everything that is not part of divine law can be dispensed with by superiors. Dominic turns the notion of 'Rule' on its head. The Rule was not the end, but rather the means to the ends of preaching and salvation. As such, when anything might be seen to impede the achievement of such ends, superiors could dispense their subjects from them. Dominic emphasizes the living authority of the superior, bound certainly within reason and custom, to meet the challenges of unforeseen situations. It was not an arbitrary power, rather this had to be directed to the purposes of the order. Some of

31 This demonstrates Dominic's willingness to abandon everything in pursuit of the ends of his order. He could have retained a headquarters in the city of Toulouse, with which he was so familiar, or even in Spain. Neither did he focus on Rome or on residence with the peripatetic curia, rather aimed directly at the scholastic hearts of Christendom.

the things that a friar could be excused from may seem shocking—
for example, common meals, the chapter of faults, or even attendance at the community Mass or the Divine Office.[32] In 1236 this
power was elaborated by a yet more surprising injunction: the Rule
of the Dominicans did not bind its subjects under pain of sin, but
only that of prescribed penance.[33] In former times, disobedience to
a religious Rule involved personal sin on the part of the subject. In
matters not involving the moral order—that is, in the rules imposed
by the Dominican constitutions—violation did not mean sin,
though a friar was still bound to do the penances prescribed by the
law and the will of the superior. This was a freedom not enjoyed
by the older orders and enabled the brethren to go about their business with a clearer conscience, yet at the same time held them
bound to personal obedience.

This dovetailed with Dominic's insistence that the religious
make his profession not to a Rule but rather to a prelate. The
novice would take his vows to obey the person of Dominic and his
successors. Benedictines professed their obedience to a Rule,
whereas the canons professed to a superior, yet remained bound to
service in particular churches. The preachers omitted all of that,
and in so doing liberated themselves from the constraints of the
canonical life, thus freeing themselves for deployment wherever the
religious superior directed them. There was no more vow of stability, or affiliation, to a particular house or shrine. The preacher
was to be a free agent, able to respond to the needs of the apostolate with dispatch. Dominic himself modeled this and became one
of the most well-travelled men in medieval Europe. He used this
travel to meet and maintain contact with individuals who could
further his project.

32   For an examination of what was possible when such exemptions
     were prudentially used, see the life of Thomas Aquinas, who was
     excused from nearly the whole concourse of Dominican community
     life and governance, so that he could focus on his academic
     endeavors.
33   While this was not enshrined until the chapter of 1236, it is clear
     that Dominic established it in practice by 1220.

More than most, Dominic knew how to "play the game." He recognized that previous movements had failed because of a lack of official sanction. He was a living presence at the curia, constantly making sure his order was not forgotten, and cultivating friendships among the resident bishops and cardinals. Dominic is a vibrant example of "networking." He knew the mechanisms of the Roman Church inside and out, and made himself and his order indispensable to the papacy and the Church at large. As a result, a symbiotic relationship grew between popes and the preachers. Dominic acquired privilege after privilege for the young order that eliminated interference from local authorities, freeing them to set down foundations throughout Europe and beyond. In turn the papacy found itself with a young, committed, and brilliant cadre of young men who could extend papal policy more widely than it had ever been. Bull after bull issued from the curia, guaranteeing the preachers papal protection and extending privileges.

Dominic knew that his young order would encounter resistance and difficulties and, to his credit, anticipated these and acquired the needed documents to speed their acceptance in the broader Church. It seems that no fewer than seventy papal documents were issued by the curia during Dominic's lifetime alone, the vast majority of which he solicited personally.[34] He possessed precisely that balance of prudence and innocence that was called for by the gospel (Mt 10:16). In his turn, Dominic reminded the institutional Church that it was there to be of benefit to such evangelical undertakings as his own, and he and the Franciscans gave renewed purpose to the governors of the Church of God. His followers would continue this practice, maintaining a steady presence with the Roman

---

34 See Patrick Zutshi, "Letters of Pope Honorius III Concerning the Order of Preachers," in *Pope, Church, and City: Essays in Honour of Brenda M. Bolton,* eds. Frances Andrews, Christoph Egger, and Constance M. Rousseau (Leiden: Brill, 2004), 269–286. For the official documents issued during his life, see *Monumenta diplomatica S. Dominici,* ed. Vladimir Koudelka (Rome: Apud Institutum Historicum Fratrum Praedicatorum, 1966).

Curia.[35] The friars were so popular with Pope Gregory IX (r. 1227–1241) that he coined a new verb. He told then Master General John the German to write down whatever the Dominicans wished, using the new phrase *Ego bullabo*, "I shall 'bull' it (command it in writing)."[36]

One might call this a devotion to embodied persons embedded in institutions. Both were considered necessary for the achievement of his dream. His order would be based on no individual heroic achievement, like Francis, nor a dry canonical exercise, but rather upon an incarnational reality, engrafted upon the true vine of Christ. In order to protect and value persons, he created flexible institutions wherein they might find home and a purpose. His achievement in the Dominican constitutions stands to this day as a model of institutional perfection.[37] This is no hyperbole. The fundamental rules of order he laid down have governed his

35   For the Friars and the curia, see my upcoming chapter, "A Most Fortuitous Alliance: The Roman Curia and the Mendicant Orders in the 13th century," in *The Brill Companion to the Roman Curia*, forthcoming 2024.

36   Thomas Cantimpré, *Miraculorum et exemplorum memorabilium sui temporis. Libri duo* (Douai, 1597), 573. Cfr. D. Mortier, *Histoire des maîtres généraux de l'Ordre des frères prêcheurs*, 8 vols. (Paris: A. Picara, 1902–1920) vol. 2, 330.

37   The first place to start in an analysis of the Dominican constitutions are: Heinrich Denifle, O.P. "Die Constitutionen des Predigerordens vom Jahre 1228," in *Archiv für Literatur und Kirchengeschichte* 1 (1885): 165–227, and id., "Die Constitutionen des Raymunds von Peñaforte 1238–1241," in *Archiv für Literatur und Kirchengeschichte* 5 (1889): 530–565. Also, indispensable is the corpus of work done by Gert Melvile, particularly his "The Dominican Constitutiones," in *A Companion to Medieval Rules and Customaries*, ed. Krijn Pansters, (Leiden: Brill, 2020), 253–281. See also, the useful early studies by Ernest Barker, *The Dominican Order and Convocation; A Study of the Growth of Representation in the Church During the Thirteenth Century* (Oxford: Clarendon Press, 1913); G. R. Galbraith, *The Constitution of the Dominican Order: 1216–1360* (New York: Longman's, 1925); H. C. Scheeben, *Die Konstitutionen des Predigerordens unter Jordan von Sachsen* (Köln –Rhein: Albertus Magnus Verlag, 1939). See also the commentary

brethren nearly unchanged for 800 years. Countless other religious institutes copied it as suited their own purposes. Even secular legislators noted its utility and flexibility. It was born at a unique nexus, for it combined the intrinsic hierarchy of the natural world and of the Church with the nascent democratic sentiments then being kindled by Christian humanism. The Dominican constitution is a masterpiece of balance in some of the most difficult questions of administration—namely, order vs. freedom, authority vs. autonomy, individual vs. community. By keeping a careful eye on the ultimate end of the whole order, the meaning of the various prescriptions comes more fully into focus.

In a further move away from monastic models, the Preachers vested supreme legislative powers in the hands of the chapters. They were to be the last word and court of final appeal for the whole order. At first these alternated between Bologna and Paris. One might speculate that Dominic wanted a clear balance between legal study—which was the specialty of the Italian university—and theology—which found its focus in the French capital. Yet particularly innovative was the manner in which these chapters were composed. They were to meet annually on a three-year cycle. For a law to be passed, it had to be ratified by three consecutive chapters. Two of the chapters would be so-called "elective" chapters, wherein "diffinitors" would be elected directly by popular vote in the provinces. The third year it would be made up of the priors of the provinces themselves. In this way the administrative wisdom of those who actually ran the order was buttressed by the those who represented the popular will of the order-at-large. It brilliantly harmonized the tension between more progressive members and conservative holders of office.[38] Each needed the other in order for laws

in R. F. Bennett, *The Early Dominicans: Studies in Thirteenth-Century Dominican History* (Cambridge: Cambridge University Press, 1937), 157–175; and, David Knowles, *From Pachomius to Ignatius: A Study in the Constitutional History of the Religious Orders* (Oxford: Clarendon Press, 1966), 49–58.

38   David Knowles, *The Religious Orders in England* (Cambridge: Cambridge University Press, 1948), vol. 3, 156.

to be passed. The purpose of this was certainly to balance aristocratic and democratic tendencies, with the idea that a combination of the two would best provide for the prudential direction of the order.[39]

Dominic rejected the frank autocracy of the older orders. In a society made up of educated clerics, there was bound to be wisdom to be tended and gleaned in many places. In this he fully embraced the fruitful medieval development of the Roman legal concept "what touches all must be approved by all."[40] In his order all authority was to be elective. Yet even then he recognized that in extreme cases immediate legislative action might be needed. Just as the Roman Republic had the relief valve of temporary dictatorship to meet emergency situations, so Dominic also instituted what was called a "Most General Chapter." This would be a blend of priors and representatives called upon in extraordinary times whose legislation would take effect immediately. It is a marvelous testament to the foresight of Dominic that only two of these were called in the entire Middle Ages (1228 and 1236). The General Chapter had plenary authority in terms of administrative and disciplinary issues. It could and did reassign members of the order at will. It also had the authority to elect the Master General, who theoretically had a life term, but in practice could tender his resignation, as happened many times.

The office of Master General was to be sort of a sitting executive officer for the whole order. He had disciplinary and administrative authority, but no legislative power, and like all the other members of the General Chapter had to submit his governance to them for judgement. He was to circulate among the provinces and priories, correcting abuses and being personally present to

39 One might speculate that this could lead to tension between the two types of chapter. Remarkably this never happened. Indeed, it is actually impossible to tell from the tenor of the legislation proposed at the thirteenth century chapters whether they were chapters of priors or chapters of diffinitors!

40 Paul A. Rahe, "The Constitution of Liberty within Christendom," in *The Intercollegiate Review* (Fall 1997): 30–36.

the members. He was the one who could meet emergency situations when they arose during the year, and who would act as a liaison with the Holy See (until the permanent position of proctor at the Curia was created in the 1250s). The Master was considered a brother like all the rest. Though he had a few concessions from the Rule for the sake of his position, he was still an equal member of the order. Should he resign his post he returned to the cloister, a friar like all the rest. As his office was elective, the representative wisdom of the order was operative in his selection, and at least in the 1200s there was such a chain of inspired leaders as to help make the Dominican order one of the fundamental forces for evangelical reform in Europe. All the provinces of the order, generally divided up by geography and language, were under his supervision. Each of these was headed by a provincial prior, also elected. This prior was in charge of annual provincial chapters, and was in turn subject to correction by them. Never before in the religious life had superiors been made so answerable to their subjects. It turned out to be a symbiotic system that extracted the best out of both friars and administrators. The old model of paternal authority was broken in favor of loyalty to a system of governance that sought the best for all, including the administrator. It was a new type of obedience. It was subjection to a Rule governed by living, embodied reason. Knowles sums this up well in contrasting the Dominican system to that of the later Jesuit order:

> Though the Dominican system was devised before the full discovery of Aristotle, it was nevertheless singularly well adapted to a mental climate in which the leading idea of Greek rationalism—a conviction of the power of the unaided human faculties to attain to a certain and adequate possession of metaphysical and moral truth— colored the whole *Weltanschauung* of the best minds, just as the system of St. Ignatius was well calculated to make an immediate appeal to a society which had lost its grasp of the body of revealed and metaphysical truth,

and of the sovereignty of rational law, and which exalted to such a degree the personal prerogative of the prince.[41]

There is one final personal contribution Dominic made to the mission of the order, and that is poverty.[42] As we have seen, apostolic, individual poverty had been in the devotional air during the previous century, and it was no new thing. Dominic had copied Diego's practice of preaching in evangelical indigence as a way to match the pretensions of the heretics with whom he disputed. It is also clear that he continued to live the communal poverty of his canonical state during the decade after Diego's death. By 1216 Dominic had made the resolution to accept no more properties or tithes saving those which they already had (and which were necessary for the maintenance of the contemplative house at Prouille). He astutely realized that the acceptance of donations, particularly of land or churches, carried with it attendant responsibilities that would compromise the necessary mobility of his friars. This was a first step toward the renunciation of all communal ownership. It does not appear that Dominic had more than a passing acquaintance with Francis of Assisi and his movement, and it is unlikely that he took the idea of absolute communal poverty from him. Like Dominic, Francis partook of the general religious tenor that elevated the practice of poverty, yet it seems that the Franciscan founder was more focused on humility, rather than the poverty emphasized by his later followers.[43] It seems over the course of 1216 to 1221 Dominic

41 Knowles, *Religious Orders*, vol. 3, 159.
42 The literature on the origins of Dominican poverty is extensive. For an excellent summary and conclusion see: Anthony Lappin, "From Osma to Bologna, from Canons to Friars, from the Preaching to the Preachers: The Dominican Path toward Mendicancy," in *The Origin, Development, and Refinement of Medieval Religious Mendicancies*, ed. Donald S. Prudlo (Leiden; Brill, 2011), 31–58. See also, Simon Tugwell, "Notes on the Life of St. Dominic," in *Archivum Fratrum Praedicatorum* 65 (1995): esp., 41–49.
43 For this, see Augustine Thompson, *Francis of Assisi: A New Biography* (Ithaca, N.Y.: Cornell University Press, 2012).

gradually began to solidify his attraction to the abandonment of property by the order. To decrease dependence upon donations, he obtained several more bulls that successively liberated the order from property ownership and renounced tithes that had been directed to it. By the end of that period the order had indeed embraced "mendicancy," and—like the Franciscans—had entirely embraced communal and individual poverty. Yet again one sees that the practice of poverty was for Dominic not an end in itself (as it became for certain Franciscan enthusiasts in the later part of the century).

Poverty too was related in a hierarchy of ends that were in place for the achievement of the purposes of the ministry. Poverty restrained distractions, allowed increased focus on study and preaching, and liberated the friars from being tied down to the often-specific stipulations of otherwise well-meaning bequests. While poverty was not mere expediency for Dominic, it came close. He expressed a fondness for it, but only a relative affection in that it brought him closer to the end in view.[44] As Thomas would explain years later, the key virtue for the religious life was obedience; it was not poverty, which dealt only with material things, or even chastity, which dealt with the body. Through obedience one offered to God that which was highest, one's own free will. Yet in line with the Dominican charism, this surrender of will was done only in and with the rule of right reason.[45] In Dominic's vision the salvation of souls put everything else in its place. All the practices of his brethren would be ordered to achieving that end. The system he created was like an efficient machine with interlocking and interchangeable parts, and it proved to be one of the most enduring administrative regimes in all of human history.

Putting the Preachers into Practice

Dominic did not live long after finishing his masterful constitutional achievement. He died quietly in his order's convent in Bologna in

44 He also specifically exempted books, which friars could freely own and use, another concession to the ultimate end.

45 Thomas Aquinas, *Summa Theologiae*, II-II, q. 186, a. 8.

1221. He had an astonishingly self-effacing personality, a man who almost blended back into the organization he created. It is sometimes difficult for the historian to attempt to access Dominic's personality, so thoroughly is he identified with his achievements. In the age of near instant sanctity, the founder's body lay humbly under the feet of his brethren for over a decade before a move was made to canonize him in 1234.[46] It seemed more than fitting that his personal humility subsumed his administrative genius in such a way that his sainthood was thus delayed. Dominic might be usefully invoked as the patron saint of administrators, or those who use the tools of law, reason, prudence, and charity to advance the goods inherent in their respective organizations, particularly those who toil to build up the Body of Christ in such roles. Yet beginnings are very delicate stages of a process. Absent the charisma of a founder, visions are in danger of wavering or diverting from their main ends. It is a credit to Dominic's patient labor and to the men that he recruited that his five successors as Master of the order were not only brilliant leaders in their own rights, but also came to be venerated as saints, a record of leadership without parallel in the history of the Church.[47] The true test of any administrative system is its responsiveness to new and unforeseen threats. Such a system must demonstrate itself flexible enough to adapt to new conditions, yet strong enough to maintain fidelity and devotion to the founding ideals. In the fifty years after Dominic's death, his followers would have to negotiate many such challenging situations.

The survival of new movements is often dependent upon the brilliance of unsung leaders whose patient labor solidifies the original beginnings and enables the group to meet new challenges and thrive in changing conditions. Blessed Humbert of Romans (ca.

---

46 Francis of Assisi was canonized two years after his death, and Anthony of Padua and Peter of Verona, O.P. were canonized within one year of their passing.

47 Bl. Jordan of Saxony (r. 1221–1237), St. Raymond of Peñafort (r. 1238–1240), Bl. John of Wildeshausen (r. 1241–1252), Bl. Humbert of Romans (r. 1254–1263), Bl. John of Vercelli (r. 1264–1283).

1190–1277) was one such man.[48] Practically unknown outside of his order today, this Dominican leader was one of the most significant churchmen of the thirteenth century. He negotiated existential threats that almost caused the demise of the mendicant orders. Insisting on regular observance, he checked tendencies to laxity within his own order, while protecting his friars from external threats. Under his tenure, he made sure to standardize the Dominican liturgy, as well as to complete its constitutional order, which still stands to this day. It was Humbert who carefully shepherded the young company of religious through its growing pains, while confronting an array of enemies. His shrewd, prudential administration ensured that the Dominicans would not only survive, but thrive as a keystone of the Christian life in the centuries to come.

Humbert was born at the end of the twelfth century in the town of Romans in southern France. Like many bright young men, his attention was drawn to the University of Paris, the intellectual epicenter of Christendom then flourishing during the scholastic renaissance. Here he studied both law and theology, an indicator of his mental aptitude. His main professor while there was Master Hugh of St. Cher. Both were mesmerized by the charismatic new

---

48   Humbert's works exist in a passable edition: Humbert of Romans, *Opera De vita regulari*, ed. J. J. Berthier, 2 vols. (Rome: Typis A. Befani, 1888). For Humbert himself, see Edward Tracy Brett, *Humbert of Romans: His Life and Views of Thirteenth-Century Society* (Toronto: Pontifical Institute of Mediaeval Studies, 1984); supplemented by the introductory material in, Simon Tugwell, O.P., *Humberti de Romanis Legendae sancti Dominici: necnon materia praedicabilis pro festis sancti Dominici et testimonia* (Rome: Institutum historicum Ordinis fratrum praedicatorum, 2008). A bit of Humbert's work can be found in translation in, id., *Early Dominicans: Selected Writings* (New York: Paulist Press, 1982), 141–149, 179–384. The only complete translation of one of Humbert's works is Humbert of Romans, *Treatise on Preaching*, ed. Walter M. Conlon (Westminster, MD: Newman Press, 1951), and even this itself is only a translation from an earlier French version. The translation of Humbert's constitutional material would be of immense benefit, and is a project that I have undertaken to complete.

Dominican Order then taking the city by storm. Humbert entered the order in 1224, followed soon after by his professor, who would later become the first Dominican Cardinal. Completing his studies, he became lector of the convent at Lyon (the equivalent of the professor of the house, who would give lectures to the brethren). Later he was elected as prior and under his rule Lyon became known as one of the premier convents of the order, producing during his tenure friars such as the prolific authors William of Peyraut and Stephen of Bourbon, not to mention Bl. Pierre Tarentaise, who would later be elected as Pope Innocent V (r. 1276). The Dominican Order was very effective in training leaders from within, giving its friars experience in various forms of government with differing levels of responsibility in the Preachers' hierarchy. Dominic had designed his order so that talent would rise to the top. Under the constitutions there was a sort of *cursus officiorum* whereby friars would be assigned increasing levels of responsibility according to their aptitude and capability.[49] The order was, by design, a school for the development of an administrative body advanced through merit.

Recognizing his leadership ability, the order elected Humbert as provincial prior for the critical Roman province in 1240 where he came into increasing contact with the papal curia. According to some historical accounts, his reputation was such that he was actually considered—though still only provincial prior—for election as Roman pontiff in 1243. When his old professor Hugh was appointed cardinal, Humbert succeeded him in his position as provincial prior for France. Therefore, while still a young man, Humbert had been given oversight of the two most integral provinces in the order. It almost seemed foreordained when, in 1254, his fellow Dominicans elected him as Master. He ruled with honor, integrity, and

49 I use *officiorum* in the sense of duties, rather than the traditional *cursus honorum* because it was not out of desire for honor that Dominican officials served. Such service was often tedious and without remuneration, hindering both study and preaching. It was truly meant to be a labor of charity.

dignity for nine years when, alleging ill health, he presented his resignation in 1263. Yet even then he was not finished. In his remaining years, he compiled many works that were the fruits of his long administrative career, providing commentaries on the "Augustinian Rule," the order's constitution, and the internal life of a Dominican convent. Not only did he continue in his service to the order after the cessation of his official responsibilities, but he was a trusted advisor to the curia, and helped to set the agenda for the Second Council of Lyon in 1274. He lived long enough to see the man he knew as a young friar ascend the throne of Peter in 1276, a stunning witness not only to the survival of the order Humbert had served so faithfully, but to its triumphant success in the medieval ecclesiastical world.[50]

It was a testament to Humbert's reputation that he was selected as Master of the Order in 1254, yet at the time he probably considered it to be an immense and undesirable burden. In that year the Dominicans were undergoing the most profound crisis in their 800-year history. Flushed with success, the first generation of Preachers had rapidly spread throughout the Christian world and had begun to undertake pastoral and academic work at the highest level. Initially welcomed as a breath of fresh evangelical air, they and their fellow mendicants, the Franciscans, enjoyed a honeymoon period during which prelates sought their assistance in ministering to the underserved and burgeoning cities of medieval Europe. By the 1240s strain had begun to manifest. Dominicans especially had cleverly leveraged papal predilection to steamroll local authorities and to establish convents wherever they went. People began to stream to the mendicants' churches to hear charismatic sermons filled with Christian fervor and deep learning. In particular, they sought the friars for confession and the deep spiritual engagement they found therein. Laity began to abandon their parishes, bringing their donations and bequests to the new movements. Such activities radically challenged the status quo of the secular clergy, leading to increasing opposition. Much as earlier monasticism had challenged

50   For this biographical material and sources, see Brett, 4–14.

the place of the secular clergy, so too did these mendicants threaten to overturn the diocesan and parochial system. A similar story was playing out in the universities, particularly Paris. Initially welcomed with open arms, the Dominicans especially had been making inroads that increased their influence and presence. Hundreds of students flocked to the friars and with them numerous professors, who maintained their teaching chairs, thus removing these positions from general circulation among the secular canons and clerks. In addition, the mendicant masters and students were often not very good "academic citizens," refusing to show solidarity with the secular masters in their struggles with the Bishop of Paris and other local interests, leading to resentment that began to bubble over in the late 1240s.[51] Even some of the laity had begun to resent the mendicants, whose growing footprints in the cities had begun to strain the resources of local charity.

This charged atmosphere was the background to Humbert's election as Master of the whole order.[52] It would be his responsibility to guide the society through the difficult and treacherous waters that threatened the mendicant movement. Throughout the controversies Humbert kept his eye on the common good of both his order and of the larger church. He demonstrated exceptional prudence in negotiating this crisis. Deeply learned and grounded in the principles of the order, he surveyed the field and began to consider his options, ever with an eye to the survival of the Dominican movement. Yet, as often happens, things got worse before

---

51   For the issues involving the friars at the university, see Donald Prudlo, *Thomas Aquinas: A Historical, Theological, and Environmental Portrait* (New York: Paulist Press, 2020), 107–150.

52   Unfortunately for the Dominicans, the previous master general, John the German, had died in late 1252, meaning that, according to the constitutions, there would be no General Chapter in 1253. A successor could not be elected until the next general chapter of 1254 (to avoid a precipitous election). At the height of the troubles, the order was leaderless. If one had to point to a constitutional weakness, it might be this. Yet the order did not alter legislation because of it.

they could get better, stretching Humbert's leadership qualities to their limit. A few months after his election, the order lost their last and most powerful ally. The aging Innocent IV (r. 1243–1254)—formerly a partisan of the mendicant orders—issued a devastating decree that deprived the new movements of nearly all of their privileges. All pastoral responsibility was stripped from them, and they were subjected immediately to their enemies, the prelates who had so opposed their rights to hear confessions, preach without a license, or to obtain bequests and donations for the faithful. Combined with an all-out assault by the secular masters at the University of Paris, this document could have been the death knell of the mendicant project.[53] In such a situation, appeal to heaven has always been the most significant recourse. Humbert ordered his friars to pray litanies every day for the relief of the order. Within several weeks Pope Innocent IV died, and was succeeded by Alexander IV (r. 1254–1261).[54] At the very least, this new pope had been protector of the Franciscan order, and was more favorably disposed than his predecessor to the new movements.

Having been given this reprieve, Humbert quickly assessed the situation and began to make the decisions necessary for reestablishing some *modus vivendi* with the papacy and the bishops. Strategically surveying the forces arrayed against him, he discerned that his greatest enemies were the secular masters at the University

---

53   In the end, we do not know why Innocent had this precipitous change of heart. It is possible that the secular master William of Saint-Amour had convinced him that the friars were flirting with heresy and threatening the stability of the institutional Church. On the other hand it may have been the pope's failing powers, as he in fact died three weeks later.

54   This led to a later legend: "Tunc dicere ceperunt cardinales et prelati: – Cavete a letaniis fratrum predicatorum." "Then cardinals and prelates began to say, 'beware the litanies of the Preachers.'" The earliest witness for this story is an early 14th century Milanese Dominican chronicler, Galvano Fiamma, see G. Odetto, "La cronica maggiore dell'ordine domenicano di Galvano Fiamma," in *Archivum Fratrum Praedicatorum* 10 (1950), n. 69, 41.

of Paris who provided the intellectual ammunition used against the friars. If his order were to overcome the threat, these arguments needed rebuttals so as to cut the strongest ground out from under his adversaries. Already the mendicant professors were meeting the challenge, including St. Thomas Aquinas in his *Contra impugnantes Dei cultum et religionem*. With that side handled, Humbert began to consider the practical details necessary to preserve the good of his order for the salvation of souls—the ultimate purpose of both the Dominicans and the Church at large. In the first place he heavily stressed cooperation and friendship with the Franciscan order. Both found themselves threatened by their current situations, yet they often weakened each other by desultory internecine warfare, sniping back and forth about minor jurisdictional or devotional issues. He enjoined his friars to end this unseemly conflict and enforced it with appropriate legislation. He also attempted to show a united front in the form of a joint encyclical issued with the Franciscan General, John of Parma, in 1255. Humbert always displayed circumspection and prudence while engaged in the order's business. He also had the foresight to impose silence on his friars vis-à-vis the outside world. He mandated that Dominicans were not to disclose the order's internal business to outsiders, nor were they ever to speak negatively in public against the hierarchy of the Church (intellectual rejoinders to Parisian masters being the exception). Humbert was very careful never to let internal matters become public knowledge. This also encouraged Dominican *esprit de corps*, unifying them against external challenges, and encouraging the friendship that is but one of the ends in a just political order.

Apart from these internal ordinances, the Master also extended concessions in a spirit of cooperation with the bishops and pastors of the Church. Recognizing that the true existential threat came from the university, he was more conciliatory to the just and traditional demands of the local churches. After all, the Dominicans were allied to the local churches as to their final end—namely, the salvation of souls. They saw themselves as elite auxiliaries in cooperating in the pastoral responsibilities of the bishops and secular priests. In light of a commitment to the common good, he offered significant compromises to local ordinaries. This was a move to generate good-will, and to separate the prelates from the camp of the secular masters for the purpose of heading off future confrontations. He agreed not to celebrate public liturgies without the ordinary's permission (this did not include the internal liturgical life of the convents, which was left untouched). In addition, he ordered his friars to seek licenses for public preaching, and furthermore promised to end competition by forbidding mendicant sermons when the bishop himself was preaching. Most significantly, he agreed not to seek legacies from the faithful and ordered his friars to encourage the laity to pay their traditional tithes to their local parishes. In light of the privileges obtained by the order in the previous thirty years, none of this was strictly necessary. Humbert could have pursued a hard line and insisted on the prerogatives obtained from the papacy, but such a tack would have only antagonized the local bishops, making local Dominican life that much harder. By voluntarily relinquishing these concessions, the Dominicans appeared magnanimous and, as a result, the tension between the friars and the secular clergy was significantly defused. His mollification of the secular clergy did much to pacify and, indeed, make friends of many of the prelates of the Church.[55]

Humbert's brilliance shines through in the final result. With the pacification of the secular clergy, the university masters found themselves without allies. By prudential accommodation, Humbert had divided his opponents, leaving the secular masters high and dry. Pleased with the attitude of the Dominicans, Alexander IV rescinded the legislation of Innocent IV, restoring the rights and privileges of the order, and in particular, ruled in their favor against the secular masters of the University of Paris, thus securing the great seat of learning for the Dominicans, and ensuring that their educational initiatives, so critical to the very mission of the order, would continue.[56]

---

55 Brett, 24.
56 Alexander suspended Innocent's legislation on 22 Dec 1254 (due to concerted lobbying by Humbert himself) and gave the friars complete victory at the university with his *Quasi lignum vitae* of 14 April 1255. See Brett, 24, 31.

Because of Humbert's triumph, men like Albert the Great and Thomas Aquinas were able to flourish, to the lasting good of the Church of God.

After this signal victory Master Humbert wanted publicly to celebrate the order as a permanent force in the Church. In order to do that, he orchestrated the General Chapter at Paris in 1255 as a demonstration of Dominican fidelity that attracted public affirmation of widespread support. To secure this he arranged an open invitation to venerate the relics of a popular Dominican martyr, St. Peter of Verona, which drew the faithful to the meeting. He also made a special effort to include bishops and aristocrats among the number of the visiting devotees. Shrewdly, he honored the King—later himself a saint—Louis IX. Already partial to the order, Humbert surprised him by cannily ordering the Dominicans to give him the honors of a Master General at his death, something calculated to please the pious king exceedingly.[57] Louis remained a firm friend of the order the remainder of his days.

Humbert also had the presence of mind to consider how the order had gotten itself into the situation in the first place. Perhaps a bit carried away by success, Humbert had gone further than Alexander IV wished in making concessions to the university. After all, Humbert's present concern had been the good of the order, and this he had secured. From Alexander's perspective however, papal authority was not being respected. Humbert deferred to the curia in the matter. In the end, the pope awarded the order more privileges than expected, while Humbert was able to retain the goodwill of the bishops for his efforts. As so often happens, in acceding to the higher good, the good of his own order was rendered even more secure, and the rebellion of the secular masters was quelled, at least for a while. This episode taught Humbert an important lesson; the good of the order must be subordinate and ordered to the good of the Church as a whole. He saw that the Dominicans had failed in

57　For the Paris chapter, see Donald Prudlo, *The Martyred Inquisitor: The Life and Cult of Peter of Verona († 1252)* (Aldershot, England: Ashgate, 2008), 235–236. See also, Brett, 36–37.

coordinating with the papacy on a regular basis. Without the presence of a consistent representative of the Preachers' interests at the court, the pope had been unduly influenced by the order's enemies. Therefore, Humbert decided to assign a circumspect friar whose job it was to collaborate with the papal curia. As a result, in 1257, he appointed a permanent procurator at the curia who would be a stable representative of the order's interests, with the particular remit of not allowing things to reach the pitch they had in the first year of Humbert's rule.[58]

Having successfully navigated the difficulties of his first years in office, Humbert was not neglectful of the common internal good of his own order. Their shared form of life was precious to him, and he did perhaps more than any Dominican in history to preserve, secure, and advance this particular form of religious profession. He was exceptionally successful in two internal matters: education and liturgy. Education for the friars was absolutely and irreducibly central to Dominican identity. It was the primary means of training the Preachers for their mission for the good of souls.[59] If that special mission were compromised it would mean the increasing irrelevance of the order for the common good of the Church. He was faced with two distinct parties within the order. One, concerned about the spiritual life of the friars, was worried that increasing attention to philosophy—particularly the newly discovered works of Aristotle—would rob the friars of their evangelical fervor. To them, this was a worldly occupation that had been superseded by revelation. Truth be told, this group was not even terribly interested in advanced theology, being content with the kind of practical theology necessary for preaching and hearing confessions. On the other hand, there were those like Albert the Great, who argued that if philosophy were neglected the

---

58 Brett, 31.

59 The best treatment of early Dominican education is M. Michèle Mulchahey, *"First the Bow Is Bent in Study—": Dominican Education Before 1350* (Toronto: Pontifical Institute of Mediaeval Studies, 1998).

Dominicans would be left behind in the wake of new discoveries and methods, and would stagnate in intellectual backwaters, all the while losing a fundamental apologetical tool against unbelievers. Humbert listened carefully to both sides, but was himself a moderate in such matters. In 1259 he convened a board of Dominican university masters.[60] He ensured that Albert and Thomas Aquinas were both appointed to the five-member committee, knowing that they would promote the cause of advanced studies in the order, while providing him political cover to advance the consensus of the university masters. The committee, chartered by Humbert, achieved an adroit balance that divided the friars according to their aptitudes for study. The regular conventual brethren were to be limited to practical theology, necessary to their daily ministry. More advanced brothers would be sent to provincial schools to continue their studies in advanced theology. The most promising students would be reserved for attendance at the great universities. Well-prepared and intellectually equipped, they were permitted to drink deeply of the draughts of philosophy. This system served the order incredibly well, permitting new studies while maintaining the good order of the fraternity, adapting every situation to the needs of each individual brother, and all subordinated to the common good. The academic conservatives were mollified and contented with the compromise. Humbert's commitment to subsidiarity is especially evident here. He left the matter to the most brilliant of his professors, while moderating their zeal for the new learning by establishing a hierarchical, tiered system that was fitted to the needs of all.

Another internal matter of significance to the Preachers was their liturgy. In the beginning, the friars celebrated according to the local missal and office wherever they found themselves. Every time they entered a new city they were confronted with a new calendar, prayers, and even rubrics. In a worldwide, travelling order, the inconveniences of such a system quickly became apparent. Humbert needed something that unified the brothers across the whole of

60   For this episode, see Prudlo, *Thomas Aquinas*, 146–157.

Christendom.[61] A previous attempt to streamline the liturgy had failed miserably in the late 1240s. Humbert saw that in this situation a strong central authority was needed that could impose the results of a standardization on the whole fraternity. To that end he committed himself to revising the order's liturgical books, despite the massive amount of work that had already fallen upon his shoulders. Using the Roman curial liturgy as a model, he reordered the missal and produced numerous normative books for the celebration of the Mass and the Divine Office.[62] While all agreed it was a masterful attempt, he was still faced with the grave task of not only communicating the new books to the order, but in cajoling those who were opposed to the new common missal and office. His prudential solutions served quickly and fairly to establish a respected rite that has been celebrated for nearly 800 years. In practical terms, he first ordered a master codex prepared at Paris. Many friars from all over the world came there, and when they arrived they had orders to procure a copy directly from the codex, which derived a subvention through a special tax to defray the expense. For houses that were unwilling, Humbert decided to bring the liturgy to them personally. He ordered a special, lightweight copy that he carried everywhere. During his indefatigable travels, he carried the books to many convents, and personally oversaw their transcription, and instructed them in the rite's celebration. Finally, he made sure that the General Chapters, whose agendas he set as Master General, continued to legislate in favor of the common ritual. Such

61   The classic study of the Dominican liturgy remains the formidable work by William R. Bonniwell, O.P., *A History of the Dominican Liturgy* (New York: J.F. Wagner, Inc, 1944). Some have suggested that the Dominican Rite has more of a Gallican influence. Bonniwell is convinced of its derivation from a Roman liturgical family, but there are interesting arguments on both sides.

62   Modelling it on the Roman liturgy was calculated to appeal to Rome and increasing liturgical centralization. The Franciscans for their part had adopted the curial liturgy with no modifications. The two worldwide mendicant orders adopting Roman-style liturgy prepared the way for the standardization of the Tridentine missal.

is an example of his personal leadership, and his willingness to commit himself to the essential missions of the order. Humbert knew that administrative imposition was not enough, but had to be accompanied by presence, skill, practical provision, and above all, charity. Quickly the order realized the benefits of such a system, and within a decade the Dominican rite was strongly established everywhere.

Another internal matter that ended up in Humbert's hands was the care of female monasteries. Here again the order was bitterly divided. On one hand was the example of holy Dominicans like Jordan of Saxony and Peter of Verona, not to mention Dominic himself, all of whom had taken special pains to affiliate female monasteries to the order and to offer them pastoral care. We possess letters demonstrating close friendships between Jordan and Peter and the nuns of various houses. After Jordan's death in 1237, there was a huge backlash. Care of nuns was time consuming and forced friars to be in permanent residence and in attendance upon a fixed location. This was seen by many as undermining the order's itinerant mission and friars increasingly began to resent such assignments. In addition, according to contemporary social ideas, there were serious dangers in frequent concourse with women. In fact, the two previous masters, Raymond of Peñafort and John the German, had worked tirelessly to disaffiliate the female monasteries, even those which had been founded by Dominic himself. Humbert knew that this was ultimately unjust, particularly for the four most ancient monasteries of the order. Therefore, he convinced the pope to place the matter in his hands. He forbade new affiliations of monasteries without the approval of three consecutive Chapters General, so as to ensure that they were capable of living the Dominican life and to see if they had enough endowments to make them financially independent. This provided a significant entry barrier and "cooling off period" for the incorporation of new houses. Then Humbert himself authored a new Rule for nuns in 1259 that became the *sine qua non* of incorporation into the Dominicans. If any nuns wanted to join, they had to accede to this new constitutional system.[63] This was essentially the Charter of the Second Order, which remained in effect until the 1930s. Humbert made it clear that the male and female branches had different missions; the sisters' was one of stability and contemplation, whereas the men's concern was preaching and mobility. In this way Humbert allowed for a limited care of female religious, maintained respect for the rights of the oldest houses, and ensured that any new houses would meet the highest standards of the order. He also rotated friars frequently as chaplains so that they did not become overly familiar with any house, and thus enabled them to return to active mission more quickly. All in all, it was an exceptionally equitable decision.

Administrators must often make difficult and complex decisions, of which later history does not always approve. One aspect of Humbert's leadership caused irritation and was overturned almost as soon as he left office. He was always dedicated to the strict observance of the Rule, and the constitutions were clear that Dominican convents were to be modest in size and decoration. Even before Humbert's term as Master, the popularity of the Preachers meant that both the faithful and their offerings poured into the churches of the order. Their early, modest foundations were not sufficient to meet the increasing demand for attendance at their sermons. Priors began to appropriate money for larger and larger convents, particularly in cities that were experiencing rapid expansion. New Gothic edifices were springing up all over Europe. Humbert resisted this in the name of primitive simplicity and observance. While he recognized the need for more space, he balanced this against his conviction that if one constitutional stricture was relaxed, then general decay would set in. Later Masters General looked the other way as massive new edifices arose, such as Santa Maria Novella in Florence or San Domenico in Naples. While there

63   See Maiju Lehmijoki-Gardner, *Dominican Penitent Women* (Mahwah, NJ: Paulist Press, 2005); and id., "Writing Religious Rules as an Interactive Process—Dominican Penitent Women and the Making of their Regula," in *Speculum* 79 (2004): 660–687.

is no way to prove causation from this correlation, it is true that Dominican strict observance began to wane in the 1270s at the same time such churches went up. While one might criticize Humbert for lack of practical vision, his first duty was to the intrinsic common good of the order he headed. According to his deep understanding of the regular life and the Dominican form in particular, he refused to back down in the face of such concessions.

Finally, the pressure and stress of his position began to bear upon him, and Humbert became ill in 1259. Still, he soldiered on for four more years. He ultimately convinced the General Chapter to accept his resignation in 1263. While he was undoubtedly happy to lay down his manifold responsibilities, and to reflect upon the survival of the order he had essentially saved, he was not yet finished. He had much more to give to the order. In his "retirement" he worked ceaselessly to write works reflective of his vast administrative experience. These writings became standard commentaries on the Dominican life. Filled with a Ciceronian conviction that those experienced in human affairs and administration will be best positioned to offer advice, he left a legacy of brilliance. While Dominicans are most known for their speculative works of theology and philosophy, Humbert's are suffused with the practical wisdom of prudence. To name just a few of these, he authored a massive commentary on the "Rule" of St. Augustine, the flexible and largely vague set of admonitions that Dominic had selected as the basis for his order. Humbert found in it a spiritual bounty ready for harvest. Though the sparse Rule is no more than twenty pages, Humbert's commentary runs into hundreds of manuscript folios. He shows himself a master of memory, and he portrays the religious Rule within the broad ambit of Church history, adducing quotations from scripture and tradition to bolster the claims of the life of perfection.

Further, he wrote a treatise on the offices within the order itself. He gives extended descriptions and practical advice not only for governing officials, but for the most humble of offices, such as the cellarer and the infirmarian. Such attention shows Humbert's comprehensive vision of Dominican life, where every office is an essential brick that makes up the whole of the wall. He also wrote vast commentaries on the Dominican Constitution itself, as well as a well-regarded handbook on the art of preaching. His work "On the Gift of Fear" was a book of preaching stories that was distributed all over Europe.[64] Finally, he continued to be of use to the Church at large, composing one of the most important preparatory documents for the Second Council of Lyon in 1274. Retirement provided the space for reflection, and Humbert continued to offer the fruits of his contemplation (and practice) to others. Indeed, in a real sense he is the 'master of praxis' to complement St. Thomas' mastership of theology and philosophy. They are two sides of one coin.

Some of Humbert's meditations give insight into his philosophy of governance. For instance, when he describes the office of procurator at the curia, he lists several essential characteristics. Such an individual must be of the highest discretion since he deals with exceptionally sensitive issues. At the same time, he needs to be amiable so as to meet dignitaries in a friendly manner. With these in mind, he must strive unapologetically to obtain concessions and benefits, pursuing the interests of the order at all times. What Humbert doesn't say is that the office of procurator helps to fill the constitutional lacuna when the office of Master General is vacant, continuing to campaign for the order even during an interregnum. When speaking of the Master General, Humbert offers more insights. The Master should also visit the curia often, out of respect for the papacy certainly, but also for the utility of the order. It is incumbent upon him to cultivate friends at the highest levels. He must be of a gracious and open disposition, yet careful to guard the internal business of the friars. He must not be afraid to honor people according to their positions, nor to court benefactors for the order. All of this shows that notwithstanding Humbert's personal austerity and dedication to the internal good of the order, he knew that he lived in a richly incarnational world where body and

---

64   A critical edition of this work is now happily available. See Humbert of Romans, *Humberti de Romanis: De dono timoris*, ed. Christine Boyer (Turnhout: Brepols, 2008).

soul together were necessary for the achievement of the final end. One worked within the circumstances that he was given, always with an eye on the ultimate goal. Humbert worked tirelessly, patiently, and prudently, and established his fraternity on the firmest of foundations.

In the end we can see the constitutional framework built by Dominic perfected under Humbert. The solid edifice left by the founder served as the administrative skeleton wherein Humbert and the other Masters could exercise their offices in prudence and justice for the advancement of the needs of the order. In truth, Humbert can be fairly called the second founder of the order. The success of institutions depends not only on the original vision, but upon the execution of the mission in subsequent ages. The Dominican order was a "school" for excellence, wherein the best would rise to the top. A friar like Thomas could be recognized for his exceptional academic abilities and freed from all external works so as to facilitate his contribution to the salvation of souls. He would be exempted from all practical administration and even from most communal obligations. On the other hand, the life of the order was richly rewarded by such brothers as Humbert. Through lower constitutional offices a friar's excellence and skill could be discerned, and he would gradually be given graver responsibilities. It was like an institution for education in prudence. The quality of Dominican scholarship and leadership in the first one hundred years is a stunning testimony to the vision of the Preachers. It was an administrative masterpiece, perfectly fitted to mission, and executed with charity and prudence. In the annals of Church history, it is one of the most transparently incarnational manifestations of grace building upon nature.

Chapter 5
Failed Saintly Administrators

While a veritable "cloud of witnesses" has paraded in testament to the marvelous possibilities of sanctity when allied to governance, still one must confront a salient reality: holiness does not of itself bequeath administrative aptitude. Since grace builds upon nature, sanctity can strengthen and deepen natural proclivities to administrative excellence, but it does not create them *ex nihilo*. Indeed, it can often happen that the holiest of people are incapable of governing well. Occasionally they are aware of this defect, as in the many cases of saints refusing episcopal promotion. This reluctance comes not only out of holiness, but from a deep self-awareness of the absence of the necessary natural gifts, aptitudes, and skills. Thomas Aquinas declined offers not only of the abbacy of Montecassino, but also of the Archbishopric of Naples, not to mention his unwavering opposition to being appointed as a cardinal.[1] He was a humble man certainly, but his lack of competence in the areas necessary to successful administration made his decisions easy. Other saints had administration unwillingly thrust upon them. They either sank or swam, and holiness was no sure guarantee of success. Their many virtues certainly enhanced their administration and blessed their subordinates, but on occasion piety could clash jarringly with the exigencies of governance. There were also deeply holy men who were abject failures in their attempts at government, often being manipulated by the wise of this world (Lk 16:8) into incautious decisions that led to disastrous consequences. The disconnect between

1   Donald S. Prudlo, *Thomas Aquinas: A Historical, Theological, and Environmental Portrait* (New York: Paulist, 2020), 75–76, 243, 275.

worldly behavior and the demands of virtue occasionally resulted in paralysis—that is, an inability to make decisions at all. On the other hand, some saints were absolutely masterful political operators whose "wisdom" as serpents occasionally seemed to clash with their "innocence" as doves (Mt 10:16). When using the machinery of the world, even for good ends, dangers exist that are not always foreseen. Occasionally charity would be occluded in the aggressive search for truth or results. Yet we know that not all saints were worldly successes, but in fidelity to Christ they soldiered on. Not always making the right calls and sometimes fighting impossible situations, at times they were "led like lambs to the slaughter" (Is 53:7). Yet their testimony of graced holiness remains whether in triumph or defeat. It is encouraging to think that the failures of this or that worldly enterprise are not what one will be judged upon, but rather the depth of faith one has in Christ and the overflow of charity one expresses in life. In that sense, failed saintly administrators offer tales simultaneously of caution and hope.

St. Cyril of Alexandria and the Audacity of Truth

The Church in Alexandria in the century after the Constantinian settlement had become one of the wonders of the ancient world. In purely secular terms, while Rome slowly declined and Constantinople was yet growing in stature, the mighty city of Alexandria stood as a testament to the endurance of Roman power. It was a city hallowed by antiquity, with connections to the pharaohs and to Alexander the Great. Its economic power was astonishing, controlling much of the trade of the eastern Mediterranean. It housed a venerable Jewish population that had seen the production of the Septuagint edition of the Old Testament. Home to perhaps a quarter of a million people, Alexandria was home to a burgeoning and already ancient Christian population.[2] Indeed in the fourth century

---

2   For an account of the city at this period of history, see: Christopher Haas, *Alexandria in Late Antiquity: Topography and Social Conflict* (Baltimore, MD: Johns Hopkins University Press, 1997).

Alexandria seemed the very bulwark of orthodoxy, as St. Athanasius its bishop stood out effectively alone in defense of the Nicene creed.[3] His witness added much luster to his local church, and conversions to Christianity multiplied. By the end of the fourth century Christians and pagans roughly equaled each other in numbers, while a determined and still numerous minority of Jews still held out. Tensions in the city ran especially high, with enthusiasts from all three groups arguing and fighting in the streets. Beyond excessive zeal, there was also the problem of Christian division. There were still minority Christian groups in the city, such as Arians and Novatians, not to mention rural monks who often exhibited more passion than good sense, and frequently became fundamentalist fanatics.

The bishop of such a city assumed a power unlike any yet seen in Christianity. Hallowed by the aura of Athanasius and supported by the wealthiest church in Christianity, the one holding this office had become a force to be reckoned with. Hundreds of years before the formation of the Papal States, the Archbishop of Alexandria had more civil power than any other figure in the Church.[4] In addition to the regular tithes of perhaps over 100,000 Christians, he held a monopoly on the Nile trade of salt, nitrates, and papyrus.[5]

3   For a brief introduction to Athanasius, see Manfred Clauss, *Athanasius der Große der unbeugsame Heilige* (Darmstadt: Verlag Philipp von Zabern GmbH, 2016). For his theology, see Khaled Anatolios, *Athanasius* (New York: Routledge, 2004). For an interesting political analysis related to realities in Alexandria, see David Brakke, *Athanasius and the Politics of Asceticism* (Oxford: Clarendon Press, 1995).

4   The unsympathetic contemporary Church historian Socrates said, "The bishopric of Alexandria exceeded the sacerdotal limit and took command of secular affairs." Cfr. Susan Wessel, *Cyril of Alexandria and the Nestorian Controversy: The Making of a Saint and of a Heretic* (Oxford: Oxford University Press, 2006), 16n5.

5   For the economic activity of the Egyptian Church, see Ewa Wipszycka, *The Second Gift of the Nile: Monks and Monasteries in Late Antique Egypt* (Warsaw: Polish Centre of Mediterranean Archaeology, 2018); Id. "Resources and Economic Activities of the

He and the local civil prefect feuded over the government of the city itself, and the Church eventually proved victorious. More than that, however, he exercised patriarchal authority in a manner that exceeded that of Rome or Antioch at the time.[6] Unlike the other chief sees, his authority over his territory was absolute. No fewer than one-hundred bishops were directly dependent upon him. He held the sole right to appoint and ordain all of them, including the metropolitan archbishops and their subordinate suffragans. When the members of the patriarchate met in synod, the bishops did not discuss anything—rather, they were handed their marching orders by the patriarch. In an ecumenical council, the Egyptians always voted as a solid bloc, deferring to the wishes of the chief bishop.[7] In addition, Egypt was the home of monasticism, a powerful if unstable force for orthodoxy during the period. The Bishop of Alexandria was considered a sort of "Supreme Patriarch" of all the monks. They deferred to him and (sometimes) obeyed him.[8] Alexandria was also exceptionally jealous of its privileges as the "See of St. Mark." It successfully kept the ancient Diocese of Antioch at arm's length, and worked strongly to limit the growing power of the imperial city of Constantinople. Alexandria truly was the "Queen of the Mediterranean," and it is no exaggeration to say the patriarch was her consort.[9]

Egyptian Monastic Communities (4th–8th Century)," in *Journal of Juristic Papyrology* 41 (2011): 159–263; and id., *Les ressources et les activités économiques des églises en Égypte: du IVe au VIIIe siècle* (Brussels: Fondation Égyptologique Reine Élisabeth, 1972).

6   The title "Patriarch" was not used until later in the 5th century, however all the power usually denominated as "patriarchal" had been attributed to the three chief sees of Rome, Alexandria, and Antioch since the Council of Nicea in 325. See Norman Russell, *Cyril of Alexandria* (London: Routledge, 2000), 9.

7   Ibid., 12.

8   Philip Hughes, *The Church in Crisis: A History of the General Councils, 325–1870* (Garden City, NY: Image Books, 1964), 47.

9   Indeed the archbishop's power over the territory of the patriarchate dwarfed the dreams of even the most fevered 19th-century ultramontane papal apologists.

When the city was ruled by a saint such as Athanasius, these tensions could be kept in check, but after his death a series of politically minded archbishops succeeded him. In particular, the figure of Theophilus (r. 385–412) gives us the picture of an ecclesiastical magnate who would stop at nothing to retain and enhance the rights of his see. He was exceptionally effective, marshalling anti-pagan sentiment into an all-out attack on the Serapeum temple in 391. He did this by means of the *parabalani*, a confraternity of burly hospital porters whom the bishop formed into an irregular militia for the purposes of maintaining his claims on power.[10] Nor did Theophilus consider maintenance of a theological tradition necessary if changing his position would improve his political fortunes. He ultimately turned against the Origenistic school that he had formerly supported, and which found its strength among the rural monasteries. These religious houses had grown overmighty, so Theophilus drummed up the anti-Origenist position as an excuse to intervene physically to break the monks' power. It is likely that many perished in his attempt to curtail their influence. Neither did consistency bother him overmuch, as he attacked the Antiochene school of Christology—which taught essentially opposite to the Origenists—simply to weaken the power of the Patriarchs of the city of Antioch. He took it as a personal affront that the Second Council of Constantinople (381) had elevated the imperial city ahead of his own in the order of precedence, and never lost an opportunity of weakening the upstart see. Theophilus displayed his exceptional political skill in the year 403. He had been summoned by the emperor himself to answer charges that he had murdered monks during the Origenist intervention. He arrived with a massive retinue and mountains of gifts, which began to be showered on the members of the imperial household. He learned that the austere Bishop of Constantinople, John Chrysostom, had incurred the wrath of the empress. Theophilus leveraged this information to engineer the synod that convened to try him for his misdeeds. At the

---

10   Russell, *Cyril*, 6. W. Schubart, "Parabalani," in *Journal of Egyptian Archaeology* 40 (1954): 97–101.

beginning of the meeting, Theophilus denounced John Chrysostom, and turned the proceedings into an uncanonical deposition of the holy John. While St. John Chrysostom was later exonerated and returned to his see, he was so exhausted by his efforts that died the next year. Theophilus was truly a master of power politics.

Present at what came to be known as the "Synod of the Oak," was Theophilus' young protege: his nephew Cyril. Cyril had been born into the ecclesial nobility of the Alexandrian church when the luster of Athanasius' triumph was at its height. He was very well educated, and wrote in flawless, creative Greek. While he was likely kept away from formal study in philosophy, he nonetheless evinces a devastating mastery of rhetoric and logic.[11] His theological depth was magnificent—indeed he is one of the finest minds among the Fathers of the Church.[12] He possessed the skill of writing the most profound theological works in the midst of astonishing secular and ecclesial turbulence. His saintliness shines forth from the pages of his formal treatises, whereas his political activities tend to cast a shade over his claims to holiness. He had learned power politics at the feet of a master, and did not scruple to use his authority to advance the cause of the Alexandrian church and that of orthodoxy. He had lived through the storming of the Serapeum and the attack on the monks of the desert, as well as having been present at the Synod of the Oak, where his uncle exiled his holy rival, St. John Chrysostom. In 412, three days after the death of Theophilus, Cyril was enthroned as the successor of St. Mark. He had prevailed over the archdeacon Timothy after a series of riots that pitted ecclesial careerists against Theophilus' nascent clerical dynasty.[13] To claim and keep the see of Alexandria was not for the faint of heart.

11   Russell, *Cyril*, 5.
12   For overviews of Cyril from a theological perspective, see Hans van Loon, *The Dyophysite Christology of Cyril of Alexandria* (Leiden: Brill, 2009), an effective recent defense of his orthodoxy vis-a-vis the Council of Chalcedon; and *The Theology of St. Cyril of Alexandria: A Critical Appreciation*, eds. Thomas G. Weinandy and Daniel A. Keating (London: T & T Clark, 2003).
13   Haas, *Alexandria*, 297.

Cyril moved quickly to consolidate his position. He knew he faced threats on a number of fronts, for the Patriarchate attracted enemies like flies drawn to honey. There were heretics, pagans, Jews, unbalanced monks, Christian factions, and a rivalrous secular prefect, not to mention the upstart Patriarchate of Constantinople. That Cyril survived his first several years at all is a testament to his consummate skill. Historians tend to underestimate the number of forces arrayed against the young bishop. He needed to establish authority swiftly. First, he used the autocratic position that he inherited to replace all priests of suspect loyalty, installing his own men throughout Egypt. Then he acted to seize the churches of heretics within the city and drive them out. He attacked the austere Novatian sect in particular. Not only had they probably supported the Archdeacon Timothy, but as schismatics they were "low hanging fruit" whose dispersal would demonstrate his commitment to orthodoxy. He shut their churches and seized their paraments.[14] In doing this he fed the Alexandrian appetite for mob action, further solidifying his church's known opposition to unorthodox groups.

Cyril's tacit acceptance of street violence worried the civil prefect of the city, Orestes. Though he was a Christian, he had the unenviable task of bringing order to the chaotic melting pot of Alexandria. He could not afford to be seen to be unduly favoring one group over the other. This was unsatisfactory to Cyril, who began importuning him to limit the activities of non-Christian groups, and to exercise increased oversight over the games and theaters. Tensions with the Jewish community were especially bad. While one must remember the context of the early Church's struggle with the synagogue, and not project recent history onto past events, it remains that Cyril was very anti-Jewish in his sentiments and in his preaching.[15] He did much to stir up an already volatile population. That said, the Jews were just as keen for factional violence in the city. When it was reported that the prefect might shut down the theaters on Saturdays (the Jewish Sabbath), they

14   Ibid., 296–299.
15   Ibid., 300.

denounced one of Cyril's servants who was present as an instigator of violence. Orestes unjustly had him flogged without the servant giving him any provocation. Cyril took this attack as a personal affront and began to plot against the prefect. After this episode, the tension simmered. One night the Jews raised an alarm, calling out that a Christian church was on fire. When panicked Christians arrived, they discovered no fire, but a mob of Jews who set about attacking and killing many of them. This drove Cyril to assemble his militia, seize all the synagogues of the city, and drive the perpetrators out of Alexandria.[16] It was a brash action that was completely in violation of imperial law, one which Cyril got away with on account of its sheer audacity.

Cyril, for his part, desired a reconciliation with the prefect, but it would only be on his own terms. One day at liturgy Cyril "spontaneously" extended the Gospel book toward Orestes in a public gesture of rapprochement. While the book was certainly a religious symbol, it was nonetheless a politically charged moment. If Orestes laid his hand on the Gospel it might look like an indication of submission on his part. Although inclined to peace, the prefect could not have this be seen as a manifestation of weakness toward the leader of a powerful faction. He refused to touch the book and thereby his faith was called into question before the whole congregation. It was a lose-lose situation engineered by Cyril, who now had extra ammunition in his struggle with the civil government. When news of the refusal began to spread it took on even greater meaning. Enthusiasts began to speculate that it had been intended as a personal insult to the archbishop by the civil authority. The fanatics in the Alexandrian Christian community raised themselves to a fit of pique (a state that they were never far from in any case). Even those who did not see eye to eye with Cyril chafed at this "insult" to their Church. A party of rural monks—always a destabilizing force—descended into the city from the desert. They cornered and surrounded the prefect, threatening him spiritually and physically. In the tumult

---

16   Socrates claims that Cyril drove all the Jews out, but this is implausible, as suggested in Wessel, *Cyril*, 36.

a monk named Ammonius hurled a rock that struck Orestes. Not able to tolerate such lèse-majesté, the prefect ordered his soldiers forcibly to disperse the crowd. He arrested and tortured the monk to death, an act well within his purview given the nature of the situation. Cyril here made a tactical error. He acquired the monk's body and attempted to "canonize" the malefactor as a martyr for the faith. The effort was met with silence by the local Christian community, the majority of whom knew quite well that Ammonius was a rabble-rouser who had committed a crime and was justly punished.[17] For once it was Cyril who was checked, and he prudently allowed the matter to drop.

Thwarted in one direction, the implacable bishop changed headings to attack the prefect from another flank. He began a campaign against the pagans of the city through preaching and writing. The famous public philosopher Hypatia had formed a friendship with the prefect that did not lack political overtones. Cyril saw this as striking at his authority, not to mention being beneath the dignity of a Christian prefect. With the city having been stirred up by incendiary preaching, some fanatical Christians led by a lector named Peter attacked Hypatia and brutally killed her. It is highly doubtful that Cyril had anything directly to do with the attack.[18] It appears the philosopher was merely an unlucky pawn in the struggle between prefect and patriarch. In spite of this, the fervid

17   Ibid., 305.
18   The brutal murder of Hypatia has been romanticized by anti-Christian writers out of all historical proportion since the time of Gibbon. She is pictured as a representative of a dying tradition of rationalism, killed by the mobs of an obscurantist Christian bishop. She has even become a sort of "martyr to science." In fact, Hypatia was not only a philosopher but an occultist, something far removed from reason. Her murder was politically motivated and perpetrated by an independent group of Christian fanatics. Cyril's attention seemed mostly focused on Jews and heretics in his early career, sensing little threat from Hypatia's rarefied paganism. See the summary in Wessel, 46, particularly 105 and 54. Wessel also establishes that the *parabalani* were not involved in the attack, either. Ibid., 57.

atmosphere cultivated in the Alexandrian Church surely con-
tributed to such violence. It was an unwieldy force to reckon with.
Sometimes Cyril was able to direct it, but other times it exceeded
his capability. It is for this reason that some have suggested that
the first three years of his rule display his inexperience combined
with a ruthlessness inherited from his uncle. It also demonstrates
that he was not all-powerful in the city, but rather had to contend
with numerous other influential factions.[19]

It is true that Cyril continued the main policy lines set out by
Theophilus. These fell into four main categories. The first is clear:
apply relentless pressure to all who were not orthodox Christians,
be they pagans, Jews, or heretics. This pressure was to employ all
available tools at the patriarch's disposal—encompassing everything social, political, and cultural. This is clear in all of Cyril's
extra-ecclesial relations. From an internal perspective the Patriarchate of Alexandria pursued three separate but related goals. The
first was to maintain the support (if not the friendship) of the
monks. Too unstable a force to control absolutely, the bishop's job
was to retain the unquestioned allegiance of the urban Church and
to blunt the more extreme forms of fanaticism, which even
Theophilus realized could not be harnessed. The next was to cultivate a warm relationship with the Roman See, one which dated
back to Nicaea and Athanasius. This was not out of any exalted
idea of Petrine primacy—rather it was due to the fact that Rome
was 1) remote, and 2) a counterbalance to the other eastern patriarchates. By honoring Rome's primacy, Alexandria secured her
own position in the East, particularly vis-a-vis the imperial capital.
An instance of this was Cyril's reluctance to name St. John Chrysostom in the diptychs at liturgy as Rome demanded. However, realizing he needed the Roman See for his ecclesiastical plans in the
East, he finally acquiesced. The remainder of his episcopate saw
warm relations between the two ancient dioceses. While it was clear
that Cyril accepted Roman primacy and never challenged it, it is
also apparent that cultivating such relations advanced his political

19   Ibid., 48.

and administrative plans. When doctrine and expedience dovetailed, so much the better for Cyril. The cultivation of Roman friendship was most directed to the final plank in the Alexandrian policy: the continual attempts to thwart the growth and authority of the upstart "patriarch" of the imperial city of Constantinople and—to a lesser extent—the ancient see of Antioch.[20]

It is clear that Cyril would occasionally make use of unscrupulous tactics, but it is equally plain that he acted from the highest motives. Unless one considers that Cyril was convinced of the rectitude of his position, and his conviction of the fact that the salvation of both believers and unbelievers rested upon many of his political decisions, then one misses the complexity of his character. As he matured as a bishop, he began to be more occupied with ecclesial matters. Having secured his position in Alexandria against all comers, he was free to pursue controversial and fundamental theology in a more peaceful environment. While he shared the outlook of his uncle, it is also apparent that there was a noticeable difference between them. In the first place, he was no theological opportunist. Theophilus changed positions on Christology several times, with the clear intention of attempting to subvert his ecclesial rivals without any concern for the truth. Cyril was immoveable in his Christology (which later became the normative Christology of the orthodox churches). Even if a modification of his position could have secured a political victory, he did not pursue it if it came at the cost of doctrine. While Cyril also aggressively promoted his supporters, he never tried to fabricate charges to get rid of priests of rival factions, as Theophilus was known to have done.[21] Cyril had the orthodoxy of Athanasius, the iron hand of Theophilus, and the sanctity to hold them both together. In spite

---

20 Antioch was, frankly, the weakest of the ancient patriarchates, often being used as a pawn in the ongoing struggle between Constantinople and Alexandria. It was seen as useful mostly because of its prestige, and for the school of Christology that had emanated from it.

21 Russell, 7.

of this, his dominant personality and consummate skill occasionally led to short-term victories that bore long-term repercussions.

This was never more on display than in the monumental confrontation with Patriarch Nestorius of Constantinople. In 428 Nestorius became bishop of the imperial city and was immediately confronted with opposing representatives of Antiochene and Alexandrian Christology. Wanting to defuse a tense theological situation, he came up with a halfway solution that pleased no one. In a sermon he declared that Mary could not rightly be called "Mother of God" since she was only the one who bore the "human person" Jesus. Partisans of both camps immediately attacked his position, for "Mother of God" was an ancient and treasured title in the Christian Church. In the meantime, he also provoked the ire of the powerful emperor's sister, Pulcheria.[22] The monks and the imperial palace began to agitate against the young patriarch. Cyril could smell blood in the water. He knew Nestorius' position was heretical. Here was a chance to assert Alexandrian dominance over Constantinople once and for all. What had been botched with Chrysostom would be rectified with Nestorius. Cyril quickly picked out the specific heresy of Nestorius, in that it divided Christ into two persons, threatening the unity of His being and the reality of the Hypostatic Union. "Christ is One!" was Cyril's cry, with the implication being that Mary had truly borne God, which confirmed the ancient piety of the Christian people.

To say Cyril lost no time is an understatement. He dispatched public letters to Pope Celestine and to Nestorius. Missive after missive arrived at the imperial palace describing Nestorius' error in detail, and each letter was accompanied with rich gifts from the illimitable resources of the Alexandrian Church.[23] The largesse and

22 Indeed, in his confrontation with the pious Pulcheria there may be a connection between his theology and a deeply anti-feminine streak. See Russell, 32.

23 It is estimated that 200 pounds of gold alone was distributed by Cyril and his agents among the imperial household in pursuance of his agenda. In the premodern world, the distribution of gifts (today seen as bribes) was far more a fundamental function of good

the public letters had the effect of hardening positions and crystal-lizing them, which is exactly what Cyril intended. Nestorius was backfooted by the onslaught, delayed in sending his letter to the pope (which had the character of excessive self-justification), and only belatedly began to recruit allies from the Antiochene school. He was totally unprepared for the forces that had been unleashed against him as he faced Cyril's *ad hoc* alliance of the papacy, the monks, various imperial officials, and his voting bloc of faithful Egyptian bishop-retainers. Cyril's quick action had resulted in the papacy granting him plenipotentiary legatine authority in the East to call an Ecumenical Council in concert with the emperor. He now had all the jurisdiction he needed to execute his designs and to pre-serve orthodoxy. He cleverly assembled the Synod at Ephesus, the last earthly home of Mary and a center of devotion to her. The Council was delayed for two weeks because many from the Anti-ochene patriarchate had not yet showed up. There was a danger that they might be sympathetic to Nestorius and tip the balance. Cyril could not let that stand. On 21 June 431 he called the Council into session, and within *one day* had accomplished all conciliar business. It was the fastest Ecumenical Council in history.[24] Nesto-rius was deposed on the basis of the Council's decision and of Cyril's legatine authority. Mary was proclaimed "Mother of God" and the unity of Christ's personhood was solemnly affirmed. At the

governance and patron/client relations. See Pauline Allen and Bronwen Neil, *Crisis Management in Late Antiquity (410–590 CE): A Survey of the Evidence from Episcopal Letters* (Leiden: Brill, 2013), 155. Cyril also miscalculated by sending separate theological tracts to Theodosius II and to the women of the imperial household. This irritated Theodosius significantly. While he supported Cyril's theology publicly, he sent a private letter to Cyril upbraiding him for attempting to circumvent him in his own family, Wessel, *Cyril,* 99–100.

24 Pope Celestine did also obtain the conciliar condemnation of Pelagianism, a problem in the West that had not really touched the East. Allen and Neil suggest that Cyril exchanged this condemnation for the concession of papal legatine authority, but I find this hard to believe. Ibid., 117.

news, the populace gathered to celebrate, and Marian processions were held throughout Christendom.

Cyril presented the Christian world essentially with a *fait accompli*. The third Ecumenical Council was successful in achieving all the aims he had set out for it. Alexandria's position as senior in the East was secured. Constantinople and—at least indirectly—Antioch had been humbled. Cyrillic theology regarding the unity of the person of Christ, truly born of the Virgin Mary, both affirmed long held beliefs and enshrined them in dogmatic formulations. It was to be Cyril's most magnificent triumph. Rarely had a person achieved so many victories over every opponent that arose against him. Yet we know that Councils rarely achieve concord. While Cyril's solution kept the peace in the East until his death in 444, storm clouds had begun to gather. The Nestorians had never really gone away, and indeed in places like Assyria in the far East of Christianity, they held the balance of opinion. Cyril's precipitate steamrolling in running through the Council business in one day had left a major loophole in the wording of the dogmatic decisions. The notion of the unity of Christ became emphasized to such an extent that Christ's divinity was in danger of utterly eclipsing His humanity. People arose in the next generation, adducing the authority of Cyril, who appeared to claim that there was no true humanity in Christ. While it is clear that Cyril himself never claimed this, his language was nevertheless loose enough to occasionally bear that interpretation.[25] After his death the Church was torn apart by a new heresy, termed "Monophysitism," which asserted that in Christ there was only a divine nature. The movement was led by Cyril's successor in Alexandria and backed by the bishop-retainers of Egypt. Cyril's impetuosity had been tempered by his sanctity and theological acumen. Those latter virtues did not burden his successor, Dioscorus. Using the prestige of the Alexandrian see, he plunged the East into violence and heresy, which was only headed off by the convocation of the Fourth Ecumenical Council at Chalcedon in 451, but not before

25　Van Loon, *The Dyophysite Christology of Cyril of Alexandria*, *passim*.

leading to a schism with the Egyptian Church that endures to the present day. The inexperienced and imprudent Nestorius had been exiled after Ephesus but lived at least until Chalcedon. When he received the acts of the Council, he found that it was close to what he had been saying all along (though his language still seemed unorthodox).[26] One can only speculate what private, high-level theological discussion might have done in the case of Nestorius, rather than Cyril's headlong plunge into Ephesus in 431.

Not everything done by a saint necessarily comports with sanctity. Indeed, as one can see with saintly popes, even decisions taken with the best of intentions can become colossal failures for many reasons. Cyril put his political acumen at the service of the Church and of orthodoxy, yet such service often elided too neatly with the prestige of his see and his short-term political goals. Indeed, Cyril's lack of foresight and excessive focus on the present situation damaged the cause of orthodoxy in the years to come and in some ways led to an enduring schism. His constant desire for decisive, precipitate action often realized stunning tactical victories, but left his flanks open to later counterattacks. One might even mark Cyril's tenure as the high-water mark of Alexandrian Christianity, for within a generation it would be racked by schism, only later to fall into the hands of Islam to suffer centuries of attrition. Rome and Constantinople became the two poles of Church leadership, and what had been the mightiest of sees became itself a persecuted backwater. While Cyril's sanctity aided him in composing some of the richest theology of the patristic period, it struggled against tendencies in the Egyptian Church and within Cyril himself that tended to exacerbate conflicts rather than quiet them. Earthly failure is no obstacle to sanctity, but neither is excessive earthly success. Cyril achieved a powerful victory for orthodoxy at

---

26   The remarkable "last testament" of Nestorius, called the *Bazaar of Heracleides* was rediscovered by chance in 1895. In 1976 the "Nestorian" Assyrian patriarch renounced the most extreme of Nestorian positions as not reflective of his church's beliefs, and in 1997 a common Christological declaration was signed between the Nestorian churches of the East and the Roman Catholic Church. It has the potential to be a great achievement of ecumenism.

Ephesus, but one which had to be counterbalanced by Pope Leo's triumph at the Council of Chalcedon twenty years later. Once Cyril triumphed, he settled down to rule his see in peace, and in the thirteen years after Ephesus the Patriarchs of the East lived in harmony with one another. Having defeated his domestic enemies, Cyril was free to work on the virtues that occasionally seemed wanting in the early years of his episcopacy.

Saintly popes, difficult situations, poor decisions

Many saints have occupied the Chair of Peter, and we have met some of them. Their virtuous actions echoed well into future generations, developing and consolidating the office of the papacy. With their far-reaching decisions they laid a foundation that undergirded the Church of Rome during the most difficult of times, helping it to endure the vicissitudes of changing fortune. Yet even the saintliest and most well-intentioned pope cannot hope to compass all of the manifold issues facing the Church of Christ during his term in office. Indeed there is no position in the world that is so universal in scope and that bears such profound responsibilities. Given that, even the greatest of popes have made poor decisions, ones which reverberated for ill throughout the Church they ruled. Because the Church is human as well as divine, it remains true that practical mistakes and miscalculations are possible. Indeed, from an apologetical point of view, the gravity of such missteps and the continued existence of the Church can themselves be considered as signs of divine preservation. Over the course of 266 office holders, the See of Rome has experienced the full spectrum of human ability. Some popes have been exceptionally good administrators but did not achieve the honor of canonization—men such as Alexander III, Innocent III, and the popes of Avignon. Even some immoral popes were excellent governors, for example Alexander VI. Yet there are also examples of saints whose decisions were imprudent, limited in vision, or downright damaging to the Church. While their personal holiness and virtue is beyond reproach, it nonetheless happened that aspects of their rule were damaging. Given the challenges of the unique position of the pope, it is worth examining several administrative cases from the history of the Church in order to illustrate the possibilities and pitfalls of the highest office, and of those who serve it.

The brilliant exploits of Pope St. Leo IX (r. 1049–1053) have been recounted above. It was he who was the hinge of the reform and purification of the Roman Church in the eleventh century. Having liberated the papacy from the scourge of the Roman clans, the Gregorians then proceeded to struggle successfully to banish simony and to limit clerical concubinage. The reform they initiated reverberated through the Latin West for the rest of the Middle Ages, and set the stage for the worldwide expansion of the Church. In spite of this, a resurgent papacy was viewed with a jaundiced eye in the Greek East, at least in some quarters. While the position of the papacy in the early centuries of Christianity had been one of vigor and preservation of orthodoxy, no strong pope had been heard of in the East since St. Nicholas I (r. 858–867) had faced down Patriarch Photios. The sun had seemed to dim over "old" Rome during the *saeculum obscurum* and the East became used to managing its own affairs, particularly since Alexandria and Antioch had fallen to Islam, and Constantinople had emerged as the ecclesiastical power broker. By 1012, the name of the pope had been removed from the diptychs (the official list of those to be commemorated at liturgy) as the long simmering dispute over the *filioque* brewed.[27] Of more immediate

---

27   This is not so much a theological problem as a liturgical problem. While much polemical ink was spilled about whether the Spirit proceeds from the Father (the Eastern position) or the Father and the Son (the Latin position), most eventually realized it was a difference in theological language, with both meaning the Spirit proceeds from the Father through the Son, as from one principle. The real problem was that the Latins added the word to the Nicene Creed unilaterally, which the Greeks considered should only have been done by a Council (if at all). See A. Edward Siecienski, *The Filioque: History of a Doctrinal Controversy* (New York: Oxford University Press, 2010).

concern, starting in 999, Norman barons (converted Viking leaders) began to seek their fortunes in southern Italy, eventually taking most of the area south of Rome and establishing their respective overlordships. This area had a unique history. Long associated with the Byzantine empire, it was Greek in language and liturgy. At the same time, the area was traditionally under the ecclesial administration of Rome. Over the previous 300 years, the Archbishop of Constantinople, backed by Byzantine authority, had been poaching areas of traditional Roman administration in the periphery, as well as in Sicily and in Illyria. Now that the Roman See had been purified and was resurgent, it would seek to reclaim its authority in those disputed areas, and the Latin Normans provided an opportunity to do so.

Yet the Normans were really too unstable a power to effect lasting administrative improvements. They imposed the Latin rite by force when confronted with unusual Greek customs, leading to animosity not only between Latin and Greek authorities, but resentment among the common people. It was not just the Greek populace that they harassed; the Norman barons also threatened the Roman ecclesiastical establishment by attacking monasteries and seizing papal lands, such as the ancient duchy of Benevento. The reform party, given their close relations with the German empire at this time, called for an army to drive them out of the peninsula. Leo and his advisors assembled an impressive alliance of Romans, Germans, Swabians, and the Lombard lords of the south. In 1053 the combined papal and imperial army met the Normans at Civitate, between Foggia and Termoli. Leo, who had led troops in his youth before ordination, accompanied the force to oversee it personally. He underestimated the skill and unity of the Normans against his rather motley force, handicapped as it was by employing a variety languages and tactics. Leo's advance was also too precipitous because he did not wait for his last ally to arrive—namely, the Byzantine general Argyros. The result was a disaster. Leo was captured and held by the Normans for the remaining year of his life. While he was treated honorably and lodged comfortably, it was nonetheless clear he was a prisoner.[28] He was generally left free to govern the Church, but was forced to accepting the Norman occupation of the south of Italy. A real opportunity had been lost. Both the general and the emperor, Constantine IX Monomachos, were sympathetic to the pope and opposed to the Normans. The Byzantines had wanted to ally with the pope and his forces, and Leo was more than happy to acknowledge any territories that they recaptured as their own, probably with a hope that his ecclesiastical governance would be recognized in turn. As it happened, Argyros was now too weak to face the Normans alone and had to send most of his forces back to Greece.

Yet there were even more serious storms brewing. The imposition of Latin rites on the people of southern Italy had aroused indignation in the East. While there had always been a hazy awareness and general toleration of distinct liturgical traditions of the Latin and Greek churches, during the first thousand years people generally remained within their own ritual territories.[29] With the rise of proto-capitalism, the Italian trading cities began bringing new knowledge of religious practices, and indeed opened Latin churches of their own in Constantinople. At this point there was no suspicion, but rather a recognition, that each worshipped God in its own particular tradition, all using customs that were believed to extend back to the time of the Apostles. In the eleventh century the Byzantines had conquered the Armenians, whose Christianity included many practices similar to the Latin Church (such as the use of unleavened bread). Many Greeks had attempted to "correct" what they considered to be improper Armenian usages, arguments that would be later employed against the West. The Greeks found themselves between two ancient "azymite" Churches. When the ham-fisted Normans forcibly imposed Latin forms, the issue came

---

28   Henry Chadwick, *East and West: The Making of a Rift in the Church: From Apostolic Times Until the Council of Florence* (Oxford: Oxford University Press, 2003), 200.

29   Andrew Louth, *Greek East and Latin West: The Church, AD 681–1071* (Crestwood, NY: St. Vladimir's Seminary Press, 2007), 307.

to a head. The stability of ancient rites of worship is one of the most important anchors of orthodoxy and identity in Christian history, and to disturb it is to upset the religious sense of the Church. People began to notice differences and then to criticize them, eventually elevating them into elaborate arguments about the illegality or even invalidity of the foreign rite. Unfortunately for the unity of the Church, this series of events began to gather downhill momentum, turning into an increasingly intractable situation that has since become almost a primer on how *not* to govern in the Church of God.

These circumstances swirled around two individuals—namely, Cardinal Humbert of Silva-Candida and Patriarch Michael Cerularius. The latter was a civil servant who had been forced into the clerical state because he had been frustrated in his political ambitions, a not unusual punishment in Byzantine Christianity.[30] He had shifted those ambitions to the ecclesiastical track and in 1043 achieved the office of patriarch. He was a man of limited imagination and theological training, but possessed nearly overmastering ambition for the prestige of his own office. He was criticized by contemporary Greeks for his affectation of purple shoes (the color only the emperors were allowed to wear), and when he was made known of papal pretensions from the *Donation of Constantine* he did not hesitate to counter by attempting to turn its unhistorical claims in favor of his own see, seeking to become a sort of "papacy of the East."[31] Humbert had different issues. He was a recognized

---

30 For Cerularius, see Franz Hermann Tinnefeld, "Michael I. Kerullarios, Patriarch von Konstantinopel (1043–1058). Kritische Überlegungen zu einer Biographie," in *Jahrbuch der österreichischen Byzantinistik* 39 (1989): 95–128. See also the older but still useful study: Anton Michel, *Humbert und Kerullarios* (Paderborn: Druck und Verlag von Ferdinand Schöningh, 1924).

31 Louth, *Greek East and Latin West*, 309. See also, Steven Runciman, *The Eastern Schism: A Study of the Papacy and the Eastern Churches During the XIth and XIIth Centuries* (Oxford: Clarendon, 1955), 39. This is an older work, and mostly pro-Byzantine, but much better written and laid out than many modern works.

leader of the extreme wing of the reform, one absolutely loyal to his vision of a purified and elevated papacy. Runciman says he was "a man of some erudition and of genuine if narrow piety, but he was hot-tempered and truculent."[32] His worldview was very nearly dualist. Whoever supported his vision of the reformed papacy was on the side of right and good, but any who opposed it was deemed evil. The Normans permitted St. Leo to have some retainers with him in his captivity in Benevento, and Humbert was among them. While there they received an alarming attack from Bishop Leo of Ochrida in Bulgaria who viciously attacked Latin liturgical practices. While Cerularius may have been behind it, there is no direct evidence. We do know that the patriarch sympathized with the contentions of the pamphlet and ordered all Latin churches in Constantinople to be closed because they used unleavened bread.[33] Indeed Cerularius sent a letter full of friendly words to Pope St. Leo, while pointedly calling himself "Ecumenical Patriarch" and addressing the pope as "Brother" instead of "Father." In it he made his proposal for a sort of "Eastern papacy." The pope could tolerate the situation no longer. It was here that St. Leo made his fundamental mistake in choosing Humbert to take the lead in responding to the challenge. In Leo's defense, his health was at the time failing, and Humbert was one of his only close allies in attendance. Further Humbert alone, it appears, knew Greek, at least to a certain extent. At this time knowledge of Greek in the West was

32   Ibid., 44. Still, his erudition was limited. He mishandled the Eucharistic controversy with Berengar badly by demanding he confess a crude physicalism in the Eucharist. This later had to be corrected under St. Gregory VII so that Berengar's confession was closer to the later doctrine of Transubstantiation. See Louth, *Greek East and Latin West,* 300.
33   It is possible that an overzealous enforcer of Cerularius' decree trampled the Latin Eucharist in the street, believing it to be unconsecrated. While only Western sources report this, I think it helps to explain the tone of the Latin response. See Henry Chadwick, *East and West: The Making of a Rift in the Church: from Apostolic Times Until the Council of Florence* (Oxford: Oxford University Press, 2003), 200–202.

as rare as Latin in the East, itself a major cause of the deterioration of relations.[34]

Yet St. Leo seemed to confuse loyalty for competence. He empowered Humbert to answer the charges. This Humbert set out to do with relish. The cardinal prepared two fiery rejoinders, but their dispatch was delayed for two reasons. First, a friendly letter had come from the emperor inviting a renewed alliance; second, Humbert's letters were excessively intemperate, and Leo compelled the cardinal to rewrite them. Eventually the pope concluded that it would be best to send legates personally. Humbert was empowered along with two others who, because they could not speak Greek, were silent observers of what now became entirely the cardinal's drama.

On the way, Humbert stopped to consult with the Byzantine commander, Argyros. This in itself was imprudent for the Latins knew that Argyros was an ally to them and an implacable enemy of Michael Cerularius. He was a personal friend of the emperor and a defender of the validity of unleavened Eucharistic consecrations. He gave them the advice to negotiate only with the emperor and to marginalize Cerularius. They followed it to the letter, much to the damage of their cause.[35] Cerularius was popular and Argyros and the emperor were not. Upon their arrival in the imperial city, they were received coolly by Cerularius and not treated according to their dignity as legates. Humbert responded in kind, leaving his letter from the pope in the patriarch's hands and going directly to see the emperor, where he was received with the dignity that he expected. Cerularius "noticed" that the seal was damaged, and charged that Argyros had tampered with the papal letter. (It seems unlikely that Cerularius decided the seal had been broken until after he had read the contents.) The letter was largely the work of Humbert. It relied heavily on the *Donation of Constantine*, then unknown in the East, and appended a long list of heretics who had occupied the see of Constantinople.[36] He even made

---

34 Indeed the Patriarch of Antioch had to send a papal letter all the way back to Constantinople in order for it to receive even a substandard translation.

35 Runciman, 45.

the charge that the East had *dropped* the word *Filioque* from the creed, rather than that the West had added it. Humbert was as poor an historian as he was a theologian. The situation simmered for a month. In his impatience Humbert started to stir up a pamphlet war with various Greek monks, and they hurled invective and polemic back and forth until the emperor, fearful of the papal alliance, forced the Greeks to apologize to the legate.[37]

However, the public spat had definitively turned public opinion against Humbert. By 16 July 1054 Humbert had had enough. With the two other legates in tow, he marched to Justinian's great basilica of Hagia Sophia. There in one of the most dismal displays in the history of Christendom, he laid a bull excommunicating Cerularius and his supporters on the high altar and stormed out, symbolically shaking the dust off his feet as he went. Cerularius probably watched from a niche. He was as exultant at the result as the emperor was appalled. Constantine had personally to guarantee the safe conduct of the legates, for the fickle Byzantine crowds had been driven to frenzy by the patriarch's agents. Cerularius later burned the bull publicly and began a public relations campaign against the Latin rites that continues to echo in the present day.

The denouement to this sorry episode was the fact that St. Leo had himself died, worn out by his labors, on 15 April. We do not know when news of his death reached Constantinople. In ordinary times it would have taken about two months, but given the extraordinary situation of the Normans in the south of Italy, the widening divide between East and West, and the language issue, it may have taken longer. The sad irony was that canonically Humbert had lost all authority upon the death of the pope.[38] The excommunication was technically

---

36   While it must be admitted there were many heretical patriarchs, Humbert clumsily added *Pope* Honorius (accused of Monothelitism) to his list, a damaging mistake to be sure.

37   Chadwick, *East and West*, 207.

38   Though the loss of legatine authority was uncertain at the time, the general tendency was to affirm that they lost it the moment the delegating pontiff died, a position that became part of the decretals within the next centuries. See Emil Herman, "Legati inviati da Leone

null and void. That did not stop Cerularius from excommunicating the legates in return. Both were closely worded and only affected the main participants. In the Greek text the pope was not mentioned, leaving any future Roman bishop to declare that Humbert had acted *ultra vires*.[39] Humbert returned from the East trumpeting his "victory" over the recalcitrant Greeks. His reports biased the West, just as Cerularius was busy publishing half-truths about the Latins that poisoned the well there. While the split of 1054 was scarcely noticed at the time, schisms become deeply entrenched with the passage of years. Whereas there were serious attempts under Bl. Urban II to heal the schism, not to mention the efforts of the Second Council of Lyons (1274) and the Council of Florence (1439), the damage had been done.[40] Wounds that had been festering for centuries had broken open because of the failures of two mediocre men, and the inability of a saint to head it all off. It would be consummated in the vicious sack of the city by excommunicated "crusaders" in 1204.[41]

The Great Refusal

By the turn of the thirteenth century the papacy had waxed strong in its influence over Latin Christendom. Having defeated the German empire on several occasions and secured the liberty of the Church, a

IX nel 1054 a Costantinopoli erano autorizzati a scomunicare il patriarca Michele Cerulario?" in *Orientalia christiana periodica* 8 (1942): 209–218. It is my suspicion that news of the pope's death arrived soon after the excommunication.

39 Runciman, 50. Indeed this is precisely what happened when, in 1965, Pope Paul VI and Patriarch Athenagoras mutually withdrew the excommunications.

40 Once again, the perspicacity and prudence of Bl. Urban II is remarkable and bears further study. See W. Holtzmann, "Die Unionsverhandlungen zwischen Kaiser Alexios I und Papst Urban II im Jahre 1089," *Byzantinische Zeitschrift* 28 (1928): 38–67.

41 For an excellent account of the sad history, and with an eye to theology, see Yves Congar, O.P. *After Nine Hundred Years: The Background of the Schism between the Eastern and Western Churches* (New York: Fordham University Press, 1959).

series of exceptionally competent popes succeeded to the throne, one after another. After the defeat of the House of Hohenstaufen by the 1260s, there were few to challenge the supremacy of the Holy See. Yet from that date a series of weaker popes caused diminishing returns that squandered much of the achievements of the previous two centuries. Indeed Martin IV (r. 1281–1285) most seriously compromised the papacy by using his papal power for the benefit of France, thereby alienating not only the Italians, but much of Europe, not to mention destroying the delicate negotiations with the Greek East. The College of Cardinals had become significantly reduced in numbers and factionalism had risen to such an extent that each successive papal conclave could stretch for months or even years before a pope could be elected, decreasing the prestige of both the college and the Holy See. Deep rifts formed between French and Italian cardinals that led to a reaction after Martin that tilted the control in the college back to the Italians. This did not, however, end the rivalries, for the Romans continued to align themselves along powerful family lines, thus creating situations where it was well-nigh impossible to come to the necessary two-thirds consensus. Indeed some, like St. Bonaventure, had virtually imprisoned the cardinals, and put them on a diet of bread and water to coerce them to elect a pontiff. At one point the city of Viterbo, tired of a seemingly endless conclave, pulled the roof off the building where the cardinals were meeting in order to expose them to the elements. When Pope Nicholas IV (r. 1288–1292) died, there were only twelve cardinal-electors, ten Italian and two French (one of whom died during the long deliberations). Evenly divided between the Roman clans, no one was able to obtain a majority.

The cardinals at the time were not paragons of ecclesial virtue, focused as they were on politics rather than on the good of the Church. Indeed, one English chronicler went so far as to say they were not "cardinals" but "carnals."[42] More concerned about the

---

42   Bartholomew of Cotton (d. Ca 1298), cf. Horace Mann, *History of the Popes*, vol. XVII (St. Louis: Herder, 1931), 254n1. St. Antoninus censured these cardinals in particular when he said, "They sought things for their own, and not for Jesus Christ." Ibid., 254n2.

diplomatic relationship of the papacy to France, they debated fruit-
lessly while wars broke out all over Europe. One of the only cardinals
of quality was the dean, Latino Malabranca, O.P. He attempted to
guide them to elect a man of experience and virtue. They met period-
ically in various locations in the Eternal City before finally settling on
Santa Maria sopra Minerva. There they wrangled for more than a
year, while Rome literally burned. It was customary to release prisoners upon the death of a pope and these added to the general atmosphere of chaos in the Holy City. Not only was there a lack of
spiritual leadership, the two leading members of the contending
Roman families both died at the same time. In the resulting anarchy,
religious houses were plundered and pilgrims robbed.[43] The cities of
the Papal States immediately began to wage war upon one another.
Particularly aggressive was the city of Orvieto, which the college
threatened with an invasion, all to no avail. The leaders of Orvieto
sent back a mocking rejoinder that when a pope is elected they would
obey him and lay down arms. The cardinals, who had essentially created the chaos, abandoned Rome and sought refuge in the hill city of
Perugia in October 1293, still divided, but at least meeting again. Facing the looming collapse of Church authority in Rome and the Papal
States, the cardinals at length realized that a pope was truly needed.

On 5 July 1294 the college was at last in a serious and somber
mood after attending the funeral of a young nephew of one of the
cardinals. Latino read a letter from a holy hermit who lived on a
mountainside in the Abruzzo, declaring that God would harshly
judge the cardinals for their lack of care for Christ's Church. Finding that the hermit was Peter Murrone, some of the other cardinals
who had met him began to talk about his holy virtues, his founding
communities of hermits and living such a life of asceticism as could
not be more opposed to their own.[44] They began to be struck by

43 Mann notes an entry from an *Icelandic* chronicle to this effect,
    demonstrating how this infamous episode echoed to the far corners
    of Christendom. Ibid., 260.
44 For Peter Murrone, see Alessandra Bartolomei Romagnoli, *Una
    memoria controversa. Celestino V e le sue fonti* (Florence: Edizioni

compunction and a sense of duty began slowly to flow back into them. The upright Latino cried out, "I elect Peter Murrone."[45] Quickly the other cardinals added their voices until the whole of the college unanimously settled upon the Abruzzese hermit. He seemed the perfect choice. Not only was he unaffiliated with any political party, Murrone was not associated with any of the existing Roman families. His Italian nationality prevented too much French influence. Further, he was the epitome of holiness and a living symbol of the best traditions of reformed Christianity that ran back to Francis and Bernard. His piety would revolutionize the Church and provide a shining beacon of holy leadership to the whole of Christendom.[46] As it turns out, the election of the man who became St. Celestine V was one of the worst decisions ever made in the history of selecting the Vicar of Christ.

The Church is an incarnational reality in which nature builds upon grace. To use St. Paul's metaphor, it is a body with Christ as head. Each member has a particular specialty that maintains the proper functioning of the body. These parts are not interchangeable—a hand cannot become a foot and vice versa. Given natural aptitudes, each can be strengthened within its own

del Galluzzo, 2013); Paolo Golinelli, *Il papa contadino: Celestino V e il suo tempo* (Florence: Camunia, 1996); Peter Herde, *Cölestin V (1294): Peter vom Morrone, der Engelpapst: mit einem Urkundenanhang und Edition zweier Viten* (Stuttgart : Anton Hiersemann, 1981); and for the original sources, see id. *Die ältesten Viten Papst Cölestins V (Peters vom Morrone)*, Monumenta Germaniae Historica: Scriptores rerum Germanicarum, Nova Series 23 (Hannover: Hahnsche Buchhandlung, 2008), which has a comprehensive bibliography, 58–62.

45   Before 1996 this "Quasi-Inspiration" was one of the three permissible methods of papal selection beside election and compromise. For the election, see Golinelli, *Il papa contadino*, 111–117. Golinelli seems to think it was by compromise, but this is as close to "Quasi-inspiration" as one can get, even though the votes of the absent cardinals were later obtained.

46   For the conclave itself, see Herde, *Peter vom Morrone*, 31–83, and Golinelli, *Il papa contadino*, 99–117.

domain, to the lasting and improved health of the whole organism of the Church. Sainthood, as a gift from God, touches every member of Christ's Body and can become enacted at any age or state in life. It does not, however, remove one's good natural proclivities, orientations, or aptitudes. If a man is ignorant of philosophy, no amount of holiness will enable him to teach it as an expert (absent the infusion of some special grace that, in any case, erases such ignorance). In reality, sanctity becomes more difficult the more one "kicks against the goad" (Acts 26:14). God certainly gives grace for seemingly impossible situations, but that grace is to augment holiness, and not necessarily to attain success. Additionally, reactive decisions are almost never good ones. The worldly cardinals—backed into a corner—essentially panicked. Even in the midst of their venal partiality, they recognized the root need for holiness in the Church and convinced themselves that piety could solve all of their problems. It was not even a statement of their own desire for conversion, but for a vicarious sanctity that might cover their sins. The aqueous virtue of the college met with the saintly unction of Peter Murrone, and as everyone knows, water and oil do not mix.

Representatives of the cardinals—none of the comfortable electors deigned to make the trip—trundled out of Perugia to the mountains of Abruzzo, puffing all the way up the hermit's mountain. The well-fed princes of the Church met Peter in his subterranean home in one of the most affecting scenes of Christian history. The bishops genuflected in front of the old, gaunt man, and he in turn prostrated himself in front of them. Peter was likely in his late seventies at this time; he had been a monk for all his life and effectively a hermit since 1256.[47] Like Francis, he attracted many followers, but preferred his life of solitary retirement.[48] Though he inspired many vocations, even in his religious life he

---

47   Golinelli dates his birth to 1209–1210. See *Il papa contadino*, 17.
48   Indeed, despite later Spiritual Franciscans who wanted to assimilate Peter to their cause, he was eminently non-Franciscan in his preference for rural rusticity and eremitism. Ibid., 247.

was no organizer.[49] Indeed it appears that members of his order (later the called Celestines) were overly focused on the person of the founder, and the order then rapidly degenerated after his death.[50] He proved incapable of maintaining office as an abbot on two separate occasions, particularly when hard pressed by a secular lord. He simply resigned and retired once again to solitude. This silence was spectacularly broken in the second week of July 1294. News had raced ahead of the delegates, and Peter already knew what they had come to announce. He was in a deep depression and had resolved to flee, but the common people among whom he lived and who knew him best would not permit it. After having prayed long and hard, he had been repeatedly admonished by his own followers to accept the tiara, and indeed not with wholly unselfish intentions. He reluctantly acceded to election for the good of the Church.[51]

Almost immediately he was besieged by the lords of both Church and state, seeking their own respective advantage in attempts to suborn him to their positions. In particular, he was deferential to Charles II of Anjou, who had been his king and who had shown himself favorable to his brotherhood. In many ways, Charles II became the leading mover of the papacy's policy.[52] Peter, now Celestine V, took it as a very great kindness that Charles took so many matters in hand, especially things with which the new pope was utterly unfamiliar. Celestine immediately (and unknowingly) alienated the curia when he placed much of the day-to-day management of the papal household in the hands of Neapolitan

49 He was able to convince Bl. Gregory X not to suppress the order following the restriction of religious Rules after Lyons II in 1274. He did this not by administrative brilliance, but by the charismatic power of his own holiness. See Golinelli, *Il papa contadino*, 69–75.

50 For the order, see Karl Borchardt, *Die Cölestiner. Eine Mönchsgemeinschaft des späteren Mittelalters* (Husum: Matthiesen, 2006); and Gert Melville, *The World of Medieval Monasticism*, trans. James Mixson (Collegeville, MN: Liturgical Press, 2016), 267–276.

51 Golinelli, *Il papa contadino*, 121–124.

52 Ibid., 133–160, Herde, *Peter vom Morrone*, 84–87.

lay lawyers. In reality, it was the cardinals' own fault for neglecting to inform him of his election personally. They pleaded with Celestine to come to papal territory, but when he did so he scandalized the leaders of Church and state alike by riding an ass the whole way to Aquila. He refused to come to the cardinals and requested that they send on the coronation regalia to Abruzzo, for he willed to be crowned there, against all advice. Again, contrary to custom, he appointed Bartholomew of Capua a notary.[53] Bartholomew was a good man; indeed, he was later a key witness in the canonization of Thomas Aquinas, but he was a layman and in the employment of Charles II. Celestine continued to antagonize the cardinals with his unconventional decisions. Everyone but Celestine could see that it was Charles II calling the shots. Even worse was his choice of vice-chancellor of the Roman Church—namely, the Archbishop of Benevento, John of Castrocoeli. This John was a social climber and totally unsuited to his position. He had no desire for the good of the Church and was a mere timeserver. Eventually the cardinals realized they had to come to the pope, even though he was in Charles II's territory. Charles had by this time, however, achieved most of his ends vis-a-vis the Church, and the cardinals were able to reassert control over at least ecclesiastical business.

"Management" of the pope therefore passed into the hands of the college, in particular Cardinal Benedetto Gaetani, whom the chronicler Ptolemy of Lucca curtly describes as the "Lord of the Curia." Celestine was quite popular among the common people, but he rubbed the nobility and princes of the Church the wrong way. While he permitted the traditional coronation banquets, the pope often absented himself, preferring to eat dry bread in his own quarters. Instead of using the curial servitors, he surrounded himself with rude, peasant monks, who themselves exhibited a truculent self-interest. Celestine blamed the monks for making him accept the papacy. In a telling remark he said, "It is a greater annoyance to me to command than it was a pleasure to

53   Golinelli, *Il papa contadino*, 139; Herde, *Peter vom Morrone*, 87.

do everything for myself."[54] The manners of Celestine (who had come from a peasant family) and those of his monks offended the curia deeply. His utter lack of education handicapped him terribly when attempting to govern. Whereas some cardinals, like Gaetani, tried to manage the affairs of the Church in the normal way, Celestine constantly undercut them. One chronicler gave the reason, "certain cardinals, lacking consciences, deceived him daily."[55] A steady flow of supplicants streamed into the pope's presence, likely drawn like moths to a flame given the knowledge of his simplicity. He would promise a benefice to one person, and then promptly assign it to another person in perfect sincerity. He seemed incapable of saying "no" to anyone, meaning that near universal satisfaction as quickly turned into near universal rage.[56] His innate generosity and desire to do well led him to the fatal error of being unable to make any hard decisions. Even when he acted decisively, it ended disastrously. For instance, one day he decided that he wanted the monks of the ancient monastery of Montecassino to conform to the Rule of his new order, exchanging their old black Benedictine habits for the white of the Celestines. He forcibly appointed one of his own monks as abbot, and this new abbot promptly expelled any monks who resisted. His unjust reign would not outlast that of the pope who appointed him.[57] One day he decided to award the extraordinary privilege of a plenary indulgence to a church in out-of-the-way Aquila, which began to draw pilgrims. While this was an original idea, it had the effect of appearing exceptionally peculiar and pulling pilgrims away from Rome and into the Kingdom of Naples. His successor abolished the indulgence, but then adapted

---

54 Mann, *History of the Popes*, vol. XVII, 291n1.
55 Ibid., 292n3.
56 As the famous canonist Johannes Andreae puts it (rather uncharitably), "He acted like an animal that lacks the light of reason. He would grant a favor in the morning, and in the evening recall it, and grant it to another." Ibid., 294n2.
57 Ibid., 299–300; Golinelli, *Il papa contadino*, 156–157; Herde, *Peter vom Morrone*, 117–118.

the idea into the first Jubilee year in 1300. Even a good idea of Celestine's it seemed would not do without reworking.[58]

His simplicity and obliviousness allowed corrupt curialists to act as they wished. A virtual industry of "fill-in-the-blank" privileges began to filter out from the papal notaries. There were so many that the next pope was forced to revoke nearly all Celestine's privileges *in toto*. Even when he tried to ameliorate ecclesiastical conditions, the situation backfired. Knowing that some of the difficulties of papal elections in the past had been due to the paucity of cardinals, he decided that he would hold a consistory. On 18 September 1294 he named no fewer than twelve new cardinals, the largest such elevation in over a century. While his intentions were impeccable, it became painfully obvious that Charles II had engineered nearly the whole series of nominees.[59] There were seven Frenchmen and five Neapolitans, of whom two were in the immediate service of Charles II. Apparently managed by Bartholomew of Capua, the whole slate was sprung upon the existing cardinals with no warning. Within a day the new princes of the Church were created. The pope later compounded the problem by irregularly elevating the terrible John of Castrocoeli to the cardinalate.[60] Celestine simply refused to consult the College of Cardinals about much that he did, and it is not clear whether he did this out of simplicity, awe, or a spiritual conviction that he was there as the direct representative of God. It is also true that he lacked one critically basic skill—namely, he was a poor speaker of Latin. It is futile for an organization to be led by someone who is ignorant of that group's

---

58   Scholars have paid particular attention to the roots of the Jubilee in Celestine's original plenary indulgence. See Chiara Frugoni, *Due papi per un giubileo: Celestino V, Bonifacio VIII e il primo Anno santo* (Milan: Rizzoli, 2000); and Arnaldo di Medio, *Le prime grandi perdonanze: Celestino V e Bonifacio VIII, due papi innovatori* (Barzago: Marna, 2002).

59   Golinelli, *Il papa contadino*, 139–141.

60   Even the pious Bl. Jacobus of Voragine says of this, "[T]he pope, who in the plenitude of his power had made twelve cardinals, in the plenitude of his simplicity made another." Cfr. Mann, 296.

primary idiom. He would not reply to public questions, nor would he deliver any directives. Living in a simple manner at the heart of the curia, it seems he was convinced that his example alone would provide the necessary direction. He was wrong. His pious activities had attracted attention beyond the curia. The party of zealots within the Franciscan order began to consider him as the "Angel Pope" sent for the purification of the Church in the end times.[61] They surmised that his papacy marked the beginning of a "third age" of the Spirit, when the old institutions would fall away.[62] Unfortunately Celestine appeared to give encouragement to these men who, emboldened, began to spread their ideas even more widely.

Many seeds were planted in his pontificate that would bear terrible fruit in the future. The irregular appointment of the incompetent, fawning Castrocoeli was enough for most of the cardinals, but the straw that broke the camel's back was Charles II's dominance over Celestine. For example, he induced the pope to redirect the entirety of the crusade tithes from England and France into Charles' coffers so that the king could regain Sicily for his realm.[63] Seeing that—under the king's influence—the pope was unlikely to go back to Rome, the cardinals obtained the king's oath that he would not interfere in a conclave should the pope die in the former's territory. Celestine promptly annulled Charles' oath such that the monarch could ensure that the cardinals were properly sealed in a conclave. This irritated the cardinals to no end; they had tried to secure the freedom of a future election but found themselves thwarted once again by the new pope.

To his credit, and as a testament to his sanctity, Celestine V came to understand that he was incompetent as pope. He knew he was making bad decisions but had no idea how to go about making good ones. As such he began to conceive of a way out. At the start

---

61 Herde, *Peter vom Morrone*, 111–114.

62 Later Spiritual Franciscans will spin this into a narrative of Celestine as the "Angel pope" deposed by the devilish and heretical Boniface VIII. See Golinelli, *Il papa contadino*, 174–176.

63 Mann, 308.

of the "Lent of St. Martin" on 11 November 1294, he decided to go into his customary solitary retreat, wishing to remain aloof from the business of the Church.[64] His advisors told him that this was impossible. Instead of bearing his responsibility he took the highly imprudent step of attempting to "assign" his power and universal authority to a commission of three cardinals. To their credit these cardinals informed him that he had no such power to change divine law in that manner, and he was persuaded to withdraw the decree.[65] He finally conceived the notion that he would resign and, after consulting friends and some of the cardinals, was relieved to find out that there was some historical precedent for such an action. It seems that while some *pro forma* protests were made to Celestine, both sides were exceedingly pleased with the possibility. I find it likely that Benedetto Gaetani not only offered legal advice, but indeed persuaded Celestine to take the step of renunciation.[66] Indeed it seems the pope placed himself in Gaetani's hands. After scenes of popular and political tumult at the news, Celestine spent a week seemingly pretending that he would not resign, all the while drawing up a writ of renunciation with Gaetani. All at once on 13 December he hastily summoned the cardinals, who found him dressed in the full pontifical regalia. He read out the writ with the decisive formula that he resigned freely and of his own will. One by one he deposited the pieces of the regalia. Petrarch records how the throne he ascended with sorrow, he now divested with joy.[67]

64 Golinelli, *Il papa contadino*, 159. The extended Advent season was common in religious orders and in some ritual traditions, such as the Ambrosian Rite.

65 Mann, 311.

66 Mann tries exceptionally hard to exonerate Gaetani (soon after elected as Pope Boniface VIII), but I remain unconvinced. Ibid., 317–318. Several contemporary sources detail Boniface's pressure on Celestine, and sympathetic sources provide no denial. Golinelli is correct, however, that Celestine needed no prodding to step down. See *Il papa contadino*, 162.

67 Petrarch, *On the Life of Solitude*, trans. Jacob Zeitlin (Champaign-Urbana: University of Illinois Press, 1924), 235.

One chronicler put it thus: "On St. Lucy's day Pope Celestine resigned the papacy, and he did well!"[68] Within two weeks the throne of St. Peter passed to Benedetto Gaetani as Pope Boniface VIII (r. 1294–1303), for good and for ill. It is likely that Celestine had recommended Boniface personally to the cardinals, and it is equally probable that this was the end that Boniface himself had been working toward for the previous several months. The former Pope Celestine V immediately promised homage and reverence to his successor and asked nothing more than to return to his hermitage. However, Boniface was a canny political operator and well aware that his enemies might use Celestine as a pawn against him. It appears he began to mistreat Celestine, after which the former pope fled from the curia and returned to his mountain. Boniface's agents pursued and captured him, and eventually bound Peter Celestine (as he came to be known) in prison. The former pope welcomed his cramped jail as a new hermitage, "I have longed for a cell, and I have received a cell." For the remaining ten months of his life he remained in that room, though it seems he was treated with respect. At length (for he was nearly 85 by this time) he began to suffer from an abscess. "He who had dominion over the whole earth, and had left it all for Christ ... lay dying on a board covered with a single cloak."[69]

Celestine finally died on 19 May 1295. He was undeniably a saint of God and as such received the honor of formal canonization in 1313.[70] Yet nearly all his acts were immediately annulled by his successor (while Celestine still lived).[71] Mann, a partisan of both Celestine and Boniface, has this to say: "[T]here is no temptation to linger on the pontificate of Celestine, pitiable in itself and deplorable in its results. The foolish acts performed in it brought

---

68   Mann, *Lives of the Popes*, vol. XVII, 323.

69   Ibid., 334.

70   Yet even this was a 'victory lap' of sorts for the French King Philip IV, who had outmaneuvered Boniface VIII and brought the papacy to Avignon.

71   Boniface VIII, *Olim Celestinus*, 8 April 1295.

ill-deserved odium on his successor ... [and] through the preponderance of French cardinals whom Celestine created, he involved the Church in one disaster after another, culminating in the Great Schism of the West."[72] Dante immortalized him as the coward of the "Great Refusal" whose actions brought terrible ruin to the church.[73] In spite of his undeniable sanctity and virtues, there has never been a Pope Celestine VI.

Exemplarity and the Paradox of Leadership

"Whoever exalts himself will be humbled, and whoever humbles himself will be exalted" (Mt 23:12). A tension approaching paradox has beset the exercise of leadership from the very dawn of the Christian religion. If the early Church added anything to the ethical doctrine of the virtuous Greeks it was the sublime teaching of humility, of a God who "emptied Himself, taking the form of a slave" (Phil 2:8). Christ, by right monarch and absolute lord of the universe, came to wash his disciples' feet, ushering in a new prototype of authority. As St. Ignatius of Antioch mysteriously put it in his letter to the Romans while on the way to martyrdom, how exactly does one "preside in the Love"? From the beginning, Church administrators have labored to reconcile the seemingly opposed aspects of servant and leader. While—given the incarnational nature of the Church—administration is natural and necessary, it too needed to be transformed in the light of the gospel. On many occasions as we have seen, this has been resolved satisfactorily for, like so many other teachings in Christianity, it is only apparently a paradox. In the imitation of Christ, leadership can be exercised as a ministry of order for the salvation of souls. On some occasions, Church leaders abandon the path of holiness

---

72   Ibid., 310.

73   Dante, *Inferno*, III. 58–60. Despite periodic doubts about the identity of the coward, the uncomfortable consensus is that Peter Murrone is among the wandering shades of outside the gates of Hell. See the summary in Robert Hollander, ed. and trans., *The Inferno* (New York: Anchor Books, 2002), 60.

and humility and act like little more than secular lords in cassocks. Sometimes, like St. Celestine V, they fail utterly to reconcile the paradox. Yet there remains one final, singular path chosen by one of the most beloved saints in history—namely, St. Francis of Assisi.[74]

Francis was a man of paradox himself, challenging both his society and ours with his radical call to abandon all for Christ and to practice the *minoritas* of a "lesser brother." The ambiguity manifested itself especially in the singularity of his call. His conversion was as personal and unrepeatable as it was dramatic and extraordinary. Coming from the burgeoning and upwardly mobile medieval bourgeoise, he added a taste for chivalric fancy. All in all, he spent a dissipated, if not actively immoral, youth enjoying the comforts of the rapidly growing towns of medieval Italy. By degree he grew tired both of the life of the merchant and of the soldier, preferring to spend more and more time alone, in remote chapels in the countryside. Following a sensational divestment of money and familial attachments in the presence of the Bishop of Assisi, Francis enrolled himself as a public penitent and spent his days wandering, repairing decrepit chapels, and begging for building materials. He lived an essentially semi-eremitical life for several years until 1208. That year, he says, "The Lord sent me brothers."

These two utterly unexpected followers completely unnerved Francis, who had no idea how to proceed as the leader of a group. He

---

74 To say the literature on Francis is voluminous is an understatement, one could call it an "industry." The two most notable recent—and excellent—biographies are: André Vauchez, *Francis of Assisi: The Life and Afterlife of a Medieval Saint*, trans. Michael F. Cusato (New Haven: Yale University Press, 2012); and Augustine Thompson, *Francis of Assisi: A New Biography* (Ithaca, NY: Cornell University Press, 2012). The sources for the life of Francis have been newly edited in Regis J. Armstrong, J. A. Wayne Hellmann, and William J. Short. *Francis of Assisi: Early Documents*, 4 vols. (Hyde Park, NY: New City Press, 1999). The best breakdown of the complicated and controversial sources for his life is in Thompson, *Francis*, "Sources and Debates," 223–410.

frankly confesses that "there was no one to tell me what to do," yet now men looked to him for guidance. In the absence of instructions, other than the form of the life of abandonment and humility he found in the gospels, he decided that he must go to Rome to get direction from the pope himself. Uncomfortable with leadership, he selected his follower Bernard as superior, but as soon as they got to Rome, Francis immediately took the lead in explaining his ideas to the curia. This pattern would be repeated for the rest of Francis' life. He needed to command in order to preserve his vision, but refused to command at the same time. It was a tension that led to spiritual agony on his part.[75]

In Rome Francis received the papal command he wished, but it directed him in a way that surprised and discomfited him. Innocent III (r. 1198–1216), a wise and far-seeing pope, directed the little band to become a fraternity dedicated to preaching, much like several other groups established during his pontificate. Francis was tonsured as a cleric, something that shocked and bemused him. The small group of lay penitent hermits had been redirected by the pope himself into the living stream of public preaching. Their elevation to clerical status was for a twofold purpose: it shielded them from accusations of heresy and gave them canonical mission to preach. It was the first step along the road that would eventually lead to becoming a legally established and well-educated order. Francis spent the remainder of his life attempting to reconcile the tensions inherent between his desire for eremitism and his new public mission, all the while navigating the difficult path between humility and leadership.[76]

After this verbal approval more and more brothers began to affiliate themselves, attracted by Francis' self-evident sanctity. This

75 Thompson, *Francis*, 35–38.
76 Indeed the majority of episodes which show Francis with some kind of inner peace after this are in eremitical settings, David Burr, *The Spiritual Franciscans: From Protest to Persecution in the Century After Saint Francis* (University Park, PA: Pennsylvania State University Press, 2001), 13. Left to his own devices, his group would likely have been much smaller, resembling the Camaldolese of St. Romuald.

growth only increased his disquiet. It was his conviction that he should only lead the brothers by example. Creating rules was exceptionally foreign to him. Such administration, to his way of thinking, put him in an unacceptable position of dominance. As Thompson puts it, "his disciples had to watch him closely and do their best to get the drift. Their leader's own call to leave the world was so intense, so personal, that he could never explain it fully, much less sketch out a program to make it practical or concrete."[77] He was a man who reacted as events came up, truly a follower taking seriously Christ's admonition of "taking no thought for the morrow" (Mt 6:34). His intense faith buoyed the little fraternity, but it would only come to fruition through much inner turmoil in Francis and many disturbances among the brethren.

Many authors in previous generations have tried to spin a narrative that Francis was a "man against the Church." Recent scholarship has thoroughly disproven their romantic constructions and demonstrated that Francis was absolutely a son of the Church and of Rome in particular. Such writers tried to make the curia into a sort of "corruptor" of the order, but in reality without powerful friends at the papal court the group itself never would have survived. As an example of Francis' desperate need for direction, around 1216 he resolved to send his brothers on missionary journeys, many of whom were illiterate or who had never left Assisi. Indeed, some of the brethren sent to Germany were treated terribly because their lack of linguistic skills, while some in Hungary were beaten and left for dead. For this he was admonished by the competent and sympathetic canonist Hugolino (later Pope Gregory IX, r. 1227–1241). In response to the growth of the brotherhood and his demonstrated inability to govern, Francis practically begged Rome for a superior who would be *gubernator, protector, et corrector*. For this, the novel and innovative office of cardinal-protector was created, and was entrusted to the friendly Hugolino.[78]

77 Thompson, *Francis*, 61.
78 Brooke, *Early Franciscan Government, Elias to Bonaventure* (Cambridge: Cambridge University Press, 1959), 68. For the office

Indeed Francis spent much of the rest of his life repeatedly attempting to resign from positions of leadership, while being ineluctably called back by the demands of charity and the need to provide a living example to his brothers. As Brooke says, between 1217–1226 "he held no office, and claimed no power, yet he remained in a very real sense the head of his Order."[79] This anomalous position caused a cascade of issues.

By 1219 Francis had once again grown tired of his life in Assisi and decided finally to undertake a mission by accompanying the fifth Crusade to Egypt. In his absence he entrusted the guidance of the order to two practical brothers, to be advised by Cardinal Hugolino. Characteristically, he failed to leave any concrete instructions. In his absence the brotherhood grew by leaps and bounds and Hugolino began to see what a leaven it could be in the contemporary Church. He desired practical results from the growth of the band, even if it meant a lessening in quality.[80] Hugolino and the two brothers worked to divide the nascent order into provinces, and they then began to seek papal privileges. While this was an absolutely normal step in the life of a religious community at the time, Francis was nevertheless enraged. He stormed back from the East and practically demanded that the pope rescind his grants. Pope Honorius III did this, somewhat bemusedly, and gave Hugolino charge over the supervision of the order. Hugolino loved Francis and would grant anything he asked regarding the order. Francis likely knew this, and his position of command was assured, despite his own "plausible deniability."[81] He also got the cardinal to relieve his two brothers from supervision of his group, for he would not do it himself. One might say that this was an astonishingly circuitous, if not

---

of cardinal-protector, see Arnold Witte, "Cardinal Protectors of Religious Institutions," in *A Companion to the Early Modern Cardinal*, eds. Mary Hollingsworth, Miles Pattenden, and Arnold Witte (Leiden: Brill, 2020), though this mainly focuses on a later period.

79   Brooke, *Franciscan Government*, 106.
80   Ibid., 71.
81   Ibid., 73.

tortuous, governance to live under. It appears that all the brothers had done was to prescribe ascetical dietary regulations and author- ize a specialized ministry to lepers. Yet to Francis they were going beyond the letter of the Gospels in terms of diet and attempting to get the brothers to specialize in a certain ministry, all of which Fran- cis considered an enemy to *minoritas*.[82] Francis personally appointed a new vicar, Peter Catani. Again, he promised the new vicar obedi- ence, but had no problem regularly giving him orders. It appears Peter knew and accepted this incongruous situation.

It is likely that Hugolino pressured Francis in early 1221 to come up with some kind of written rule for the burgeoning order. They lacked a uniform regular observance and had no systematic formation. Anyone who showed up, Francis readily accepted into the brotherhood.[83] The effect was that—while many holy men ar- rived—others were totally unsuitable and left or wandered about without permission. The situation was becoming intolerable from an institutional perspective. Francis likely put it off for as long as he could, for "composing a rule was a task for which Francis could hardly have been less suited."[84] What came to be known as the Rule of 1221, or the *Regula non Bullata*, is a wandering and homiletic document, quite characteristic of Francis. It contained a catena of his favorite passages of scripture, and a strict call to ab- solute obedience, which seemed to be his chief concern at the time. For him it was obedience to legitimately constituted superiors that best exemplified *minoritas*. Yet, with an astonishing lack of self- awareness, he did not confront his own peculiar position in the order and continued to "rule" in a charismatic way, parallel to the institutional authorities he set up.

That year he also resigned as Minister General and appointed his friend Elias. Here again we see Francis' autocratic tendencies

82 Thompson, *Francis*, 110–111.
83 Indeed this was the most common early complaint about the Franciscans, Kajetan Esser, *Origins of the Franciscan Order* (Chicago: Franciscan Herald Press, 1966), 138–147. Cf. Thompson, *Francis*, 316.
84 Ibid., 138.

at work. There was no election, as was common in other orders; Francis simply appointed Elias as he had Peter Catani, by the force of his personal will. It was likely the worst decision he ever made. When the friars were at the General Chapter, Francis would sit at Elias' feet in a gesture of humility, but whenever he wished to add something he would tug on the Minister General's habit, and his request was translated by Elias into a command. In 1223, with the help of Hugolino, he streamlined his rule using better Latin and legal language, and finally this new document was promulgated by the pope, thus becoming the *Regula Bullata*.

Tired, sick, and emotionally exhausted, Francis finally retired from public life to spend the remainder of his earthly journey in eremitical seclusion. During this period, he made his presence continually felt by communicating rebukes, correction, and even curses to the lax and disobedient.[85] As death approached, Francis had one final gift for his friars, a legacy that was to prove a double-edged sword. He composed a final *Testament*. It begins with a rambling series of memories about the primitive brethren at the founding of the fraternity. He then pleads that the brethren obey the Minister General in all matters yet—practically in the next breath—he issues a series of commands to them. This is not a discordant part of Francis' character, but rather integral to it. In particular it seems Francis was tortured by his brothers' repeated attempts to curry favor with the curia and to acquire papal privileges. It must be noted that this was not an "anti-institutional" stance by Francis, who was known for his devotion to the papacy, to Hugolino, and indeed to any ordained cleric. Rather, it was the tension that resulted when the "lesser brethren" sought privileges that would place them in positions of power. It seemed a traducing of the absolute humility Francis himself practiced. In the final part of the *Testament*, he lays a heavy curse on friars who are remiss in celebrating the Divine Office or who might fall from Catholic orthodoxy. He concluded with a final admonition that has puzzled many, both then and now. He avers that the *Testament* was not a new rule, but rather an invitation

85   Ibid., 382.

to observe the *Regula bullata* in a more Catholic way." He ends by commanding the friars not to add anything new to the rule, or to expound upon it, and closed his *Testament* with a blessing. All in all, it was a terribly confusing document, lacking definite legal jurisdiction, and at the same time bearing ambiguous but charismatic authority. It was open to misinterpretation from the beginning; it was a mandate that refused to command, a directive that forbade direction. Indeed, it was a commentary on a rule that proscribed such commentary. Such a legacy could not but produce questions and dissension.

Francis' handpicked successor, Elias, has been the subject of historical vilification from his own time up to ours, but for widely varying reasons. Later Franciscan heretics and earlier modern biographers saw him as the root cause of the Minorites' "slide" from original purity. The last fifty years have seen a certain clearing of Elias' name. It is clear that there was no original "poverty controversy" that Elias caused by relaxing the strictures of the order. "Spiritual Franciscanism" only appeared fifty years after his Generalate and became potent nearly a century later.[86] That said, Elias is not thereby innocent. Francis demonstrated himself a poor judge of character when he selected Elias as vicar. What even modern scholars fail to see is that the primary cause of the turbulence of the Franciscan order in the century after the founder's death was Francis' stunning lack of administrative foresight. Indeed some (not all) of Elias' faults came from following the example laid down by the saint himself.

Elias was never ordained, remaining a lay brother his whole life. This was in harmony with Francis' model from the beginning. While he honored all priests, and was happy to have some join the brotherhood, all members were equally to be "lesser brothers." Francis himself never passed the rank of deacon and was happy to have a multiplicity of lay brothers, rejoicing in their simplicity. Elias

---

86   Burr, *Spiritual Franciscans*, 16 and *passim*. For the early history of the order, see: Michael J. P. Robson, *The Franciscans in the Middle Ages* (Woodbridge, Suffolk, UK: Boydell Press, 2006).

merely continued this tack. This was in opposition to the slow trend developing since Innocent tonsured the original brothers. An increasing clericalization was underway, given the necessity for preaching and pastoral work, both of which demanded a deeper level of education and literacy. Francis was worried about these trends, and during his life only the force of his personality and holiness had kept the two factions from fighting. After his death, Elias continued Francis' policy of admitting many lay members, who were increasingly seen as "useless" by the clerical portion.[87] The priests demonstrated their disquiet by their deposition of Elias at the 1227 chapter. Chastened, but not humbled, Elias turned his skill toward the erection of the *Sacro Convento* at Assisi, one of the greatest and most quickly completed churches in medieval Christendom. He demonstrated notable talent not only for architecture, but also for amassing and managing large amounts of money, an odd trait for a Franciscan. He continued to outrage the clerical membership when, fearful of a plot to steal the recently canonized Francis' body, he secretly had it translated and sealed in concrete at the *Sacro Convento* without the knowledge of either pope or order.[88]

While Elias was thus busy in Assisi, the order itself was occupied in trying to take Francis' pastiche of regulations and assemble a kind of administration that could oversee a fraternity of thousands and operate on an international basis. Francis' insistence on absolute corporate poverty was astonishingly original and ultimately unworkable. A group of one hundred friars could not simply live off the land in a medieval city. They needed a place to live, to worship, to care for their sick, and to attend to various bodily needs. In other words, they needed property, which meant money in some form. How to square that with Francis' original intentions

---

87 Brooke, *Early Franciscan Government*, 160.
88 For this episode, see Helmut Feld, *Franziskus von Assisi und seine Bewegung* (Darmstadt: Wissenschaftliche Buchgesellschaft, 1994), esp. chapter 9, "Bruder Elias von Cortona und der Bau der Grabeskirche San Francesco in Assisi."

would cause an immense amount of discord and schism in the coming years. Yet the early clerical friars, along with Hugolino, had developed a brilliant legal fiction. Any time a substantial donation was made to the order, the transaction would be handled through a lay proctor. This "spiritual friend" of the order would take care of all the temporalities associated with a convent. When a property was purchased, ultimately ownership was transferred to the pope himself, who permitted the friars to "use" the movables and immovables in perpetuity.[89] The friars remained theoretically poor, but they received the use of all the facilities they needed and the papacy gained prestige and an immense portfolio of property. It was a dazzlingly original conception, one of the most innovative administrative solutions in the history of the Church. Of course, in later years, some puritans would come to challenge it, considering that perpetual use was synonymous with actual ownership.

In a certain restricted sense, of course, they were right (as puritans are always right, in a restricted sense). However, it permitted the massive growth of the Franciscan order, their penetration into every city in Christendom, and their attainment of academic, scientific, and pastoral achievements of the highest level. It was a decision that "kept body and soul together" in the best incarnational sense. Hugolino, now Pope Gregory IX, ratified this decision in 1230 with the bull *Quo Elongati*, while also annulling the validity of Francis' *Testament* for the order, thereby trying to eliminate the rise of a rival vision of Franciscan perfection. This move also opened the floodgates for the acquisition of many papal privileges and concessions (something clearly against the will of Francis).

It should be stressed that all of this happened while Elias was out of power. For all his many faults, he was not some original villain who sought to lessen the strictures of the rule, particularly as regarded poverty. That tendency was accelerating even before the founder's death, and it must be said that like many other things, he approached it with ambiguity rather than with condemnation. In 1232, Elias, using a virtual army of Italian lay brothers, packed the General Chapter and

89   Burr, *Spiritual Franciscans*, 6–15.

had himself re-elected as Minister General. While in office he did much good, sending the brothers out to found hundreds of new convents and building on a massive scale using the exemptions offered by *Quo Elongati*. Yet in many ways he followed his master's example. Like Francis, he ruled the order autocratically. Still, as Brooke presciently remarks, "government in [Francis'] tradition but without his grace was doomed."[90] During his whole tenure he refused to call a General Chapter, and repeatedly packed the administration of the order not with those most worthy, but with the ones who demonstrated the most friendship. These were mostly from the lay brother class, generating increasing resentment from the rising clerical contingent.

While Elias did nothing to mitigate the Franciscan rule, he more and more came to consider himself exempt from it. Success had gone to his head. He was honored by the leading powers of Church and state. A friend of St. Francis and personally selected by him, he began to live like a prince. Riding horses and enjoying sumptuous foods, he required members of the order to travel to him to be received, rather than be compelled to visit remote convents. Opposition gradually began to build to his rule, and delegations were sent to the pope. Gregory IX ordered a general chapter in 1239 that witnessed discreditable episodes from both sides of the debate, but which ended up with Elias being overthrown. It was not for a diminution of the rule, rather Elias was disbarred for his autocracy and partiality toward lay brothers (both of which, frankly, he inherited from Francis himself). His emphasis on the laity was ironically anachronistic in the clerical atmosphere of thirteenth century religious orders. Unlike Francis, though, who took his duty of exemplarity with staggering seriousness, Elias was a hypocritical Franciscan who did not practice what he required of others. He did not help his case when he absconded and joined the party of the excommunicated emperor, Frederick II. In spite of his innocence regarding later historical misconstructions, Elias was a bad leader from the start, possessing some administrative skill, but whose autocratic tendencies ultimately undermined him.

90   Brooke, *Early Franciscan Government*, 176.

Following his exile, the order was placed in the hands of Albert of Pisa, perhaps the most experienced administrator in the order. He and his successors refined legislation, began to draft constitutions, and solidified the clericalization of the order. This accelerated under Haymo of Faversham (r. 1240–1243) who exemplified a very Dominican approach to administration.[91] A tension arose in the 1240s and 1250s, not about poverty, but about the level of scholastic education, urbanization, and clericalization in the order. On one side were those who wished to follow a more rural, eremitical life, and a simple observance of the rule rather than the settled life of the massive convents then being reared in the cities of Europe.[92] The first stage of this tension ended with the triumph of the mendicant professors at Paris and ushered in the final period of clericalization that tended to reduce the lay brothers to the class of *conversi,* or lay penitents, attached to convents merely for their functions in fulfilling manual labor.[93] The key figure in solidifying the Franciscan tradition was to be St. Bonaventure. He was able to finally unify the deep Franciscan charism with the best traditions of incarnational administration. Just as he authored what was to become the definitive, "authorized" version of the life of St. Francis, so also did he call a General Chapter in Narbonne in 1260 for the final creation and redaction of the Franciscan constitutions. This was a magnificent, balanced legislation that settled the trim of the Minorite ship. All previous editions of the constitutions were to be destroyed. As Minister General, he formally revoked all edicts and concessions of his predecessors (implicitly including Francis). In this way he cleared the field of all contradictory decisions, and

---

91　Indeed it has been said he was a Franciscan "Dominican" in terms of his administration and scholastic outlook. He had been drawn to the Franciscans, but then heard of the Friars Preachers. He went to Bl. Jordan of Saxony, who charitably did not want to "poach" him from the Minorites. See Brooke, *Early Franciscan Government*, 202.

92　Burr, *Spiritual Franciscans*, 34.

93　Again, an original concern of Francis. He wanted his brothers to live by the work of their hands, begging was not originally a prioritized category. Thompson, *Francis*, 55–56.

offered the order a fresh start.[94] He achieved an administrative triumph of the first order. To the eyes of most he had preserved the genius of Francis while also accepting contemporary realities, thereby assuring the continuation of an elite body of preachers, scholars, and spiritual masters. It took a saint to save the efforts of another saint, "for there are many gifts, but one Spirit" (1 Cor 12:4). As Brooke puts it so well, Bonaventure had completed the transition from a

> small group of simple men, pledged to the literal observance of the Gospel, living in voluntary poverty, and preaching penitence to all ... [that] by 1239–1240—still more by 1260—[had] become a large, efficient, and powerful organisation, composed predominantly of clerics and learned men, and governed in accordance with a constitution which took cognisance of the details of daily life, and which required for its enforcement a complicated executive and administrative machinery.[95]

This was no diminution, but rather a fulfillment or the extension of the idiosyncratic call of the poor man of Assisi, now made accessible to the whole world. Francis' immense personal sanctity had to be "translated" such to be made available to the whole of the community, and to perpetuate his tradition of holiness in the world.

---

94   Brooke, *Early Franciscan Government*, 211.
95   Ibid., 4.

Chapter 6
Shepherds and Guardians

No position is so critical to the growth and maintenance of the Church of God than the office of bishop. From the foundations of Christianity, the bishops have been the "overseers" of the flock. Indeed even the pope acquires his title from the fact that he rules as "Bishop of Rome." The bishops, as successors of the Apostles, are the pillars and foundation of the Church. Without them, the triple office of governing, teaching, and sanctifying would be impossible. As St. Ignatius of Antioch wrote while on his way to martyrdom in in the year 107 AD, "Where the Bishop is, there is the Catholic Church."[1] Indeed it is the only office whose responsibilities are described in detail in the New Testament. Given the axial nature of such a position one can plainly see how a bishop's sanctity can affect the quality of his ministry and the holiness of his charges. Many have served with honor and dignity in this most sacred office. Others, tempted by the power and prestige that such a position brings, have corrupted and demeaned their sacred duties, an abuse made worse by the sublimity of the

---

1   St. Ignatius of Antioch, "Letter to the Smyrneans," chapter 8. "See that you all follow the bishop, even as Jesus Christ does the Father.... Let no man do anything connected with the Church without the bishop. Let that be deemed a proper Eucharist, which is [administered] either by the bishop, or by one to whom he has entrusted it. Wherever the bishop shall appear, there let the multitude [of the people] also be; even as, wherever Jesus Christ is, there is the Catholic Church. It is not lawful without the bishop either to baptize or to celebrate a love-feast; but whatsoever he shall approve of, that is also pleasing to God, so that everything that is done may be secure and valid."

}285{

episcopal call. Most enduringly, however, a select few, fortified with supernatural grace, have borne witness to the astonishing possibilities of this vocation. Harnessing their natural talents to the gifts of the Holy Spirit, they have become exemplars of the office— men to whom later bishops and leaders in every age could look to with admiration and be ignited with the desire to imitate. Men such as this have arisen in every age of the Church, and it is instructive to take several examples from early Christianity, from the medieval period, and from the time of the Catholic Reform.

The first and second letters to Timothy and the epistle to Titus are in a certain sense instruction manuals for the governance of the Church after the departure of the Apostles. As it is written:

> If anyone aspires to the office of bishop, he desires a noble task. Now a bishop must be above reproach, the husband of one wife, temperate, sensible, dignified, hospitable, an apt teacher, no drunkard, not violent but gentle, not quarrelsome, and no lover of money. He must manage his own household well, keeping his children submissive and respectful in every way; for if a man does not know how to manage his own household, how can he care for God's church? He must not be a recent convert, or he may be puffed up with conceit and fall into the condemnation of the devil. (1 Tm 3:1–7)

In a few short lines, the author lays out all the essential qualities for episcopal office. To be a successor of the Apostles is a noble task indeed, the very life of perfection, for it is through their ministry that others are perfected in grace.[2] The ideal bishop needs not only to avoid sin, but to be "above reproach," which involves the prudential management of one's public reputation, and a care for honor, particularly the honor of the Church and of God. This includes a responsibility to be "dignified," which means activity that comports with the office in question; officeholders are to

2   Thomas Aquinas, *Summa* II-II, q. 184, a. 7.

"look" and "act" the part. Indeed, the text stresses the practice of all the cardinal virtues in this passage. Note that he does not require intellectual brilliance in the bishop, but simply an aptitude for teaching and a gentle and sensible demeanor. Such a man must also be hospitable, an attitude that includes charity certainly, but which also has the implications that he should be a "public man," who opens his house to guests, even those outside of the household of the faith. It is surprising that, even in the first century, the letter cautions about avarice, almost as if the author knew the worldly temptations that would arise in the course of the history of the episcopal office. He also appeals to the necessity for the bishop to know *oikonomia* or the proper management of the household, which, in an Aristotelian sense, fits one for the government of larger entities.[3]

What should surprise the reader is the "secular" orientation of this passage. The writer certainly assumes that the bishop must be schooled in the theological virtues, but he does not mention it here. This is an almost philosophical analysis of the office of bishop, as seen from the outside. Correct governance in the Church of God proceeds from prudence allied to the other cardinal virtues. When taken together, these will allow the "father" and "householder" of the local Church to govern in good order, so as to facilitate the cultivation of deeper levels of virtue and grace among his charges. In other words, it is essential for the Church of God to have rulers who combine administrative acumen with the life of holiness. Embedded in the world and suffused by the reality of the Incarnation, it is necessary to have pastors who can negotiate the delicate balance of being in the world, but not of it.

Episcopal Holiness in the Early Church

Examples of bishops who possessed astonishing holiness and ruled in sanctity abound in the first centuries of Christianity. Leading their flocks through persecution, they often merited the crown of

3   Aristotle, *Politics*, Book I, c. 3–13.

martyrdom for themselves. While it is instructive to look at their tenures in office we are often limited by the lack of primary sources, and also by the very real historical conditions that limited the full expression of the life of a bishop in the Church during that age. The legalization of Christianity by Constantine in 313 marks the first time that bishops could publicly take up their offices in an atmosphere of peace, and sources about their respective rules begin to multiply in the fourth century. Dozens of examples of brilliant theologians who occupied a bishop's throne present themselves to us. New conditions created new problems as these men delicately negotiated the ongoing Christianization of the Roman empire and the problems of heresy, and all the while they were likewise confronted with an entirely new category of Church-state relations. Even the internal question of how to govern the Christian people in times of peace was a novelty.

Yet the Catholic Church, always willing to incorporate the good traditions of predecessor cultures, knew that the Romans were master administrators. It was not their skill in armed conquest that made them seem a permanent fixture in world history, but rather their ability to govern well, to bring law and order, and to raise up men from the status of conquered peoples to that of equal citizens.[4] It was no mistake that the Church took this tradition of legal and administrative excellence of the Romans and applied it to ecclesial life. Just like its inheritances from Athens and Jerusalem, so too would the excellent qualities of pagan Rome flow into the Church's living tradition. Just to take one example, our modern idea of territorial dioceses is a direct holdover from the geographical divisions of the later Roman empire. The term is taken directly from a Greek word that means "administration." This Roman expertise would help to streamline and make efficient Church governance in the fourth and fifth centuries, speeding the Christianization of the whole

4   Even their greatest poet, Virgil, affirmed these characteristics in *Aeneid*, VI, 850–853: "But you, Romans, remember your great arts; To govern the peoples with authority, to establish peace under the rule of law, to conquer the mighty, and show them mercy once they are conquered."

of Late Roman civilization, not to mention making it easier to incorporate barbarian elements in subsequent ages. Indeed, there was nothing good in the precursor cultures that was not taken and ennobled through the revelation of the gospel, making it into a tool for the good and for the salvation of souls.

These traditions came together stunningly during the episcopal election held in the city of Milan in 374. For years the city had been under the control of an Arian bishop, and his death brought out the orthodox and heretical factions in large numbers, each seeking to secure the bishop's throne for themselves. The situation rapidly deteriorated and the government was forced to call in troops to quell a brewing riot. Milan was not a simple, provincial town. It had become a *de facto* capital of the West, situated as it was nearer to the areas of barbarian activity than Rome. Order had to be maintained in an imperial city. The man delegated with this delicate task was the local Roman governor, Aurelius Ambrosius. Ambrosius (hereafter Ambrose) was of an aristocratic family, though one of recent origin.[5] Even during the difficult transition into late antiquity, the Roman nobility was still imbued with the immemorial commitment to public service that was so characteristic of the best elements of the old Roman upper class.[6] He was the son of the Praetorian Prefect of Rome and distant cousin to the great pagan senator Symmachus. In spite of this, his family had some connections to Christianity, though

---

5   For considerations of the aristocracy of the late antique period, see Michele R. Salzman, *The Making of a Christian Aristocracy: Social and Religious Change in the Western Roman Empire* (Cambridge, MA: Harvard University Press, 2002).

6   Henry Chadwick, *The Church in Ancient Society: From Galilee to Gregory the Great* (New York: Oxford University Press, 2009), 350. For Ambrose, see Neil B. McLynn, *Ambrose of Milan: Church and Court in a Christian Capital* (Berkeley, CA: University of California Press, 1994); J. H. W. G. Liebeschuetz, *Ambrose and John Chrysostom: Clerics between Desert and Empire* (Oxford: Oxford University Press, 2011); and the elegant but somewhat dated effort in Angelo Paredi, *Saint Ambrose, His Life and Times* (Notre Dame, IN: University of Notre Dame Press, 1964).

Ambrose was not baptized and was educated in the manner common to pagans of the late empire. He was a brilliant student and quickly became a renowned lawyer, attracting the attention of those in authority. He was selected as an attorney in the Prefecture of Pannonia (Hungary) where he came to know many in the poorer ranks of society for the first time as individuals, rather than just an underclass.[7] He acquired a reputation for advocacy and incorruptibility, and was admitted to the governor's inner curia of advisors in 367. By 370, as a result of his administrative aptitude, he was appointed governor of Aemilia-Liguria, a territory that included the imperial capital of Milan. In this position he was styled *clarissimus*, the third highest rank in the civil hierarchy. In this role, he spent most of his time in court as judge of the first instance, in both civil and criminal cases, while also being charged with preserving public order. He also had the responsibility to maintain public buildings and to supervise the civil service.[8] All in all it was a testament of his estimation in the eyes of those in power that they would entrust such authority to a man who was only about thirty years old at the time. When he heard rumors of the nascent civil unrest in Milan, Ambrose traveled there immediately. Upon arrival he deployed his troops in such a way as to prevent violence while also respecting the freedom of the Christians to the election. It was imperative to head off partisan bloodshed. Having lived in Rome in the 350s, he had seen firsthand the factional violence that results from disputed elections and theological controversies. Despite his precautions, both factions in this ordeal had occupied positions in the old Cathedral of Milan. In order to forestall fighting in the nave of the church itself, Ambrose bravely interposed himself between the two parties in the name of civic order. He gave a stirring speech on the necessity of concord and peace, particularly in the imperial city. It was also probably his intention to give a gesture of official approval to the Nicene party.[9] A trained rhetor, known by all as a powerful speaker, his words had a decided

7   Paredi, *Saint Ambrose*, 74.
8   Ibid., 110.
9   McLynn, *Ambrose of Milan*, 13.

effect. As he spoke, a young boy in the crowd cried out, "Ambrose! Bishop!" Quickly the call was taken up by all, both Catholic and Arian, and echoed off the walls of the basilica. The parties were certainly moved by his appeal to harmony, but the outsider Ambrose also had the advantage of not openly belonging to either party. In fact, it seems not to have bothered the excited crowd a bit that Ambrose was technically not even a Christian.[10]

Ambrose was utterly taken aback, yet at the same time strangely moved by the outpouring of support. He asked for a short delay to acquire imperial permission and to secure the assent of the local bishops. He probably did this in order to give the local populace time to reflect and retract their decision. They did not. The requisite permissions having been received, on 30 November 374 Ambrose found himself baptized. Over the next several days he was advanced through the various minor and major orders, and on 7 December was consecrated and solemnly enthroned as Archbishop of Milan—an astonishing turn of events, both for the Church and for Ambrose himself.[11] From the beginning, Ambrose was no ordinary bishop, as he was "still bathed in the aura of a senatorial governorship."[12] It is likely the largely lower-class Christian populace of Milan saw this as a key advantage in a city that was filled with the officials of the imperial court. Ambrose might be the grand

10   Such spontaneous acclamation was not unheard of in the early Church. Augustine would become ordained in nearly the same way and there are other instances as well.

11   McLynn considers this daily procession of progressive ordinations more for public consumption, but it was required for canonical regularity, though it did have a dramatic propulsive character leading to the consecration on 7 December. There is no reason why it might not have been canonical, sanctifying, and politically expedient all in one. McLynn, *Ambrose of Milan*, 51. See also the interesting study: John Gibaut, *The Cursus Honorum: A Study of the Origins and Evolution of Sequential Ordination* (New York: Peter Lang, 2000), esp. 138–142.

12   Peter Brown, *Through the Eye of a Needle: Wealth, the Fall of Rome, and the Making of Christianity in the West, 350–550 AD* (Princeton, NJ: Princeton University Press, 2014), 123.

patronus who would be able to mediate between the community and the emperor, he would be one who "knew his way along the corridors of power."[13] On that score, Ambrose was not to disappoint. In addition, his lack of open affiliation with either the Nicene or Arian parties appealed to both sides at once. Some of the more enlightened members of the congregation may have even dared to hope that the unaffiliated but successful career official might mediate the growing dispute and bring peace to an unsettled church.

It appears that in responding to the vocational call, Ambrose immediately disposed himself to receive the many graces necessary for his new position.[14] He demonstrated the authenticity of his conversion, first of all in a conventional way by divesting himself of all of his property. Yet even in doing this he showed providential foresight. He made provision for his sister, Marcellina who was a nun in Rome, by carving out a trust to take care of her temporal needs. All the rest of his property he deeded to the Diocese of Milan, an immensely popular move from a political standpoint. While making himself individually poor, he thereby retained the use of his holdings for the good of his people. The lands of the Diocese of Milan—rooted in the original bequest of Ambrose—would grow to become some of the most extensive in Christendom, with holdings located as far away as Sicily. This stabilized the diocese and made it capable both of extensive building programs and exceptional charitable care for the poor of the city.[15] Ambrose also

---

13   Chadwick, *The Church in Ancient Society*, 351.

14   Other conversions of life upon receiving ordination are not completely unheard of in the lives of the saints, one may recall also the example of St. Thomas Becket.

15   McLynn, *Ambrose of Milan*, 55, 70. McLynn stresses that Ambrose's holdings were not substantial so as to underscore the delicacy of his initial position as bishop. However I consider that even though specific records have not survived, the amount of patronage he was able to marshal, the churches he was able to construct, and the later massive patrimony of the Milanese Church clearly demonstrate not only substantial initial holdings throughout the central Mediterranean, but also exceptionally good management.

shrewdly appointed his brother (and best friend) Satyrus as manager of the temporalities of the local church.[16] In so doing he left them in safe, trusted, and responsible hands, while freeing himself up for his pastoral responsibilities in taking care of the spiritual needs of the diocese. In doing this he also obtained the presence and counsel of Satyrus, which was to prove an invaluable aid to his initial governance of the diocese. We can witness the reliance Ambrose placed upon his brother by reading the moving eulogy he preached after Satyrus died at a young age in 378.[17] While he was only able to enjoy his brother's counsel for four years, these were some of the most precarious of his tenure, and their teamwork firmly established Ambrose in the city.

Ambrose had to walk a veritable tightrope in his early reign in attempting to reconcile Arian and Catholics, all the while negotiating with the officials of the later empire. He was convinced that internal harmony within the Christian community was necessary in order effectively to meet and deal with the external world. He also knew that he was not yet fully competent in theology and was open to the charge that his election violated Paul's principle concerning new converts. He threw himself into the study of the Fathers, even avoiding preaching for the first couple years of his reign. What did occupy him in his early years was the necessity of carefully reintegrating the Arian clergy of the city into his church. In the first place, he did not launch a frontal attack. His first theological works and sermons dealt with the exaltation of virginity, at that time a neutral topic in the factional debates and praised by both sides. This emphasis on an area of agreement softened the opposition. In these early efforts he honed his theological acumen, while becoming the spokesman of a movement that would come to dominate Christianity in the coming centuries.[18] He was able to leverage the weak-

16 Paredi, *Saint Ambrose*, 124.
17 Ambrose, *De excessu fratris Satyri*, Patrologia Latina 73. McLynn usefully traces how Ambrose transformed his private grief into a moment of community building that would stand him in good stead in future conflicts. McLynn, *Ambrose of Milan*, 77.
18 McLynn, *Ambrose of Milan*, 60–61.

ening of the Arian party under the short-lived Julian the Apostate and the concomitant success of the Nicene party of Athanasius. Citing the liberal religious policies of Valentinian I (r. 364–375)—who was largely content to let the Church police itself—Ambrose offered generous terms of reconciliation to Arian clergy. They could keep their churches and benefices. All they had to do was sign the Nicene Creed and accept the validity of the Catholic sacraments. This done, they were able to peacefully reintegrate into the Church under the leadership of Ambrose.[19] It is likely that Ambrose wanted to effectuate this reintegration quickly for several reasons. Beside the internal peace of his church and the salvation of souls, he wanted to present a common front to the world. In addition, given the history of the Church politics in the fourth century, he knew that the Church was always only one emperor away from a new wave of persecution. In this he was terribly prescient, for when a new emperor emerged who was indeed Arian, Ambrose was able to withstand the conflict with a unified congregation at his back.

Even apart from the death of his beloved brother, the year 378 was Ambrose's *annus horribilis*. That year the Eastern Emperor Valens (r. 364–378) was killed at the Battle of Adrianople. Not only did this battle signal the end of the dominance of the Roman legionary infantry and the rise of medieval cavalry, it was the first major disaster in a seemingly endless series that would threaten the very foundations of the empire itself. Refugees from the Roman Balkan provinces streamed into the city of Milan. By convention the Christian bishops were the ones who had competence over refugees, and all of Ambrose's administrative skill was necessary to give them aid. In addition, he melted down church plate to ransom as many captives as he could.[20] Worse still, the Gothic victors had been converted to Arian Christianity. Just when the Roman

19   Paredi, *Saint Ambrose*, 127; Chadwick, *The Church in Ancient Society*, 355.
20   In this he was criticized by some contemporaries. Church plate was intimately related to the liturgical life and prestige of the local Christian population. Most were willing to give anything to charity, except that. Paredi, *Saint Ambrose*, 173.

world had seemed on the cusp of eliminating the Arians, they returned in the form of the migrating barbarian peoples. Ambrose would be menaced by the specter Arianism for the remainder of his life. While the orthodox emperor Gratian (r. 375–383) had to spend his time on the Rhenish and Danubian frontiers, Ambrose was left to tolerate the co-rule of his nephew Valentinian II (r. 375–392) in Italy, although in reality he was controlled by his Arian mother, Justina, who would later prove a terrible thorn in the bishop's side.

In the meantime, Ambrose had proven himself a capable administrator of the Church of Milan, and thus began to attract political attention for such skill. His diocese was efficiently run, incorruptibly managed, and able to express its power in many direct and indirect ways. He capably fulfilled the traditional episcopal duty of hospitality, which meant that his house became a hub of activity and a venue for the informal activation of patronage networks. He had immense tact, a reserve imbibed through his aristocratic upbringing and reinforced by his careful training and career in civil service. As Liebeschuetz writes, "Ambrose knew the dangers of unrestrained *parrhesia*, and he was also blessed with an instinct which warned him precisely how far he could go in a given situation."[21] Many remarked upon his noble bearing and consummate diplomacy. He knew precisely how to word his petitions and directives to achieve the maximum effect. He became a trusted associate of emperor Gratian, so much so that the emperor wanted him to become his personal chaplain. Ambrose knew that he could do more good where he was than as a prelate-courtier and carefully and methodically talked Gratian out of the plan.[22] He was a person who knew how to leverage relations with the powerful. Gratian himself was disposed to religious toleration of the various Christian factions, particularly given the grave need for unity in the face of

---

21   J. H. W. G. Liebeschuetz, *Ambrose and John Chrysostom: Clerics between Desert and Empire* (Oxford: Oxford University Press, 2012), 80.

22   Paredi, *Saint Ambrose*, 185.

external threat. Ambrose bided his time and instead focused his energies against the remaining traces of paganism in the empire. In one famous episode he convinced the emperor to finally remove the Altar of Victory from the Roman senate. This drew the ire of his relative, the pagan senator Symmachus, who brought his case to the court. Though the senator argued eloquently for the old religion, Ambrose—trained as he was in rhetoric—was able to surpass him and win the day.[23] As time went on he gradually worked upon Gratian, using utilitarian arguments when necessary. As an adept public speaker, Ambrose knew how to fit his arguments to audience and occasion. He convinced the emperor that heresy weakened the empire, as did any form of religious disunity. In this sense the orthodox Nicenes, committed as they were to church unity, were at one with the good of the empire. Having secured himself political influence, Ambrose was able to convince Gratian to take action against Arian heretics so that they could not do harm to the orthodox.

Ambrose knew how to strike while the iron was hot. Coming off these victories at the imperial court, he leveraged his increasing prestige with the Italian bishops to convene the Council at Aquileia in 381. At this Council Ambrose took the lead, and it was there he began to work out his conception of Church-state relations that would come to dominate Catholic thought. Ostensibly called to debate the continuing rift between Arians and Catholics in Italy, Ambrose turned the Council essentially into a court in which he acted as both judge and prosecutor. There were no debates. Backed by imperial and papal approval, Ambrose charged and summarily dismissed the Arian bishops in Italy. This forceful handling of the situation shows how far he had come from his tentative first steps in Milan. Now, backed by ecclesiastical and temporal power and to assure the victory of the orthodox party, he acted resolutely. He

23   Ibid., 233. The victory, however, was managed by Ambrose to appear as a direct confrontation, whereas in reality Symmachus was never able to press his suit very far. McLynn, 264. Ambrose knew how to manage public relations as well.

declared that in such matters the state was the adjunct of the Church. The Church could not enforce its own decisions, but an orthodox emperor might. The independence and superiority of the spiritual power would not only become a cardinal principle through the duration of his career, but would establish itself as a bedrock of Catholic political theology. Indeed, if Ambrose had not acted decisively, the rise of an emperor sympathetic to the Arians—not to mention the eruption of the Arian Goths in the coming years—may have swamped the Catholics in Italy. Ambrose established a firewall that endured in the most trying of circumstances.

Ambrose's attention to community solidarity was one of the keynotes of his episcopacy. From the very beginning he sought to soften internal dissonance, especially by focusing on the poor of the city as full and integral members of the Church, whose presence was necessary to secure the salvation of the rich. His success in generating authentic Christian community is matched by few bishops in history. He knew how to engender charity through his powerful sermons, his careful patronage, and his acute sense of the needs of his congregation. This *communitas* would find itself severely tested when his friend Gratian was murdered in 383 after failing to put down a rebellion in Gaul. In Milan Gratian was succeeded by Valentinian II, a man overshadowed by his Arian mother, Justina. Quickly, she moved to secure rights for her co-religionists in the imperial city, but Ambrose was ready. Through his efforts at reconciliation and attention to the common good, Ambrose had united the Catholics of Milan to such an extent that they were willing to follow him anywhere in his defense of the true faith. In 385 she demanded that Ambrose hand over one of his basilicas to Arian clergy for their use.[24] He refused point-blank. Summoned before the imperial council, he arrived surrounded by thousands of the faithful. Thwarted but not defeated, the imperial government removed itself to Aquileia to lick its wounds. They were back in 386 with an order for the dismissal of Catholics in the civil service, an

24   Paredi, *Saint Ambrose*, 244–246; McLynn, *Ambrose of Milan*, 159–219.

edict of toleration for the Arians, and a renewed demand for a basilica. Ambrose was implacable. In a response worthy of the Spartan Leonidas, he challenged the empress to come and take a basilica, with himself and his faithful inside it. More than this, during the dispute Ambrose even discovered the relics of two early martyrs, Gervasius and Protasius, and trumpeted the find as a sign of approval from heaven. This fortified the resistance of his faithful. Moreover, he initiated the tradition of antiphonal singing to keep their spirits up during their occupation of the basilica.[25] Justina ordered the basilica to be surrounded by imperial troops, with the intention of forcing and entrance and effecting violence. When thus threatened, Ambrose responded, "May God permit you to do what you threaten. I shall suffer what a bishop should suffer, and you will do what servants are accustomed to do."[26] In the end, realizing that the people and their bishop would not back down, Justina withdrew the troops, thwarted in her attempts to Arianize the western imperial capital. Ambrose's church would not bend to political expediency.

Augustine had been present for all this. A restless seeker, he had almost despaired in his search for truth. When he met Ambrose, however, he encountered something very new to him—namely, a person of deep Christian faith but also imbued with wisdom and learning. It was key to his conversion as described in his own *Confessions*. Paredi puts it best when he says:

> During those years of struggle for the freedom of the Church at Milan, Augustine came to recognize the meaning of Catholicism and what the Church is—not a wan group of ascetics separated from the actualities of life, but a great living tree, a faith which acts as a leaven

25 Indeed one of the faithful who surrounded Ambrose with support in the basilica was none other than Saint Monnica, the mother of Augustine, both of whom were present in Milan for these events. These firsthand accounts can be read in Augustine's *Confessions*.

26 Paredi, *Saint Ambrose*, 244–255

against the forces of evil in or outside of man, a well-or-
dered organism, a precise creed, a teaching, and a principle of authority. He had feverishly sought for the truth,
and he found in Ambrose the only truth which could sat-
isfy him, a truth lived in love.[27]

For Augustine, Ambrose would always represent the ideal bishop,
one whose example he sought to follow as he too later took up the
crozier. Augustine tells us in particular about one of the most time-
consuming but necessary parts of the bishop's office at that time.
Soon after the legalization of Christianity, Constantine had invested
bishops with the authority of a magistrate, particularly to decide
civil cases.[28] This had the effect not only of lightening the
administrative burden of the civil service, but also of instantly
enhancing the powers of the episcopal office. Ambrose had much
experience as a judge in his role as governor, and he transferred his
expertise to what was called the *episcopalis audientia*—that is, a
sort of small-claims court to which the faithful would turn in times
of need, and which the civil power would enforce. Ambrose had a
simple rule for this, "Never refuse to intervene when there is a
possibility of doing good, especially when the interests of God and
the Church are at stake."[29] Whereas Augustine found this service
enervating and tedious, Ambrose knew that it cemented the
Christian community together under his leadership.[30] They looked
to the bishop for justice, and he believed that he could provide it,
tempered by the leaven of the gospel. He was firmly convinced that
the clergy ought to be a leadership class in society, set apart yet still
engaged with the world. They were there to defend the weak and

27   Ibid., 293.
28   Chadwick, *The Church in Ancient Society*, 349.
29   Cf. Paredi, *Saint Ambrose*, 135.
30   See Peter Brown, *Augustine of Hippo* (Berkeley, CA: University of
     California Press, 2000), 189–191; and Neil B. McLynn,
     "Administrator: Augustine in His Diocese," in *A Companion to
     Augustine*, ed. M. Vessey (Chichester, West Sussex: Wiley-Blackwell,
     2012): 310–322.

to check the powerful. Indeed, they could be a new Roman aristocracy in the classical sense of *aristoi*, or "the best."

Ambrose left a comprehensive statement of his sense of duty in his *De Officiis*.[31] This was a manual for the Christian clergy in the tradition of the influential Ciceronian treatise of the same name. The bishop was to be above all seen as the visible head of the *communitas*, attended by officials and clergy wherever he went. Order was critical, particularly in the society where that value was rapidly decaying. Such order enabled the bishop to meet with civil officials on similar terms, and to visibly reinforce the presence of the whole Christian community. McLynn sees this work as a "complex exercise designed at once to make the church intelligible to the *saeculum* and to annex the latter's traditional territory."[32] It attempted to unite the values of the stoic sage with that of the celibate holy man, creating an "elevated and demanding" (to use McLynn's words) vision of the clerical office. It is an image that is familiar to us, but one must realize that it presented something stunningly new in the 380s. A bishop was to be honored, attended, and well-comported in his public life, while remaining celibate, temperate, and self-controlled in private. It was a novel and enduring attempt to permanently elevate the social position of a Christian bishop, while at the same time maintaining a strict commitment to gospel values. The Christian Church was no longer hidden and persecuted. Its clergy now moved in the highest levels of the state and had to address men of all social classes.

Ambrose was sensitive to the need to understand the customs of one's society, and to creatively integrate them in such a way as to balance secular influences with Christian ethics. He knew that the bishop had a responsibility to entertain, and he welcomed both Christians and non-Christians to his home. He was particularly

31   See the excellent edition: Ambrose, *De officiis*, ed. Ivor J. Davidson, 2 vols. (Oxford: Oxford University Press, 2001). Peter Brown denominates the work "a call to duty" for contemporary Christian clergy, id., *Through the Eye of a Needle*, 127.

32   McLynn, *Ambrose of Milan*, 255.

attentive to the business that could be accomplished at his own table, over a fine meal.[33] At the same time, however, he advised the clergy not to banquet except at their own homes. Invitations to private dinners, particularly from those who were not Christian or who held secular power, might compromise one's position as representative of the whole Christian community. Ambrose also refused to recommend people for imperial service, likewise for the sake of allaying charges of favoritism or to subject himself and the Church he ruled to opprobrium should such persons show themselves unworthy of office.

Yet patronage was the very lifeblood of the premodern system. Ambrose was acutely aware of this and remained a powerful and effective patron. This he did informally, through extensive personal contacts throughout the government, Church, and civil service. He could act with decisiveness, such as when a client who was a minor official found himself falsely accused of mishandling money: "As soon as I saw your letter, I saw the prefect.... The prefect immediately granted forgiveness and ordered the letter of confiscation to be countermanded."[34] While he was capable of extreme public theater when the situation demanded it, he preferred to do things in a low-key manner. While remaining always deferential to the Roman See, Ambrose was able to secure appointments for a cadre of like-minded bishops throughout the dioceses of northern Italy, something accomplished by his judicious application of informal patronage. Similarly, he advised clergy to avoid adjudicating cases over money unless some injustice could be rectified, such as in the civil judgments in his episcopal court. He also refused publicly to have anything to do with arranging marriages, yet through his public preaching on the merits of virginity, not to mention his extension of Church supervision over betrothals and the Christian marriage ceremony, he once again demonstrated his exceptional ability to be "in the world, but not of it."

By the end of his life Ambrose had become a figure of renown

---

33   Paredi, *Saint Ambrose*, 126.
34   Cfr. Brown, *Through the Eye*, 145.

throughout the empire, respected and in some cases feared by the officials of both Church and state. He had been given high-level political commissions, such as several delicate diplomatic negotiations between competing claimants for the throne. Indeed, he was the first bishop in history entrusted with such delicate offices.[35] He showed extraordinary skill in negotiation and peacemaking between different contending authorities. Ambrose did not see these as opportunities to enhance his authority or to secure merely political advantage—rather, he envisioned them as a pastoral duty. In attempting to get violent men to keep the peace and assure the security of the churches, he was trying to preserve the delicate work that he and the other Catholic bishops had begun at the legalization. He saw this work as essential, as the Church traversed the long road to bring the mission of the gospel to perfection.[36] At times he encountered leaders who were friendly to him, while others were actively hostile; but Ambrose knew how to deal with all types of men. At the end of his life, Ambrose was able to enjoy the reign of the solidly orthodox emperor Theodosius, who had done so much to establish the Church in the late empire. Yet one day a terrible massacre of Gothic prisoners carried out under his command reached the ears of Ambrose. The elderly bishop denounced the emperor in no uncertain terms and ordered him to do penance. As Ambrose preached, "A bishop can at times give orders which are bitter, like the rind of a walnut, but the fruit within is sweet."[37] Theodosius was genuinely conscience-stricken for his rash act and agreed to be enrolled with the public penitents for Easter. While McLynn is right in stating that this was politically opportune for Theodosius (similarly as was penance for Henry II in the death of St. Thomas Becket), nonetheless it was one of the crucial turning points of Western civilization. As Paredi says, "For the first time in history a monarch publicly recognized the fact that he was also subject to the eternal laws of justice, and a bishop vindicated for

35   Paredi, *Saint Ambrose*, 210.
36   Ibid., 213.
37   Cfr. Ibid., 301.

himself the right of judging and absolving even kings."[38] While Ambrose was doing something wholly new and not without risk, the image of the penitent lord of the Roman Empire beseeching absolution from a bishop of the Church burned itself into the conscience of the West, laying the groundwork for what would become Christendom.[39]

Many scholars point to the fact that Ambrose is both surprising and very hidden.[40] The shocking things he did became normative for Church administrators, but it was he who created many of the standard operating procedures of the Latin clergy. He established a new pattern for clerical virtue and comportment. He provided a novel pattern for Church-state relations. Perhaps most importantly, he created a model for future bishops of the Roman Church, one that existed and operated alongside the powers of this world while remaining faithful to the words of Christ. He toiled incessantly to govern his Church, and was constantly available for consultation, for his house was open to everyone.[41] In an age that valued secretaries, he wrote all his works himself so as not to trouble anyone else. Indeed he applied himself so assiduously to his church that, after his death, it took no fewer than five bishops to accomplish the same amount of work that he had done.[42] He had created a new form of the old Ciceronian republic, this time a Christian one where the plebeian poor were integrated into a new and exalted

38   Ibid., 310.
39   Paredi quotes Hans Lietzmann in this regard, "Ambrose was certainly one of the great men of human history, even before he became a bishop, and he by no means regarded his office as a sinecure when he was the pastor and the political confidant of three emperors.... Theodosius was not wrong in giving way to this man, in whom the classical dignity proper to the Roman sense of what the state demands was combined with a profoundly earnest, Christian conception of the meaning of life." Ibid., vi.
40   Peter Brown says, "Hindsight has made him both larger than life and strangely unremarkable." Id., *Through the Eye*, 121.
41   So much so that the young Augustine might enter unannounced and discover Ambrose reading a text by himself.
42   Paredi, *Saint Ambrose*, 375.

community.[43] McLynn is right to foreground Augustine's description of Ambrose as *satis episcopaliter*, for it is truly Saint Ambrose who would be imitated in later centuries by Catholic bishops when they sought to act "in a properly episcopal manner."[44]

The Ambrosian Model Enacted: Medieval England

Ambrose has stamped the abiding pattern for a Latin bishop. It is one that has endured in many ways into the present day. He was at once a man of learning, diplomacy, and careful administration. One can find bishops who live up to Ambrose's ideal in every age of the Church, but it is instructive to choose a few examples and see how they were able to function in quite distinct settings and times. Medieval England was a robustly Catholic country, thoroughly integrated into the European continent by religion, learning, and history. Its government enjoyed warm relations with the papacy and with the domestic church, punctuated by periodic bouts of struggle. The famous episode of Thomas Becket is a case in point. He was a royal administrator appointed to the see of Canterbury. In that role, he became an implacable and unexpected defender of the liberties of the Church against his erstwhile friend Henry II. Facing a fractured and dangerous political climate, he was forced into exile. When he was finally able to return, he was brutally murdered by men in the pay of the king (though not necessarily with his knowledge). Becket's martyrdom steeled the English Church and fortified it for future struggles with the monarchy. The murdered archbishop cast a long shadow over the rest of the Middle Ages, and his cult reinforced the see of Canterbury significantly, bringing with it prestige and an innumerable train of pilgrims. His successors in that office were serious men. They were by tradition the first counselors of the realm, but were also able to enforce the rights of the Church. In this they often fought side by side with the nobility in the intent of limiting royal consolidation of power. For this reason, by the early 1200s the

43 Brown, *Through the Eye*, 175.
44 Augustine, Confessions, 5.13; cfr. McLynn, *Ambrose of Milan*, 377.

kings of England had withdrawn themselves from the counsel of the nobility and of the Church at Canterbury, choosing to focus more on raising loyal courtiers and court advisors to positions of eminence. The epic failure of King John to enforce his claims over France, the Church, or the nobility resulted in the signing of *Magna Carta*, engineered by the brilliant Archbishop Stephen Langton. At King John's death in 1216, he was succeeded by the child Henry III, who would not rule in his own name until 1227. During the minority, and into the early years of Henry's reign, the young king was dominated by Peter des Roches, the powerful Bishop of Winchester. Des Roches had been his tutor and guardian, and as such, insinuated himself into the government of the inexperienced Henry. This bishop was a political opportunist who, in 1232, orchestrated his rivals' fall from power, becoming the king's primary advisor. An effective—if Machiavellian—administrator, he began to seize the lands and castles of Henry's rivals in order to undermine *Magna Carta* and establish more centralized royal authority. As a Frenchman he was hated by most of the English aristocracy and the native English clergy. All these knew that he was not governing for the benefit of either the Church or the common good, but solely to circumvent the customs of England enshrined in the Great Charter and to augment royal power. Many nobles rebelled and des Roches sent troops against them, setting the stage a potential civil war.

Into this situation stepped Edmund Rich of Abingdon, a retiring scholar from Oxford who was more at home in the monastery than in the chancery. Des Roches had been able to sideline the Church during this conflict because no fewer than three consecutive candidates for the see of Canterbury had been quashed by the papacy, mostly because they were partisans of des Roches and the king.[45] At length, in 1234, the Canterbury chapter voted for

---

45 Key sources for Edmund of Abingdon are C. H. Lawrence, *The Life of St Edmund [by Matthew Paris]* (London: Sandpiper Books), 1999; and, ID., *St. Edmund of Abingdon: A Study in Hagiography and History* (Oxford: Clarendon Press, 1960); and, Edmund of Abingdon, *Speculum religiosorum and Speculum ecclesie*, ed. Helen P. Forshaw (London: Oxford Univ. Press, 1973).

Edmund. Both the king and des Roches acquiesced, thinking that the scholar would pose no threat to their plans. Edmund came from a middle-class family in the little town of Abingdon, near Oxford. He felt called to a life of monasticism, a predilection he retained for most of his life, and which enabled him to maintain a calm center in a crisis. Having spent a year at the Augustinian priory of Merton, he went up to Oxford to begin his formal studies.[46] For the rest of his life, whenever he took leave or made a retreat, he would return to such religious houses. Before his entrance into the clerical state, he had made over his whole patrimony in favor of a hospital at Abingdon. At the University, Edmund stood out for his incorruptibility and piety. He attended daily Mass before teaching, a practice "unusual among lecturers at that time."[47] In order to support themselves while at school, clerics were often awarded benefices at which they were not expected to reside. While common, he refused to accept such a sinecure without making provision for the spiritual needs of the residents. He did finally accept a benefice, but worked with pastoral energy to improve it, resigning once he had spent much of his income on repairs and service books.[48] Edmund completed his studies at Oxford with success and was appointed a secular canon of the Cathedral of Salisbury, an ancient and powerful see in England.

Salisbury was a bustling city at the time, and Edmund witnessed the construction of the beautiful, new Gothic cathedral during his tenure. While there his talents did not go unnoticed. The canons appointed him treasurer, which denoted one who had care of the fabric of the church, and the charge of its paraments and sacred vessels.[49] One can imagine that this was a significant responsibility given the ongoing construction, and not an easy task. Edmund had to manage an entire staff of guards, sacristans, and laundresses and ensure that the church ran well. He was expected

46 Lawrence, *The Life*, 8.
47 Ibid., 17.
48 Ibid., 37, 123.
49 Ibid., 38.

to pay for this out of his own income as a canon (to which a benefice was attached for the purpose). He did this while maintaining a reputation for open-handed generosity, often housing and paying the expenses of poor clerical scholars. One of these scholars reported at Edmund's canonization proceedings what Lawrence calls "a hint of mismanagement."[50] The young man reported that Edmund was disinclined to inspect his stores and disdained to hear accounts of household management. This is likely hagiographic retrojection. A saint was not supposed to have his mind on things of this world, and so the story is likely meant to emphasize his charitable nature: "[D]o not let your right hand know what your left hand is doing" (Mt 6:3). It is unlikely that someone who was habitually improvident would have been entrusted either with the office of treasurer, nor later raised to the see of Canterbury. He is known to have avoided litigation (the favored pastime of medieval clerics) at all costs, preferring instead mediation and negotiation. Unfortunately, litigation would be a major part of his episcopacy.

Having settled on the canon as a compromise candidate, the chapter informed Edmund of his election, much to his horror. His refusals went beyond the normal protestations of humility, and he was only prevailed to accept election when they told him that his renunciation would do damage to the Church, and might result in the see becoming occupied by a foreigner. Unfortunately for the shy, retiring Edmund, he was immediately thrust into the national crisis that had been precipitated by the Bishop of Winchester. Upon consecration, Edmund immediately set to work attempting to head off the incipient civil war. His purpose in peacemaking was itself revealing—namely, he believed conflict should be headed off because it imperils innocent subordinates.[51] His first act was to convene all the bishops of his province, consult them, and coordinate a united front against Peter des Roches. He also made use of the mendicant orders, sending the Minorite Agnellus of Pisa as mediator to the rebels, thinking the memory of Francis might jar them

50 Ibid.
51 Ibid., 132.

to their senses. This done, he went to confront the king. The two sides met, and Edmund had to calm a sharp exchange between Henry and Bishop Alexander Stavensby (St. Dominic's old professor from Toulouse). He was able to prevail upon Henry the need for a truce. Unfortunately, peace talks broke down, and the resultant violence caused the death of the Earl Marshal, Richard of Pembroke, who had led the rebellion. Edmund personally went to the king to intercede for the defeated rebels and almost single-handedly ended the nascent civil conflict, bringing peace back to the realm. By preserving the unity of the episcopal bench, he was able to persuade Henry to abandon Peter des Roches and his retinue. Few Church leaders have faced such crises in the first days of their respective rules. Edmund demonstrated that, although he was by nature a monk and a scholar, he would not back down where the gospel or the Church was at issue. A sort of iron entered him in a manner akin to that of Thomas Becket after his consecration.

Having quelled this national disaster, Edmund turned to the administration of the Church. The see at Canterbury had been languishing since the death of the powerful Stephen Langton in 1228 and needed serious attention. The appointment of senior staff was especially critical for the primatial see, for they not only administered the diocese, but coordinated with the suffragans of the whole province, and provided support to the archbishop as the representative of the entire English Church to the crown and the papacy. To his credit, Edmund knew where his weaknesses were, and appointed men of sterling reputation and renowned capability. He relied heavily on his younger brother, Robert. Wisely he gave him no official position, but let it be known that he had the authority to act in his name. This informality allowed the settling of many difficult cases, and Robert was an exceptionally good administrator of the temporalities of the diocese, and served as an incorruptible Vicar General during the many times Edmund was forced to travel. He also appointed Eustace of Faversham from the Canterbury Cathedral Chapter as his personal chaplain, a mark of respect for the chapter that would later be lost on them. Most significantly, he lured the Chancellor of Oxford University, Richard de Wych, to become chancellor of the diocese. Richard would prove himself not only the best and closest of collaborators, but would himself carry on Edmund's work after the latter's death, as we shall see. Edmund was very careful with his retainers and servants. He made them promise that if they were ever guilty of scandal, they would receive their just wages, and immediately depart his service.[52] All in all, the careful development of his domestic *familia* enabled him to right the foundering see, for Edmund had that talent possessed by all great leaders of discerning competence and entrusting responsibility accordingly.

He also maintained excellent relations with his episcopal confreres, particularly following the fall of Peter des Roches as royal advisor. One of his closest allies was the radical reforming Bishop of Lincoln, Robert Grosseteste.[53] Having attended Oxford together they remained friends, with Edmund tempering the more extreme sentiments of Robert when the need arose. Edmund was a practical man, whereas Robert was often lost in abstractions. On one occasion Robert had assailed the practice of clerics serving as secular judges. It was technically against canon law, but Edmund saw that the result would be not only the emptying of the judicial benches of England (leading to a crisis in the administration of justice), but also the loss of many honorable and incorruptible judges who were rending good service. In tempering Robert's extremism, Edmund was able to accomplish great good. On other occasions Edmund gave support to Robert's efforts to purify the Church, though he often permitted the more temperamental Robert to assume the leading role. In addition, Edmund remained great friends with the Archbishop of York, a major rival to Canterbury in ecclesial

52   Lawrence, *The Life*, 141.
53   For more on this remarkable churchman, see R. W. Southern, *Robert Grosseteste: The Growth of an English Mind in Medieval Europe*, Rev. Ed. (Oxford: Clarendon Press, 2011); C. Colt Anderson, "Robert Grosseteste's Theology of Pastoral Care," in *A Companion to Pastoral Care in the Late Middle Ages (1200–1500)*, ed. Ronald J. Stansbury, (Leiden: Brill, 2010); and, James McEvoy, *Robert Grosseteste* (New York: Oxford University Press, 2000).

politics. This itself was remarkable given the hundreds of years of tension existing between the two sees. While the irenic Edmund was able deftly to manage the Church, he was also able to delicately manage ecclesiastical affairs with the king. Whenever there was a clash of jurisdictions, Edmund was unafraid to defend the rights of the Church. None of this was done to aggrandize power personally, for he considered that the privileges and rights of the Church in England were given to him as a trust from previous generations, and it was his responsibility to defend them. He made sure to continue to secure the competence of Church courts over marriages, probates, and clerical malfeasance. He was also able to cultivate excellent relations with the papal legate, Cardinal Otto. This was a delicate situation; a papal legate technically had more power than the primate when he was in the country. Edmund did not see this as a threat to his authority, rather he knew that close cooperation with Rome's representative would end up benefiting the Church. Even though Otto was only a deacon, Edmund cleverly recognized and even underscored his authority. For instance, at the baptism of the king's son, Otto performed the baptism, while Edmund reinforced his own position by performing confirmation immediately after. In this way the respective offices were affirmed.[54]

Where Edmund tended to founder was in the area closest to home. Unlike many bishoprics in England, the see of Canterbury was so ancient that it had a peculiar form of governance. Pope Gregory had sent St. Augustine as the abbot of a monastery of Benedictine missionaries. The chapter of Canterbury was then founded not as a community of secular canons, but rather as a capitular monastery. Secular canons (as Edmund had been in Salisbury) were much more attached to and dependent upon the local bishop. The ancient monastic chapter of Canterbury, however, was exceptionally

---

54 The nationalist chronicler Matthew Paris considered this to be a massive slight, but historians have been much more supportive of good relations between the legate and Edmund. See Dorothy Williamson, "Some Aspects of the Legation of Cardinal Otto," in *English Historical Review* 64 (1949): 145–173.

independent, both in spirit and by ancient privilege. They often quarreled with the archbishop over revenues and exemptions. One of the monks of the chapter had tried to forge a privilege of Thomas Becket in favor of the chapter. This forger was detected and expelled by Cardinal Otto and Edmund working together, but the episode left a bad taste in the mouths of the monks. They decided to appeal to Rome without telling their archbishop. When Edmund came to Rome on official business in 1237, he was chagrined to find members of his own chapter already there, litigating against him. He was able to smooth matters over with the pope and when he returned in 1238 he brokered a very fair deal as regarded monastic rents and liberties. Edmund made a heartfelt appeal to the monks, personally appearing in chapter and calling upon them to make peace. Yet all the monks saw was his large retinue of secular clerks and mendicants, and their bitterness endured through this act of humility. They dispatched another secret appeal to Rome. When they lost that, they then appealed to the king. The temerity of the monks—who had first lost trust by forging a charter and then relied on constant litigation against their bishop—eventually became too much. When Edmund learned that the monks had appealed to Rome yet again (for another cause), he realized the time for moderation was past. He deposed the priors in chapter, causing the monks to walk out on the archbishop. He laid an interdict upon them, essentially depriving them (and himself) of the massive income from pilgrims coming to the tomb of Thomas Becket. They ignored the interdict and continued to celebrate the sacraments, illegally electing another prior with the king's tacit approval. Edmund could brook the matter no longer, and made ready to undertake the arduous journey once again to Rome.[55] It is likely that the forced sojourn hastened his death. At the Cistercian abbey of Pontigny in France he fell ill. At

---

55 The hagiographers wanted to make this into an exile, to make a parallel to the case of Thomas Becket, but it is likely Edmund decided upon the journey on his own. See C. H. Lawrence, "The Alleged Exile of Archbishop Edmund," in *The Journal of Ecclesiastical History* 7.2 (1956): 160–173.

this development many of his servants panicked, thinking they would be abandoned and exiled should he die. Edmund spent his final days patiently writing letters of safe conduct and recommendation for his *familia*. All of this was recorded by his faithful, stalwart companion, Chancellor Richard de Wych. Edmund succumbed in late 1240 and was buried at the abbey of Pontigny. He would be canonized just six years later by Pope Innocent IV as a model bishop.

Though Edmund was dead, he left a precious legacy for his chancellor and friend, Richard de Wych. Richard too had been born to a middle-class family and followed a career path very similar to Edmund's.[56] He was drawn to a life of scholarship like so many of the great minds of the thirteenth century. He went to Oxford (and perhaps Bologna) and acquired a specialization in administration and canon law. When his improvident elder brother inherited the family lands from his father, he knew the former was not up to the task. Richard dutifully left his studies and took over management of the estates. He rectified the accounts and improved them, returning them to profitability. This done, he returned the whole of the patrimony to his brother and, like Cincinnatus, returned to the plow of his studies. By 1229 he had received his doctorate in canon law. Unlike Edmund, Richard was a born administrator. He began to attract attention, and within five years

---

56 For Richard's life see: David Jones and Ralph Bocking, *Saint Richard of Chichester: The Sources for His Life* (Lewes, East Sussex: Sussex Record Society, 1995); Delbert Wayne Russell, *La vie Seint Richard, evesque de Cycestre* (London: Anglo-Norman Text Society from Birbeck College, 1995); David Jones, "The Medieval Lives of St. Richard of Chichester," *Analecta Bollandiana* 105:1 (1987): 105–129; E. F. Jacob,"St. Richard of Chichester," in *The Journal of Ecclesiastical History* 7:2 (1956): 174–188; J. R. H. Moorman, "Great Pastors—II. St Richard of Chichester (c. 1197–1253)," in *Theology* 56: 392 (February 1953): 51–54. A recent effort is mostly interested in the *topoi* in his life, rather than a biographical study. See Katherine Harvey, "Perfect Bishop, Perfect Man? Masculinity, Restraint and the Episcopal Body in the Life of St Richard of Chichester," in *Southern History* 35 (2013): 1–22.

he was appointed to the prestigious office of Chancellor of the University of Oxford. It was during this time (1235–1237) that Richard consolidated the office of chancellor, beginning to assert authority over all the scholars for the purpose of uniting them under a common representative and ordinary.[57] This set the life of the school on a much firmer, safer, and more centralized foundation. Former Oxford masters like Robert Grosseteste wanted Richard for their own diocesan chancellors. It was ultimately St. Edmund who was able to lure Richard from Oxford to the even more illustrious office as Chancellor of Canterbury.

Given his blisteringly fast career trajectory leading to that point, Richard could assure himself that even greater things were in store. He became personal private secretary to the archbishop and keeper of the seals. His administration was efficient and capable, and showed particular capacity to settle difficult disputes about jurisdiction and money. Yet service in the tempered and moderate regime of Edmund introduced Richard to a deeper level of spiritual awareness than he had previously possessed. During his three years with Edmund he matured significantly. Richard became known as an opponent of the new breed of royal administrator "whose primary concern was to augment the revenues of their royal master so as to make them adequate to sustain his expensive undertakings in France as well as at home."[58] These officials sought only the private good of the king to the detriment of the common good of both Church and state. Opposition to them brought opprobrium, something that would stunt his meteoric career, itself an indicator of his spiritual growth.

After the death of his patron, Richard knew he would not be welcomed back in England. Inspired by Edmund, he knew that—if he wanted to continue along the road of sanctification and be of service to others—he needed further education in theology. He went to live and study with the young Dominican order, receiving ordination at the late age of 46 in 1243. It is likely that, had not

57   Jacob, "St. Richard," 177.
58   Ibid., 179.

events intervened, Richard would have professed into the Order of Preachers and continued his career among the scholarly friars. As it was, King Henry III tried to force one of his courtiers into the see of Chichester. Robert Grosseteste lost no time in demonstrating that the king's nominee was utterly untutored in theology, much to the embarrassment of the king. The appointment was quashed, but in revenge the king decided to assume the estates and incomes of the whole diocese and to funnel them into his own personal accounts. In light of this situation, the Chapter of Chichester decided to elect Richard of Wych as the new bishop, knowing his skill, his allegiances, and his relation to St. Edmund. Henry was livid, but Pope Innocent IV quickly saw the wisdom of such an appointment. He consecrated Richard as a bishop himself in Lyon in 1245. Henry forbade Richard from taking possession of his see, even posting guards at the gates of the city to prevent his entrance. "[He] came to his diocese as a man in trouble—homeless, poor, outcast—yet he made light of his suffering and devoted himself to his people and to the Church which he loved."[59] Richard, as a student of Edmund, knew that episcopal residence was the key to sound administration. He knew of a parish that was directly dependent upon Canterbury near Chichester, run by a poor priest named Simon of Tarring. He lived with Simon in his poor parsonage, administering his diocese as best as he could from there, knowing that the king's bailiffs who had occupied his estates could not legally trespass on a parish of Canterbury.

His patience, equanimity, and administrative skill in spite of everything eventually won over the king, who finally admitted defeat in June of 1246 and allowed Richard at last to take possession of his episcopal see. His dedication and poverty had already won over the people and the clergy, and they were to be solidly behind him for the remainder of his reign. His Dominican biographer, Ralph of Bocking, who had known him personally, remembered him as the "sweet-tempered man with the happy face."[60] Like Edmund he was a pacific

59   Moorman, "Great Pastors," 51.
60   Cfr. Jacob, "St. Richard," 182.

figure and a reconciler. He knew from bitter experience how terrible could be the conflicts between bishop and chapter, so worked to cement good relations with his canons. Fortunately for him they were secular (unlike Canterbury) and so were more directly beholden to his person. Still, he respected their customs and rights, and valued their advice. The charters of his episcopacy demonstrate excellent relations between himself and his dean. He stipulated that the dean and the canons "should not make answer to the bishop in anything, except in chapter, and that they should be subject to the judgement of the chapter."[61] In fact, he likely unified them by making a central concern of his episcopacy the care of the fabric of the Cathedral. He streamlined accounts by creating a common fund for maintaining the cathedral, created an endowment for the choir boys (and young scholars) resident in Chichester, and worked tirelessly to raise money for the care of the Mother Church. In this he impressively reversed the financial fortunes of his diocese, wounded by the exactions and inattention of the king's bailiffs during the previous conflict.[62] Because of this he could continue the spirit of generosity and hospitality he had learned from St. Edmund.

Richard was interested in more than simply his chapter and cathedral, for his pastoral attention reached the whole of his diocese. He was known by the adjective *prudens* which—in the medieval period—meant more than simply wise judgment, but rather indicated one who was adept at both theology and legal administration. Such men merited this title because they knew both the end

61 Ibid., 184.
62 Occasionally this irritated his stewards, who themselves were trying to rectify the situation. "It is not my fault that the diocese is impoverished: why then should I be punished for the sins of others by not being able to give due honor to guests and to relieve the poor." See Moorman, "Great Pastors," 53. One example was when his steward delayed a delivery of wheat owed to a convent, because of the precarious situation of the diocesan stores. When Richard heard about this he ordered him to send double the amount. After that—though he retained the steward—he never again fully trusted him with important matters. Jacob, *Saint Richard*, 183.

and the means whereby to attain it. He was very devoted to the laity of his diocese, who found him much more approachable and available than most bishops they had experienced. Indeed many of the problems in the diocese had stemmed from the time of Bishop Ralph Neville (r. 1222–1244), who had been Chancellor of England. He had been so rarely in his diocese that the chapter had to beg him to come for just one celebration of Easter. Informed as he was of the injustice and neglect of the royal officials, Richard was acutely aware of the plight of his direct tenants, and treated them with the utmost respect, occasionally returning their rent money when they were having difficulties. While he did not avoid litigation, he always made it a point to separate the cause and the person. Those in legal cases against him were astonished that he continued to treat them as persons with kindness and charity. With that said, he could be strict in the cause of justice. When the laity of Lewes had violently seized and murdered a suspected thief who had tried to take sanctuary at the altar, the bishop ordered them to disinter him with their own hands and carry him to church so he could receive a Christian burial. He was no less tough on arrogant nobility, such as a local lord who had unjustly detained a priest. Richard made him carry the log the priest had been chained to around the village as penance. Known for tempering his justice with open-handed generosity to all, Richard made a permanent mark on the hearts of his lay faithful.

Being a wise man, he knew the spiritual condition of the laity was unable to be corrected without a solidly formed clergy. Most of his efforts primarily focused on improving the quality of his parish priests, many of whom suffered from ignorance or poverty. In particular, a serious danger was absenteeism—that is, the granting of a benefice to a distant person who had no intention to effect the cure of souls in the living. This happened for several reasons. Many benefices were in the hands of religious houses, who used the income to finance their own monasteries and priories. Another issue were incumbents who were too greedy or venal to appoint a vicar. Deepening the problem was the growing issue of multiple benefices. In order to augment wealth, clerics sometimes collected the incomes of several different livings, further diluting the pastoral care of their territories. Finally, some benefices had incumbents (usually noblemen) who were independently wealthy and had no attachment to the land at all. Richard met all these challenges head on, working to reform vicarages and livings so as to assure the proper pastoral care of his people. He did this by issuing one of the most famous set of diocesan constitutions in English medieval history.

The constitutions breathe the reforming spirit of the Fourth Lateran Council in 1215. While they are dependent upon the Oxford constitutions of 1222 and the injunctions of Richard le Poore, Bishop of Salisbury, they disclose Richard's particular genius and insight into the burning issues of reform. In the first place he dealt with basic catechesis. He offered a primer to his parish clergy on the sacraments and how properly to administer them. These simple explanations would also enable them to explain the rites to the people in a language they understood. He spent a long section on the qualities necessary to be ordained a priest, and on the requirement for uprightness of life, and for celibacy in particular. In the statues he was particularly keen to reform and standardize the clerical "middle-management" of the deans and archdeacons who were so critical for diocesan management in the Middle Ages. These were to be trustworthy and well-trained men who took their responsibilities seriously. They were not to charge for deferring penances nor were they to attempt to increase their authority at the expense of the bishop. The archdeacons were to be regular visitors to the parishes, compiling reports and assessing competencies. Above all they were not to farm out their duties, but to attend to them personally. He imposed the requirement of residence for the occupation of benefices, foregrounding the care of souls. In so doing he often leaned upon the mendicant orders who could assist him while he undertook the long process of reforming the diocesan clergy. In the short term, he specifically demanded proper liturgical care, mandating clean churches and vestments, gilt or silver vessels, and clean linens. Four times a year the rural chaplains and pastors were to come together at a meeting under the presidency of the deans and archdeacons to give accounts, listen to the statutes read aloud, and renew their obedience to the bishop. He also instituted supervision for the deans and archdeacons, requiring each of them to keep and render accounts to his own household.

By the end of his life he became widely known in both Church and state. Even the formerly hostile King Henry III had become a grudging admirer, at least for his administrative skills, and appointed him a collector of the crusading tax. He was also well known to the pope, who commissioned him as a crusade preacher. Both positions required tact, skill, and great acumen. He was also an organizer, causing all the scattered charters of the diocese to be collected into one large cartulary for convenience, consultation, and good governance. Indeed, one unfriendly historian avers that because of this it demonstrated that Richard was a "shrewd administrator with a definite church policy."[63] What was meant as a criticism redounds rather to the bishop's credit. Out of his own possessions (including selling his horse) he had personally endowed a hospital for sick and aged clergy. Among his own people he was remembered as *facetus, largus, curialis, vultu hilaris*—that is, "witty, generous, courteous, with a smiling face." Richard died in 1253, and in his will left all his earthly possessions to those in his diocese. Ever the doctor of canon law, however, he promised to take up the king's damages to the property of the diocese in the court of heaven. Like Edmund, he was almost immediately hailed as a saint, and canonized just eight years later. Such men demonstrated the enduring relevance of Ambrose's model and bore witness to the presence of sanctity among bishops in every age.

A Saint in the Ambrosian See

The sixteenth century presented monumental new challenges to the Catholic Church. Long plagued by corruption, the Church had been making piecemeal efforts to reform itself during the previous century. The Protestant Reformation gave new impetus to such

63   Cfr. Jacob, *Saint Richard*, 183.

endeavors. In terms of the curia and the administration of the Church, the chief question at hand was whether the model of governance in place for over a millennium—and rooted in biblical principles—would be able to adapt and conform itself to the new needs of the age. If it were not able, then the radical new ecclesiologies of the reformers might very well overwhelm the existing structures. The root of the question was whether a purification was needed, as called for by many holy laity and churchmen, or rather the revolution desired by Luther and Calvin. Confessional historiography in the past viewed the history of Catholic government in the sixteenth century as a desperate attempt to hold on to the vestiges of medieval power, with the Council of Trent being no more than a tool to help the papacy "circle the wagons." Recent historians, however, have painted a very different picture. The "Catholic Reform" was already in full swing, particularly in places like Spain and in the reformed religious orders, well before Luther's advent. Some of the most creative voices of reform, such as Thomas More, Erasmus, Cajetan, and Reginald Pole, came from within the Catholic Church itself. Their calls for purification did not fall on deaf ears, for all of Christendom knew and felt the desire for an enduring restoration. The key was to preserve what was good, while pruning the bad. Such a negotiation was exceptionally delicate even in a time of peace, but in the midst of religious conflict, rising nationalism, and a resurgent Muslim threat, it became nearly impossible. It must not be denied that the papacy, particularly the inept Clement VII (r. 1523–1534), dithered. One can justly say that Clement fiddled while Rome and the rest of the continent burned.

It was not until twenty-five long years had elapsed after the excommunication of Luther in 1520 that the Council of Trent was able to take its first, feeble steps. The gathering strength of this Council, arguably the most significant in the history of the Catholic Church, creatively and assertively legislated in both dogma and discipline to right the foundering Barque of Peter. Though the delay had cost the Church nearly all of northern Europe, Trent established the necessary structure for the stabilization and later globalization of the Catholic Church. The matter remained, however, as how to bring it to a successful conclusion and to implement its decrees. Trent was the longest Ecumenical Council in history, with periodic sessions lasting from 1545–1563.[64] The political and religious considerations that affected the Council were severe.[65] In spite of that the Council did astonishing work under a series of brilliant cardinal legates, though at times they were hampered by papal policy, particularly under the intemperate Paul IV Carafa (r. 1555–1559). After his virtually disastrous pontificate, it remained the task of the new pope, Pius IV (r. 1559–1565) to try to pick up the pieces, and try to finish the Council that Paul IV had nearly destroyed.[66] In order to do this he needed close and trusted aides and, like all popes of the age, called upon his family.[67] In this case, nepotism was exceptionally successful, for Pius IV called his nephew Carlo Borromeo from Milan to serve at his right hand. It was to be one of the most fortunate appointments in the history of the Catholic Church.

Carlo was "to the manor born." A son of the powerful and ancient Borromeo family of Lombardy, his mother was also a scion

64 For the fascinating history of the Council, see the magisterial work by Hubert Jedin, *Geschichte des Konzils von Trient*, 5 vols. (Freiburg: Verlag Herder, 1950–1975). Only the first two volumes have been translated into English. For a brief introduction to more recent historiography, see John W. O'Malley, S.J., *Trent and All That: Renaming Catholicism in the Early Modern Era* (Cambridge, MA: Harvard University Press, 2002).

65 Indeed the ten years preceding the Council were taken up with just the delicate political question of *where* to hold the meeting.

66 As an indicator of the tenor of Paul's pontificate, while he was dying the people of Rome rioted, decapitating his statue, and removing all signs of the Carafa family on churches throughout the city, almost burning down Santa Maria sopra Minerva. As a sign of how the rest of the Church felt about Paul IV, the first act of Pius IV was to pardon the rioters and to put Carafa's cardinal-nephew on trial, sentencing him to death.

67 For the institution of the "cardinal-nephew," see Birgit Emich, "The Cardinal Nephew," in *A Companion to the Early Modern Cardinal*, eds. M. Hollingsworth, M. Pattenden, and A. Witte (Leiden: Brill, 2020): 71–90.

of the influential Medici clan.[68] Like many saints in Church history, he demonstrates that privilege is not the inherent problem—rather, it is how one employs it. At twelve he was tonsured and given the revenues of a monastery that was entailed to the family. While this was a common abuse, from even this early age Carlo was insistent that any money not used for his education be employed for the good of the monastery itself. He began to attend the University of Pavia to obtain a degree in law but was recalled by the death of his father in 1554. Much like the story of Richard of Chichester, Carlo's elder brother Federigo considered himself unsuited for the task of managing the family patrimony. At the tender age of sixteen, the young cleric found himself placed in charge of the massive holdings of the Borromeos, and acquitted himself so creditably that he was able to broker a fair solution to litigation between his family and the court of Spain. Such early administrative success was merely a sign of the later extraordinary things he would accomplish. Having rectified the family situation, he returned to Pavia, where, in 1559, he obtained doctorates in both canon and civil law at the age of 21. Carlo was clearly marked for great things, and his career was accelerated even more dramatically by the election of his uncle as Pope Pius IV on Christmas day of that year.

Needing trusted associates in the Holy City that had been so abused and impoverished by Paul IV, Pius called upon his young relative. In early 1560, Carlo found himself created a cardinal-deacon. He was successively made administrator of the Papal States and of the Archdiocese of Milan, and appointed personal secretary

---

68   There is an extensive bibliography on Carlo, but little in the way of formal biography apart from older, confessional books. See Danilo Zardin, *Carlo Borromeo: cultura, santità, governo* (Milan: V & P, 2010); and the excellent essays in *San Carlo Borromeo: Catholic Reform and Ecclesiastical Politics in the Second Half of the Sixteenth Century*, eds. John M. Headley and John B. Tomaro (Washington, DC: Folger Shakespeare Library, 1988), hereafter *SCB*. There is a fine translation of his biography from 1610 in Giovanni Pietro Giussano, *The Life of St. Charles Borromeo (1610)* 2 vols. (London: Burns and Oates, 1884).

to Pius IV. He was also put in charge of distributing honors and benefices. It was in this office that he made a significant mark on the curia. He would only dispense favors to those who had personally reformed their lives. Though he was only in Rome for four years, during that time the curia and the clergy of Rome were largely remade in a Borromean image. He curbed the infamous extravagance of the curia and the cardinals, and made it a rule that the clergy could only wear a somber black. He also knew the importance of cultivating friendship and creating a network of sympathetic associates. In a humanist vein he gathered like-minded cardinals and prelates to his *Noctes Vaticanae*, an evening ecclesiastical salon of sorts, where they would meet and discuss theological and spiritual themes. Each of the prelates was known by a faintly ironic epithet, like "Nestor" or "the Constant One." Carlo's nickname was "Chaos," hearkening back to the original condition of confusion out of which God brings order. The irony was that Carlo—who was actually bringing order—was throwing Roman society into chaos.[69] Indeed one of Carlo's interventions in the *Noctes* is a sermon against *luxuria*, a capacious term encompassing the lasciviousness, excess, and corruption found in contemporary Rome. This network formed the basis for the extension of his administrative efforts.

It was in his role as secretary of state that Carlo had carefully to negotiate the convocation and management of the last sessions of Trent. Suspended since 1552, the success of the Council hinged on the final meetings between 1562 and 1563. Bound up in this was not only the hiatus caused by Paul IV, but the rapidly deteriorating European situation. General tolerance had been extended to

---

69 These have never been translated, but can be found in: *Noctes Vaticanae seu sermones habiti in Academia a S. Carolo Borromeo Romae in Palatio Vaticano instituta. Praemittitur opusculum Augustini Valerii inscriptum Convivium noctium Vaticanarum. Omnia nunc primum e MSS. codicibus Bibliothecae Ambrosianae eruta Ioseph Antonius Saxius praefatione et notis illustravit* (Milan: Ex typographia Bibliothecae Ambrosianae apud Ioseph Marellum, 1748).

the Protestants by the Religious Peace of Augsburg in 1555. While the emperor, Ferdinand I, was staunchly Catholic, he ruled over a bitterly divided empire. He was eager to see quick reform among the Catholic ranks and perhaps indults for such things as clerical marriage and communion under both kinds so as to attract Protestants back to the Church. His nephew, Philip II of Spain, was mounting ever higher in power as a result of his worldwide empire and wanted purification and absolute fidelity to Catholic doctrine. Whole regions, such as Britain and Scandinavia, had been irreparably lost, while France teetered on a knife's edge. There religious warfare and dynastic instability threatened the peace of Christians, not to mention the ever-present French insistence on an independent Gallican church. While theological liberals and accomodationists had largely been removed from the field, there remained radical reformers who wanted a wholesale Catholic purification "in head and members." The danger was that the Council, prodded by the civil powers, would assert control over the reformation of the papacy, perhaps leading toward the slippery slope to the conciliarism of the fifteenth century. This might have resulted in an eclipsing of papal power and a diminution of the unity of the Church at the very moment that decisive leadership was most needed. Borromeo's delicate task, then, was to balance all these competing interests, and to safeguard the honor and primacy of the Holy See, all the while brining an Ecumenical Council to fruitful conclusion.

Carlo's main strategy in accomplishing all this was to mollify the civil ambassadors as much as possible. He was hampered in this because his presence was required in Rome; therefore, he operated through the cardinal-legates who were present in Trent. He wanted above all to maintain the vision of a free Council, but it is nonetheless true that it was being conducted from Rome behind the scenes.[70] One example of this is seen when Carlo sent the legates

---

70   Foundational for understanding this period of Carlo's life is, Msgr. Robert Trisco, "Reforming the Roman Curia: Emperor Ferdinand I and the Council of Trent," in *Reform and Authority in the Medieval and Reformation Church*, eds. Guy Fitch Lytle and Uta-

an unpublished bull, listing the matters that Pius would consent to have discussed in the Council. This allowed the legates cover should they open up controversial issues and gave them guidelines as to what topics were off limits, yet all this was accomplished privately.[71] In this Carlo shows himself exceptionally adept and—one must admit—a bit Machiavellian. The young man was clearly in control of events, and managed papal policy with a judicious prudence far in advance of his age. His chief concern as papal secretary was to preserve the honor and rights of the Holy See. The secular nations were clamoring for papal reform. Carlo went on a concerted charm offensive, repeatedly detailing Pius' own efforts at Rome in an attempt to preempt the Council from making precipitous decisions. He made it clear to the legates that they were able to open all areas of reform to discussion, but they must not make it appear that the secular powers had imposed this course of action on the Council. Carlo knew that the future implementation of the Tridentine decrees would depend on both the perceived freedom of the Council Fathers in deciding them, as well as an authoritative papacy to implement them. Indeed, Carlo must have had a private post service, for he and the legates maintained constant communication, an exceptional achievement in remote governance for the premodern world. But Carlo was still more prudent, and cultivated correspondents and informants both inside and outside of the conciliar deliberations, all the while keeping the lines of communication open with secular powers.[72]

Matters almost came to an unfortunate head in 1562. Pius was ill and many considered him near death. The secular powers chose this moment to propose a reformation of the College of Cardinals and of papal elections, matters which the papacy had already reserved to itself. A further and more serious danger was that if the pope died during a sitting Council, the secular powers might

Renate Blumenthal (Washington, DC: Catholic University of America Press, 1981): 143–333.

71 Ibid., 168.

72 Ibid., 250.

convince the assembled bishops to attempt to elect a new pope, as they had at Constance in 1415. Carlò had to act quickly. First, he promised that papal legislation on all such matters would be immediately forthcoming. He informed the legates to keep the ambassadors placated and to hold them at arms-length. He quickly composed a bull entitled *In eligendis*, later promulgated by Pius IV on 9 October 1562. It has been qualified as a "statesman's masterpiece."[73] It firstly asserts the rights of the cardinal electors to elect the pope even while a General Council is in session. It then describes a reformation of the papal election process and avers to a reorganization of the College of Cardinals in a much more realistic manner than had been theoretically discussed at Trent. It also presented the Council and the ambassadors with a *fait accompli* that demonstrated that the Roman See could reform itself without assistance from the Council (and headed off the politically and theologically troublesome image of a Council dictating reform to the Holy See).

Pius was able to endure his illness and rule for another two years, allowing Carlo to continue his work on the Council. The young secretary of state was particularly concerned with the French contingent, who had arrived at Trent with all sorts of Gallicanizing sentiments, leaning in the direction of a French national church (mostly as a political expedient to divide their Habsburg enemies). Carlo was constantly cast into the role of attempting to control the rumor mill. Each faction was busy manufacturing propaganda for the advancement of its own aims. He was constantly engaged in a public relations effort that tried to reinforce the papacy's commitment to self-reform, while at the same time trying to thwart misinformation coming particularly from the French and certain radical German officials. In this Carlo was undermined by Pius' private correspondence with some of the more reactionary members of the Council, wherein the pope imprudently expressed his lack of confidence in two of the cardinal legates.[74] It was largely due to Carlo's

73 Ibid., 212.
74 Ibid., 234.

inspired leadership that effective reform decrees were passed that saved the honor of the Holy See, and in which traditional dogmas of Catholicism were reaffirmed. Likely with a profound sense of satisfaction, Carlo was informed of the solemn conclusion of the Council of Trent, which ended with the traditional request to the pope to confirm and ratify each of its decrees. The lumbering ship was finally brought to shore, and to general satisfaction. The outlines of this Council would guide Catholicism for centuries.

During these years Carlo himself was maturing. Much like Richard of Chichester, while in the midst of administration, he too began to have contact with many holy men. His work on the Council, while highly successful, was at the same time pragmatic and often expedient. He needed something deeper to anchor his spirituality. The pious mediations of his colleagues in his *Noctes Vaticanae* began to sink in. Constantly surrounding himself with men of high moral caliber and deep spiritual appreciation, his company began to have an effect on him. One person in particular who was to leave a profound impression on Carlo was the saintly Archbishop of Braga in Portugal, Bartholomew a Martyribus, O.P.[75] Bartholomew was a moderate, who was single-mindedly dedicated to the pastoral reform of his diocese. He had written a sort of spiritual and practical instruction manual for bishops, the *Stimulus Pastorum*.[76] Carlo was so moved by the work that he caused it to

---

75   Raul de Almeida Rolo, *L'évêque de la reforme tridentine: sa mission pastorale d'après le vénérable Barthélemy des Martyrs* (Lisbon: Centro de Estudos Históricos Ultramarinos, 1965). Bartholomew was made a saint by equipollent canonization by Pope Francis in 2019.

76   This book went through many editions, most recently, Bartolomeu dos Mártires, *Stimulus pastorum: ex sanctorum floribus ardentioribusque verbis praecipue concinatus* (Braga, 1963). This edition was given as a gift by Paul VI to all the Council Fathers at the close of Vatican II. There are three translations, one in Portuguese: *Estímulo de pastores*, trans. Raul de Almeida Rolo (Braga: Movimento Bartolomeano, 1981); and in German, *Stimulus pastorum zur Spiritualität des Hirtenamtes*, trans. Marianne Schlosser (St. Ottilien, Eos Verlag, 2018); and in English, *Stimulus*

be published for the first time, and it remained his favorite "mirror" for prelates. During the time of Bartholomew's visit to Rome, Carlo's elder brother Federigo died at the age of 28. This seems to have precipitated a spiritual crisis in the young man. He felt profound guilt that he had not given himself totally over to the gospel, and resolved to leave the world ever more completely. He was dissuaded from this by Bartholomew, who advised him how necessary it was to have good and holy administrators in the Church. Carlo resolved that he would no longer be an absent administrator and, having satisfactorily concluded the Council, petitioned Pius IV to allow him to become resident Archbishop of Milan. Though Pius was understandably worried about losing such a powerful advisor, he consented and in 1563 Carlo was ordained and consecrated as bishop. It has been said that Carlo's personal example in Rome was of even more lasting influence than his successful conclusion of the Council.[77] He knew that Rome was the key to the whole success of the reform, but that it must come from within the primordial see itself. This meant surrounding the pope with solid advisors. As he wrote regarding the Roman cardinals of his time: "This reform vexes them a great deal, and not only if one looked to them would it never be made but they will try to obstruct it in every way they can, but we who have to render to God an account even of their omissions of this council do not have to look to them but [rather] to do always what is fitting without regard [to anyone]."[78] Carlo would take the good beginning he made in Rome to the great see of Milan.

Though he still had to fulfill his duties in Rome up to the death of his patron Pius IV in 1565, he nonetheless began to make significant plans for the diocese. He began by appointing strong vicars to start laying the groundwork for his efforts but knew that, in the long run, personal residence was absolutely necessary

---

Pastorum, trans. Donald S. Prudlo (South Bend, IN: St. Augustine's Press, 2022).

77 Trisco, "Carlo Borromeo and the Council of Trent," in *SCB*, 63.
78 Cfr. Trisco, "Reforming the Roman Curia," 316.

for a bishop (and prescribed by the Council itself).[79] His first vicar was Nicolò Ormanetto, who had been in the household of the reforming English cardinal, Reginald Pole. He was precisely the kind of man that Borromeo needed. Beside being efficient and committed to reform, he was also an outsider from Verona, able to speak with all of the different factions of the diocese from a position of impartiality, and free of any previous attachments to the powerful Borromeo family. He and Carlo agreed that the central focus of all reforming trends must start with the diocesan clergy. To that end Carlo had Nicolò call a plenary diocesan synod in 1564 at which no fewer than 1200 priests were present. There the decrees of Trent on the reformation of Church life were read and their implementation initiated. Beside entrusting the diocese to Ormanetto as vicar general, he appointed two sub-vicars, each with responsibility for civil and criminal cases, thus removing such matters from the plate of Nicolò and, later, Carlo himself. Following this, the vicar general made a comprehensive visitation of the whole diocese, compiling reports that would be invaluable to Carlo upon his arrival. Key to the reformation of the clergy was the removal of corruption and enforcing the duties of residence. He also wrote key tracts for the entire Tridentine period on the proper construction of churches and on regulating sacred music, in order to restore dignity and functionality to the liturgy.[80] A particular concern was the necessity of good preaching. Carlo was aware that the Protestant movement found its strength in popular preaching and for far too long in Catholicism such an activity had been considered the specialized province of the religious orders. To the end of correcting this, Carlo had homiletic manuals published and made a practice of inviting powerful preachers to Milan for the ongoing formation of his diocesan clergy. For the purposes of stimulating fraternity, an always difficult matter with diocesan clergy, he formed a confraternity of St. Ambrose for his priests, which would unite them in prayer and

79   John Headley, "Introduction," in *SCB*, 15.
80   Ibid., 20.

fellowship. The crowning achievement, and one that set the pattern for the Church up to the present day, was his creation of one of the first formal seminaries in Christendom. Here he would train the next generation of priests. To that end he called thirty members of the new Jesuit order to assist Nicolò in his efforts at education. The formalization of the formation of clerics, following the desires of the Council, was one of Carlo's signal accomplishments.

All these preparations having been set forth, Carlo made his solemn entrance into the city of Milan amidst much rejoicing in September of 1565. The delight of the Milanese was certainly in the return of a beloved son, but in reality it went much deeper. It was a study in miniature of the rebuilding of the Church itself, which had been foundering for so long. The Ambrosian see had been without a resident archbishop for *eighty* years. Carlo would incarnate the reform in his own person and become a living exemplar of the duties of a bishop. Indeed, here one finds the model of Ambrose, who had done so much to form our concepts of the Latin episcopacy, remade and repristinated in Borromeo's image: the "ideal" Tridentine bishop, resident, full of pastoral energy, and on fire for the purity of the Church. Carlo wasted no time. Within a month he convoked his first provincial council, attended by ten of his suffragan bishops. There he shared his vision with them, firing them with the desire to bring the reform to their dioceses as well. Above all he inspired them with the personal character of his plan: "We ought to walk in front," he told them, "and our spiritual subjects will follow us more easily." Not all were fully on board with his energy or ideals. The Bishop of Brescia was frank; he thought Carlo wildly impractical. He later wrote that Carlo was "exhaustingly zealous, full of holy willpower, and an imprudent rigor."[81] Yet such was his tireless passion that he won many over. As one historian wrote, "He was an administrative genius who worked to give substance to Tridentine spirit, he did not always win approval or were his suggestions warmly received, but no one ever doubted

81   Cf. Ibid., 25.

the sincerity and selflessness of his approach."[82] Numerous bishops, fired by his ardor, began the implementation of the Council in their territories.[83]

Almost immediately after this synod, Carlo was called away to be present at the deathbed of his uncle, the pope. Pius died attended by Carlo and St. Philip Neri. On 20 December the 27-year-old cardinal found himself as one of the Grand Electors for the new pope, coordinating the coterie of prelates in support of the policies of the deceased Pius IV, and largely opposed to the remaining supporters of Paul IV. In a letter after the conclave to the cardinal of Portugal, Carlo gives us a portrait of a cardinal wishing nothing other than the good of the Church:

> Although my grief at the death of my uncle the Sovereign Pontiff was great and proportioned to the paternal love he ever showed me and the veneration I bore him in return, yet no sorrow, however bitter, could ever distract me for a moment from my desire to do everything for the benefit of the Holy See.... [W]hilst I recognised the obligation resting upon me to act in union with the other Cardinals, I yet saw that there were some matters connected with the vacant see that were the special concern of my office. The times were fraught with evils for the Church. There were dangers to be guarded against on every side.... It seemed to me that I ought to do all in my power to procure the election of a Pontiff who would worthily replace him who with so much prudence had known how to uphold the authority and dignity of the Apostolic See in the hour of peril.... In proceeding

82 John B. Tomaro, "San Carlo Borromeo and the Implementation of the Council of Trent," in *SCB*, 78.

83 Indeed one of his suffragans, Nicolò Sfondrato of Cremona, would afterward become Pope Gregory XIV, one of the first of many popes influenced by Carlo. Indeed, as one of Carlo's correspondents himself said, "La riforma romana è figliuola della milanese." Cfr. Headly, "Introduction," in *SCB*, 18.

to the election of a Pope, it is clear that I was bound to observe great care and diligence, and to exclude every consideration except the service of religion and of the Faith. This I did; for all my efforts and wishes were directed solely toward the good of the universal Church, and to the exclusion of any kind of personal or private interest.[84]

With extensive experience of delicate negotiations, Carlo managed the candidacy of the reformer Giovanni Morone and obtained a majority of the conclave's votes for him, but fell short of the required two-thirds. After a brief attempt to elect his old teacher, Cardinal Sireto, Borromeo had to go to the powerful French-backed candidate, Cardinal Farnese. Borromeo pointedly told him he would not back him in *this* conclave (a prudential and non-committal assertion), but invited him to help come up with a compromise candidate acceptable to all. They finally settled on the Dominican Michele Ghislieri, who was promptly elected, taking the name of Pius V (r. 1565–1572), likely in thanks and homage to Borromeo for his support in the conclave.

Carlo returned to his diocese—satisfied with the election—and to his task of patient reformation. Needing significant attention was the apparatus of Church governance. He made sure to appoint only men of proven worth, and paid them good wages so that they would not be subjected to the temptations of venality in their work. In particular, he wanted good relations with the powerful canons of the cathedral, but was aware that in many dioceses such canonical appointments often became sinecures. For the sake of reform he gave his cathedral chapter specific tasks. He instructed them to be especially and continually devoted to the sacrament of confession, making it available at all times. This dovetailed with a general trend in post-Tridentine spirituality that focused on this sacrament as a primary means not only of purgation, but of spiritual perfection. He

84   Cf. Giovanni Pietro Giussano, *The Life of St. Charles Borromeo (1610)* (London: Burns and Oates, 1884), 72–73.

was also careful only to appoint solid theologians, knowing the kind of education necessary to become a good confessor. He also organized his vicars and deans in such a way that they gave him frequent reports on their charges. This was particularly important for him in the area of pastoral visitation, which he conducted with extraordinary regularity.[85] His vicars would produce detailed reports prior to each episcopal visit, which made the time he spent at them exceptionally productive, for armed with the necessary information beforehand he could get directly to the heart of cases. A special concern was the condition of the lives of the religious in the city. Over the previous centuries they had grown increasingly lax, corrupted by excess wealth and a lack of proper episcopal oversight. He sought to restore regular observance in the cloisters, and particularly enforced the religious enclosure of nuns. This brought him into conflict with many members of noble families who had taken the veil, and he had to engage in a conflict with two of his own aunts just to get them to install a visitor's grille in their convents.

The difficulties of the situation of the religious were some of the most intractable problems of his reign, even drawing the worried attention of the pope. In 1569 the canons of Santa Maria della Scala claimed immunity from diocesan jurisdiction, though their assertion had never been legally established. When Carlo commanded them to observe diocesan statutes, they rebelled. Carlo came in full episcopal regalia for a visitation, and such was the extent of their dissent that their lay supporters discharged firearms, harming Carlo's pastoral staff. Threatened with excommunication, they finally relented. Pius V very reasonably wanted them treated with severity, but Carlo preferred an amicable reconciliation, one that later made Santa Maria into a stronghold of diocesan power. A similar situation manifested itself with the order known as the *Humiliati*. What had been a thriving lay order in the thirteenth century had, by Carlo's time,

85 They were so well conducted that they even inspired a young Angelo Roncalli to make a scholarly analysis of them. See Angelo Roncalli [John XXIII] and Pietro Forno, *Gli atti della visita apostolica di S. Carlo Borromeo a Bergamo (1575)* (Florence: L.S. Olschki, 1936).

degenerated into essentially a real estate management firm ensuring the wealth of a few well-heeled monks.[86] Carlo so vigorously pursued its reformation that they sought to assassinate him, attempting to kill him while he was at prayer in his chapel. Carlo fortunately survived when the gun misfired. He suppressed the order with the pope's assistance and distributed their holdings to charity and to more productive religious associations.

At the heart of Carlo's mission was a pastoral sense of the needs of his faithful. All the reforms detailed above were directed to the benefit of the lay members of his diocese. Even during the Council of Trent, he had been concerned with the religious life of the laity. It was by his suggestion that the Council ordered the composition of a catechism. This book, later known as the "Roman Catechism," was the first such official effort in the Church's history. It was intended directly for parish priests, and even included a preaching plan intended to introduce the faith and catechize the laity through the course of the liturgical year. He was interested in the most minute details of education at every level, from the seminary down to the catechism classes he organized for children. He would visit these personally and always had a supply of apples to reward the students.[87] Though by nature of a clerical bent, Carlo learned during the course of his ministry to trust lay catechists who were properly trained.[88] This would mark a significant moment in the integration of the laity into the Church's teaching ministry. His pastoral heart was on full display in the famine of 1576. He personally relieved 3,000 people for three straight months from his own funds, and went on many public processions, barefoot and clad in sackcloth, to beseech God's mercy on his people. When the civil authorities of the city fled, Carlo was present daily, ministering to the people's needs.

86 By the 1560s, there were only 170 "monks" for the 94 well-propertied monasteries of the order.
87 Headly, "Introduction," in *SCB*, 20.
88 See the insightful chapter by Paul Grendler, "Borromeo and the Schools of Christian Doctrine," in *SCB*, 158–171.

While he was able to speak to all people on their own levels, and to bring desperately needed reform, Carlo never forgot the intimate union between pastoral duty and doctrine. Whether defending his see against secular encroachments, religious heterodoxy, or clerical corruption, he was a tireless promoter of the idea that truth and mercy were two sides of the same coin. He always acted *satis episcopaliter*, though his motto was *Humilitas*. He saw no contradiction. His actions as a bishop were the highest expression of humility: utter, complete, and humble service to his position as the successor of St. Ambrose. He lived simply, devoutly, and penitently, but when he executed his office he bore the weight of tradition, history, and doctrine. Holding no fewer than eleven diocesan synods before his death in 1584, Carlo was a living example of the truth that the Church always has the power to reform from within, drawing on the inestimable treasures endowed upon her by Christ and the saints. The eminent contemporary historian Cardinal Baronius writes, soon after Carlo's untimely passing at the age of 46, that he was "a second Ambrose, whose early death, lamented by all good men, inflicted great loss on the Church." Canonized in 1610, he became a powerful example for the bishops who followed him, an incarnation of the unity between sanctity, administration, doctrine, and practice.

Conclusion

The two millennia since the Incarnation have provided the Church with a plethora of holy men and women who have demonstrated that Christian leadership and administration is no mere paradox. For the good of others and for the salvation of souls, they have accepted the burden of government and in so doing modeled themselves on the supreme governor, who is none other than God Himself. In light of their rational natures and their acceptance of the grace of God they have authentically mirrored the divine image in their souls. Such individuals refused the abandonment of all rulership, an untenable position that might be gleaned from a facile reading of Scripture. Rather, they acknowledged that their authority was borne by their humility, and their administration was their service to their fellow believers. For them, there was no dichotomy in bringing authority to bear when the needs of the Church of God demanded it. These saints knew that governance was indispensable. The administration of justice, the punishment of the evildoer, and the exercise of power—these things were not necessary evils, but were positively willed by the God who created us as embodied souls in an incarnational universe. Such activities, like all earthly endeavors, might indeed be poisoned by sin and by self-will, yet they could also be exalted and made sublime through cooperation with grace.

The characters we met in this book illustrate the achievement of what seems like an impossible command by Christ—namely, to be "as prudent as serpents, and as innocent as doves" (Mt 10:16). The imperative itself indicates that to be both wise and pure is not only possible, but an end to actively pursue. In the first place one must remain embedded in the doctrine of the Church and in the living-out of the natural and supernatural moral law. As even the ancient philosophers demanded, these saints knew how to govern themselves before they sought to govern others. This point is particularly lost today, when most people consider individual moral behavior to be utterly separate from administrative or governing competency. Such a dualism would have seemed completely foreign to these saints. For them, there was no separation between the good and the useful, and that "effectiveness" had to be judged according to the higher standard of moral probity. Further, they knew that their moral behavior was not only salvific but necessarily exemplary for their followers. All hypocrisy is a corrosive force, antithetical to the achievement of God's reign on earth.

Christ had brought the fulness of truth, therefore fidelity to his word and to his Church provided the fundamental environment in which to exercise good governance. While much of this book has emphasized the innovations that these brilliant men and women made in adapting the Christian life to their respective time periods, we need to remember that the good administrator in the Church of God is Janus-faced. Like the Roman god of old—the embodiment of prudence—the saintly administrator must look to the past as much as to the future. Any innovation needs to be organic, grown from the same soil that provided nutriment for the Church from its beginning. It must be grafted into Christ, for the only true life to the Christian believer flows from Him. This means that administration needs to be traditional and evolutionary at the same time, while avoiding all revolutionary sentiment. The Church is very much like what was described by Edmund Burke, "Society is a partnership of the dead, the living, and the unborn," except in a Catholic sense all three were united vertically to God through Christ and His life-giving Spirit.

Yet such fidelity to orthodoxy and the moral life is not enough. There were also techniques of good governance, many of which the Church acquired wholesale from the practical Romans. The Roman Church assumed certain institutions of law, administration, and politics intact and "baptized" them, as it were. God willed the Incarnation and the early spread of the Church to take place in a Hebrew religious society, in a Greek cultural space, within the political sphere of the brilliant Roman people. This was no accident. These are the three essential cultures. Remove one of them and Christianity is no longer Christianity. It is Jewish, Greek, and Roman in its very incarnational constitution. The early Church took all that was good in these precursor cultures and refined and elevated them through the leaven of the Gospel. Unjust elements were purified, and in the refiners fire the finest natural elements remained, upon which grace would build. The members of the Church used these elements to forge the Church upon earth, subordinating power and authority to the purpose of the salvation of souls. Administration is indeed an art. Brought to a high level of excellence by the Romans, it could be learned and practiced. When united to grace, such an art becomes a fulfillment of the divine governance of the universe itself. Saints who immersed themselves not only in doctrine and morals, but soberly assessed their natural talents before applying them to the cause of the Gospel became Holy Administrators, exercising power and authority for the good of all. They had become "the wise," for the end and fulfillment of all wisdom is simply—as the Philosopher says—to order.

Index of Scripture Passages

General Index

Peter, Pope St., 16, 30, 32, 44, 48,
50, 63, 115, 150, 153, 166,
169–171
Piacenza, Council of (1095), 180
Primicerius notariorum, 40–41,
64–66
Priscillianists, 42
prudence, 14–15, 63, 68, 128,
142, 173, 181, 213, 220, 224,
226, 234, 236, 287, 330, 336
Polypticum, 53, 61, 66
Paul the Hermit, St., 81
Petronax, 104–105
Praemonstratensians, Customary
of the, 192, 209
Pataria, 163–165, 169, 173, 186–
187
Pelagius, Pope, 57–58
Pulcheria, 248
Peter of Verona, St., 228, 232
parabalani, 241, 245
Photios, Patriarch, 253
Pole, Reginald, Cardinal, 319, 328
Ptolemy of Lucca, 266
Paul IV, Pope (Carafa), 320, 322,
330
Pius IV, Pope, 320–322, 324–325,
327, 330
Pius V, Pope (Michele Ghislieri),
331–332
Philip II of Spain, Emperor, 323

Ralph of Bocking, 314
Rex et sacerdos/rex-sacerdos sys-
tem, 142, 145, 167, 174
Rich, Edmund, of Abingdon, St.,
9, 305–315, 318
Richard of Chichester, 321, 326
Richard le Poore, 317
Richard of Pembroke, 308
Richard of Wych, 9, 308–309,

312–318
Robert of Arbrissel, 187
Robert of Molesmes, St., 120
Roman Catechism, 333
Romanitas, 4, 11, 13–15, 38–39,
43, 61, 63
Rufinus of Aquileia, 87, 90

sacellarius, 66
saeculum obscurum ("shadowy
age"), 139, 151, 253
Salian Conrad II, Emperor, 145
satis episcopaliter, 304, 334
Satyrus, 293
Schism of 1054, 260
scrinium, 46, 49, 65
secundicarius, 65
Seigneurial Revolution, 143
Seljuk Turks, 181
Simon Stylites, St., 85
simony, 119, 146–147, 150, 152–
154, 161, 164–165, 167, 175,
179, 196, 253
Siricus, Pope, 21
Sireto, Cardinal, 331
Sixtus II, Pope, 30
Stephen of Bourbon, 222, 203
Stravensby, Alexander, Bishop,
308
Sturm, St., 105
Sulpicius Severus, 90
Symmachus, 21, 289, 296
Sylvester II, Pope, 142, 196
Sylvester III, Pope, 147
synodality, 6, 152
Synod of the Corpse (897), 139
Synod of Ephesus (431), 249
Synod of Sutri (1046), 146
Synod of Lombardy, 153
Synod of the Oak, 242
techne, 3